INUYASHA

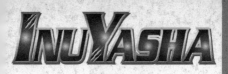

VOL. 5
VIZ Media Edition

Story and Art by
RUMIKO TAKAHASHI

English Adaptation by Gerard Jones

Translation/Mari Morimoto
Touch-Up Art & Lettering/Wayne Truman
Cover Design/Hidemi Sahara
Graphics & Design/Sean Lee
Editor (1st Edition)/Julie Davis
Editor (Action Edition)/Julie Davis

Editor in Chief, Books/Alvin Lu
Editor in Chief, Magazines/Marc Weidenbaum
VP of Publishing Licensing/Rika Inouye
VP of Sales/Gonzalo Ferreyra
Sr. VP of Marketing/Liza Coppola
Publisher/Hyoe Narita

Printed in Canada

Published by VIZ Media, LLC
P.O. Box 77010
San Francisco, CA 94107

1st Edition published 1999
VIZ Media Edition
10 9 8 7 6
First printing, September 2003
Sixth printing, November 2007

RATED T+ FOR OLDER TEEN

PARENTAL ADVISORY
INUYASHA is rated T+ for Older Teen and is recommended for ages 16 and up. This book contains violence.

ratings.viz.com

viz media

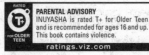

www.viz.com

store.viz.com

INUYASHA

VOL. 5 — VIZ Media Edition

STORY AND ART BY
RUMIKO TAKAHASHI

CONTENTS

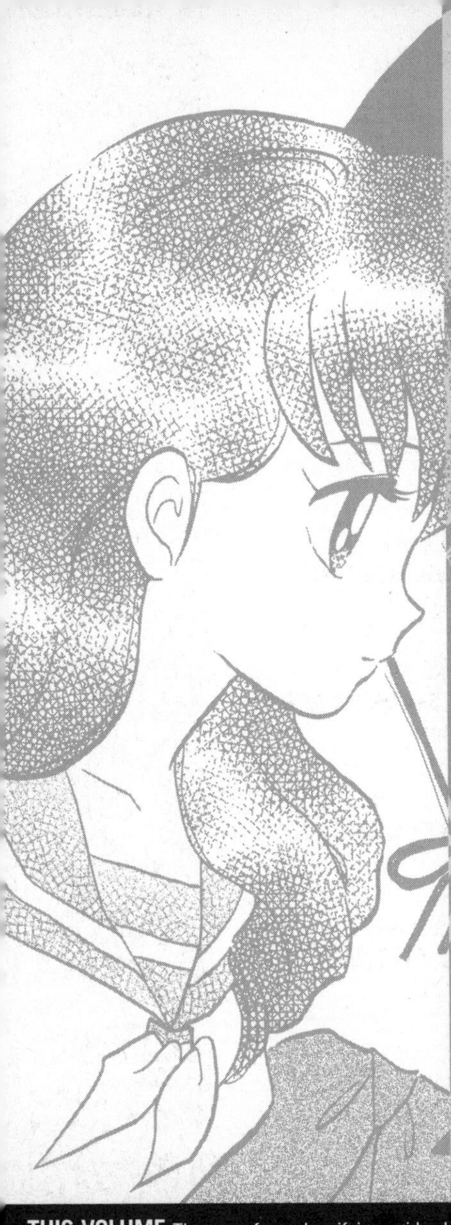

Long ago, in the "Warring States" era of Japan's Muromachi period (Sengoku-jidai, approximately 1467-1568 CE), a legendary doglike half-demon called "Inu-Yasha" attempted to steal the Shikon Jewel, or "Jewel of Four Souls," from a village, but was stopped by the enchanted arrow of the village priestess, Kikyo. Inu-Yasha fell into a deep sleep, pinned to a tree by Kikyo's arrow, while the mortally wounded Kikyo took the Shikon Jewel with her into the fires of her funeral pyre. Years passed.

Fast forward to the present day. Kagome, a Japanese high school girl, is pulled into a well one day by a mysterious centipede monster, and finds herself transported into the past, only to come face to face with the trapped Inu-Yasha. She frees him, and Inu-Yasha easily defeats the centipede monster.

The residents of the village, now fifty years older, readily accept Kagome as the reincarnation of their deceased priestess Kikyo, a claim supported by the fact that the Shikon Jewel emerges from a cut on Kagome's body. Unfortunately, the jewel's rediscovery means that the village is soon under attack by a variety of demons in search of this treasure. Then, the jewel is accidentally shattered into many shards, each of which may have the fearsome power of the entire jewel.

Although Inu-Yasha says he hates Kagome because of her resemblance to Kikyo, the woman who "killed" him, he is forced to team up with her when Kaede, the village leader, binds him to Kagome with a powerful spell. Now the two grudging companions must fight to reclaim and reassemble the shattered shards of the Shikon Jewel before they fall into the wrong hands.

THIS VOLUME The gang faces horrifying spider-head demons,

CHARACTERS

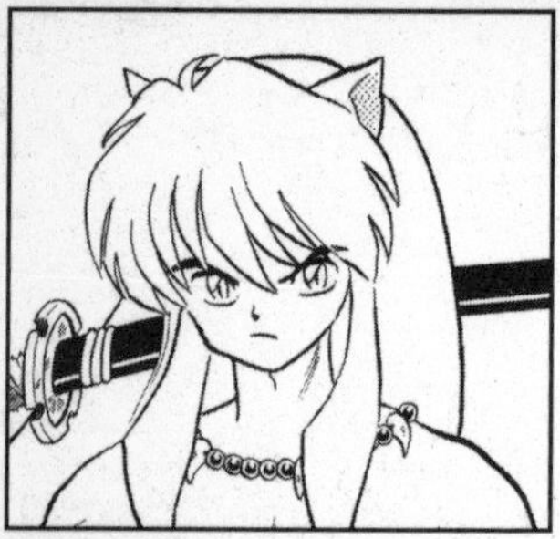

INU-YASHA
A half-human, half-demon hybrid, Inu-Yasha has doglike ears, a thick mane of white hair, and demonic strength. Hoping to increase his demonic powers, he once stole the Shikon Jewel from a village, but was cast into a fifty-year sleep by the arrow of the village priestess, Kikyo, who died as a result of the battle. Now, he assists Kagome in her search for the shards of the Jewel, mostly because he has no choice in the matter—a charmed necklace allows Kagome to restrain him with a single word.

KAGOME
A Japanese schoolgirl from the modern day who is also the reincarnation of Kikyo, the priestess who imprisoned Inu-Yasha for fifty years with her enchanted arrow. As Kikyo's reincarnation, Kagome has the power to see the Shikon Jewel shards, even ones hidden within a demon's body.

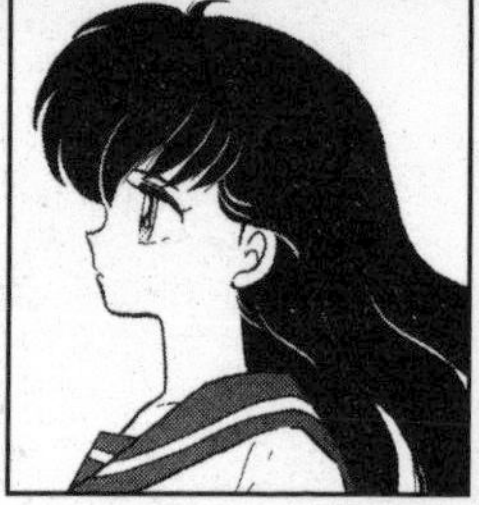

KAEDE
Kikyo's little sister, who carried out the priestess' wish that the Shikon Jewel should be burned with her remains. Now fifty years older, Kaede is head of the village, and helps Kagome and Inu-Yasha in their quest to recover the jewel. It was Kaede's spell, activated by a spoken word, that bound Inu-Yasha to Kagome by means of a string of prayer beads.

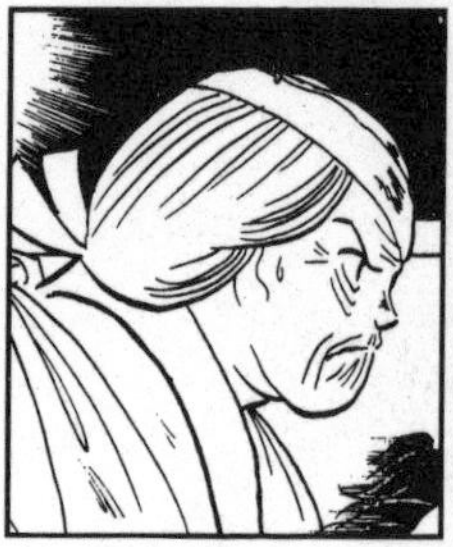

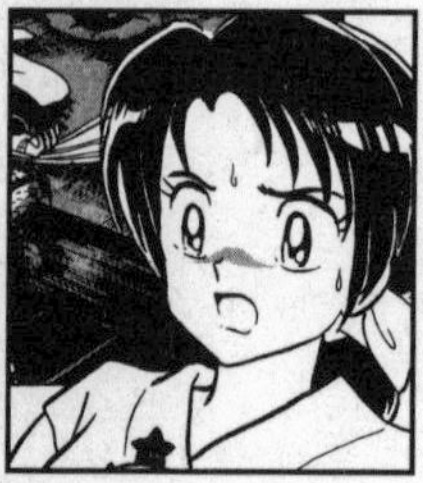

NAZUNA
Orphaned when the Spider-Head demons killed her father, Nazuna was taken in by a kindly old monk who promised to protect her. Her father's death has left Nazuna with a natural distrust of demons.

KIKYO
A powerful priestess, Kikyo was charged with the awesome responsibility of protecting the Shikon Jewel from demons and humans who coveted its power. She died after firing the enchanted arrow that kept Inu-Yasha imprisioned for fifty years.

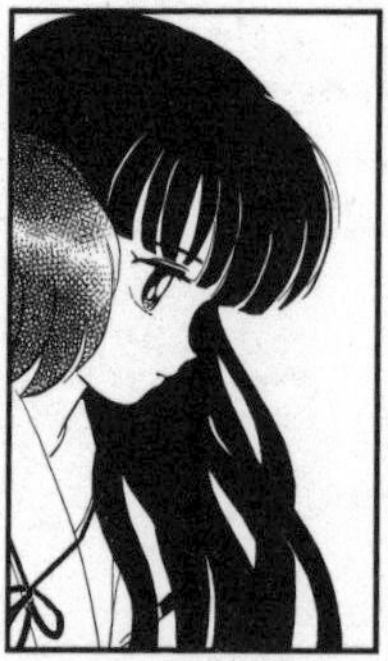

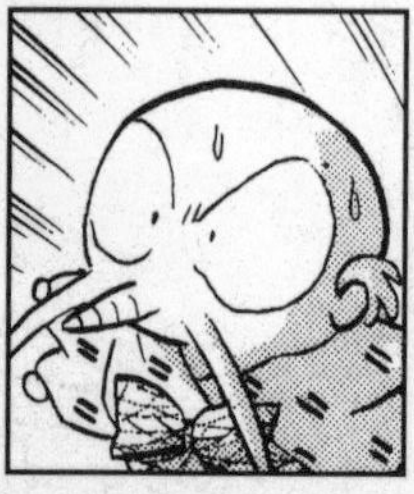

MYOGA
Servant to Inu-Yasha, this flea-demon often offers sage advice, but he is also the first to flee when a situation turns dangerous. His bloodsucking seems to have the ability to weaken certain spells.

SHIPPO
A young fox-demon, orphaned by two other demons whose powers had been boosted by the Shikon Jewel, the mischievous Shippo enjoys goading Inu-Yasha and playing tricks with his shape-changing abilities.

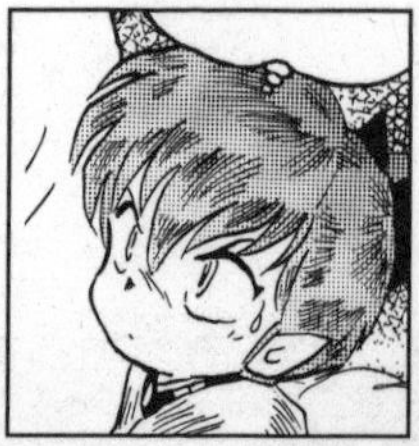

SCROLL ONE

SPIDER HEAD

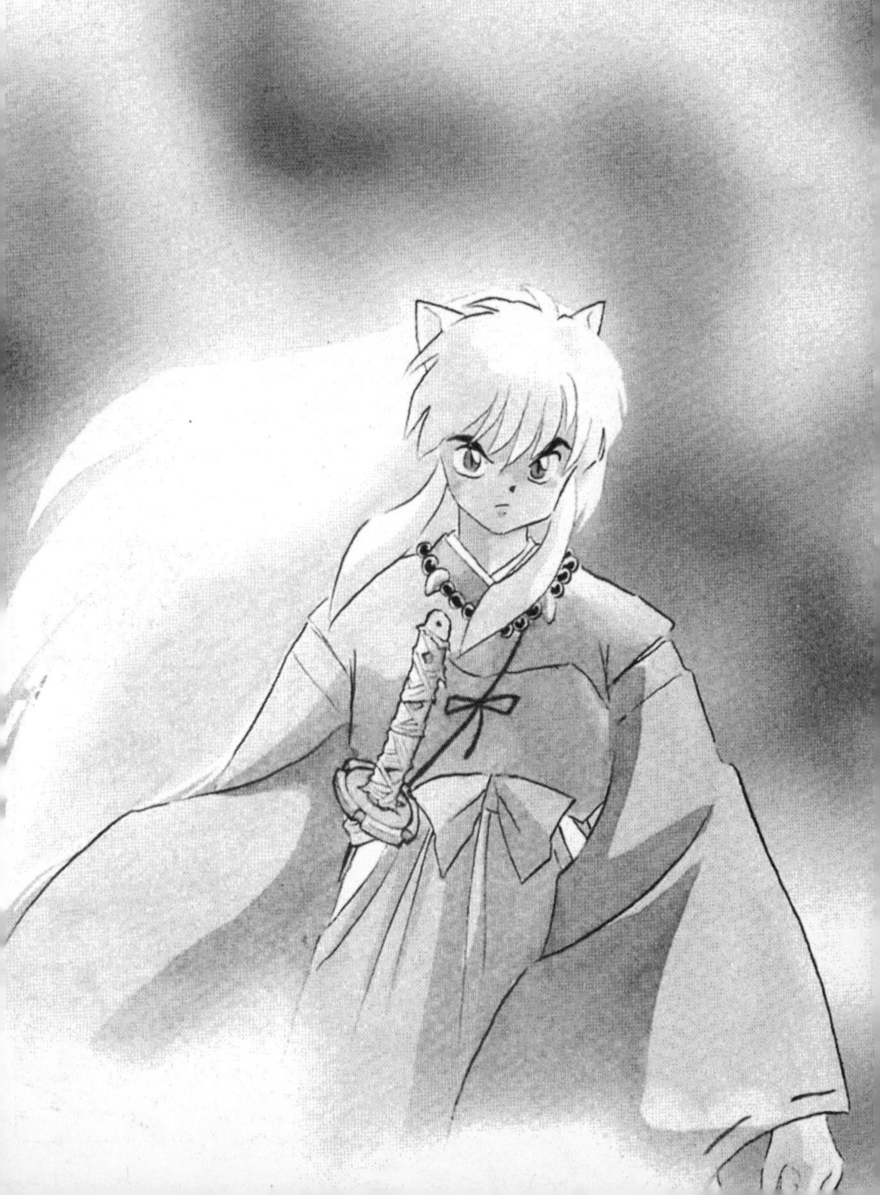

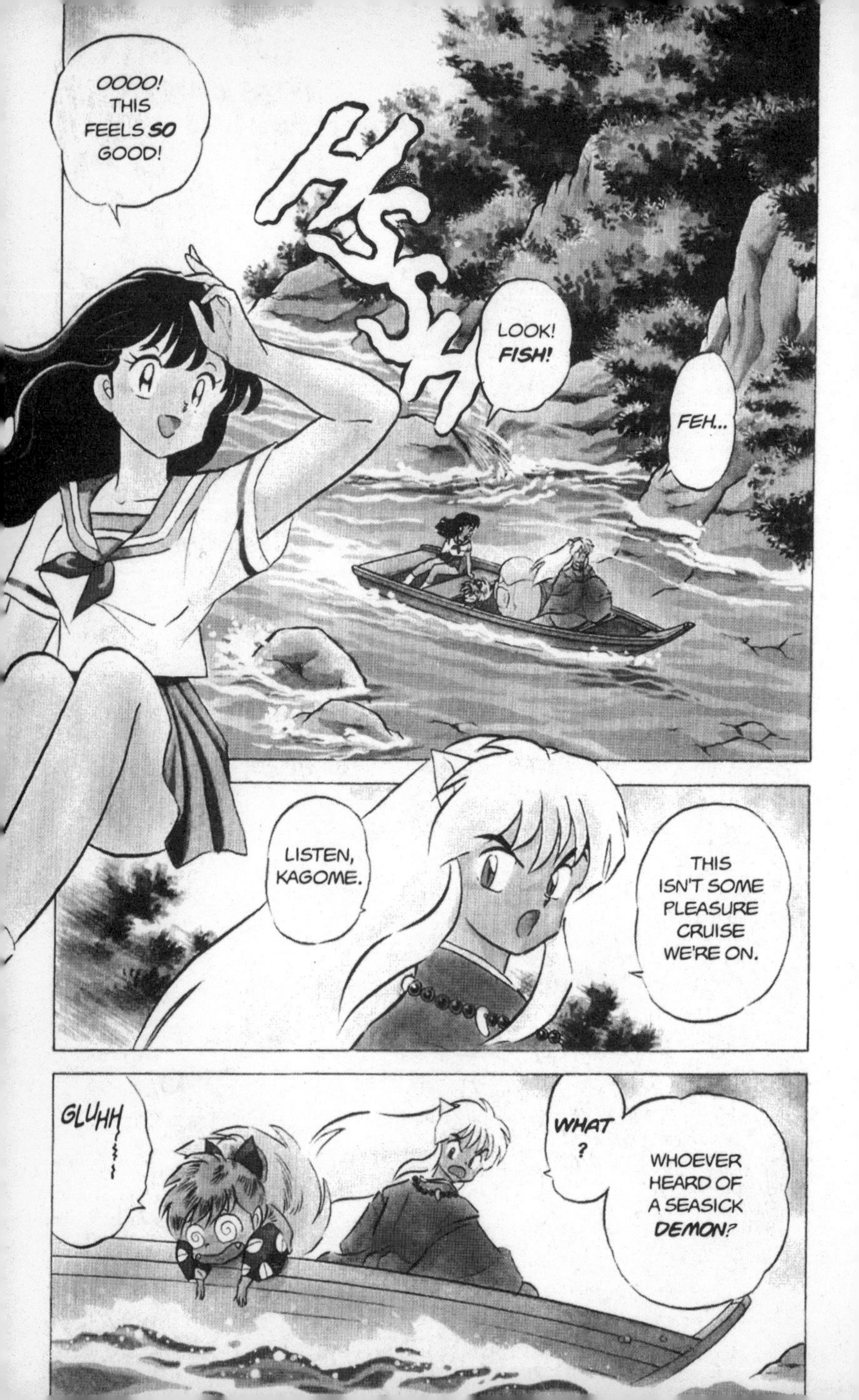
OOOO! THIS FEELS **SO** GOOD!
LOOK! ***FISH!***
FEH...
LISTEN, KAGOME.
THIS ISN'T SOME PLEASURE CRUISE WE'RE ON.
GLUHH
WHAT?
WHOEVER HEARD OF A SEASICK ***DEMON?***

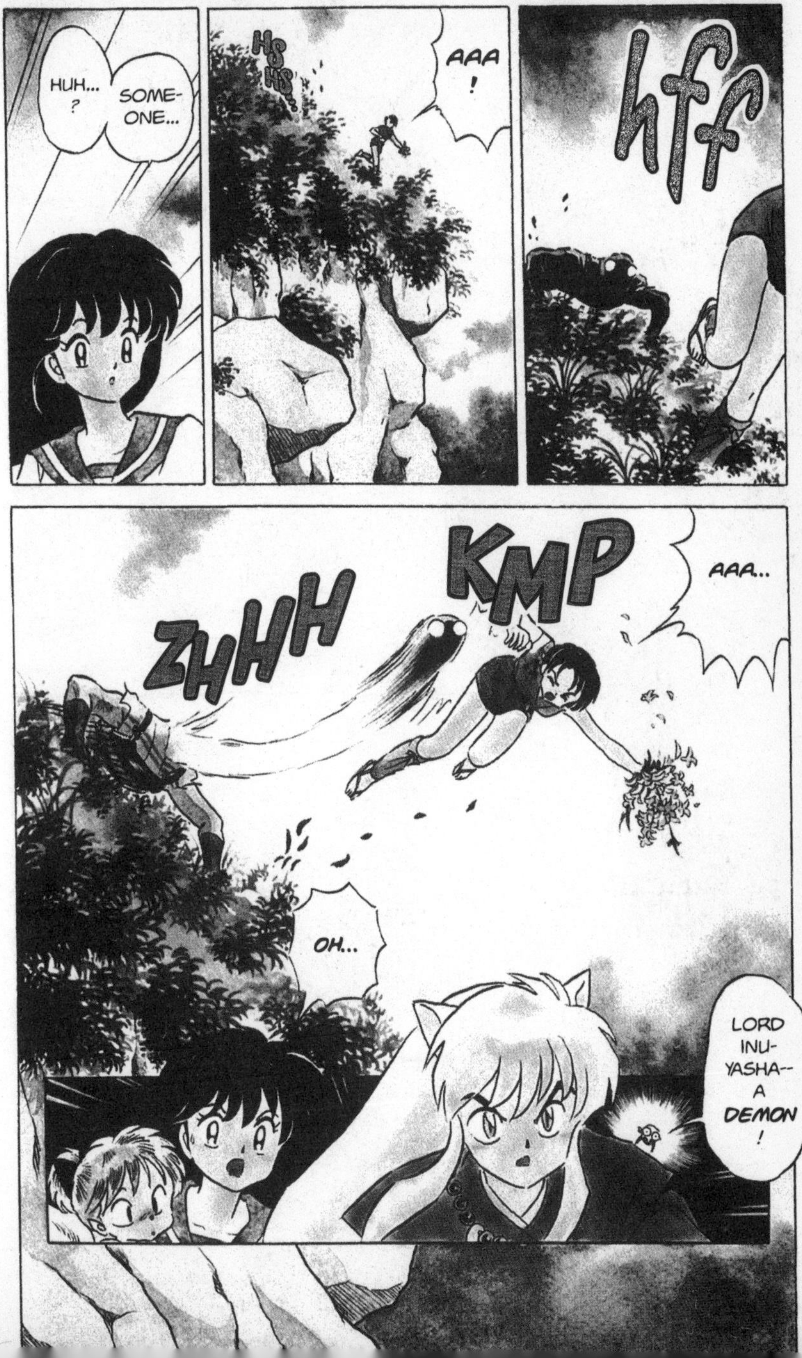
HUH... ?
SOME-ONE...
HS HS...
AAA !
hff
ZHHH
KMP
AAA...
OH...
LORD INU-YASHA-- A DEMON !

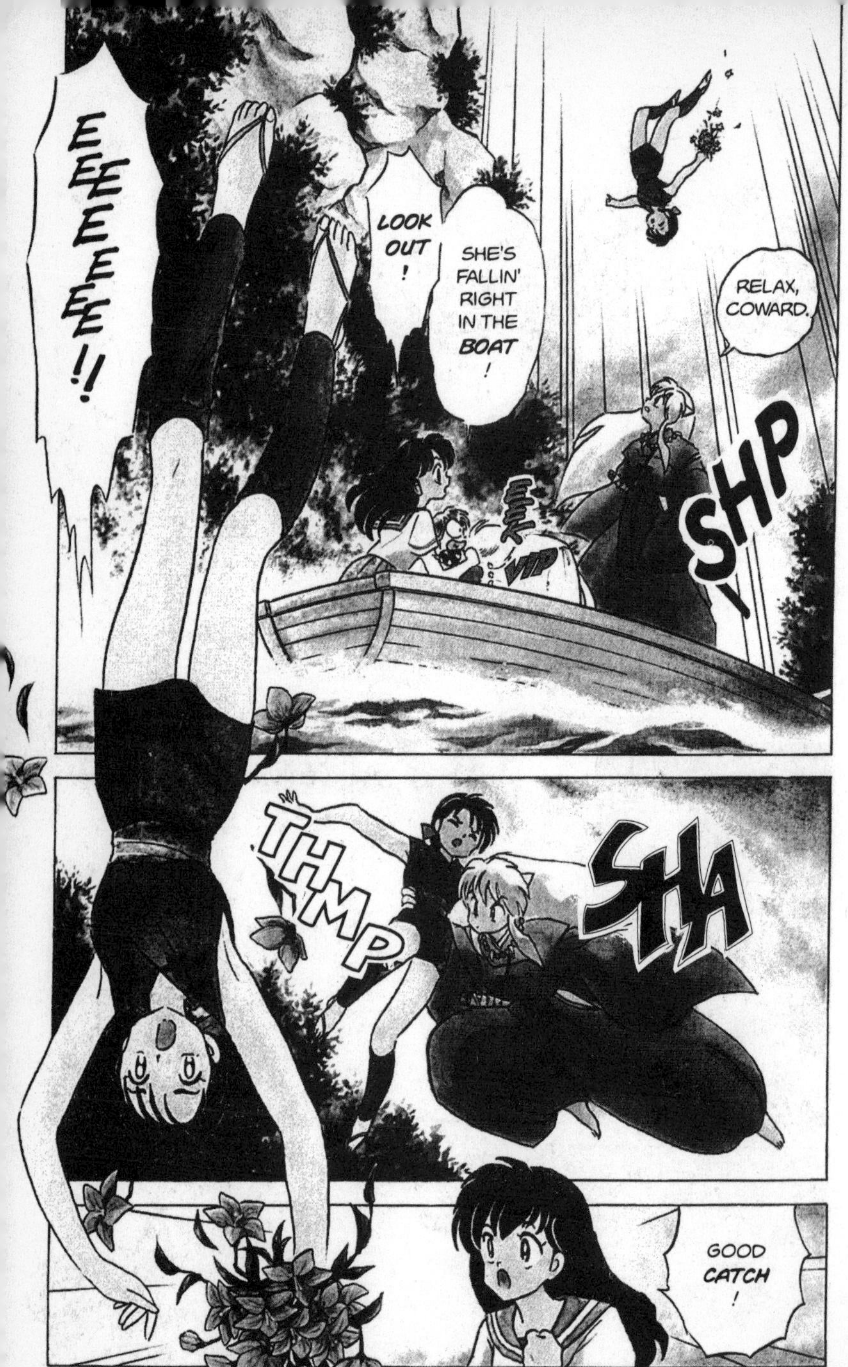
EEEEEEEEE!!
LOOK OUT!
SHE'S FALLIN' RIGHT IN THE BOAT!
RELAX, COWARD.
EEK
VIP
SHP
THMP
SHA
GOOD CATCH!

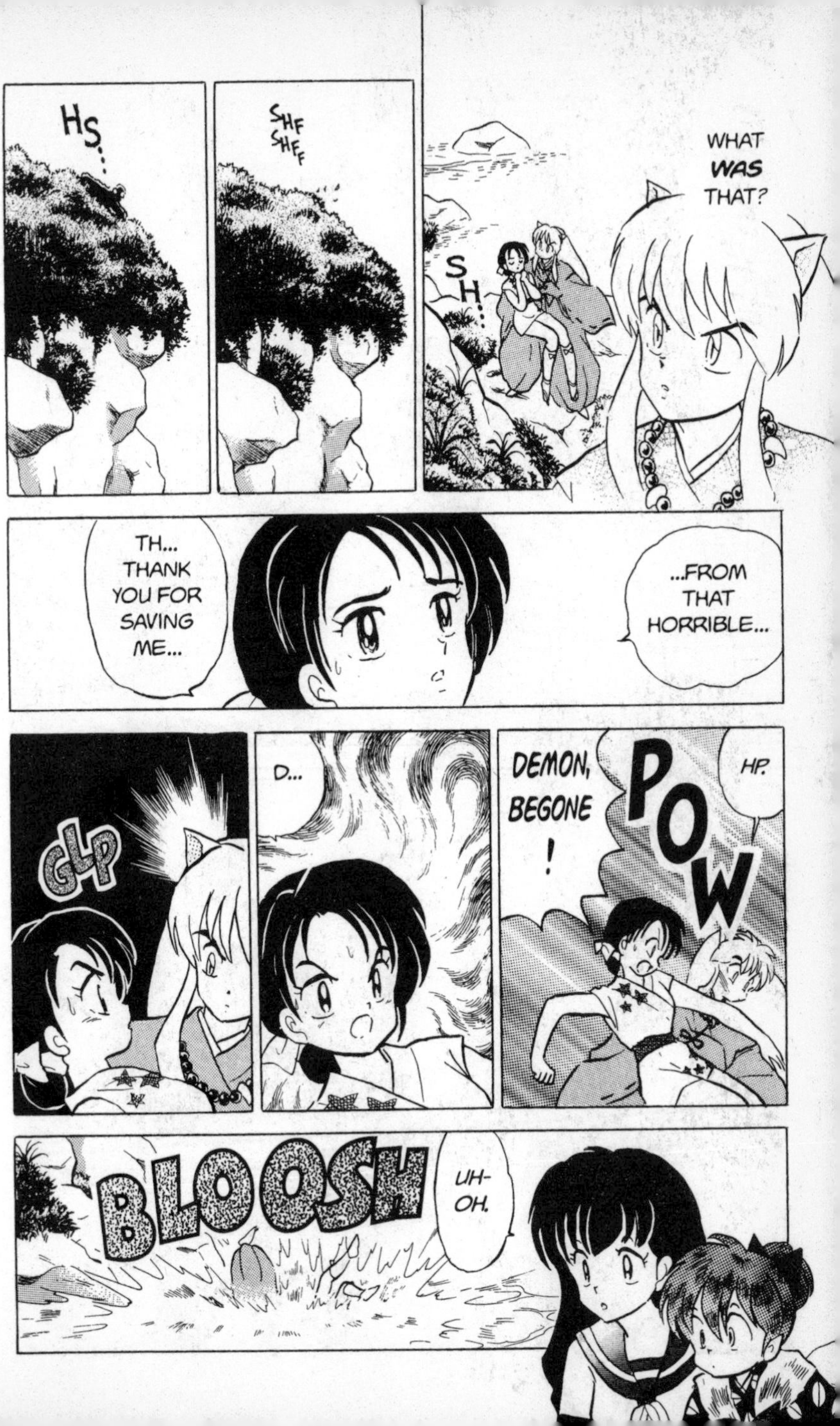
HS...
SHF SHFF
WHAT WAS THAT?
SH...
TH... THANK YOU FOR SAVING ME...
...FROM THAT HORRIBLE...
GLP
D...
DEMON, BEGONE!
POW
HP.
BLOOSH
UH-OH.

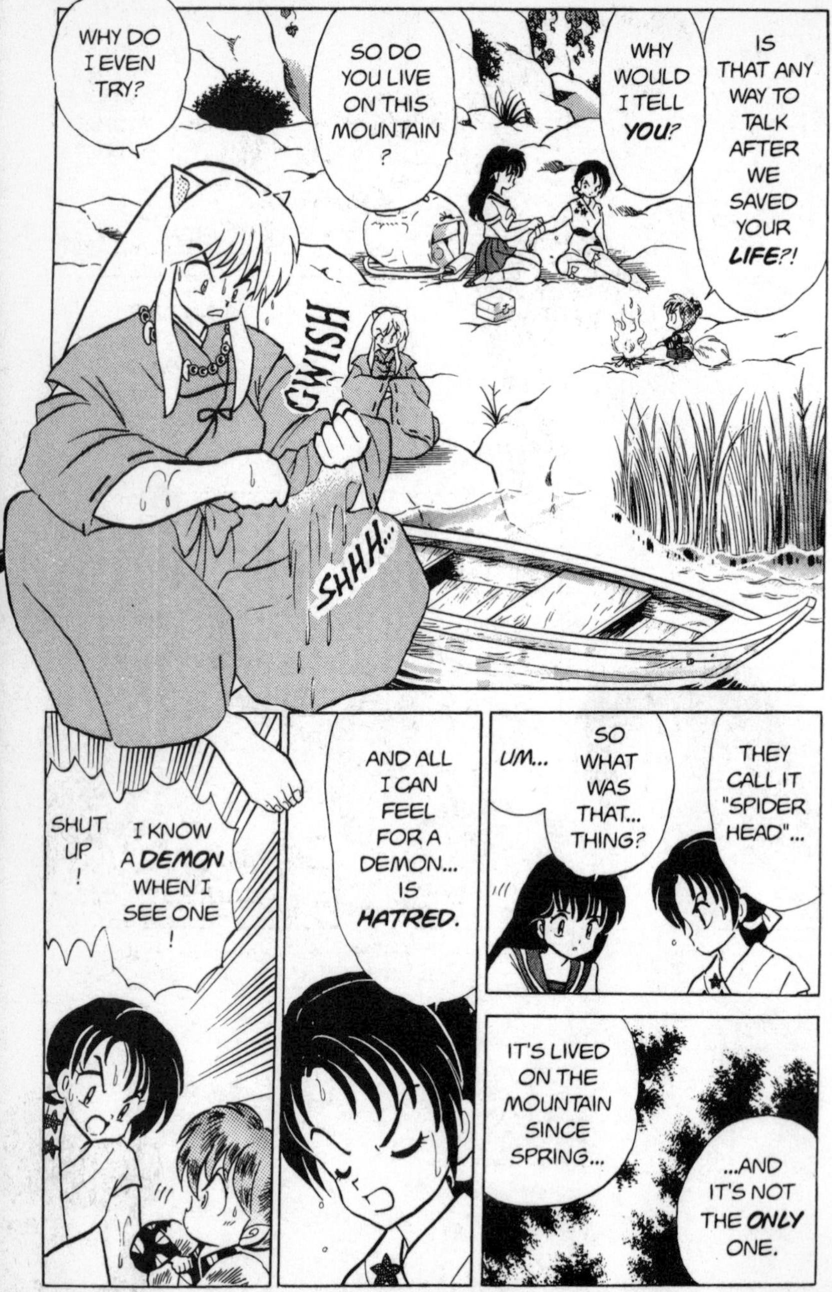
WHY DO I EVEN TRY?
SO DO YOU LIVE ON THIS MOUNTAIN?
WHY WOULD I TELL YOU?
IS THAT ANY WAY TO TALK AFTER WE SAVED YOUR LIFE?!
GWISH
SHHH...
SHUT UP!
I KNOW A DEMON WHEN I SEE ONE!
AND ALL I CAN FEEL FOR A DEMON... IS HATRED.
UM...
SO WHAT WAS THAT... THING?
THEY CALL IT "SPIDER HEAD"...
IT'S LIVED ON THE MOUNTAIN SINCE SPRING...
...AND IT'S NOT THE ONLY ONE.

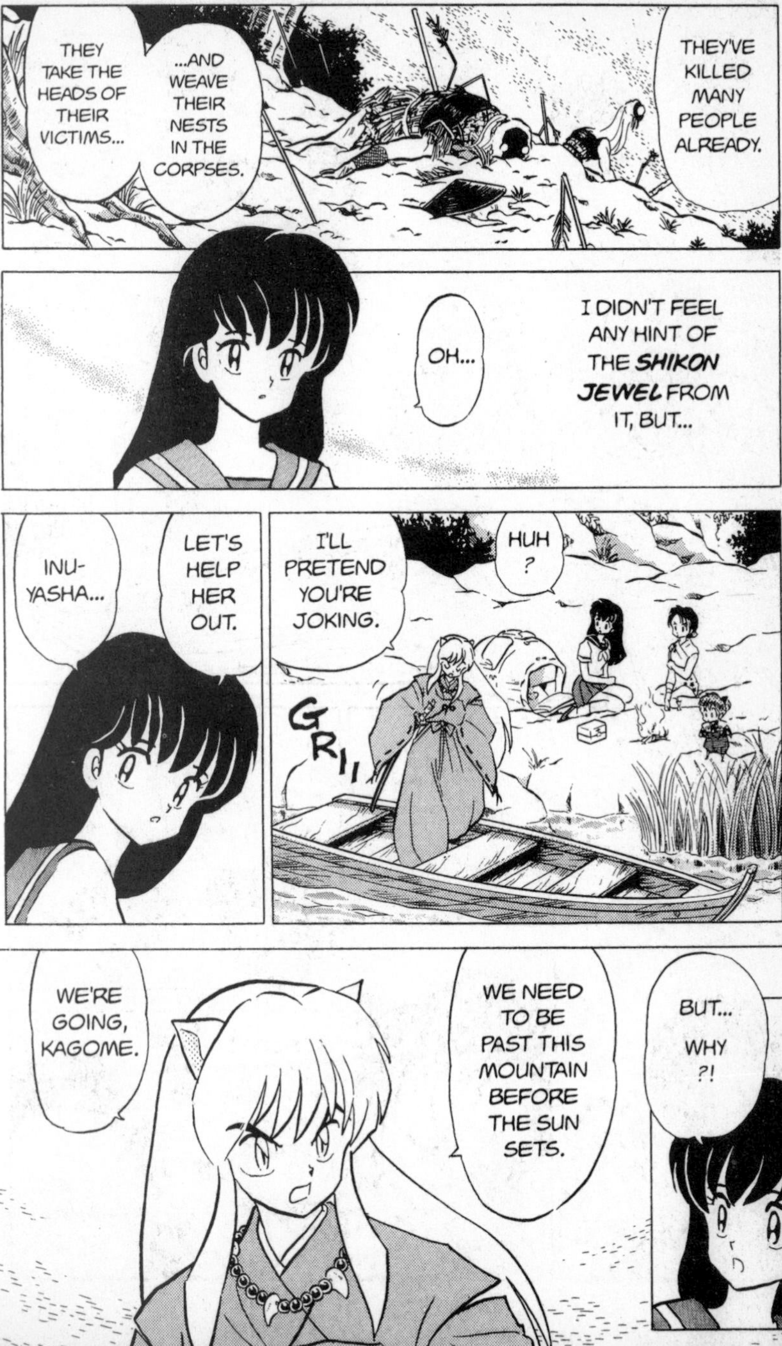
THEY TAKE THE HEADS OF THEIR VICTIMS...
...AND WEAVE THEIR NESTS IN THE CORPSES.
THEY'VE KILLED MANY PEOPLE ALREADY.
OH...
I DIDN'T FEEL ANY HINT OF THE *SHIKON JEWEL* FROM IT, BUT...
INU-YASHA...
LET'S HELP HER OUT.
I'LL PRETEND YOU'RE JOKING.
HUH?
GRII
WE'RE GOING, KAGOME.
WE NEED TO BE PAST THIS MOUNTAIN BEFORE THE SUN SETS.
BUT... WHY?!

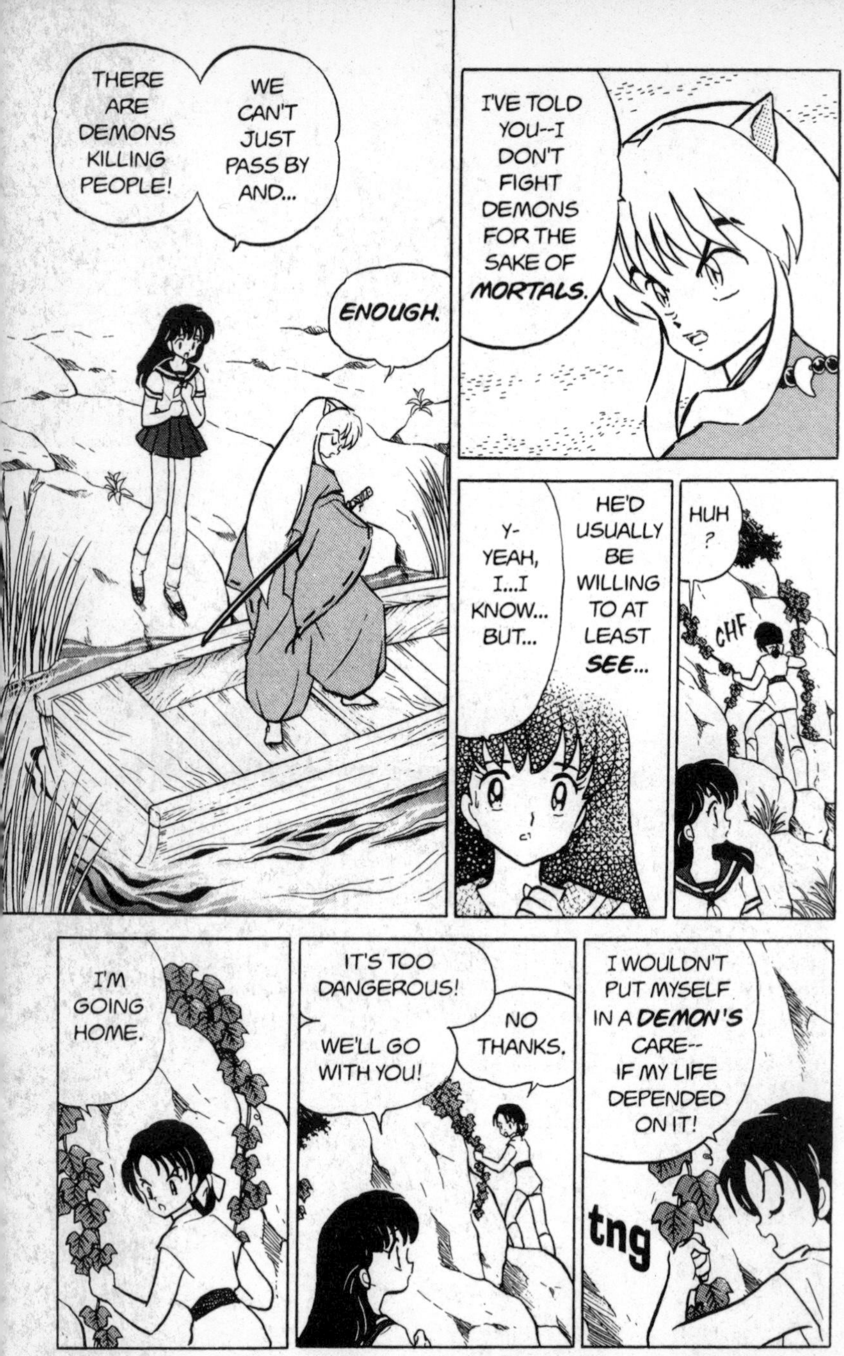
THERE ARE DEMONS KILLING PEOPLE!
WE CAN'T JUST PASS BY AND...
ENOUGH.
I'VE TOLD YOU--I DON'T FIGHT DEMONS FOR THE SAKE OF MORTALS.
Y-YEAH, I...I KNOW... BUT...
HE'D USUALLY BE WILLING TO AT LEAST SEE...
HUH?
CHF
I'M GOING HOME.
IT'S TOO DANGEROUS!
WE'LL GO WITH YOU!
NO THANKS.
I WOULDN'T PUT MYSELF IN A DEMON'S CARE-- IF MY LIFE DEPENDED ON IT!
tng

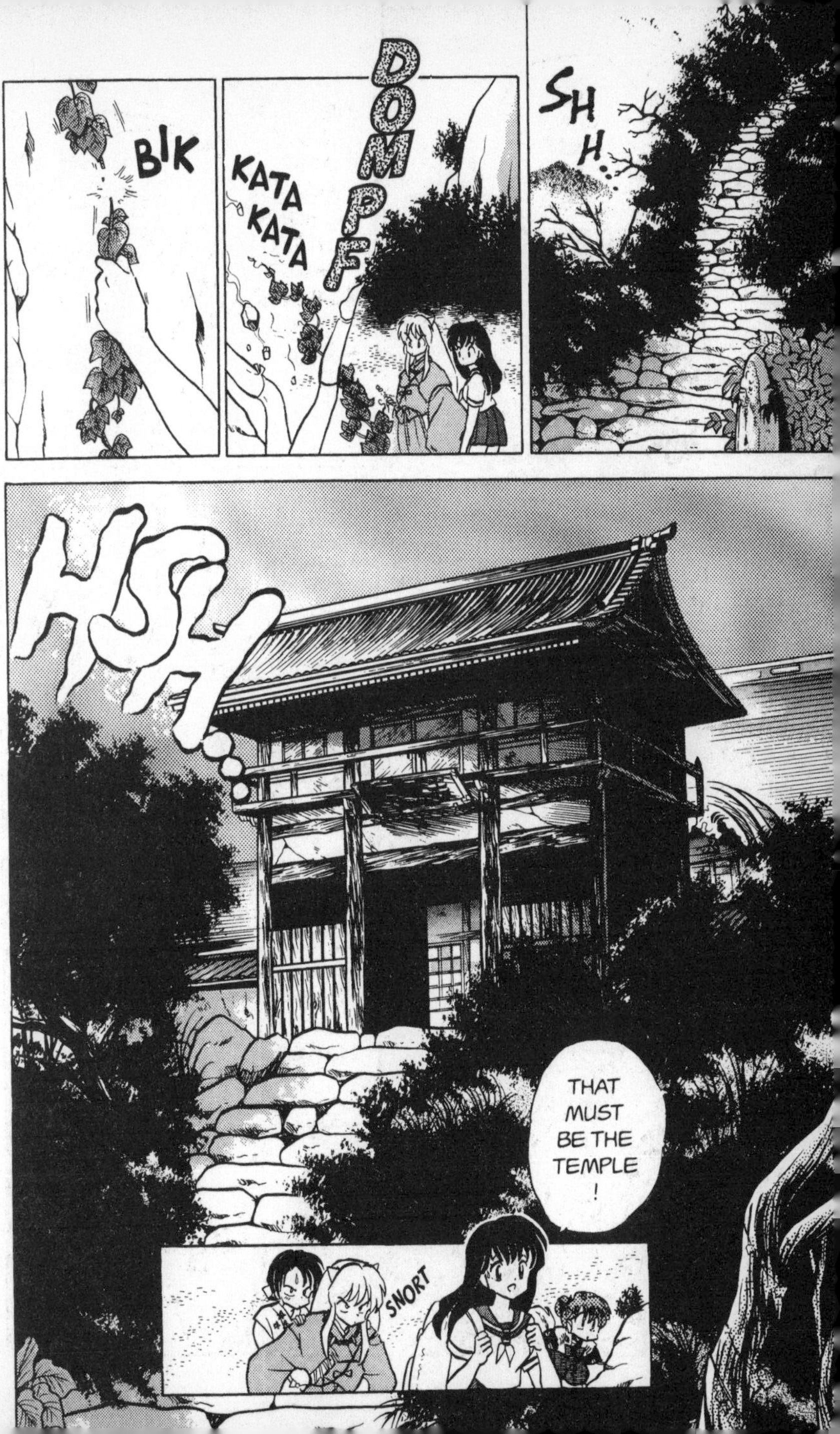
BIK
KATA KATA
DOMPF
SHH...
HSH...
THAT MUST BE THE TEMPLE!
SNORT

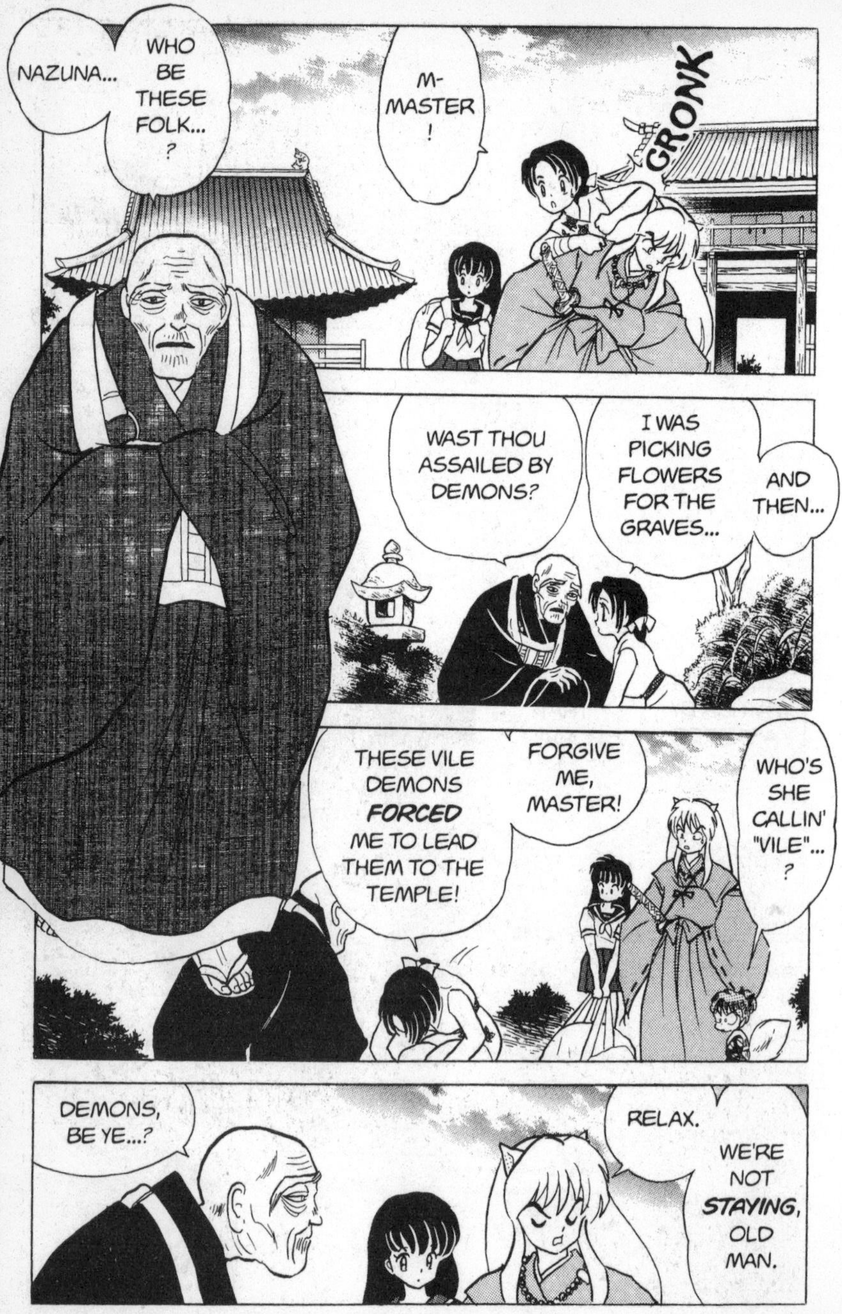
NAZUNA...
WHO BE THESE FOLK...?
M-MASTER!
GRONK
WAST THOU ASSAILED BY DEMONS?
I WAS PICKING FLOWERS FOR THE GRAVES...
AND THEN...
THESE VILE DEMONS *FORCED* ME TO LEAD THEM TO THE TEMPLE!
FORGIVE ME, MASTER!
WHO'S SHE CALLIN' "VILE"...?
DEMONS, BE YE...?
RELAX.
WE'RE NOT *STAYING*, OLD MAN.

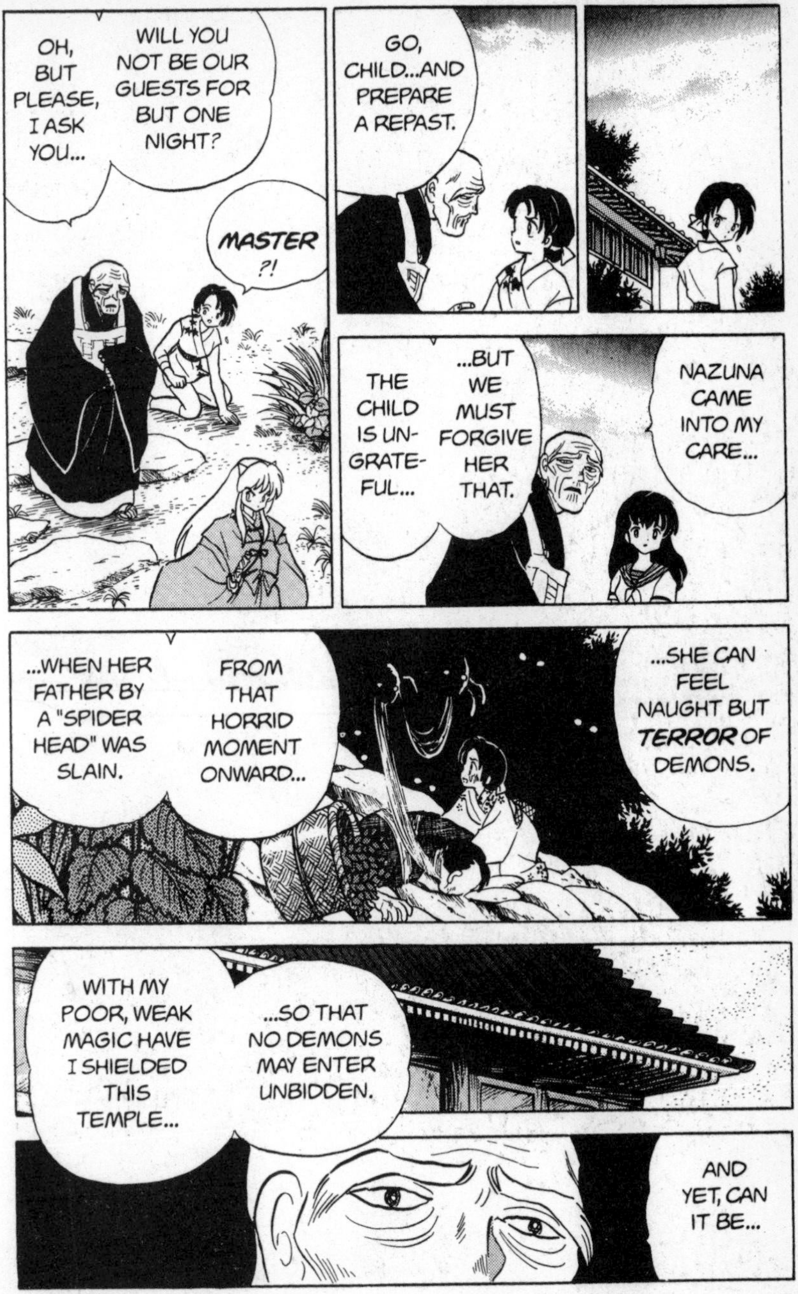
OH, BUT PLEASE, I ASK YOU...
WILL YOU NOT BE OUR GUESTS FOR BUT ONE NIGHT?
MASTER ?!
GO, CHILD...AND PREPARE A REPAST.
THE CHILD IS UN-GRATE-FUL...
...BUT WE MUST FORGIVE HER THAT.
NAZUNA CAME INTO MY CARE...
...WHEN HER FATHER BY A "SPIDER HEAD" WAS SLAIN.
FROM THAT HORRID MOMENT ONWARD...
...SHE CAN FEEL NAUGHT BUT TERROR OF DEMONS.
WITH MY POOR, WEAK MAGIC HAVE I SHIELDED THIS TEMPLE...
...SO THAT NO DEMONS MAY ENTER UNBIDDEN.
AND YET, CAN IT BE...

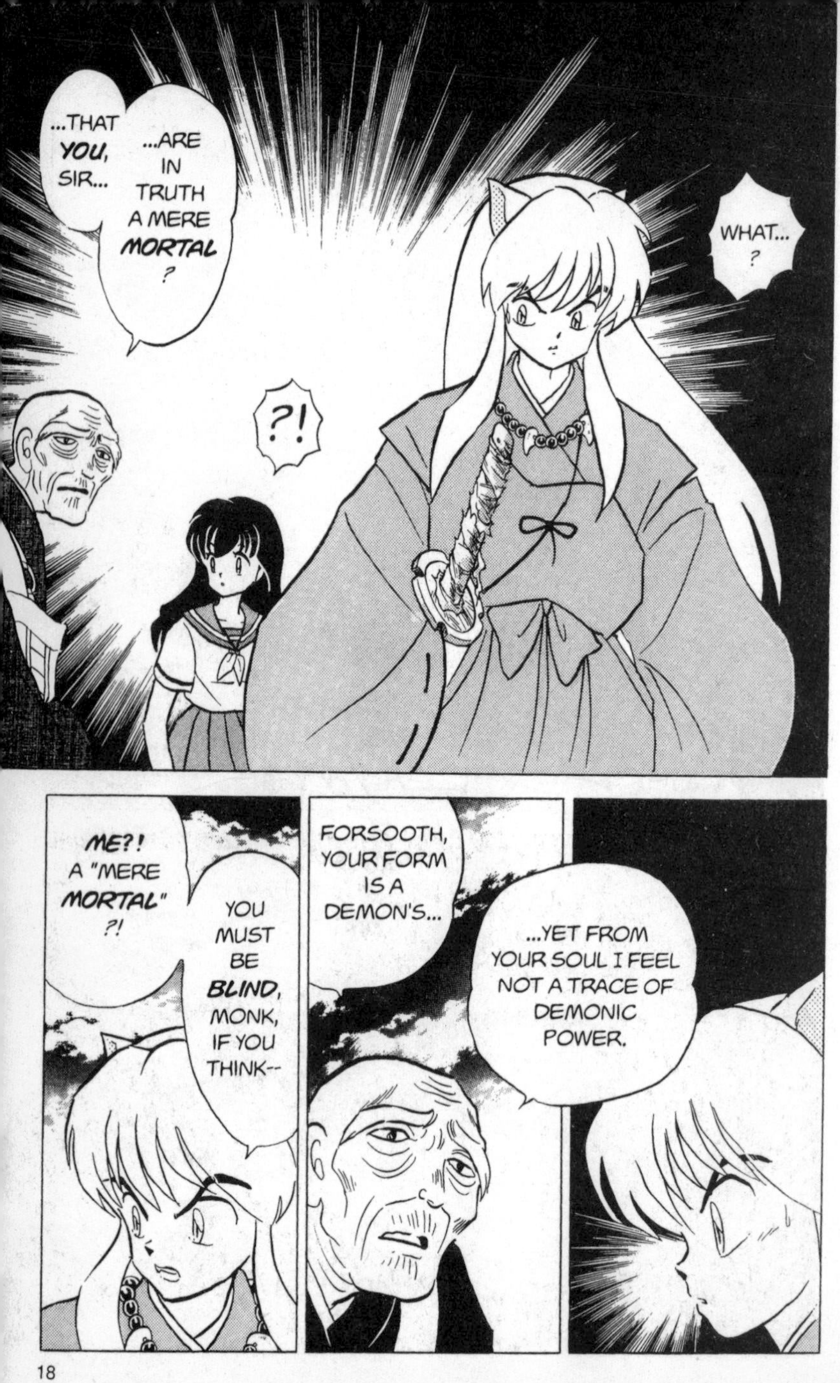
...THAT YOU, SIR...
...ARE IN TRUTH A MERE MORTAL?
WHAT...?
?!
ME?! A "MERE MORTAL"?!
YOU MUST BE BLIND, MONK, IF YOU THINK--
FORSOOTH, YOUR FORM IS A DEMON'S...
...YET FROM YOUR SOUL I FEEL NOT A TRACE OF DEMONIC POWER.

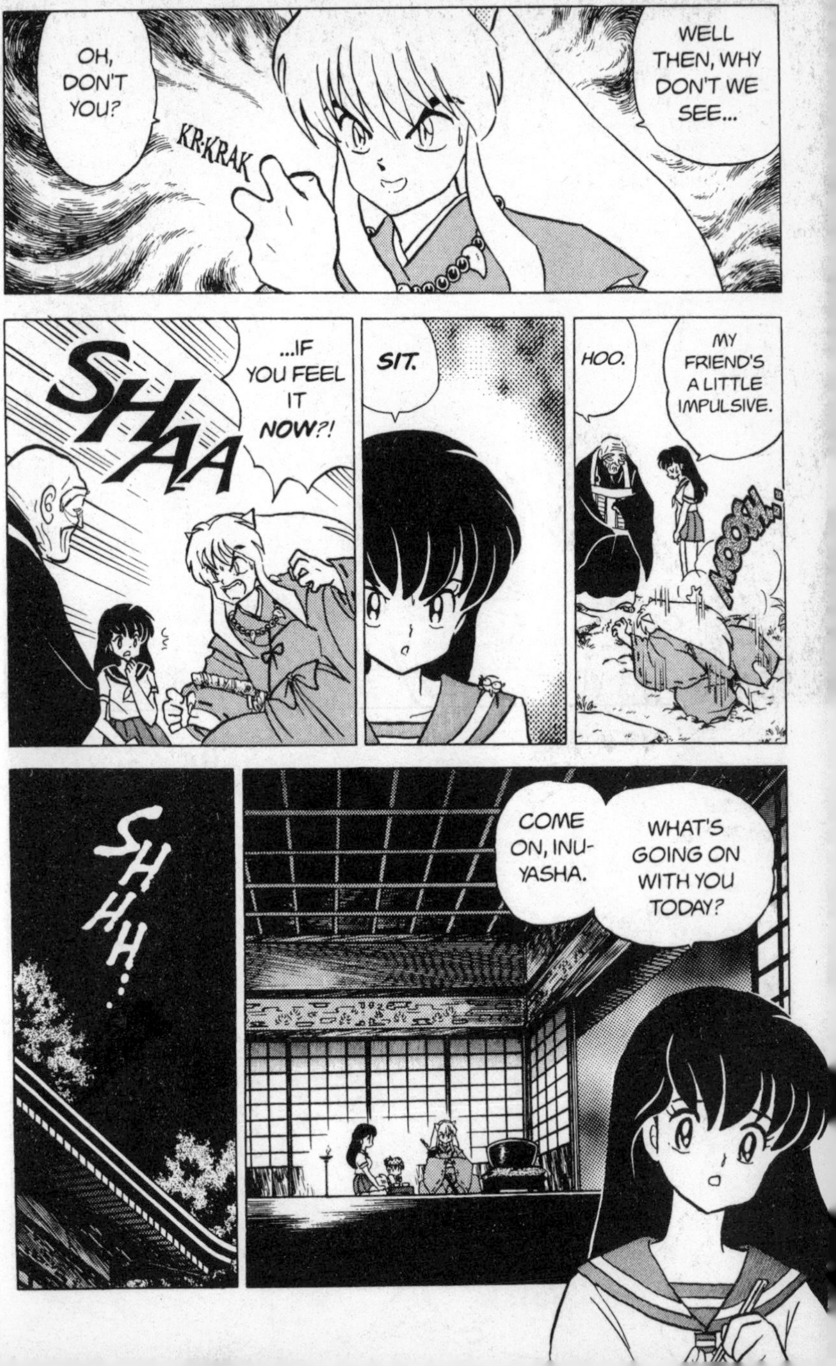
OH, DON'T YOU?
KR-KRAK
WELL THEN, WHY DON'T WE SEE...
SHAA
...IF YOU FEEL IT NOW?!
SIT.
HOO.
MY FRIEND'S A LITTLE IMPULSIVE.
WOOF!!
SHHH...
COME ON, INU-YASHA.
WHAT'S GOING ON WITH YOU TODAY?

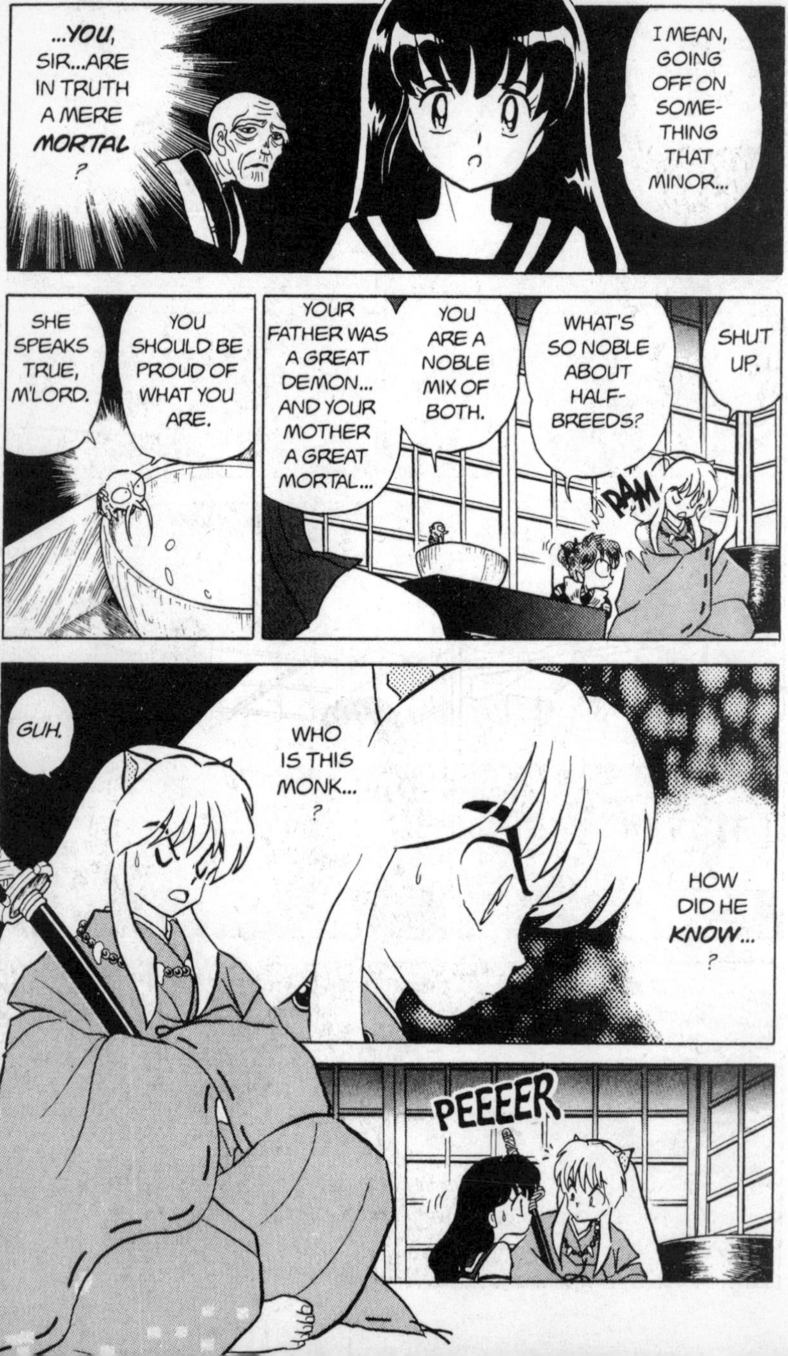
...YOU, SIR...ARE IN TRUTH A MERE MORTAL?
I MEAN, GOING OFF ON SOMETHING THAT MINOR...
SHE SPEAKS TRUE, M'LORD.
YOU SHOULD BE PROUD OF WHAT YOU ARE.
YOUR FATHER WAS A GREAT DEMON... AND YOUR MOTHER A GREAT MORTAL...
YOU ARE A NOBLE MIX OF BOTH.
WHAT'S SO NOBLE ABOUT HALF-BREEDS?
SHUT UP.
BAM
GUH.
WHO IS THIS MONK...?
HOW DID HE KNOW...?
PEEEER

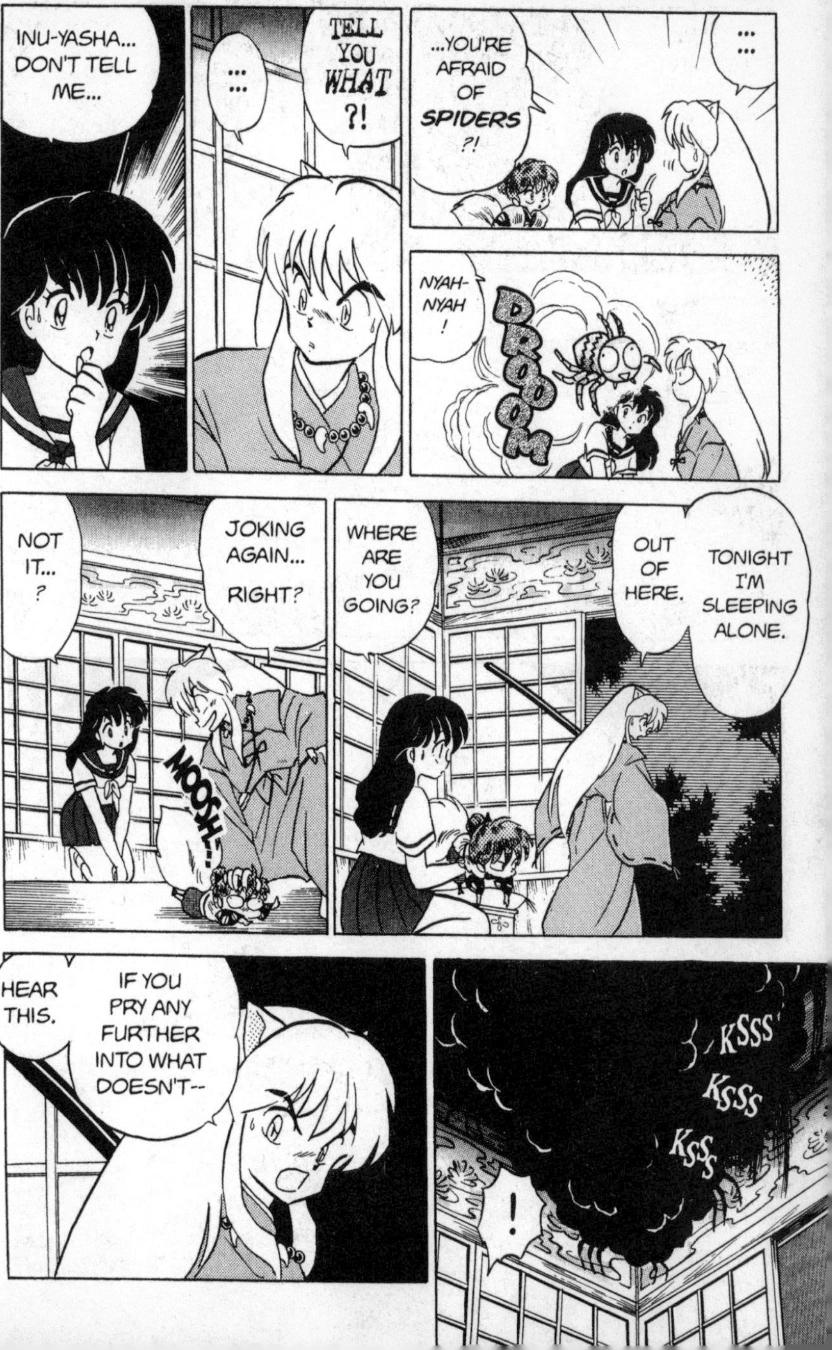
INU-YASHA... DON'T TELL ME...
... ...
TELL YOU WHAT ?!
...YOU'RE AFRAID OF SPIDERS ?!
... ...
NYAH-NYAH !
DROOOM
NOT IT... ?
JOKING AGAIN... RIGHT?
MOOSH...
WHERE ARE YOU GOING?
OUT OF HERE.
TONIGHT I'M SLEEPING ALONE.
HEAR THIS.
IF YOU PRY ANY FURTHER INTO WHAT DOESN'T--
KSSS
KSSS
KSSS
!

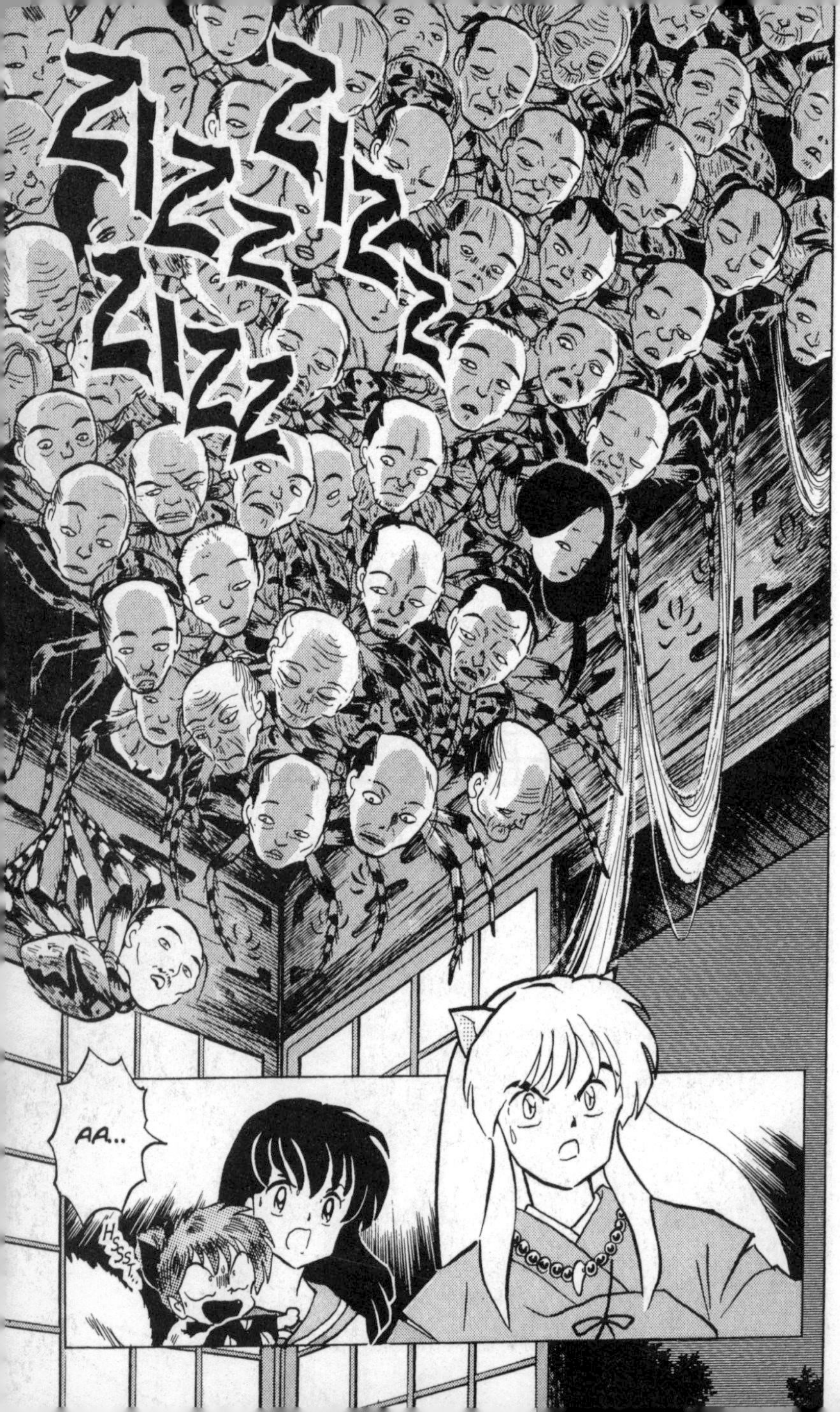

ZZZZ
ZZZ
AA...
HSSST...

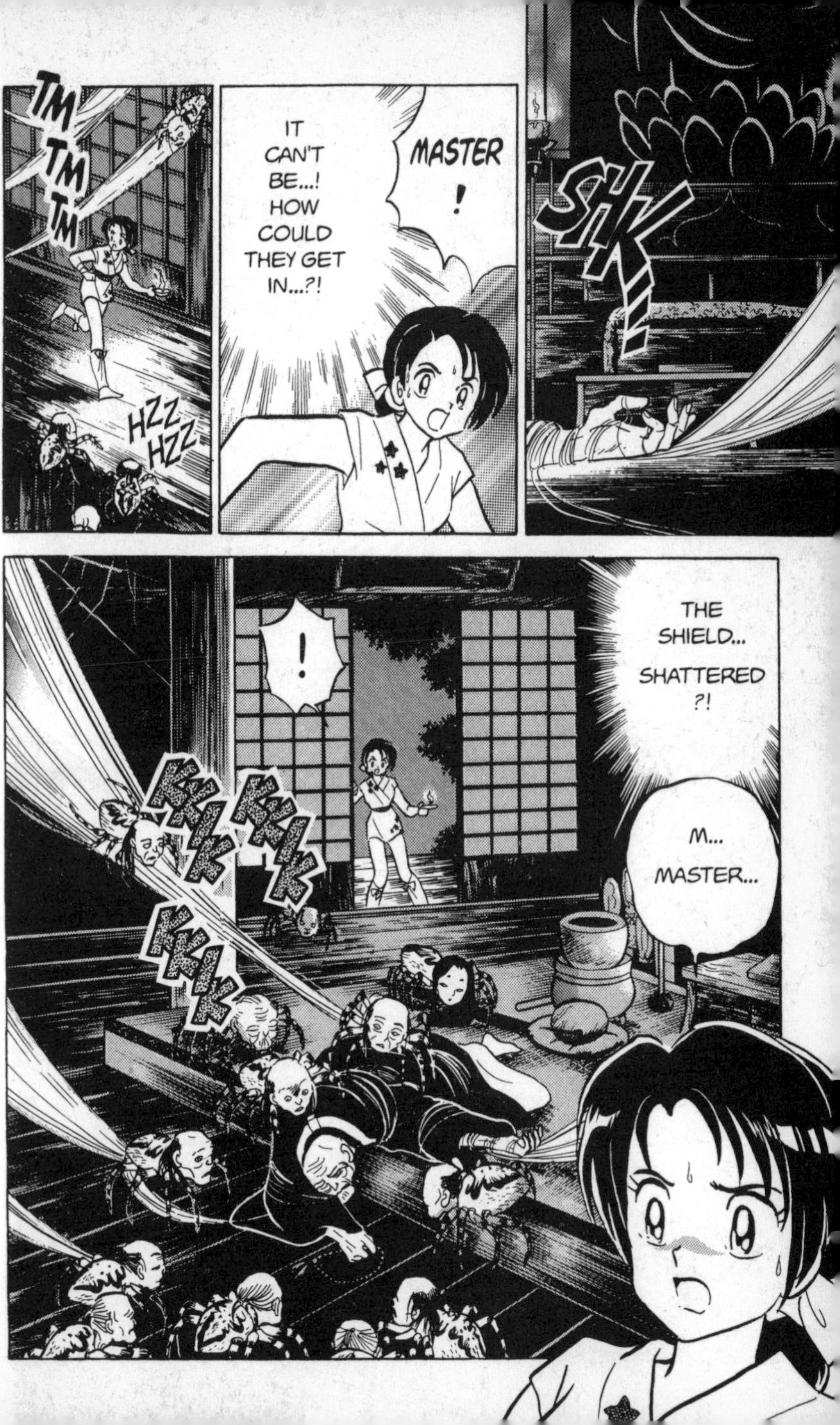
TM TM TM
HZZ HZZ
IT CAN'T BE...! HOW COULD THEY GET IN...?!
MASTER !
SHK
!
THE SHIELD...
SHATTERED ?!
KKKK
KKKK
KKK
M... MASTER...

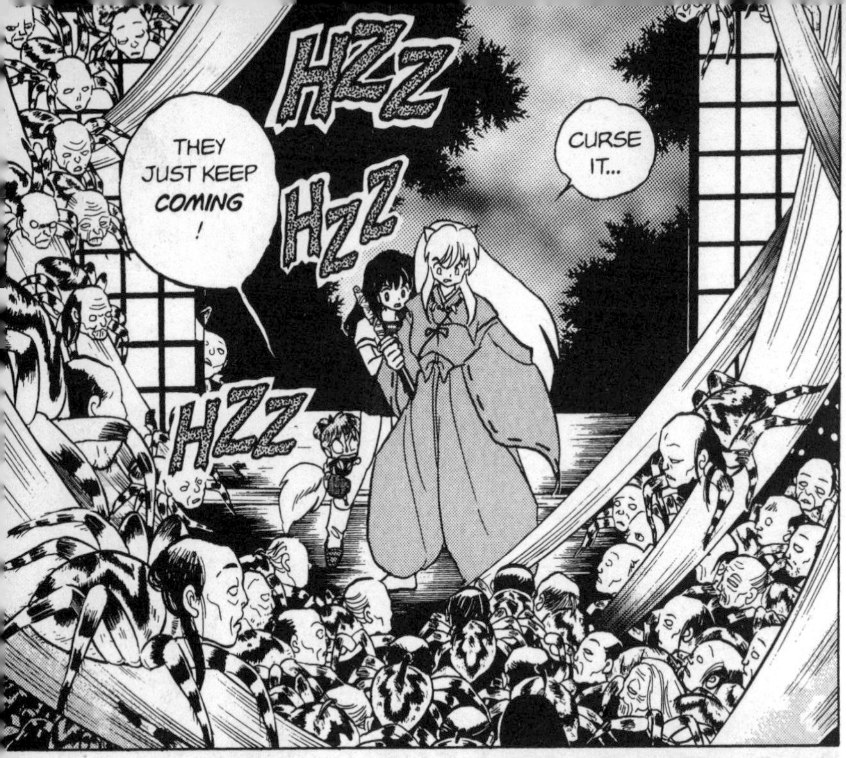
HZZ
THEY JUST KEEP COMING!
HZZ
CURSE IT...
HZZ
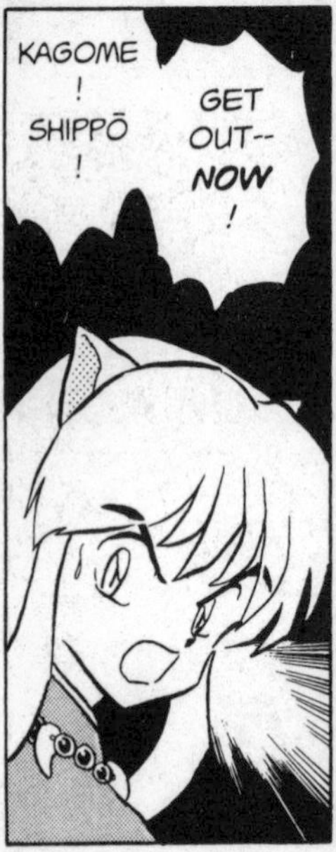
KAGOME! SHIPPŌ!
GET OUT--NOW!
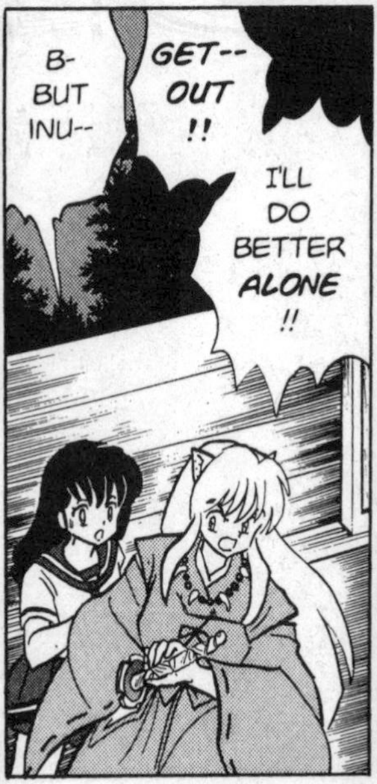
B-BUT INU--
GET--OUT!!
I'LL DO BETTER ALONE!!
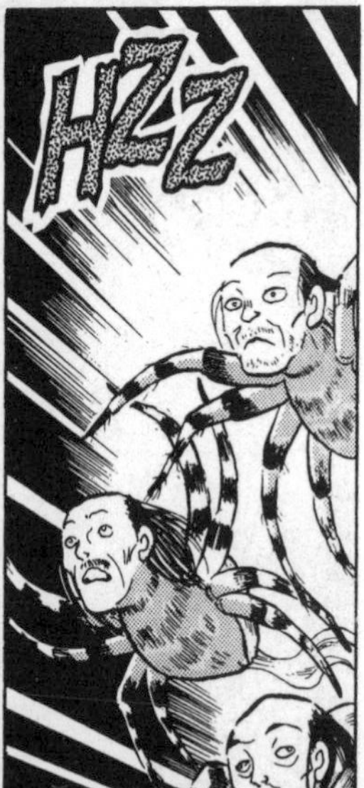
HZZ

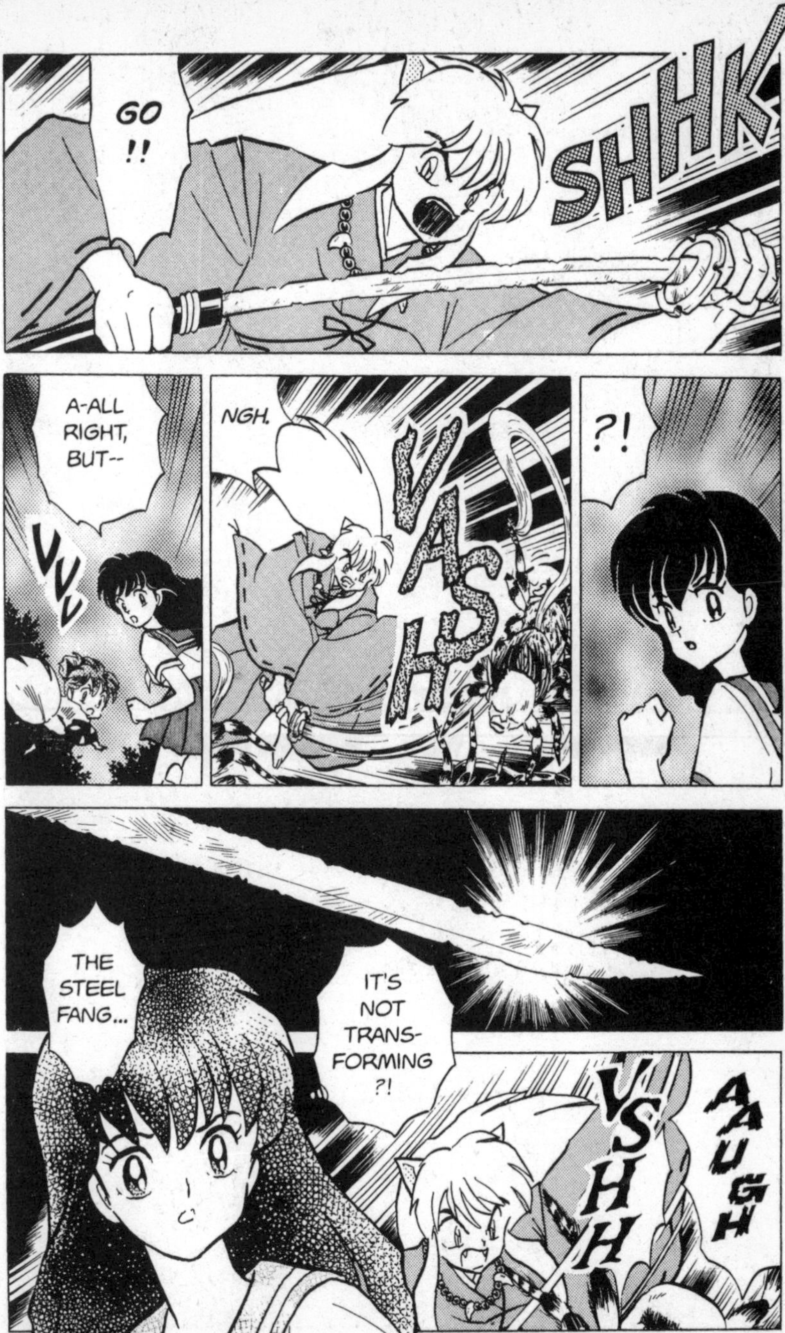
GO !!
SHHK
A-ALL RIGHT, BUT--
VVV
NGH.
VASH
?!
THE STEEL FANG...
IT'S NOT TRANS-FORMING ?!
VSHH
AAUGH

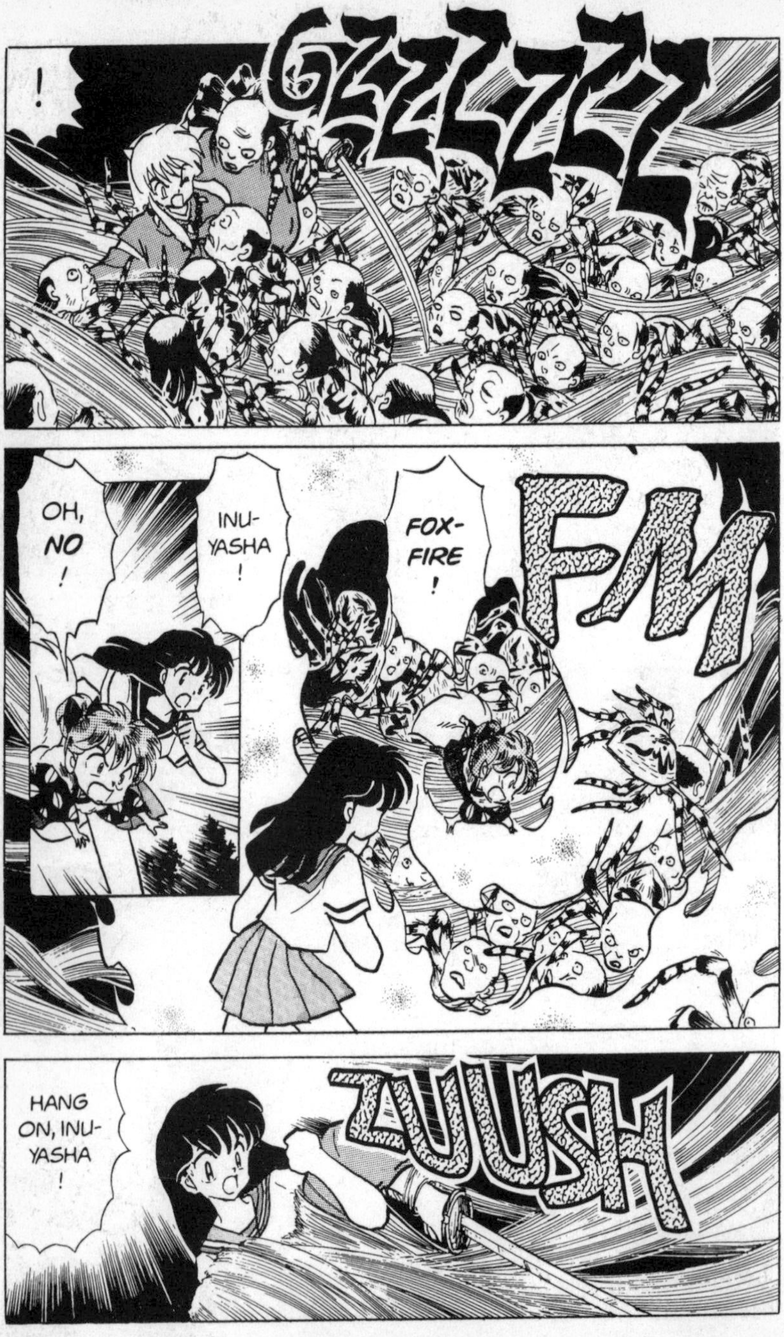
!
GZZZZZT
OH, NO!
INU-YASHA!
FOX-FIRE!
FM
HANG ON, INU-YASHA!
ZUUSH

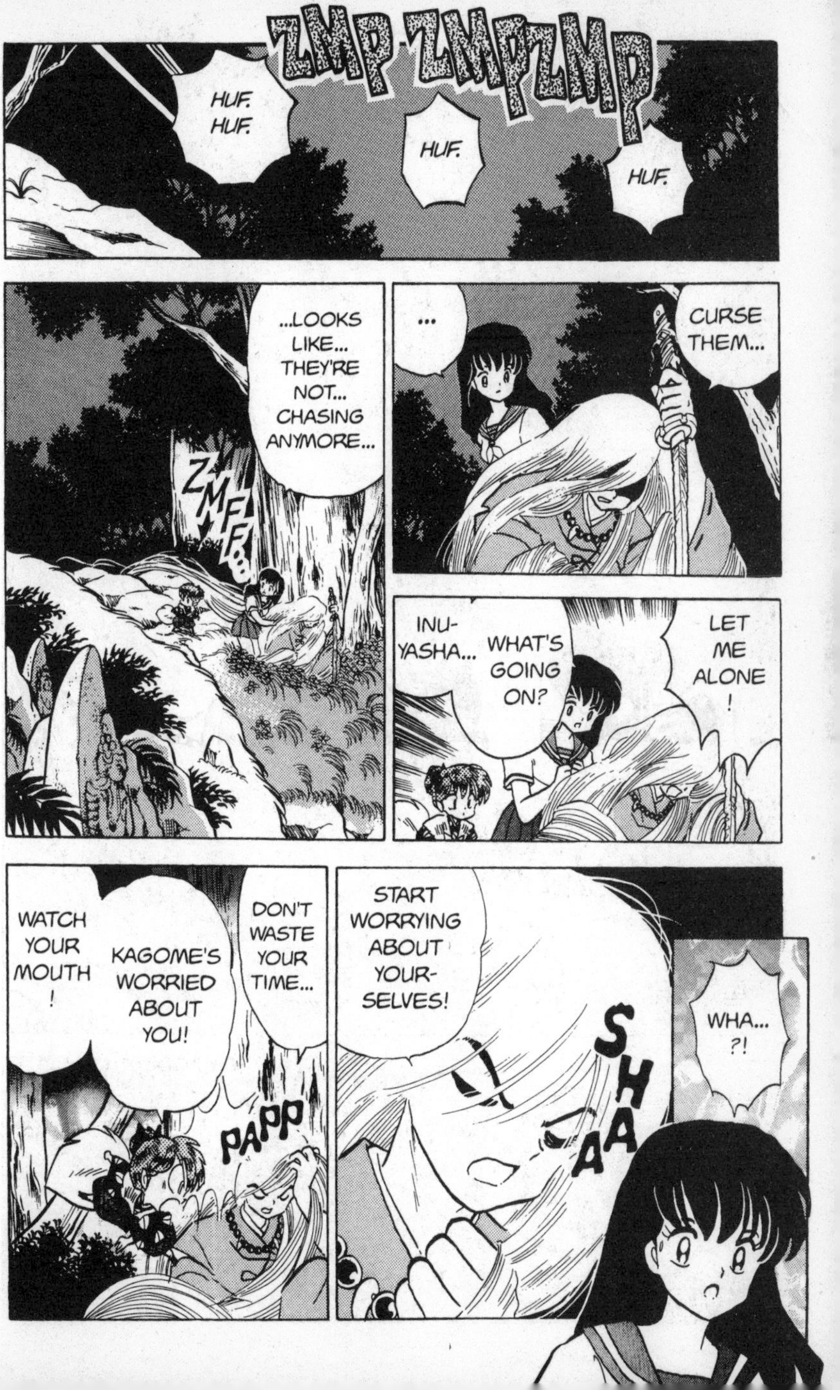
ZMP ZMP ZMP ZMP
HUF. HUF.
HUF.
HUF.
...LOOKS LIKE... THEY'RE NOT... CHASING ANYMORE...
ZMFF
...
CURSE THEM...
INU-YASHA...
WHAT'S GOING ON?
LET ME ALONE!
WATCH YOUR MOUTH!
KAGOME'S WORRIED ABOUT YOU!
DON'T WASTE YOUR TIME...
PAPP
START WORRYING ABOUT YOUR-SELVES!
SHAA
WHA...?!

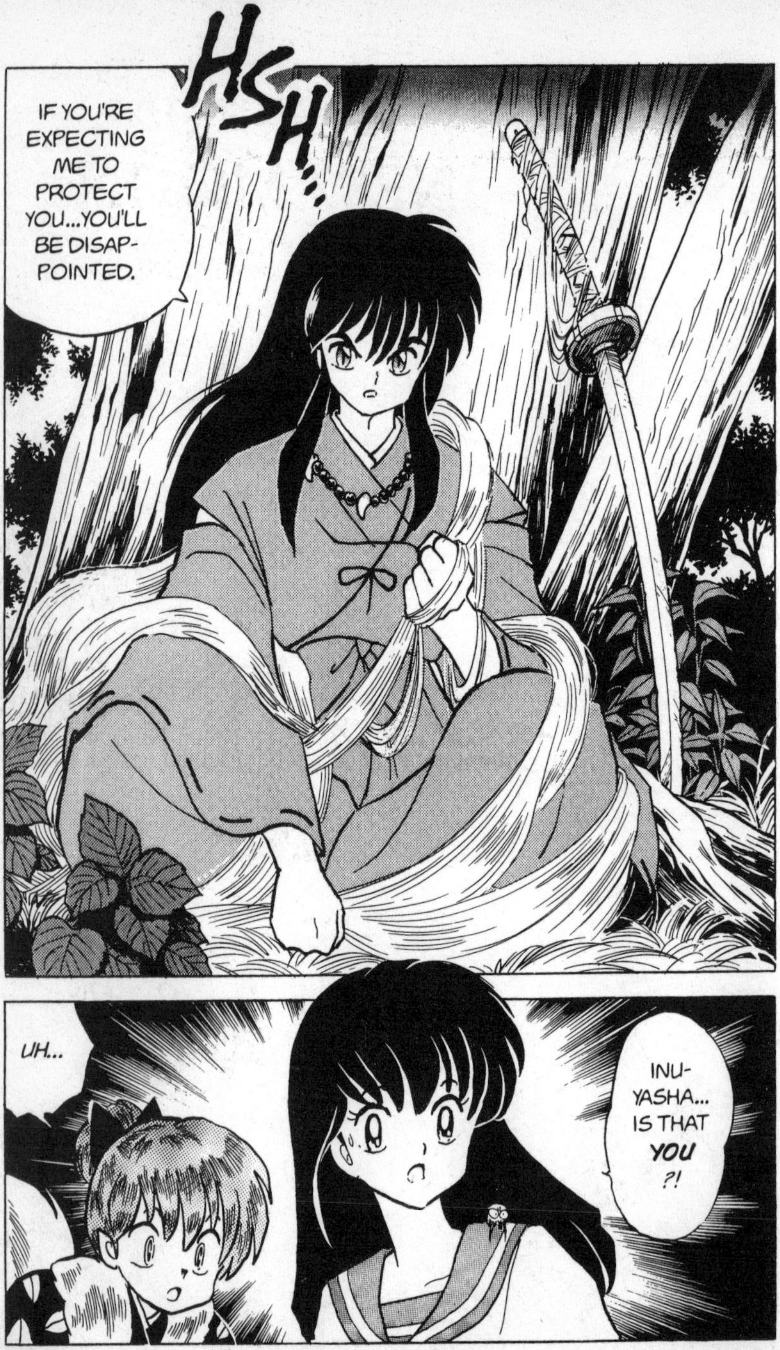
HSH...
IF YOU'RE EXPECTING ME TO PROTECT YOU...YOU'LL BE DISAP-POINTED.
UH...
INU-YASHA... IS THAT YOU ?!

SCROLL TWO

NEW MOON

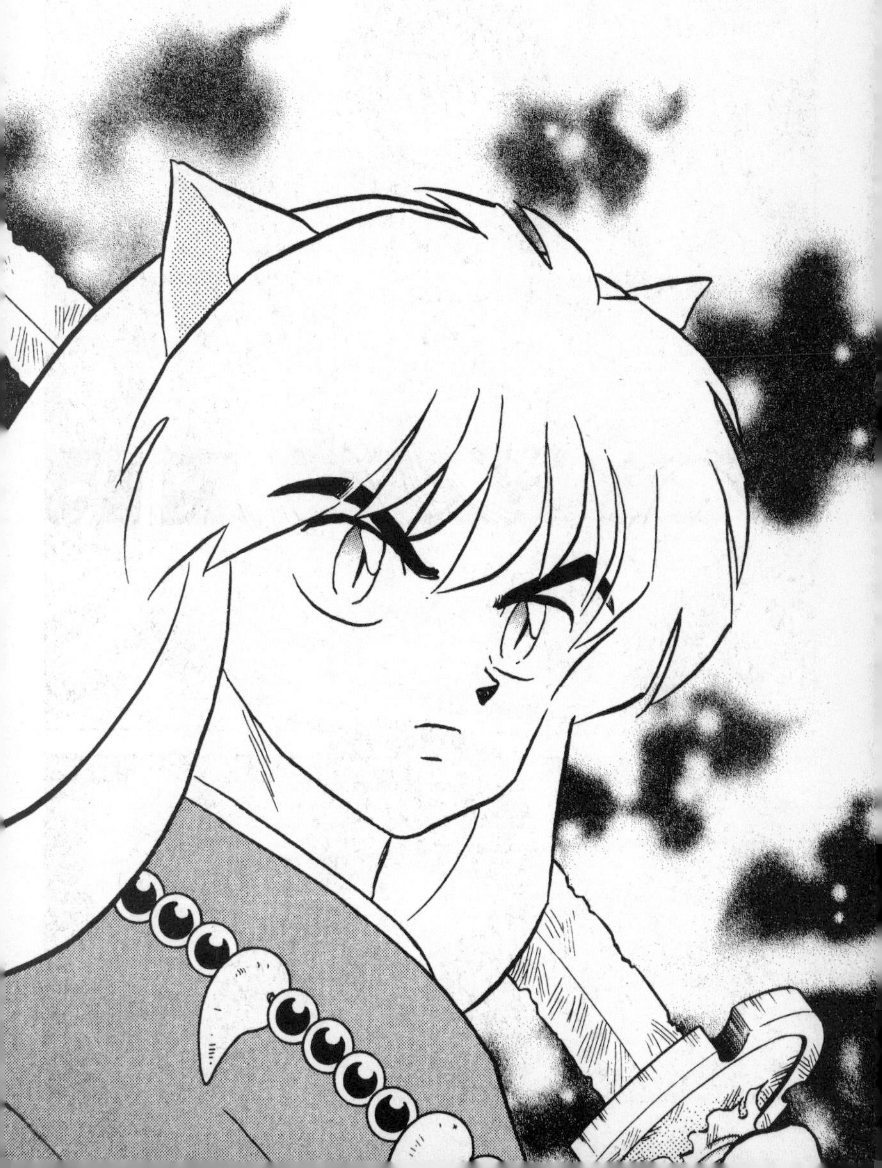

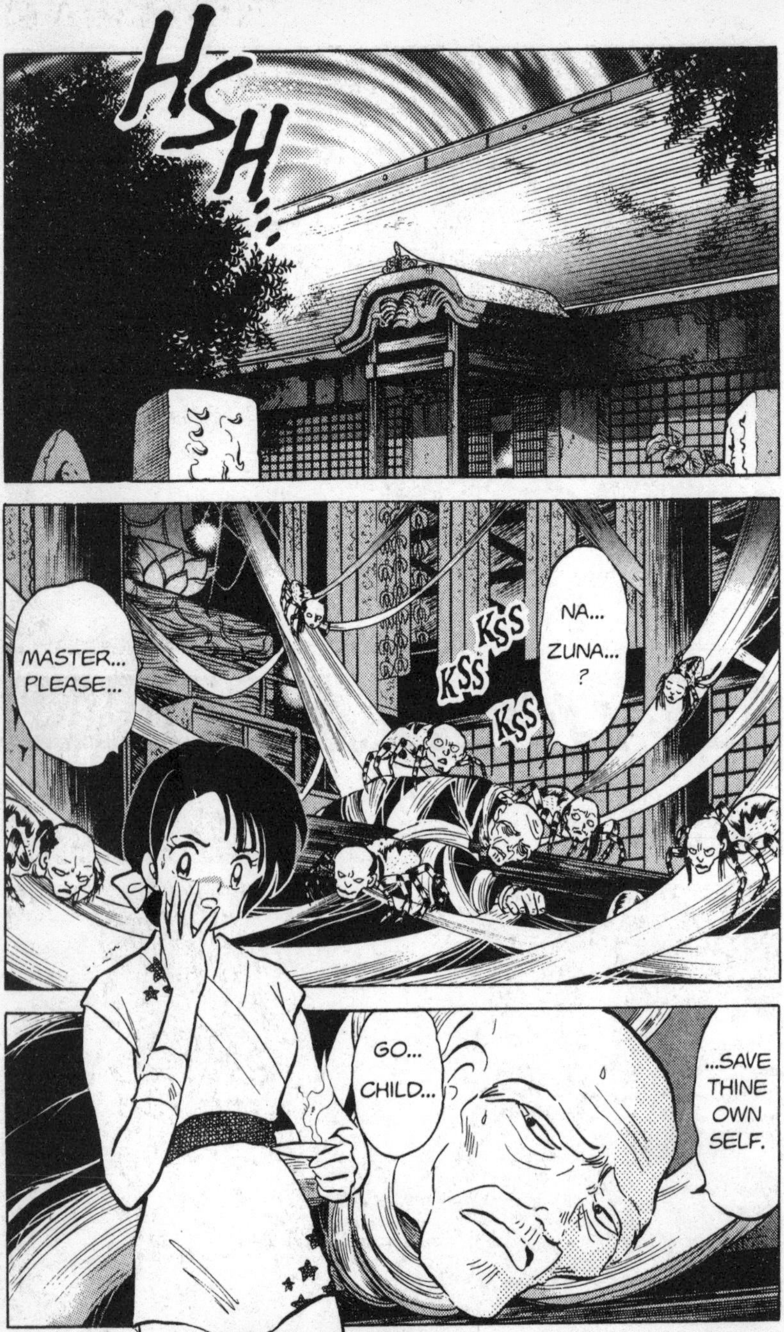
HSH!!
MASTER... PLEASE...
KSS KSS KSS
NA... ZUNA...?
GO... CHILD...
...SAVE THINE OWN SELF.

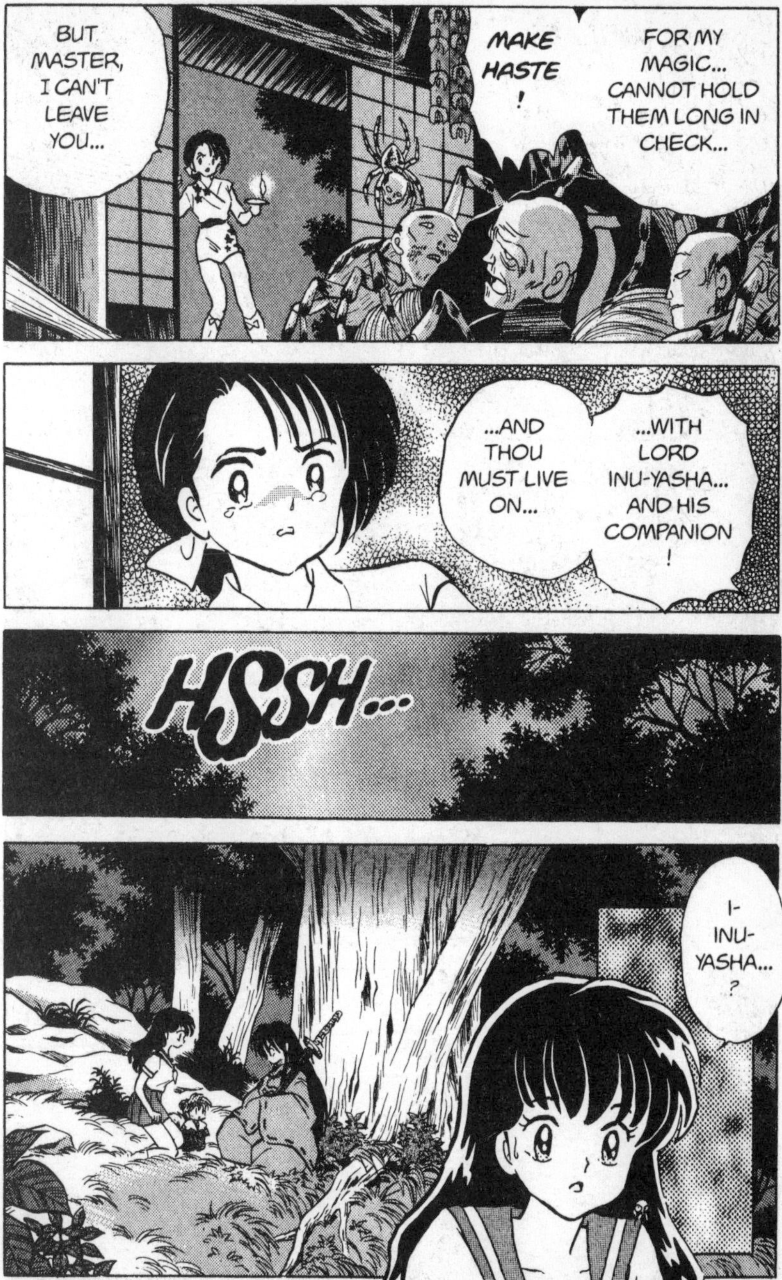
BUT MASTER, I CAN'T LEAVE YOU...
MAKE HASTE!
FOR MY MAGIC... CANNOT HOLD THEM LONG IN CHECK...
...AND THOU MUST LIVE ON...
...WITH LORD INU-YASHA... AND HIS COMPANION!
HSSSH...
I- INU-YASHA...?

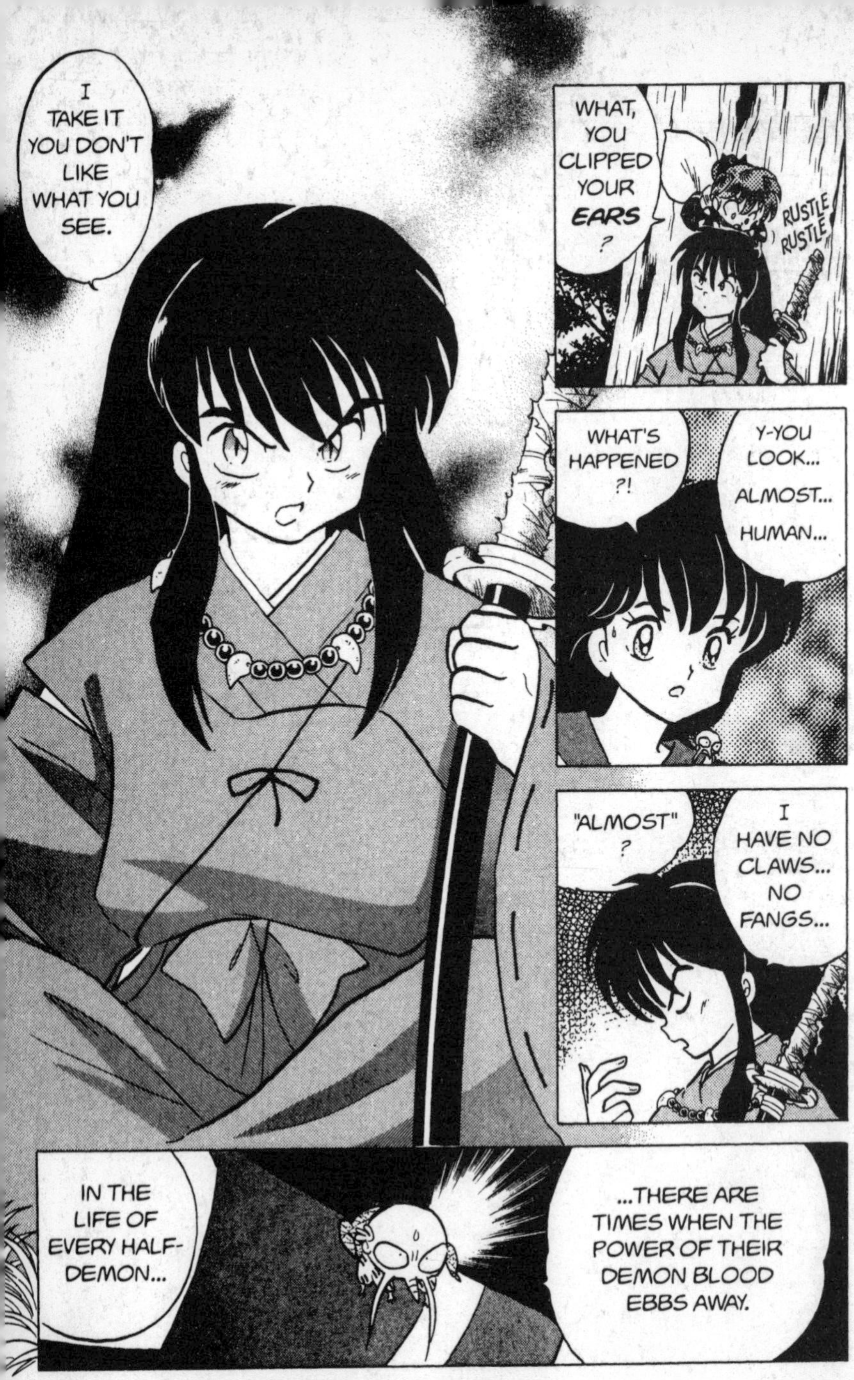
I TAKE IT YOU DON'T LIKE WHAT YOU SEE.
WHAT, YOU CLIPPED YOUR *EARS* ?
RUSTLE RUSTLE
WHAT'S HAPPENED ?!
Y-YOU LOOK... ALMOST... HUMAN...
"ALMOST" ?
I HAVE NO CLAWS... NO FANGS...
IN THE LIFE OF EVERY HALF-DEMON...
...THERE ARE TIMES WHEN THE POWER OF THEIR DEMON BLOOD EBBS AWAY.

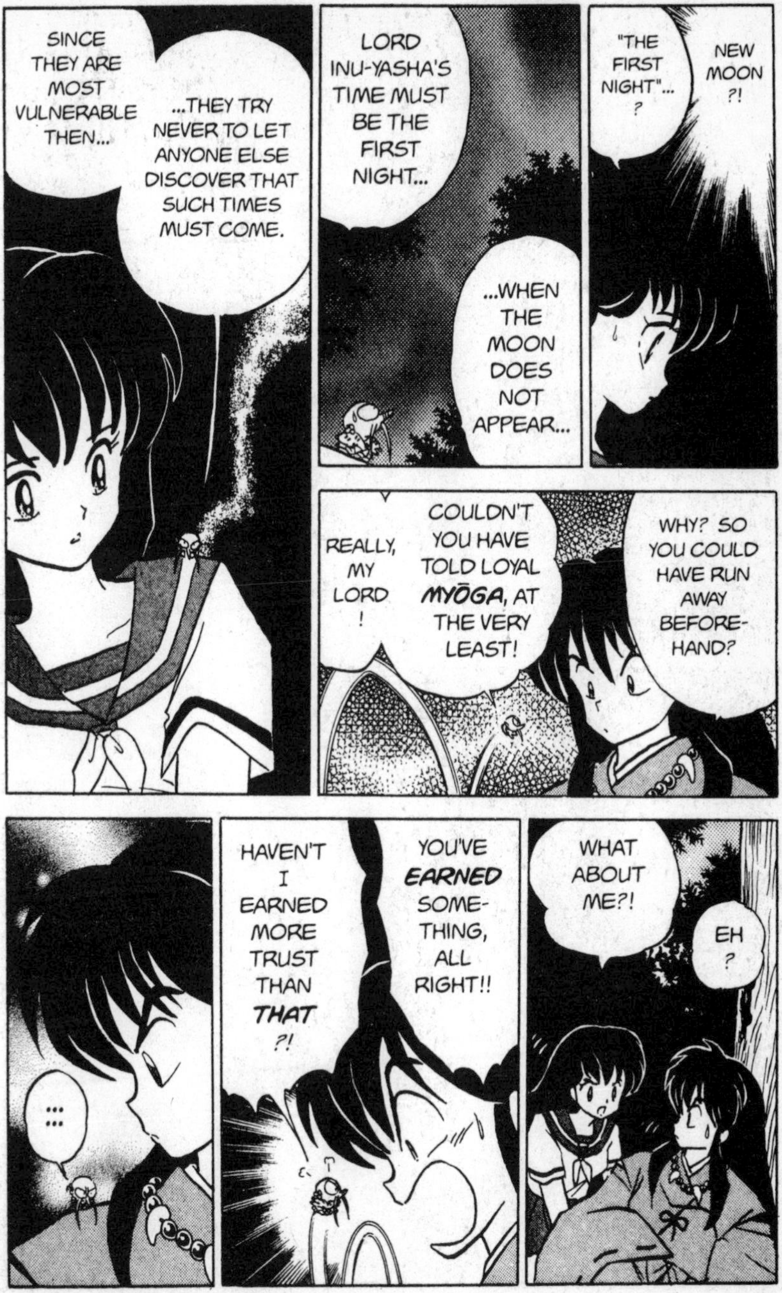
SINCE THEY ARE MOST VULNERABLE THEN...
...THEY TRY NEVER TO LET ANYONE ELSE DISCOVER THAT SUCH TIMES MUST COME.
LORD INU-YASHA'S TIME MUST BE THE FIRST NIGHT...
...WHEN THE MOON DOES NOT APPEAR...
"THE FIRST NIGHT"... ?
NEW MOON ?!
REALLY, MY LORD !
COULDN'T YOU HAVE TOLD LOYAL MYŌGA, AT THE VERY LEAST!
WHY? SO YOU COULD HAVE RUN AWAY BEFORE-HAND?
......
HAVEN'T I EARNED MORE TRUST THAN THAT ?!
YOU'VE EARNED SOME-THING, ALL RIGHT!!
WHAT ABOUT ME?!
EH ?

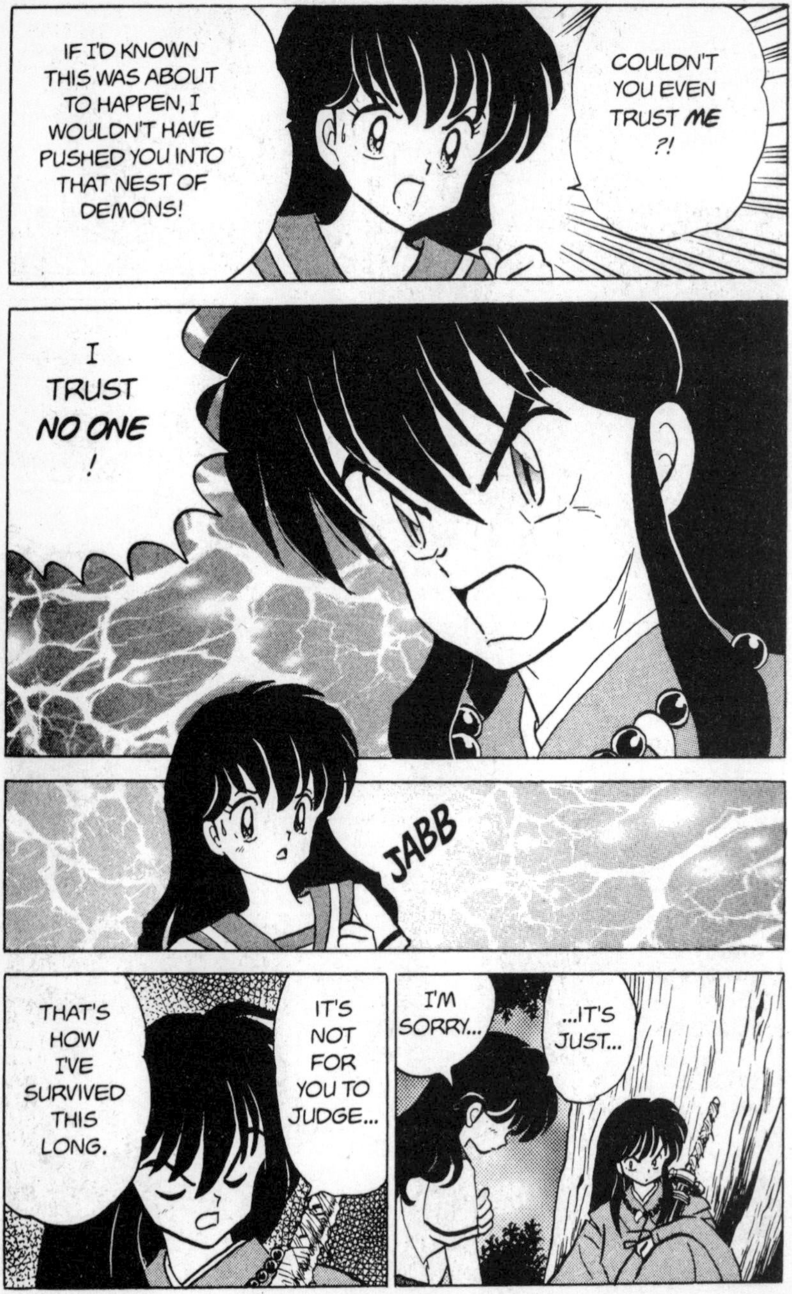
IF I'D KNOWN THIS WAS ABOUT TO HAPPEN, I WOULDN'T HAVE PUSHED YOU INTO THAT NEST OF DEMONS!
COULDN'T YOU EVEN TRUST *ME* ?!
I TRUST *NO ONE* !
JABB
THAT'S HOW I'VE SURVIVED THIS LONG.
IT'S NOT FOR YOU TO JUDGE...
I'M SORRY...
...IT'S JUST...

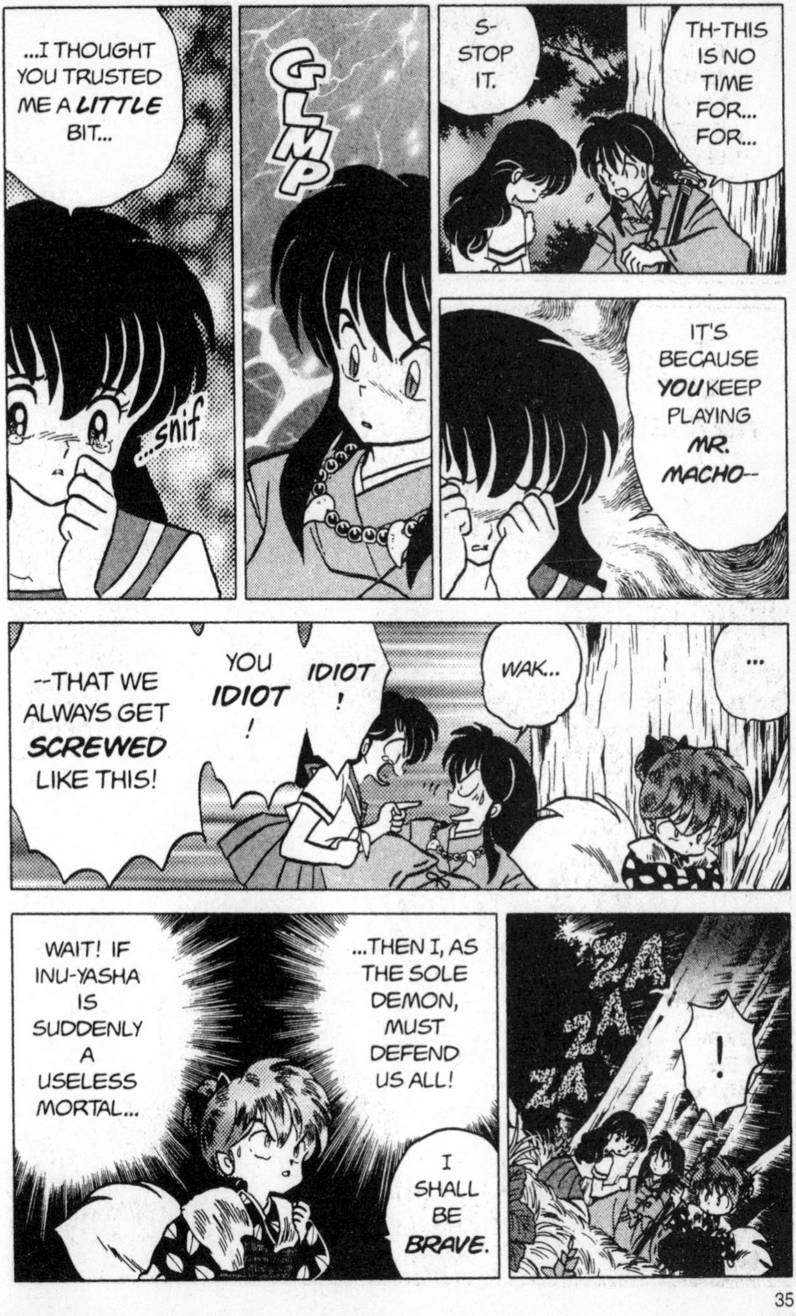
...I THOUGHT YOU TRUSTED ME A LITTLE BIT...
GLMP
...snif
S- STOP IT.
TH-THIS IS NO TIME FOR... FOR...
IT'S BECAUSE YOU KEEP PLAYING MR. MACHO--
--THAT WE ALWAYS GET SCREWED LIKE THIS!
YOU IDIOT!
IDIOT!
WAK...
...
WAIT! IF INU-YASHA IS SUDDENLY A USELESS MORTAL...
...THEN I, AS THE SOLE DEMON, MUST DEFEND US ALL!
I SHALL BE BRAVE.
ZA ZA ZA
!

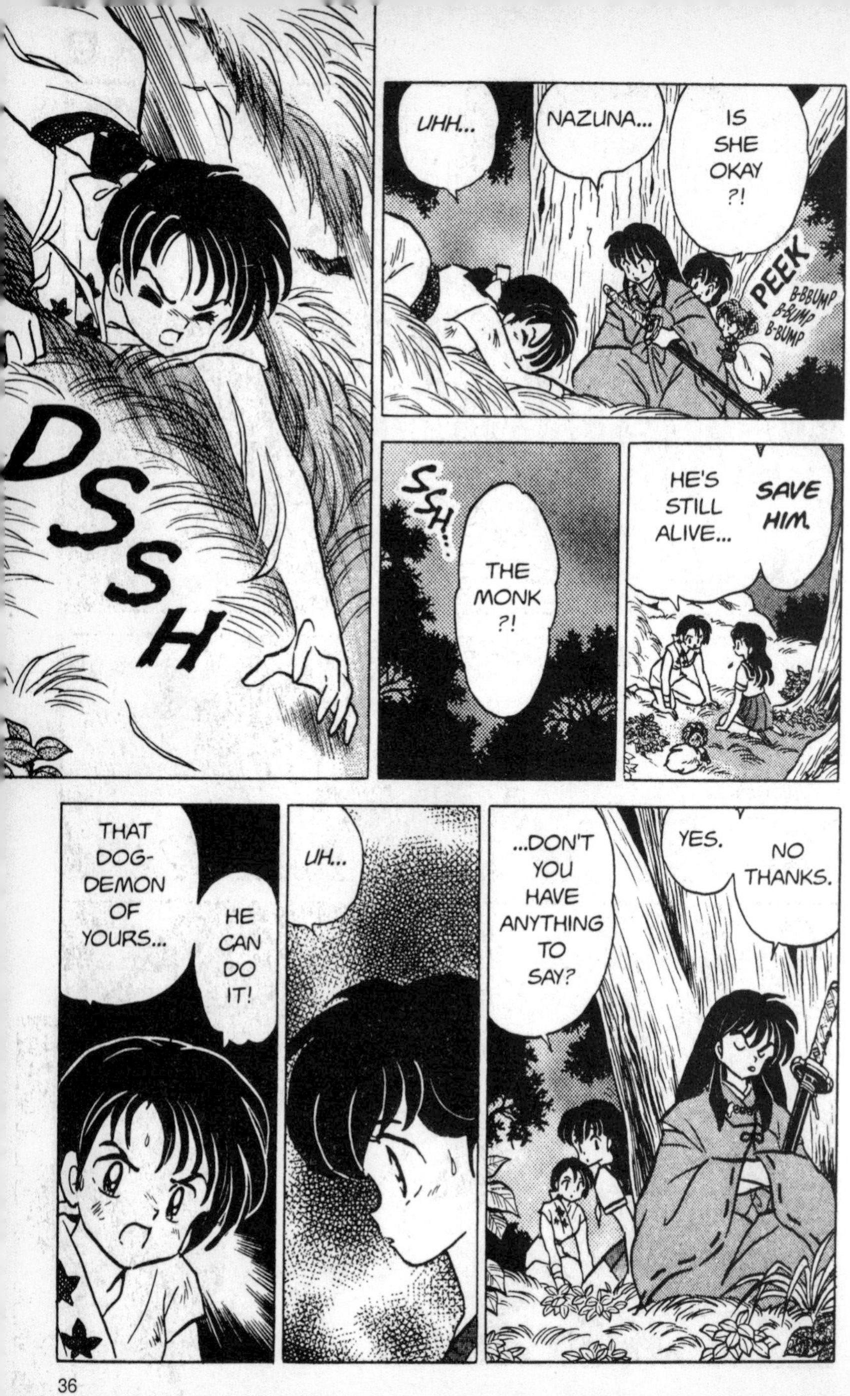
DSSH
UHH...
NAZUNA...
IS SHE OKAY ?!
PEEK
B-BBUMP B-BUMP B-BUMP
SSH...
THE MONK ?!
HE'S STILL ALIVE...
SAVE HIM.
THAT DOG-DEMON OF YOURS...
HE CAN DO IT!
UH...
...DON'T YOU HAVE ANYTHING TO SAY?
YES.
NO THANKS.

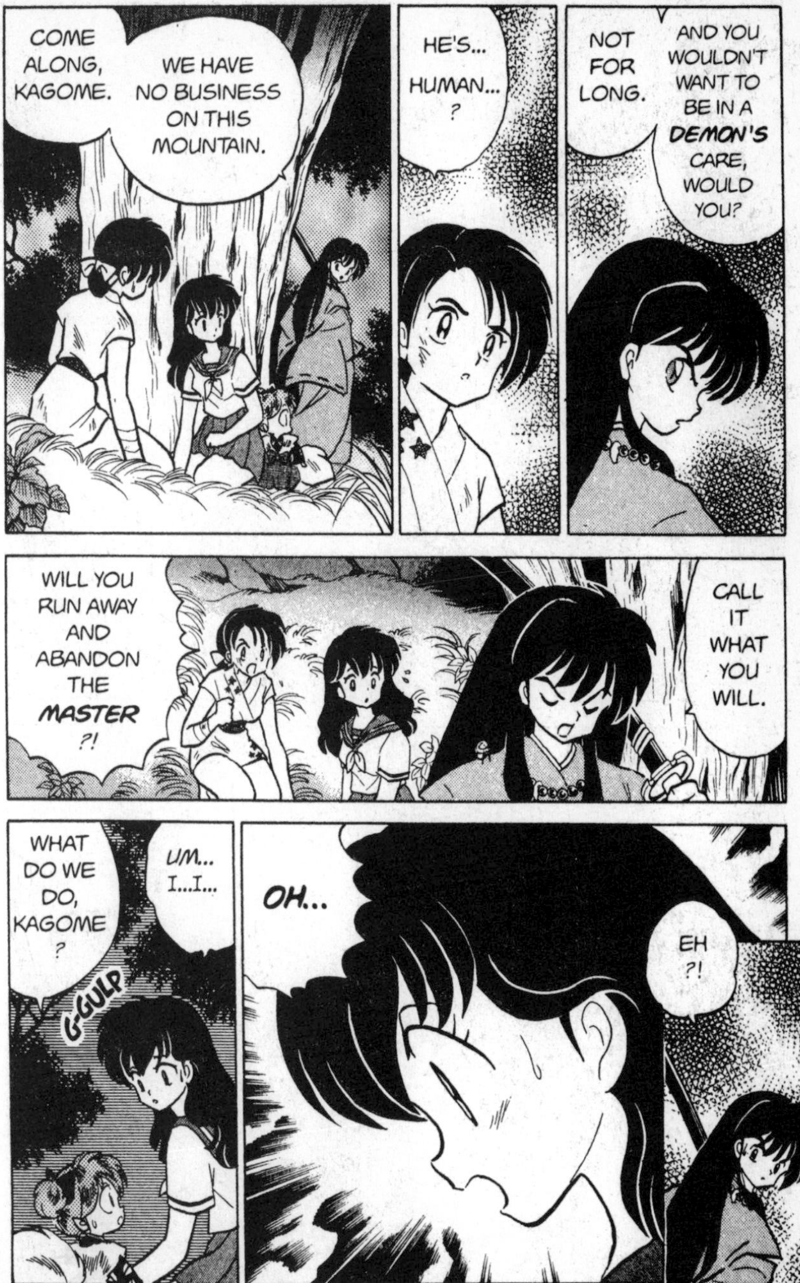
COME ALONG, KAGOME.
WE HAVE NO BUSINESS ON THIS MOUNTAIN.
HE'S... HUMAN...?
NOT FOR LONG.
AND YOU WOULDN'T WANT TO BE IN A DEMON'S CARE, WOULD YOU?
WILL YOU RUN AWAY AND ABANDON THE MASTER?!
CALL IT WHAT YOU WILL.
WHAT DO WE DO, KAGOME?
UM... I...I...
G-GULP
OH...
EH?!

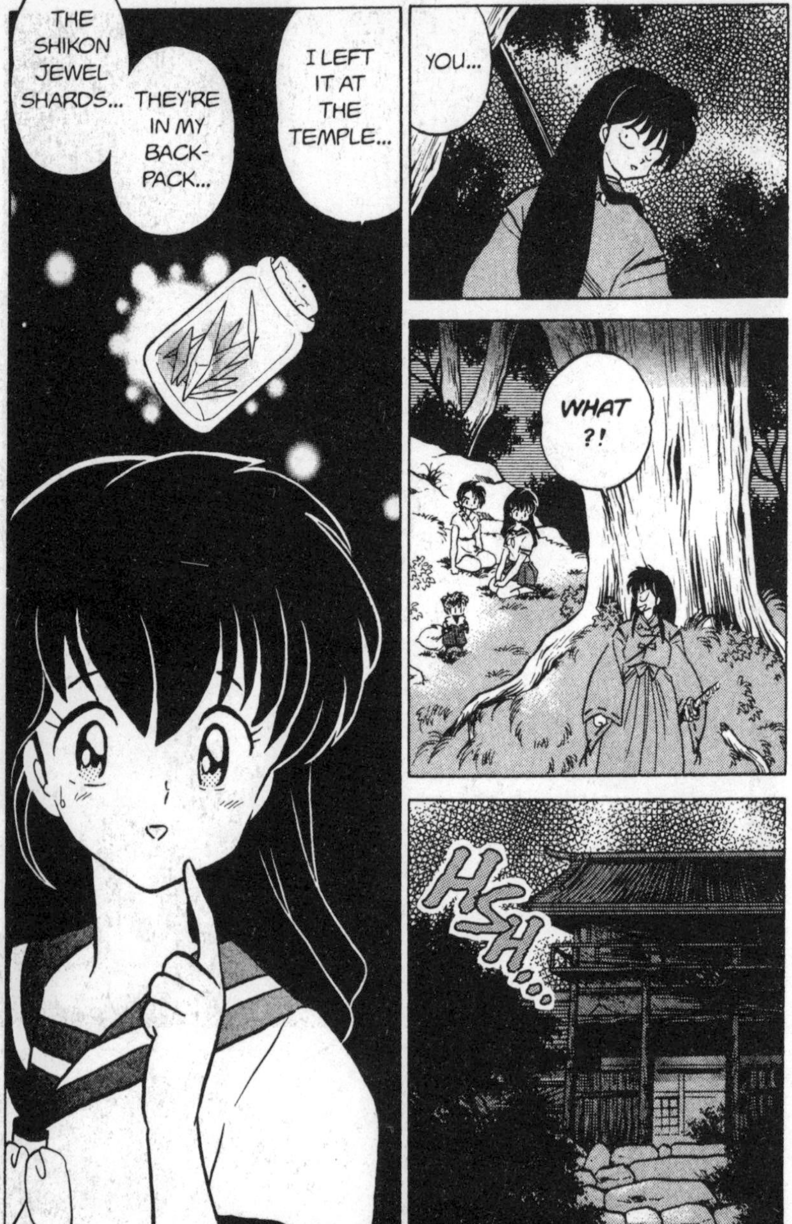
THE SHIKON JEWEL SHARDS...
THEY'RE IN MY BACK-PACK...
I LEFT IT AT THE TEMPLE...
YOU...
WHAT?!
HSH...

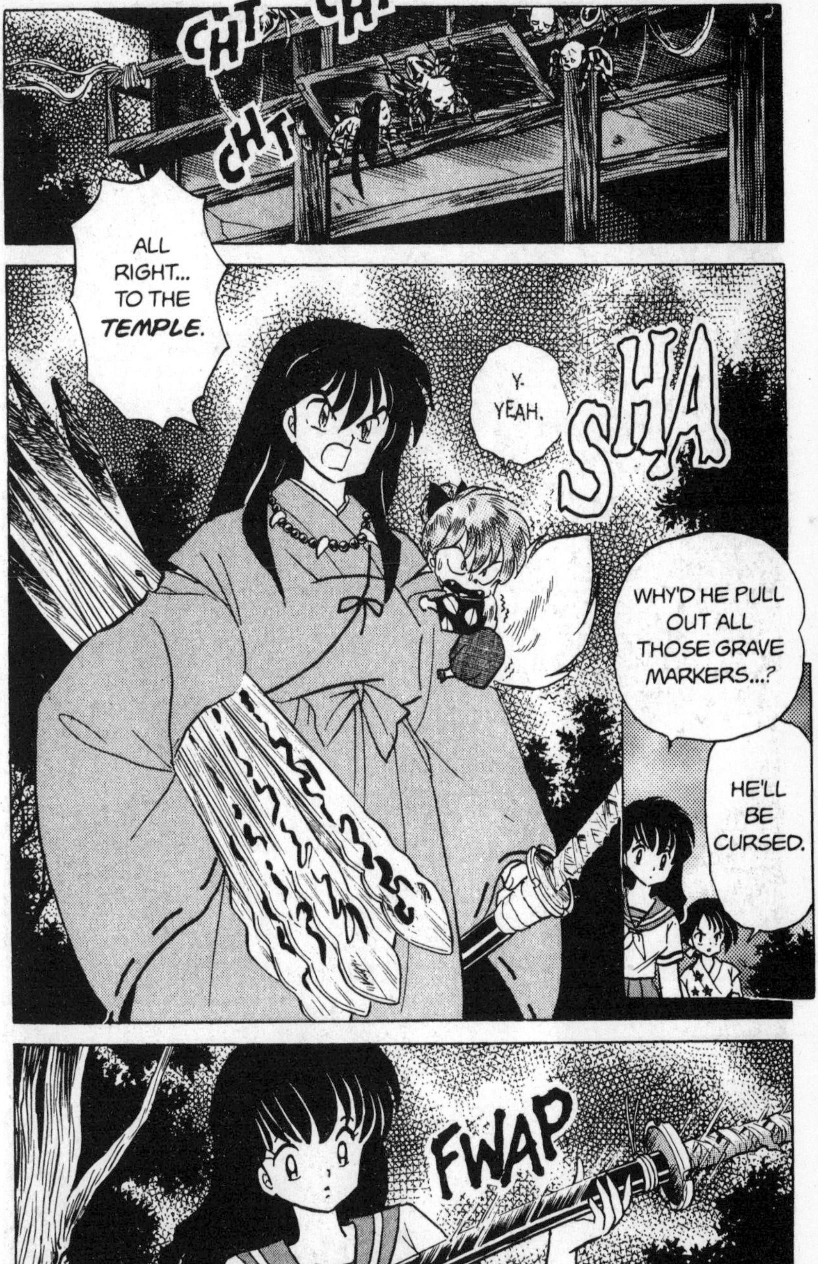
CHT CHT
CHT
ALL RIGHT... TO THE *TEMPLE*.
Y-YEAH.
SHA
WHY'D HE PULL OUT ALL THOSE GRAVE MARKERS...?
HE'LL BE CURSED.
FWAP

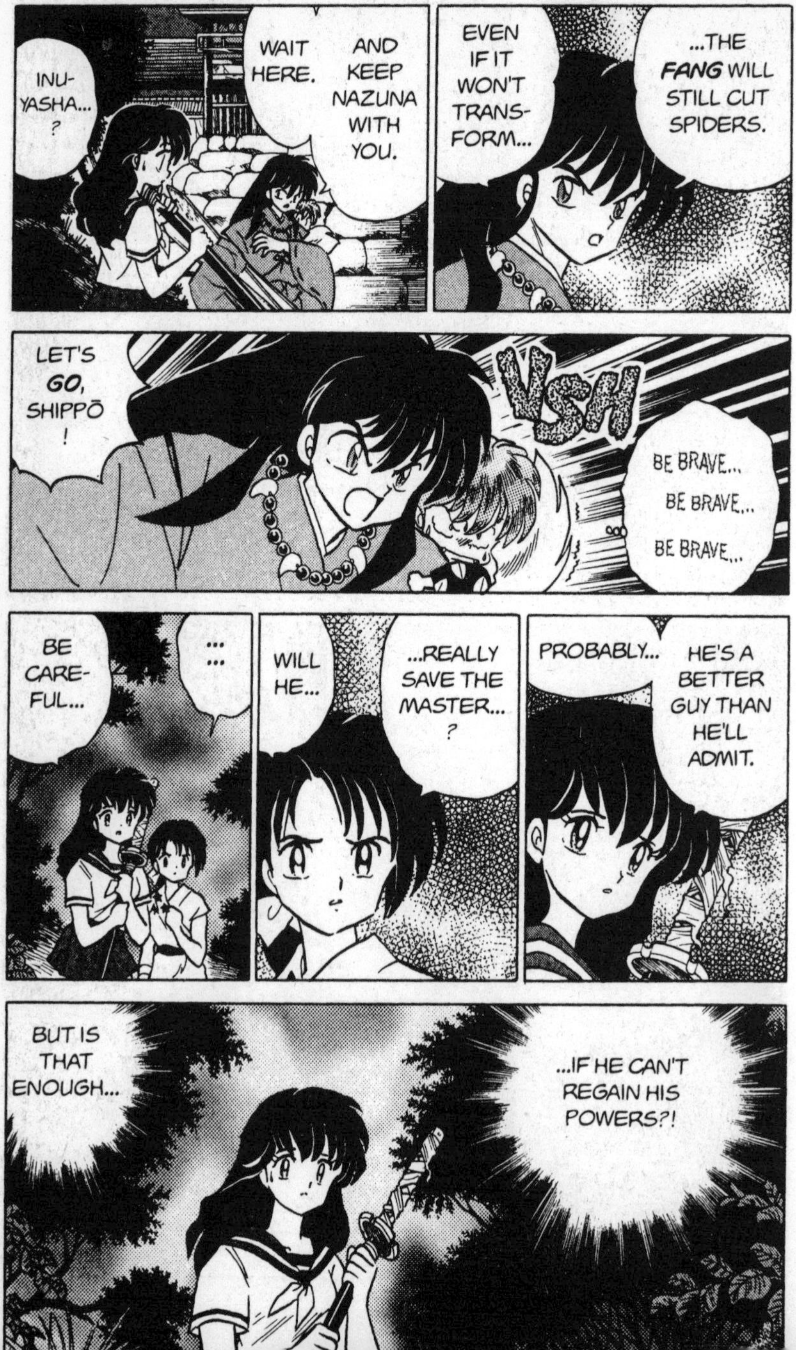
INU-YASHA...?
WAIT HERE.
AND KEEP NAZUNA WITH YOU.
EVEN IF IT WON'T TRANS-FORM...
...THE FANG WILL STILL CUT SPIDERS.
LET'S GO, SHIPPŌ!
VSH
BE BRAVE... BE BRAVE... BE BRAVE...
BE CARE-FUL...
......
WILL HE...
...REALLY SAVE THE MASTER...?
PROBABLY...
HE'S A BETTER GUY THAN HE'LL ADMIT.
BUT IS THAT ENOUGH...
...IF HE CAN'T REGAIN HIS POWERS?!

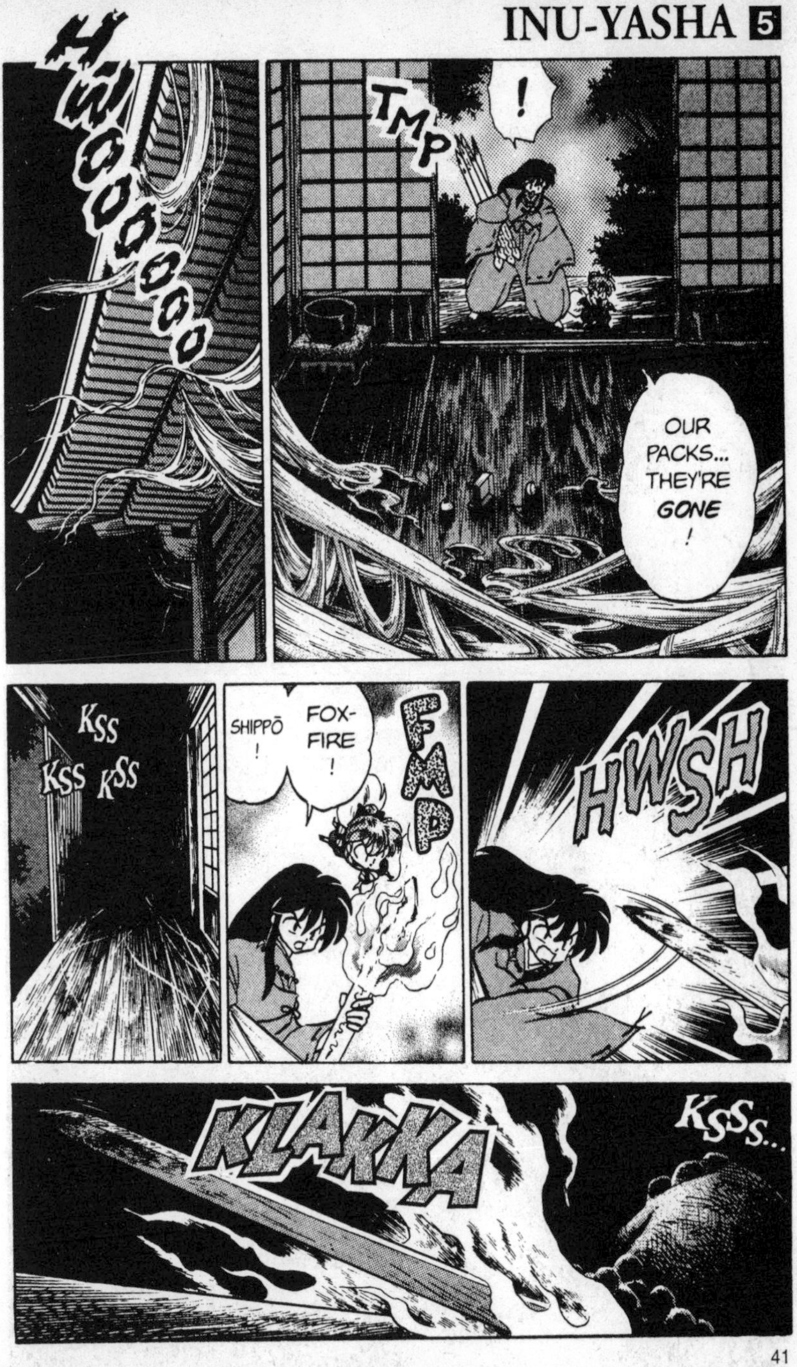
TMP
!
OUR PACKS... THEY'RE GONE!
HWOOOOOOOO
HWSH
FMP
FOX-FIRE!
SHIPPŌ!
KSS
KSS KSS
KLAKKA
KSSS...

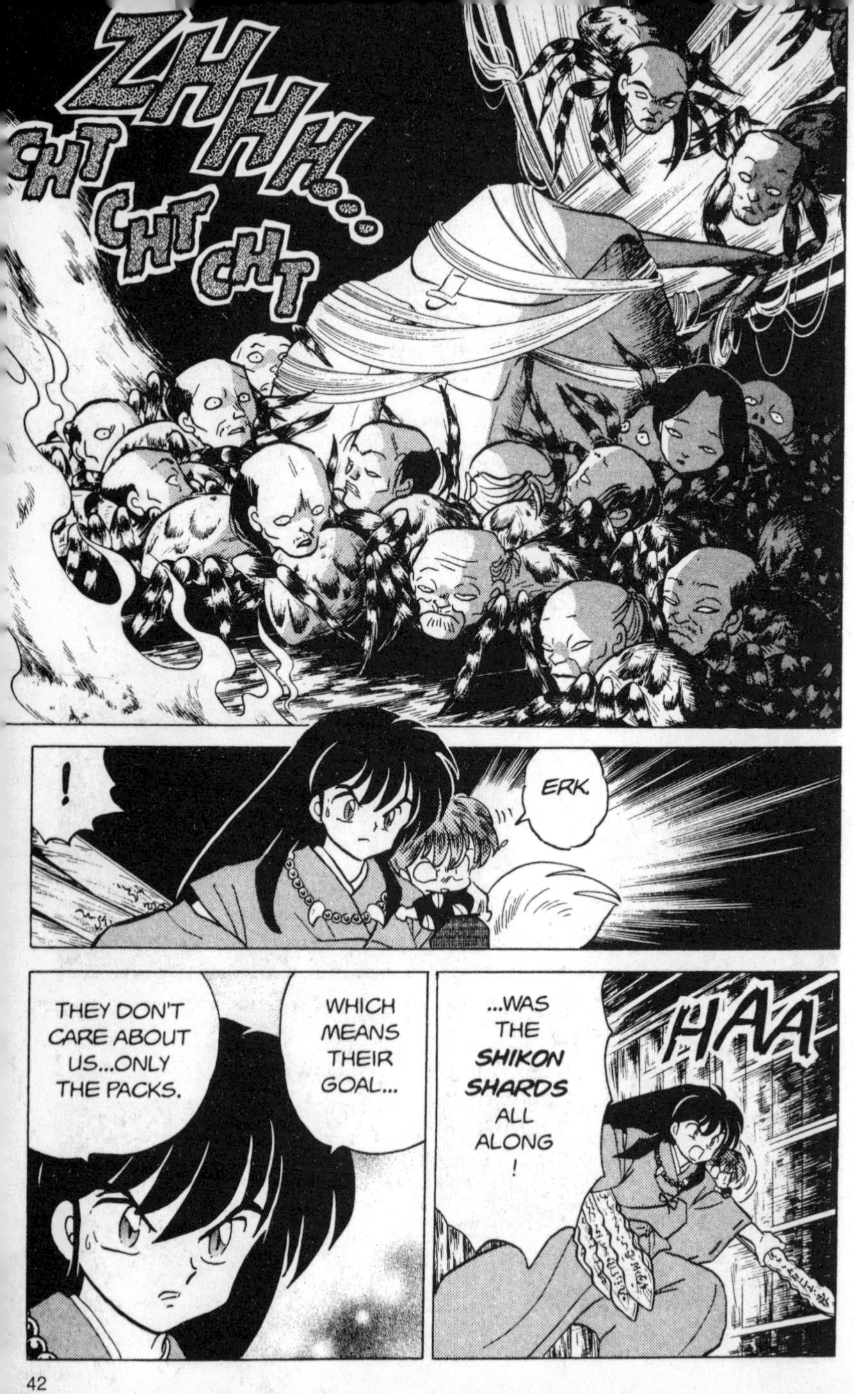
ZHHHH...
CHT CHT CHT
!
ERK.
THEY DON'T CARE ABOUT US...ONLY THE PACKS.
WHICH MEANS THEIR GOAL...
...WAS THE SHIKON SHARDS ALL ALONG!
HAA

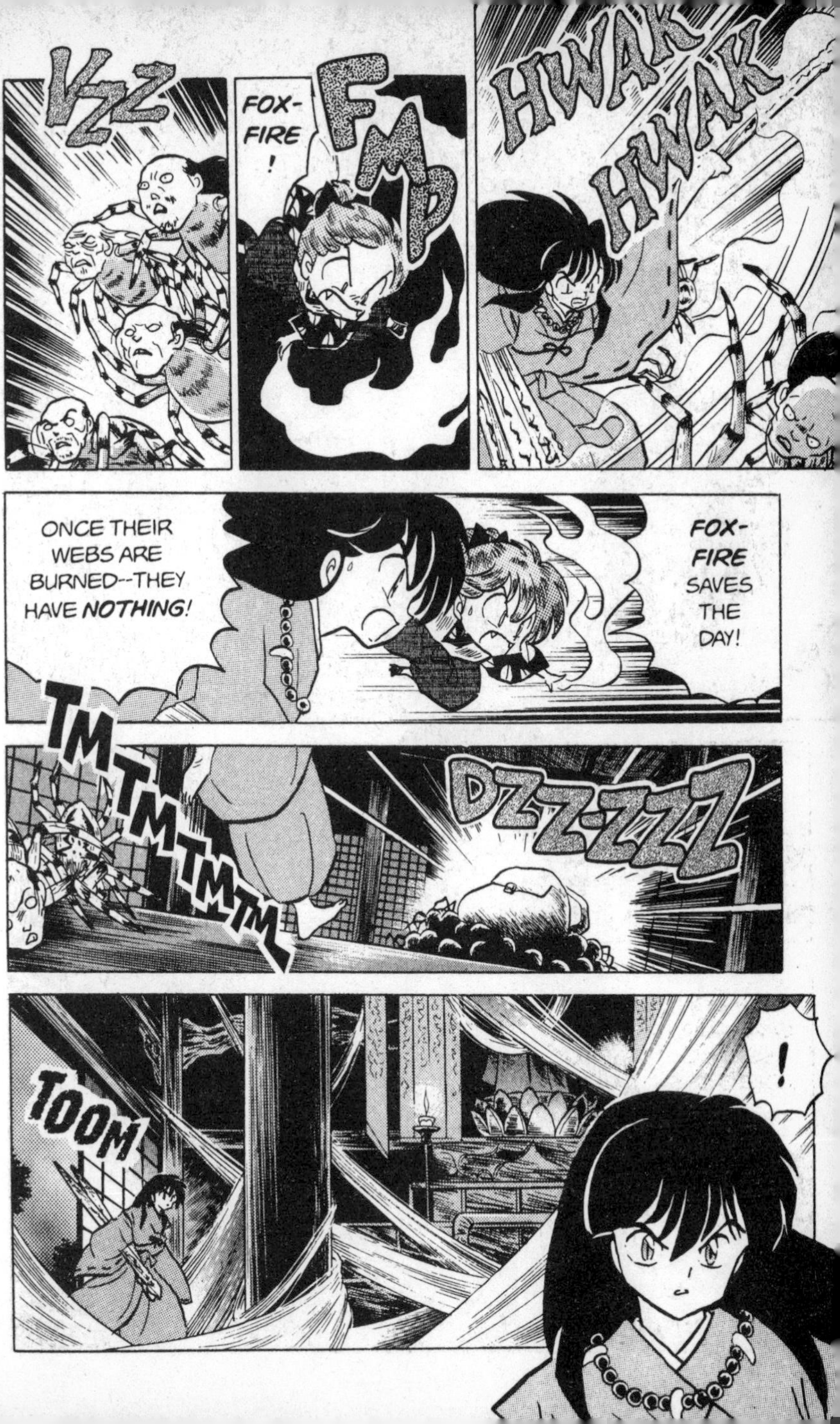
VZZ
FOX-FIRE!
FMP
HWAK HWAK
ONCE THEIR WEBS ARE BURNED--THEY HAVE **NOTHING**!
FOX-FIRE SAVES THE DAY!
TMTMTMTMTM
DZZ-ZZZ
TOOM
!

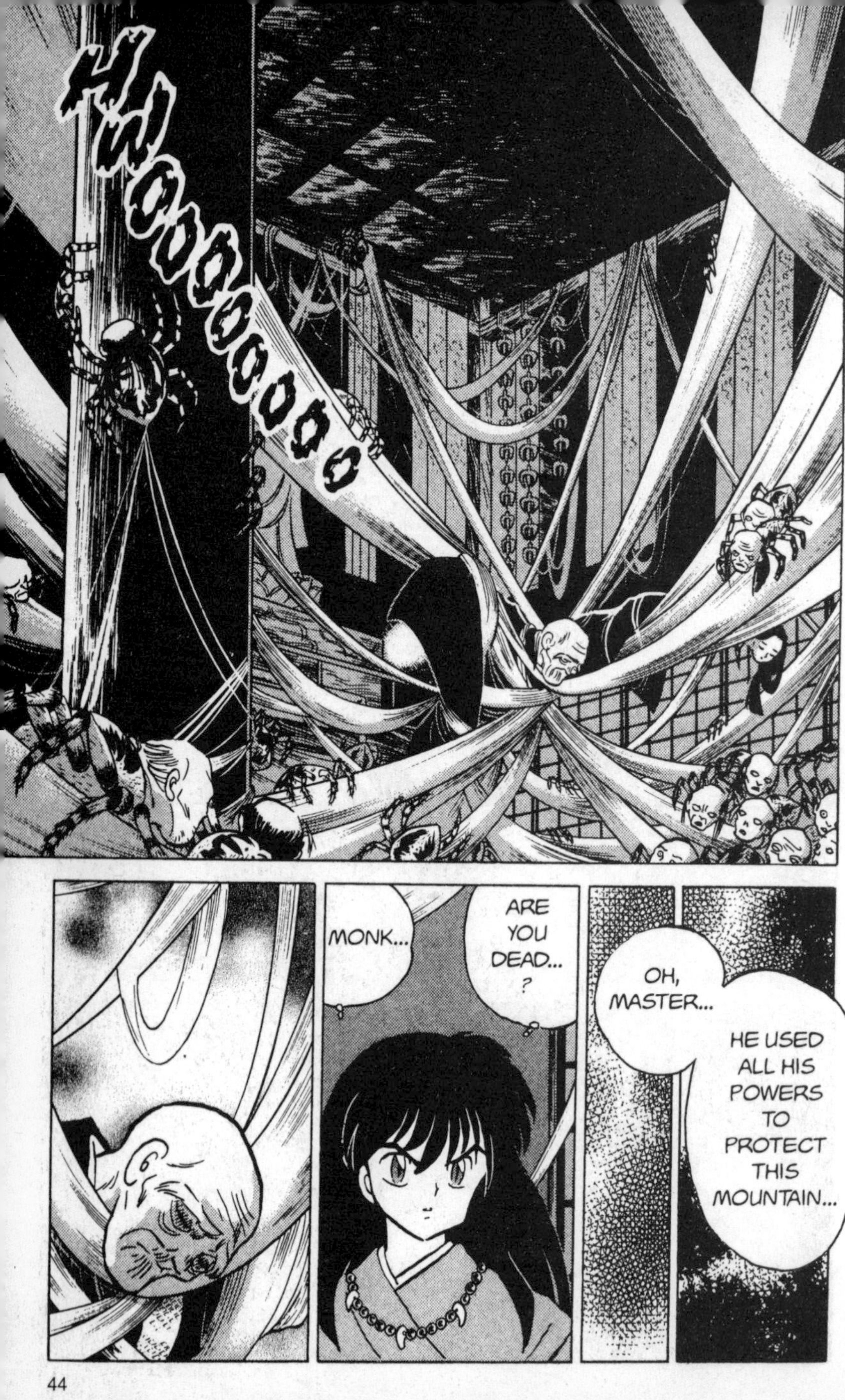
HUOOOOOOOO
MONK...
ARE YOU DEAD... ?
OH, MASTER...
HE USED ALL HIS POWERS TO PROTECT THIS MOUNTAIN...

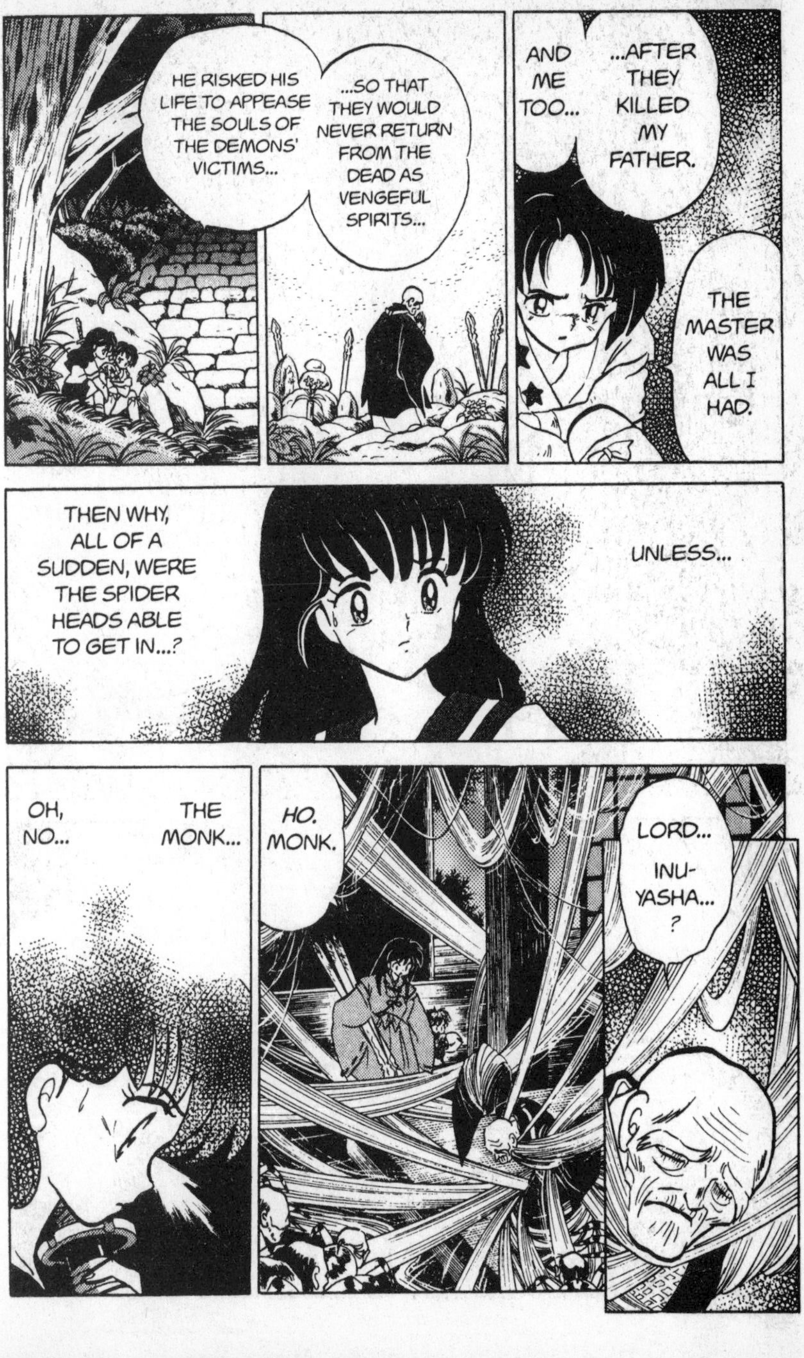
HE RISKED HIS LIFE TO APPEASE THE SOULS OF THE DEMONS' VICTIMS...
...SO THAT THEY WOULD NEVER RETURN FROM THE DEAD AS VENGEFUL SPIRITS...
AND ME TOO...
...AFTER THEY KILLED MY FATHER.
THE MASTER WAS ALL I HAD.
THEN WHY, ALL OF A SUDDEN, WERE THE SPIDER HEADS ABLE TO GET IN...?
UNLESS...
OH, NO...
THE MONK...
HO. MONK.
LORD...
INU-YASHA...
?

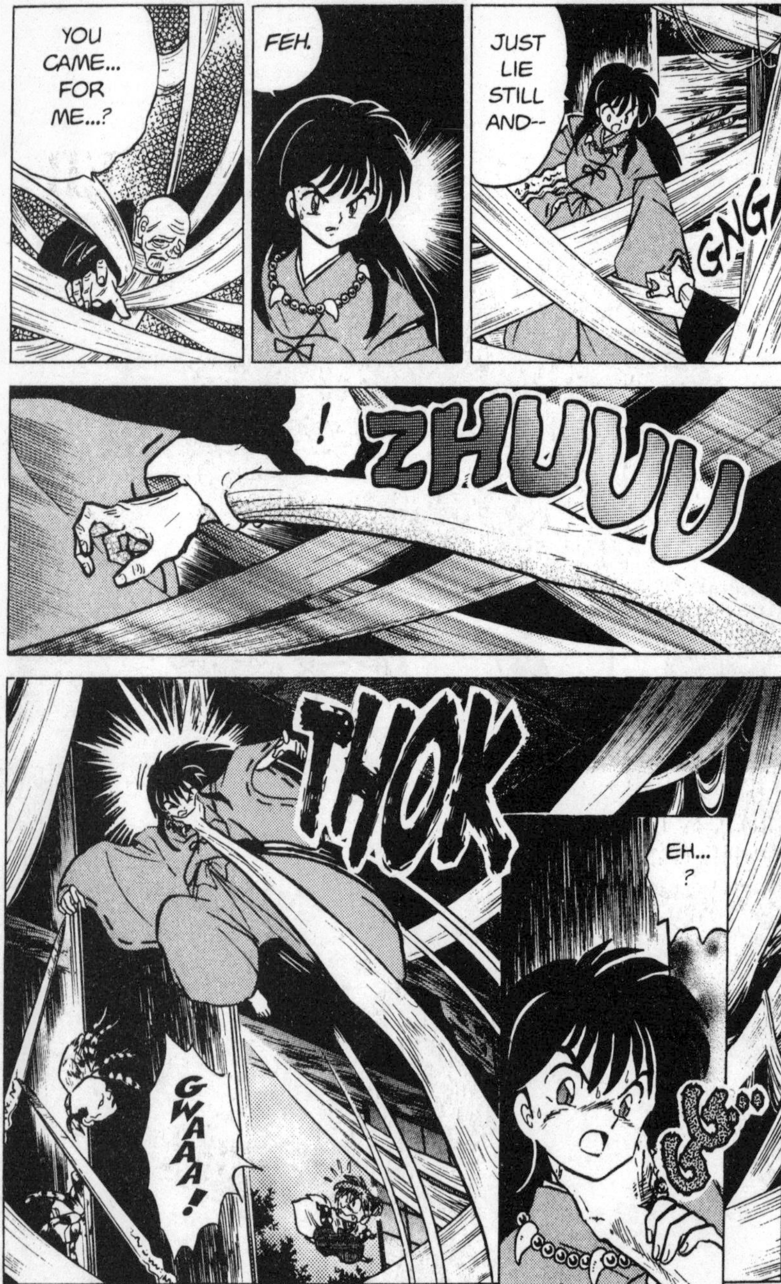
YOU CAME... FOR ME...?
FEH.
JUST LIE STILL AND--
GNG
!
ZHUUU
THOK
GWAAA!
EH...?

SCROLL THREE

THE SPIDER'S WEB

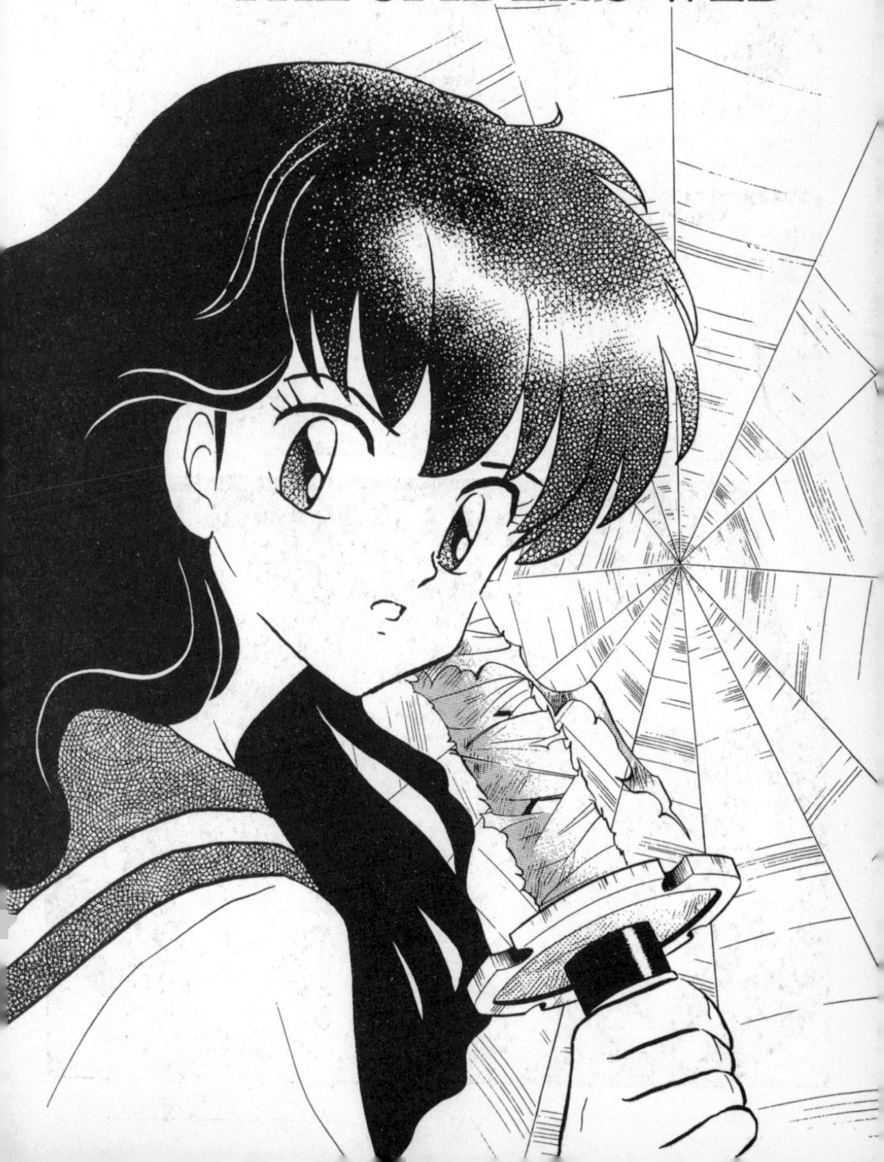

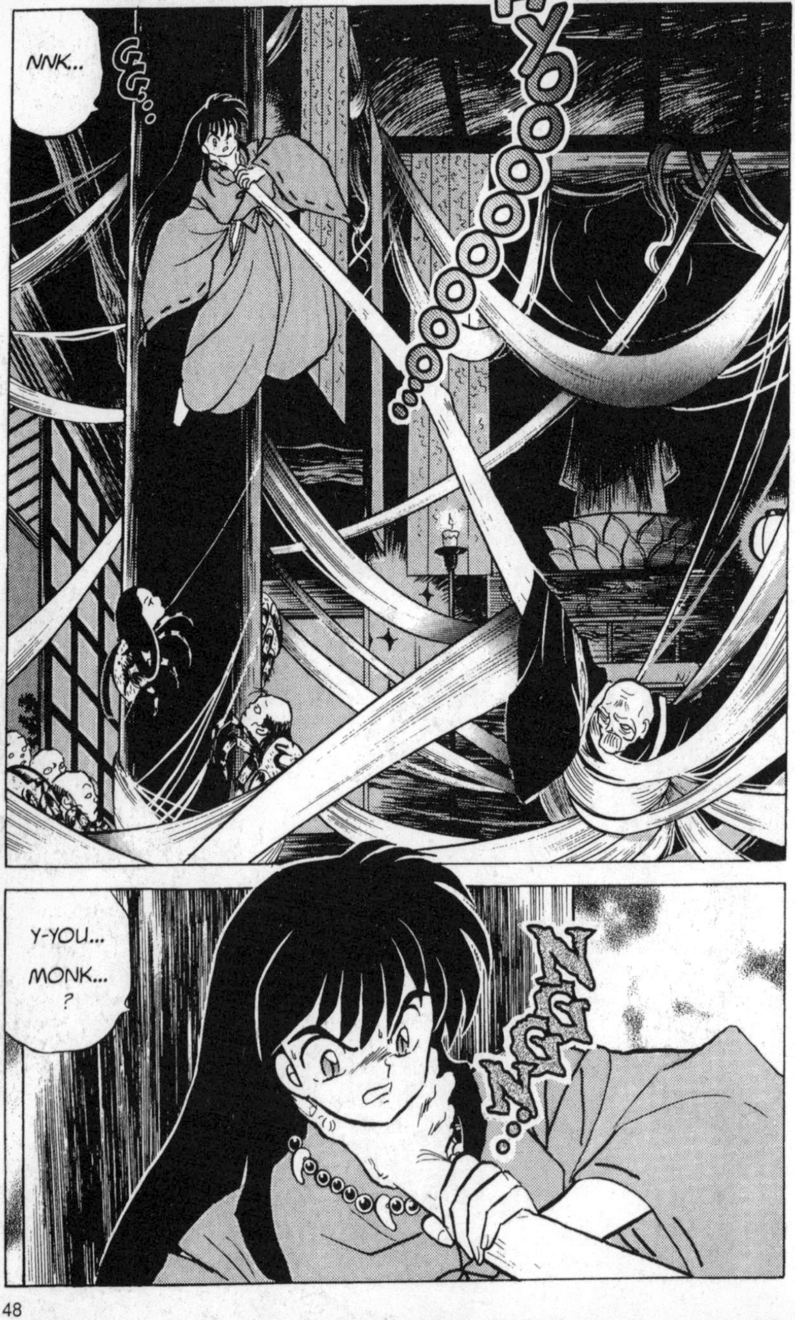
NNK...
GG...
HYOOOOOOOOOOOO...
Y-YOU...
MONK...
?
NGGN...

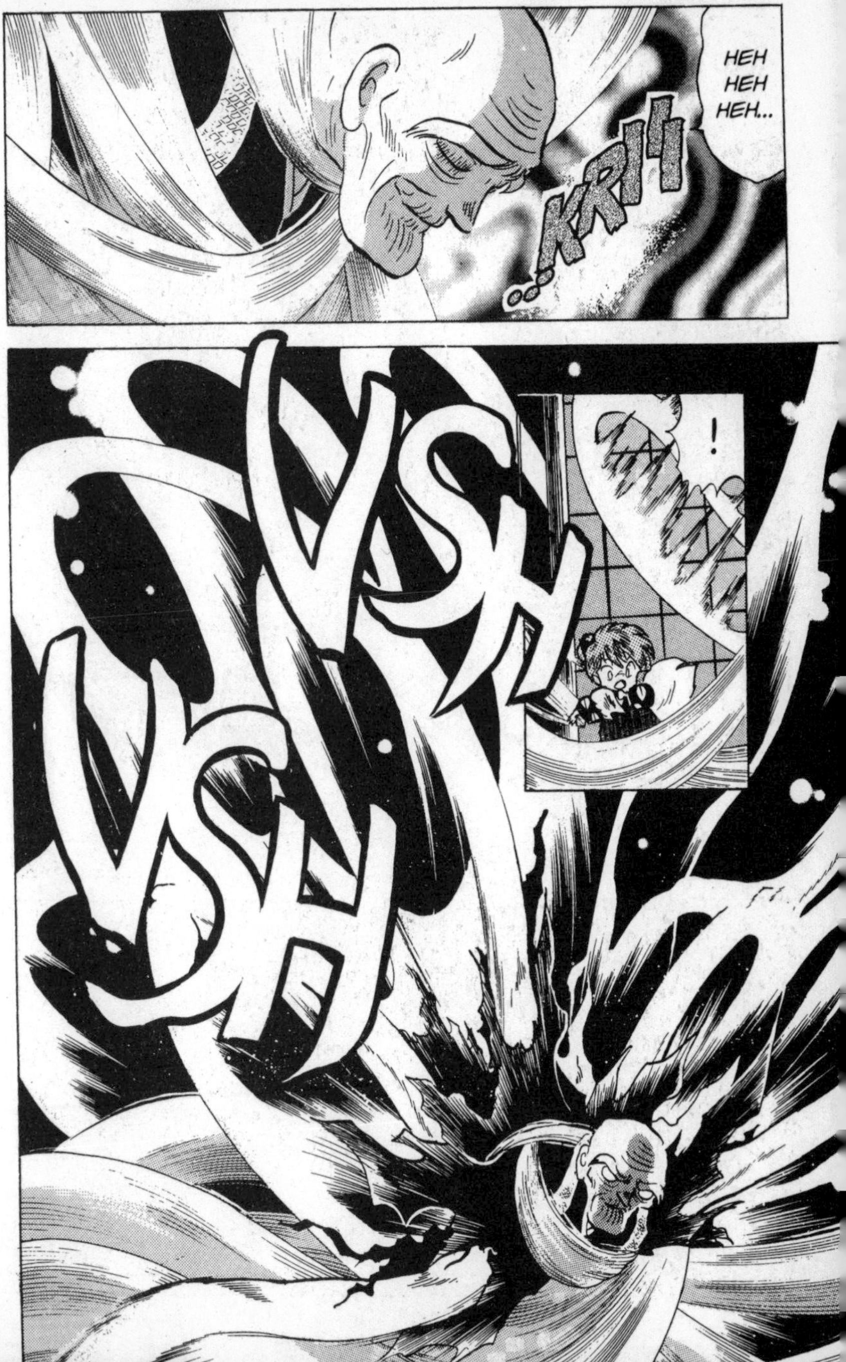
...KRII
HEH
HEH
HEH...
!

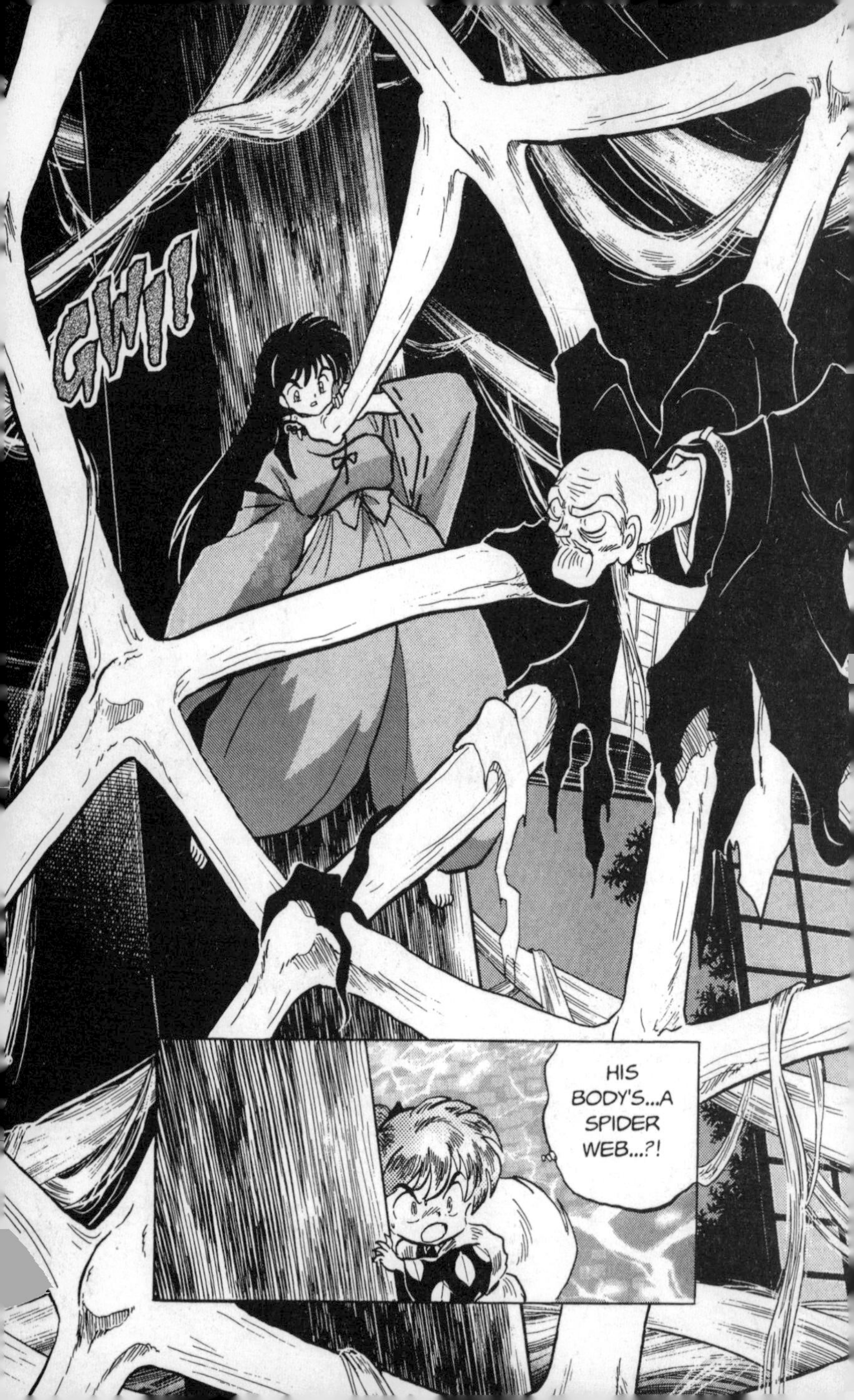
GWI!
HIS BODY'S...A SPIDER WEB...?!

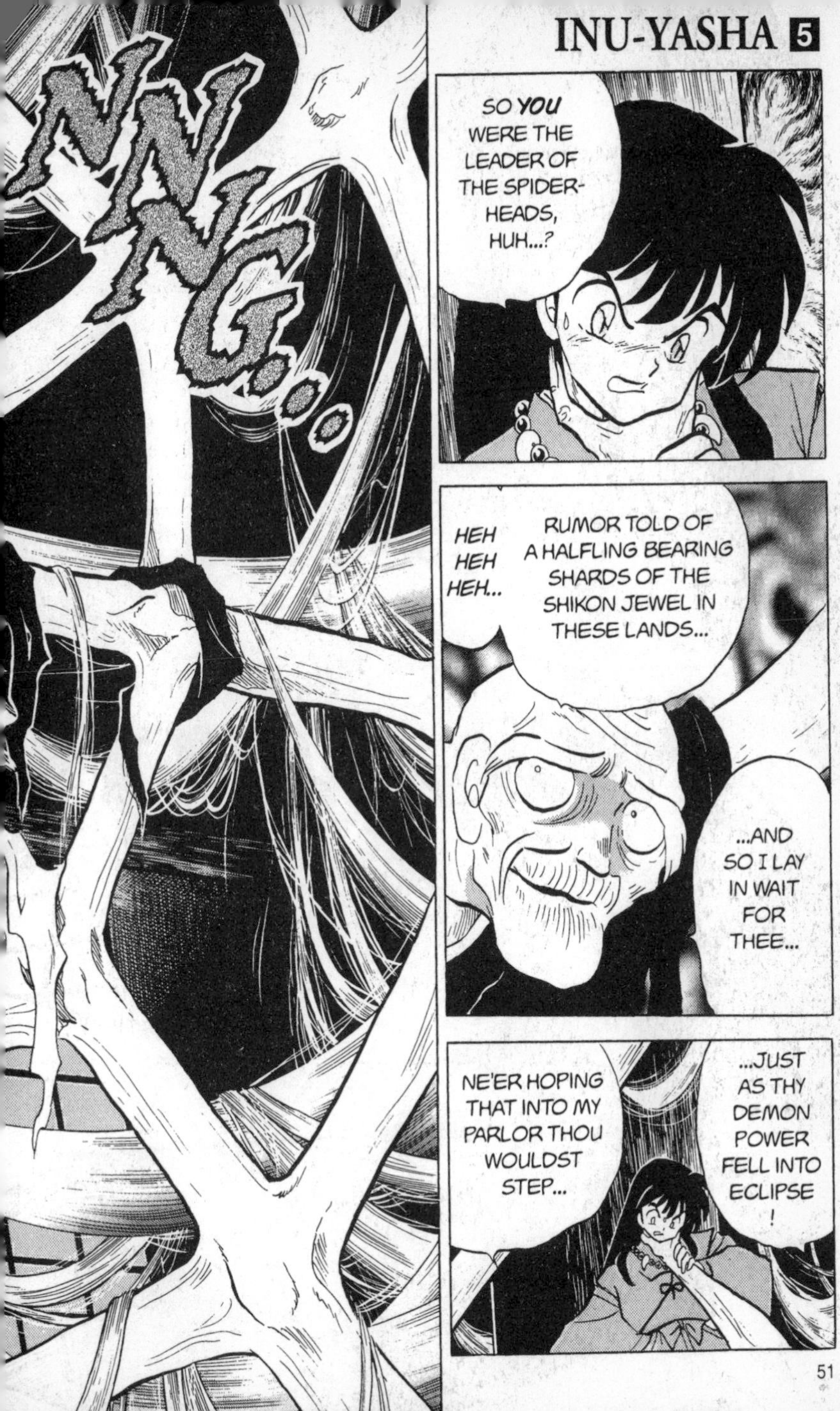
NNG...
SO *YOU* WERE THE LEADER OF THE SPIDER-HEADS, HUH...?
HEH HEH HEH...
RUMOR TOLD OF A HALFLING BEARING SHARDS OF THE SHIKON JEWEL IN THESE LANDS...
...AND SO I LAY IN WAIT FOR THEE...
NE'ER HOPING THAT INTO MY PARLOR THOU WOULDST STEP...
...JUST AS THY DEMON POWER FELL INTO ECLIPSE !

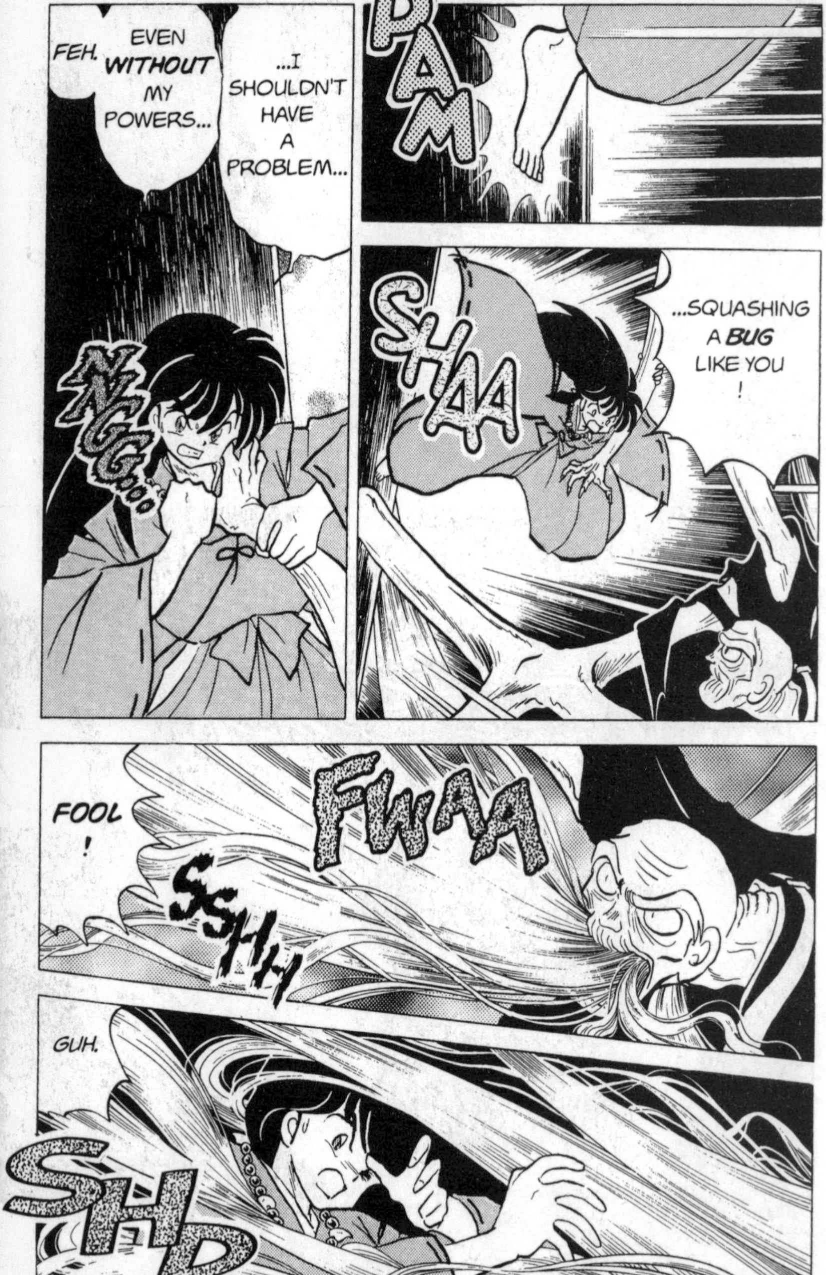
FEH.
EVEN WITHOUT MY POWERS...
...I SHOULDN'T HAVE A PROBLEM...
NNG...
PAM
SHAA
...SQUASHING A BUG LIKE YOU!
FOOL!
FWAA
SSHH
GUH.
SHP

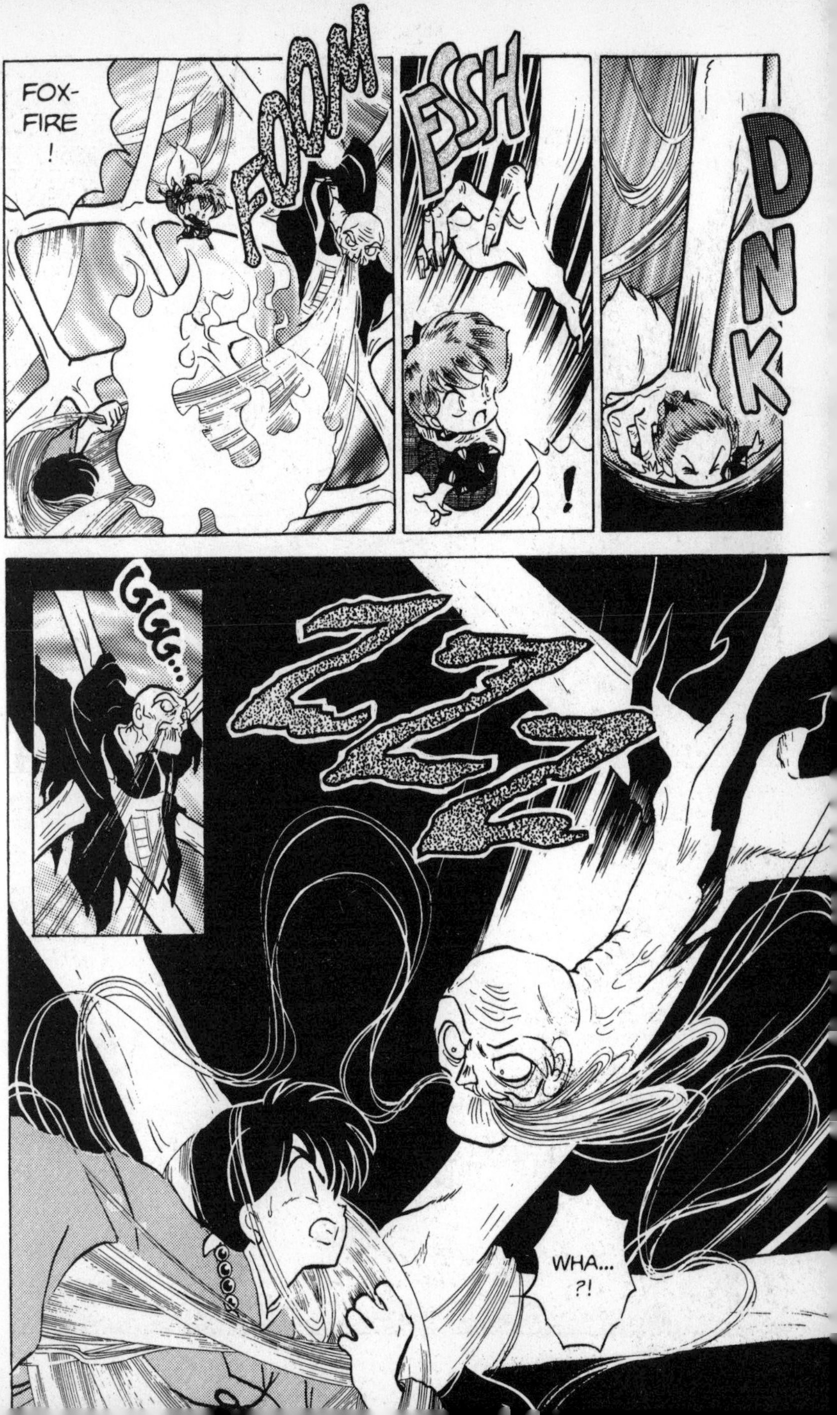
FOX-
FIRE
!
FOOOM
FSSH
!
DNK
GGG...
ZZZ
WHA...
?!

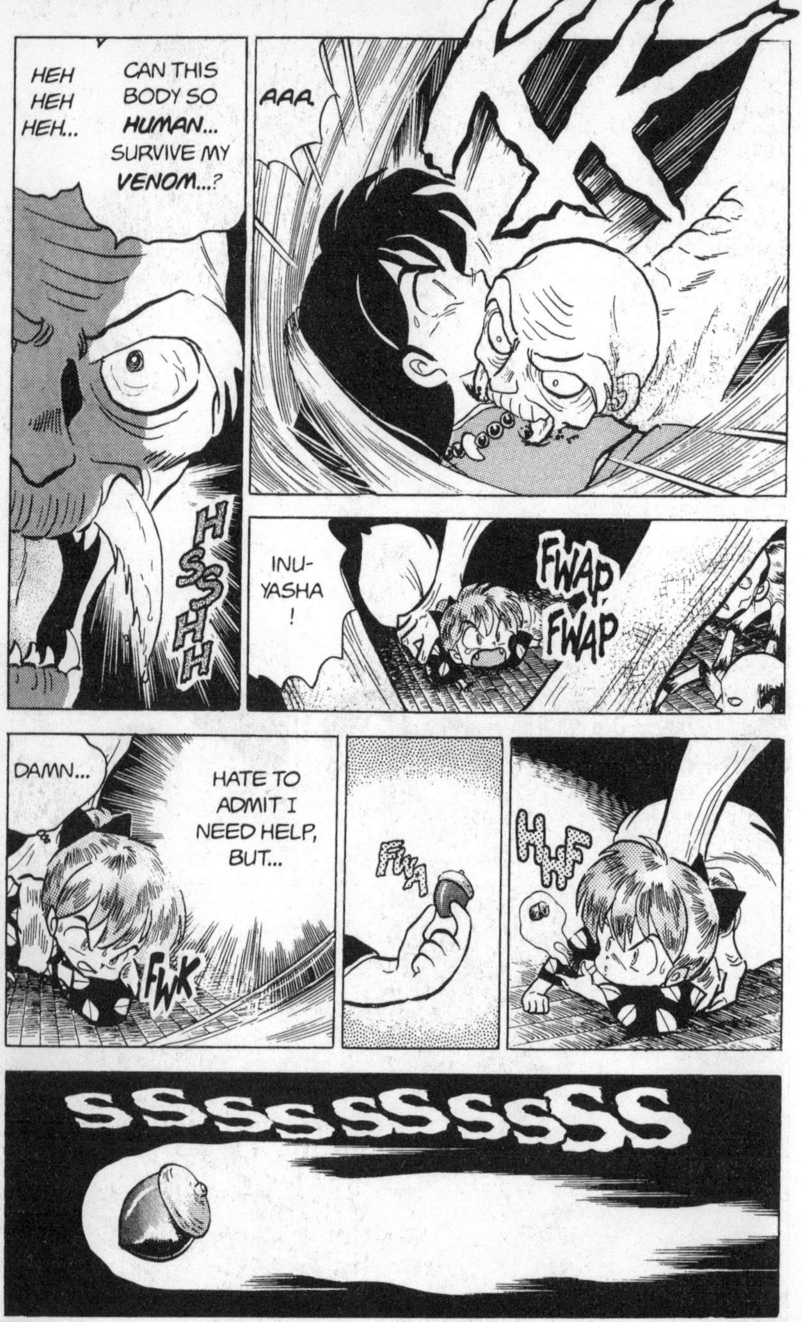
HEH HEH HEH...
CAN THIS BODY SO HUMAN... SURVIVE MY VENOM...?
HSSHH
AAA.
INU-YASHA !
FWAP FWAP
DAMN...
HATE TO ADMIT I NEED HELP, BUT...
FWK
FWA
HWF
SSSSSSSSSSS

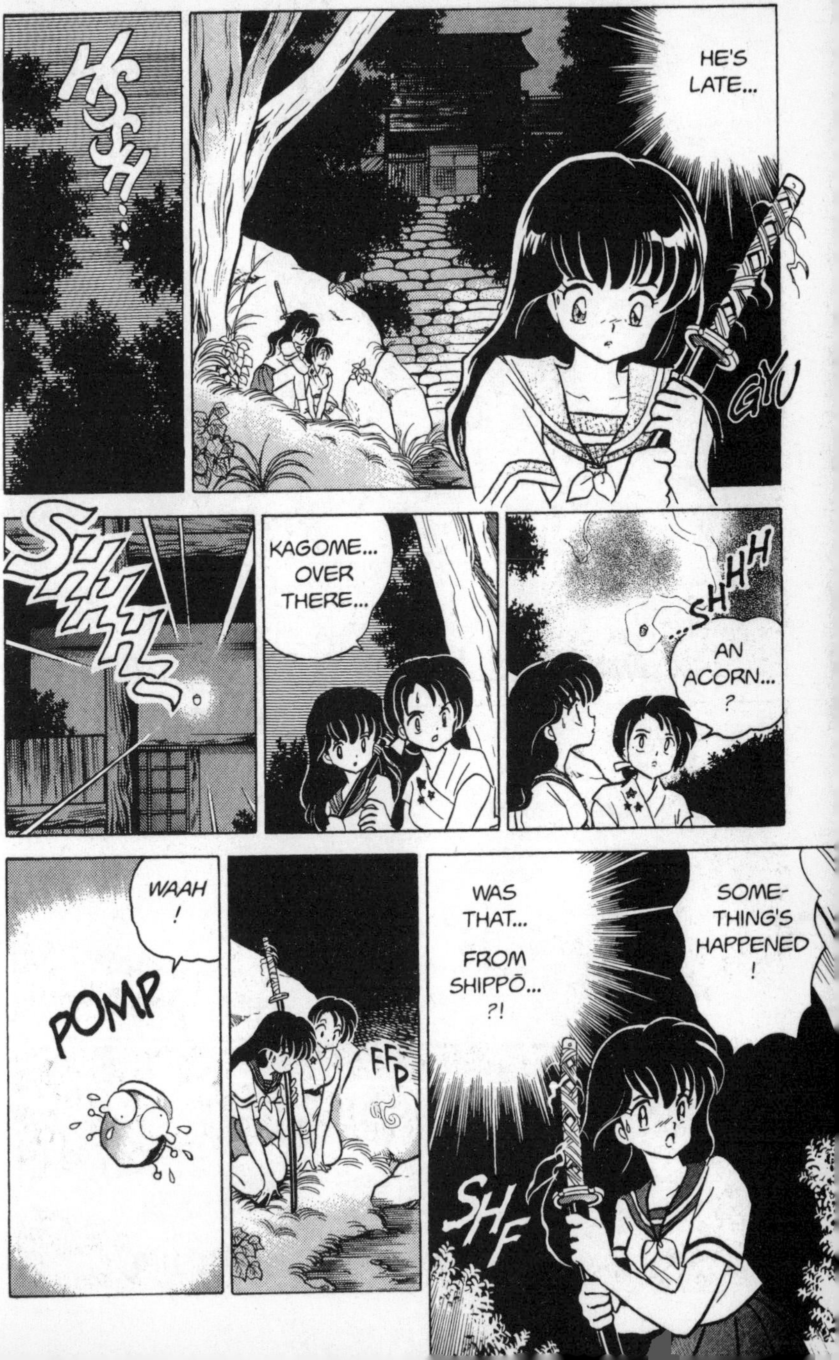
HSSH...
HE'S LATE...
GYU
SHHHH
KAGOME... OVER THERE...
...SHHHH
AN ACORN... ?
WAAH!
POMP
FFP
WAS THAT... FROM SHIPPŌ... ?!
SOME-THING'S HAPPENED!
SHF

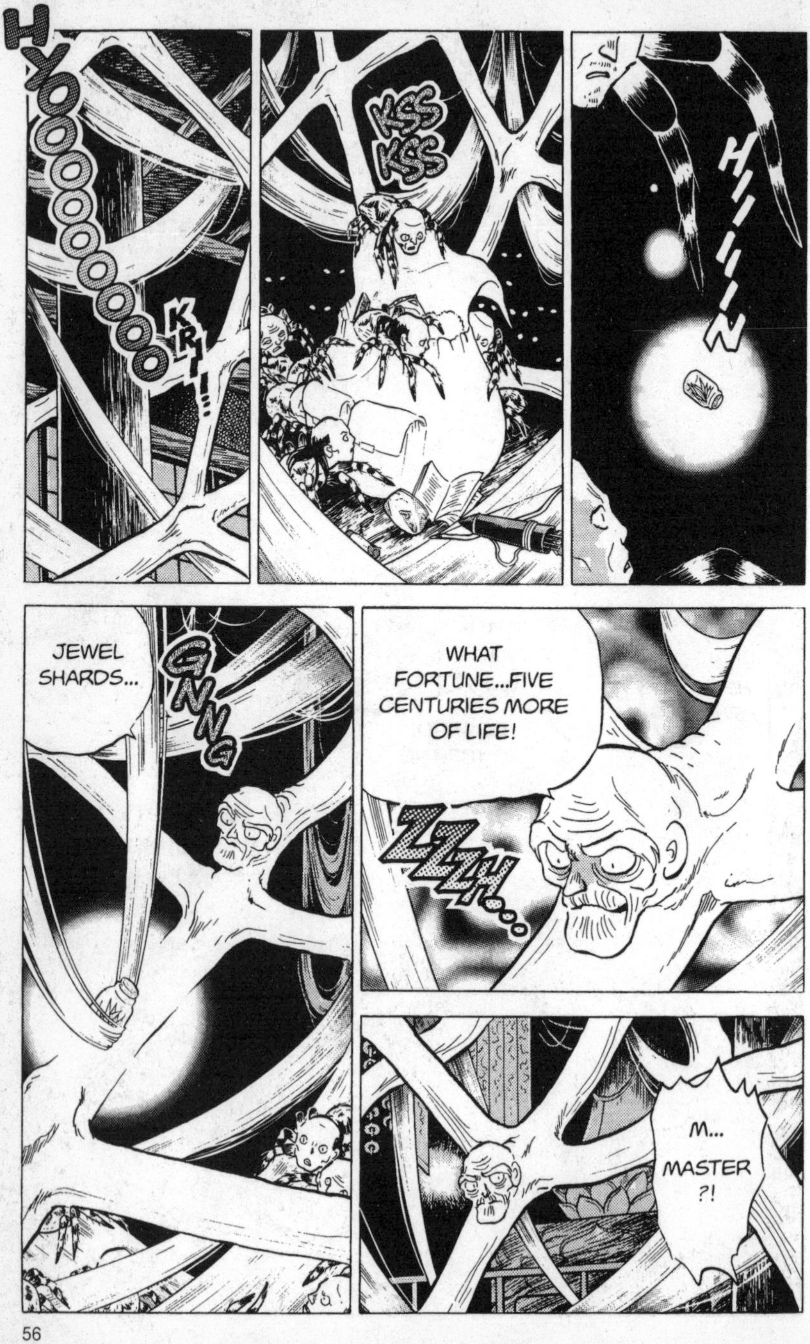
HYOOOOOOOO
KRI!!
KSS KSS
HIIIIIIN
JEWEL SHARDS...
GNNG
WHAT FORTUNE...FIVE CENTURIES MORE OF LIFE!
ZZZH...
M... MASTER ?!

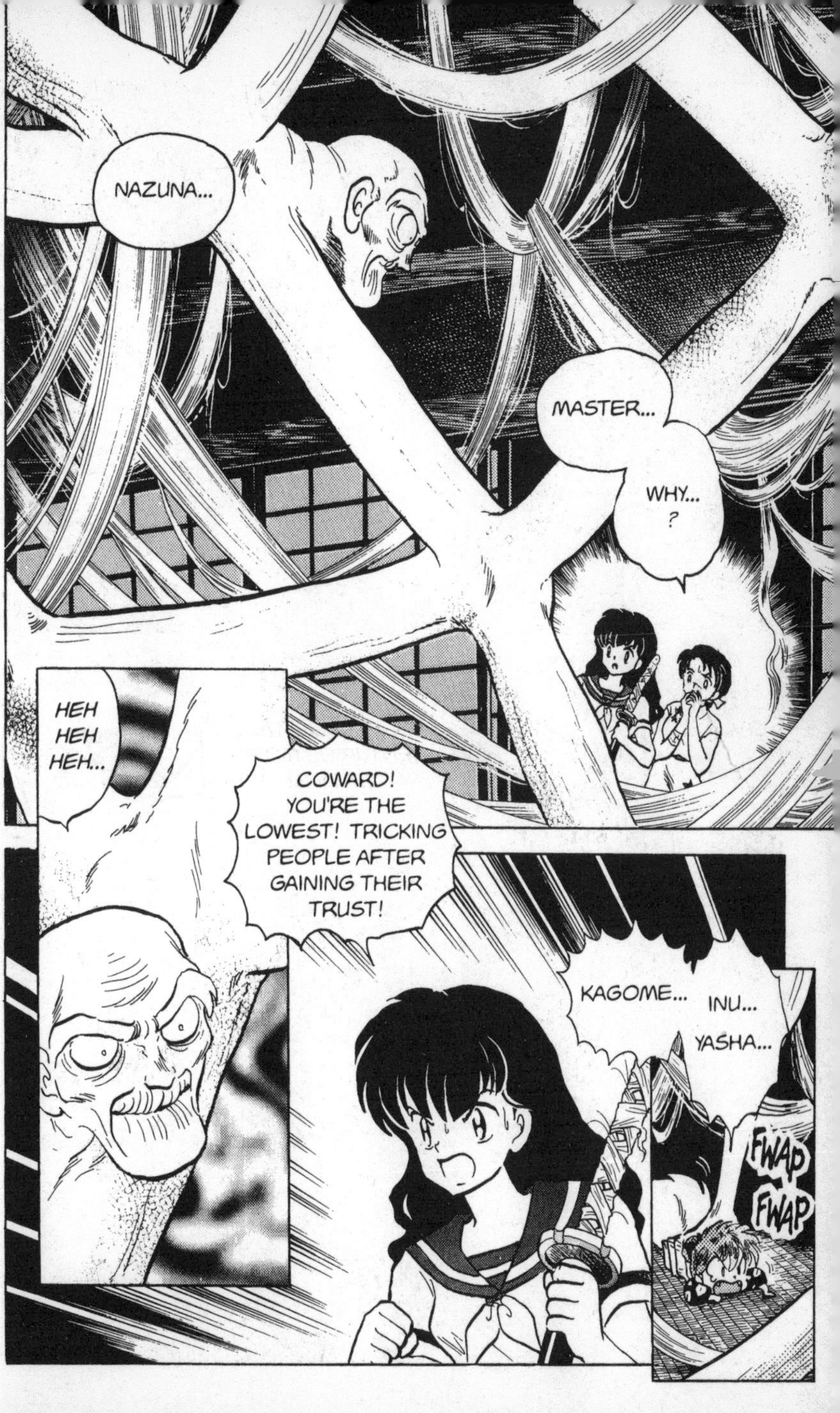
NAZUNA...
MASTER...
WHY... ?
HEH HEH HEH...
COWARD! YOU'RE THE LOWEST! TRICKING PEOPLE AFTER GAINING THEIR TRUST!
KAGOME...
INU... YASHA...
FWAP FWAP

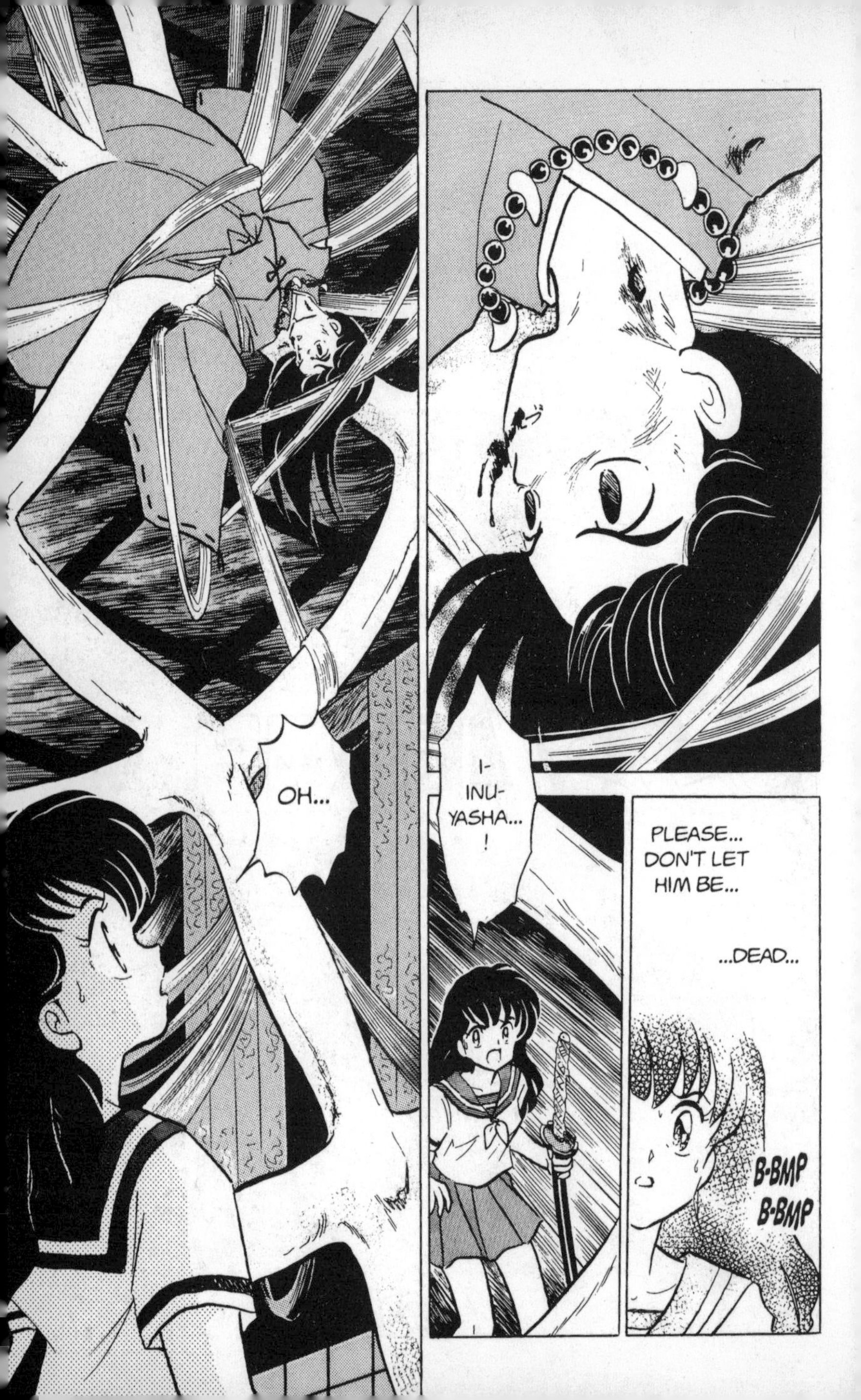
OH...
I- INU-YASHA... !
PLEASE... DON'T LET HIM BE...
...DEAD...
B-BMP B-BMP

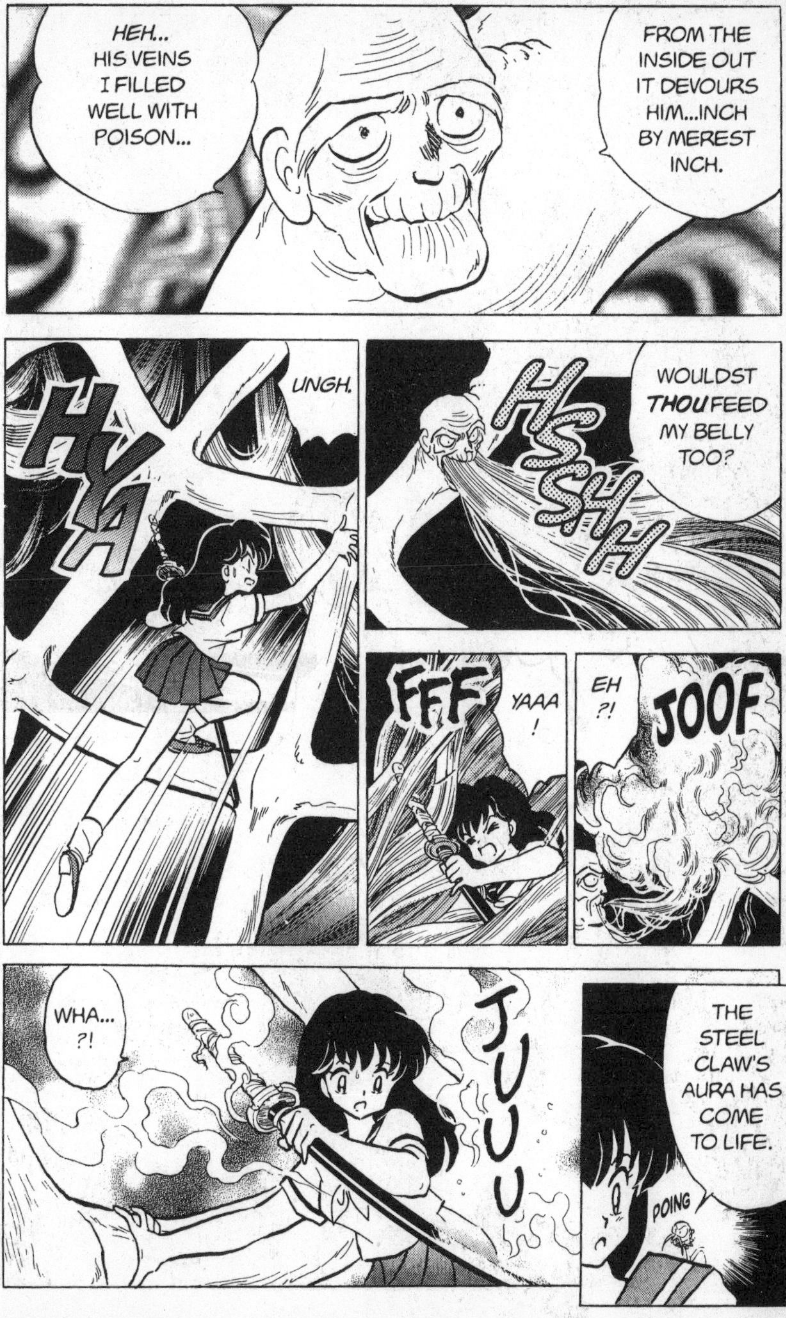
HEH... HIS VEINS I FILLED WELL WITH POISON...
FROM THE INSIDE OUT IT DEVOURS HIM...INCH BY MEREST INCH.
HYA
UNGH.
HSSHH
WOULDST *THOU* FEED MY BELLY TOO?
FFF
YAAA!
EH?!
JOOF
WHA...?!
JUUU
THE STEEL CLAW'S AURA HAS COME TO LIFE.
POING

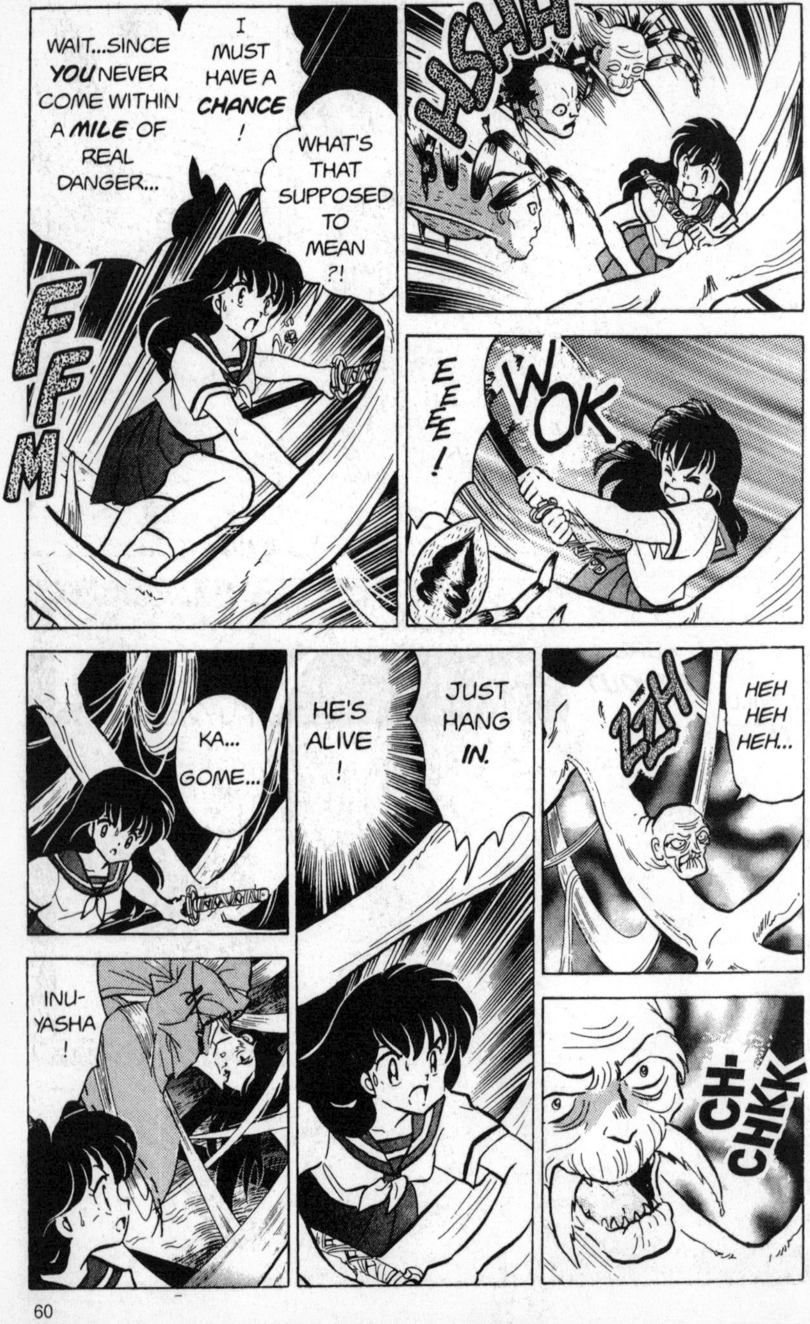

WAIT...SINCE YOU NEVER COME WITHIN A MILE OF REAL DANGER...
I MUST HAVE A CHANCE!
WHAT'S THAT SUPPOSED TO MEAN?!
FFM
HSHH
EEEE!
WOK
KA... GOME...
INU-YASHA!
HE'S ALIVE!
JUST HANG IN.
ZZH
HEH HEH HEH...
CH-CHKK

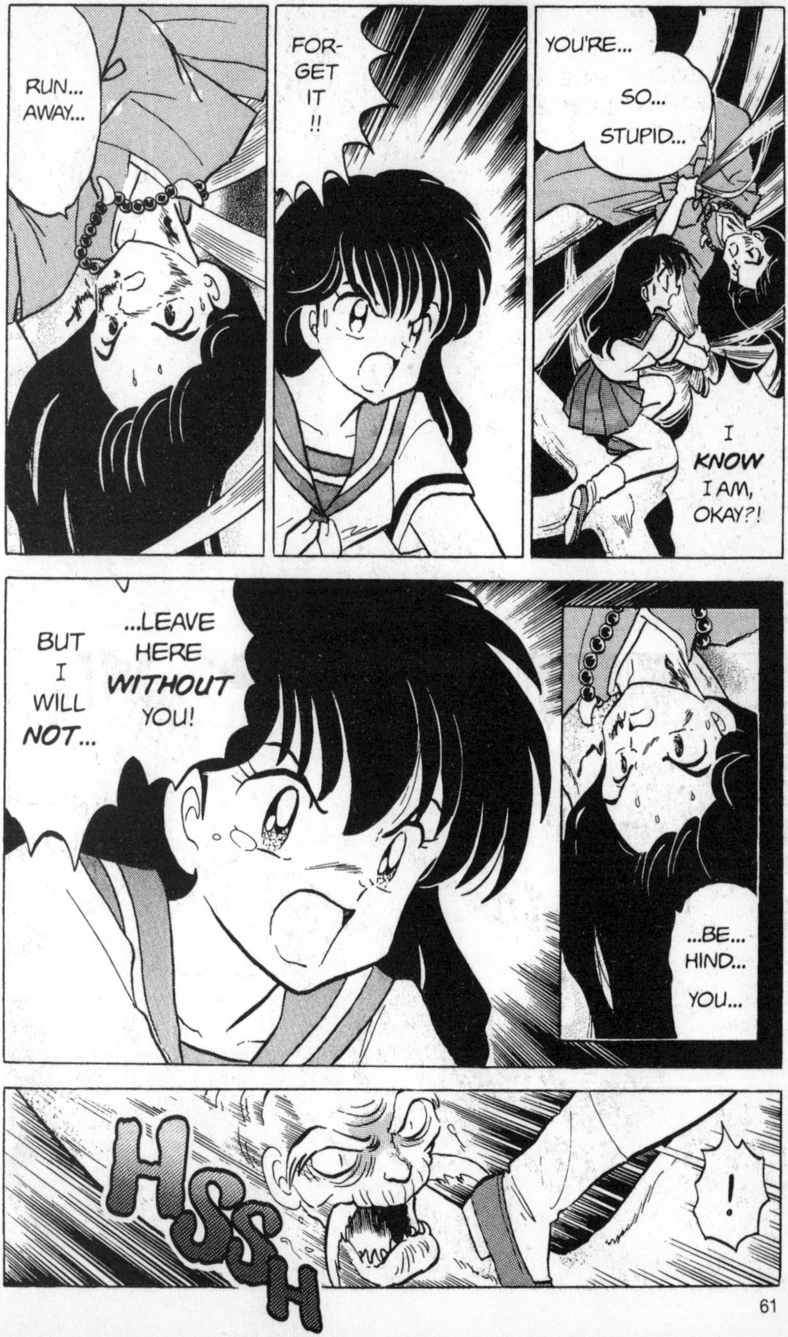
RUN... AWAY...
FOR-GET IT !!
YOU'RE...
SO... STUPID...
I **KNOW** I AM, OKAY?!
BUT I WILL **NOT**...
...LEAVE HERE **WITHOUT** YOU!
...BE... HIND... YOU...
HSSSH
!

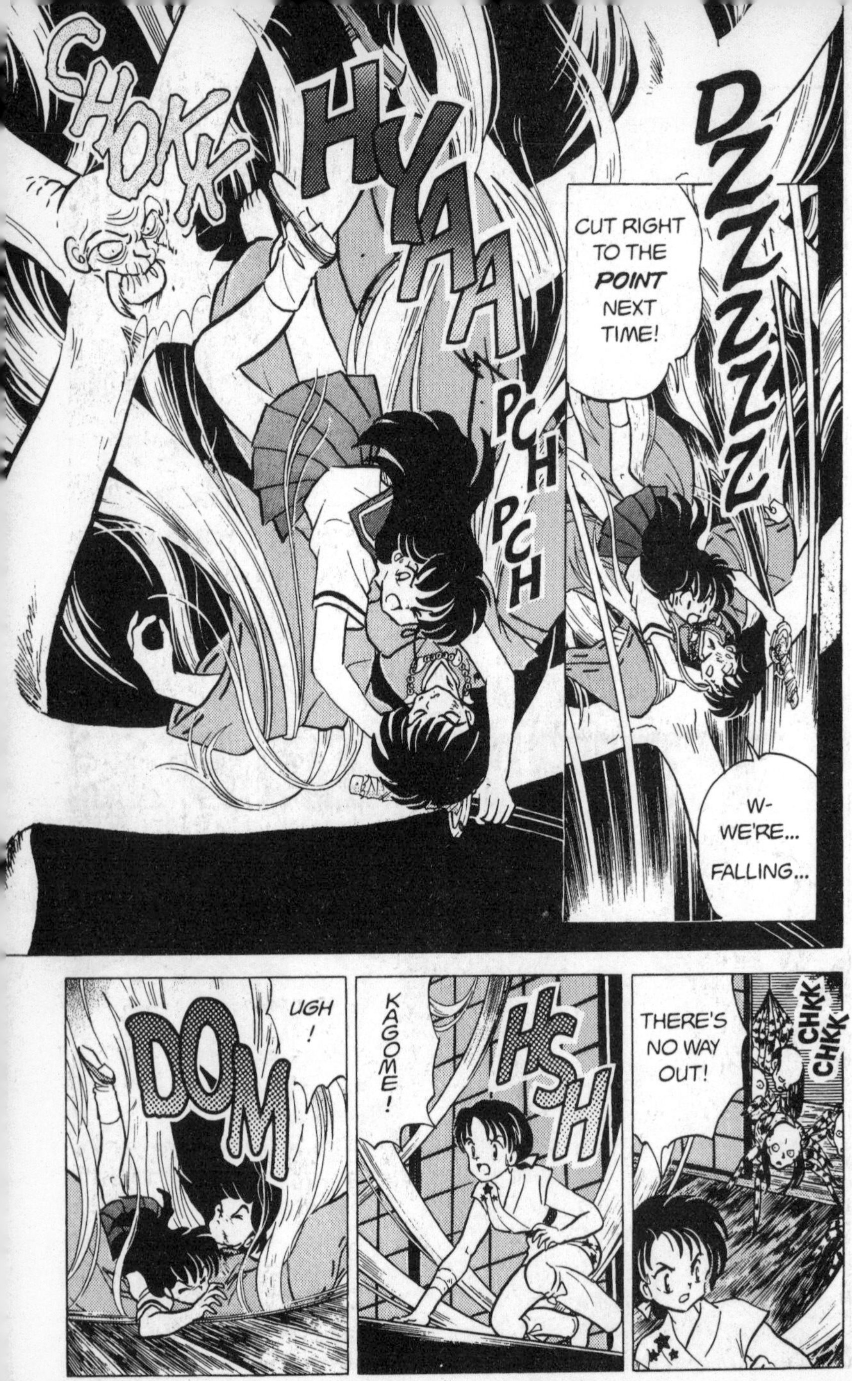

CHOKK
HYAAA
PCH PCH
DZZZZZZ
CUT RIGHT TO THE ***POINT*** NEXT TIME!
W- WE'RE... FALLING...
DOM
UGH!
KAGOME!
HSH
THERE'S NO WAY OUT!
CHKK CHKK

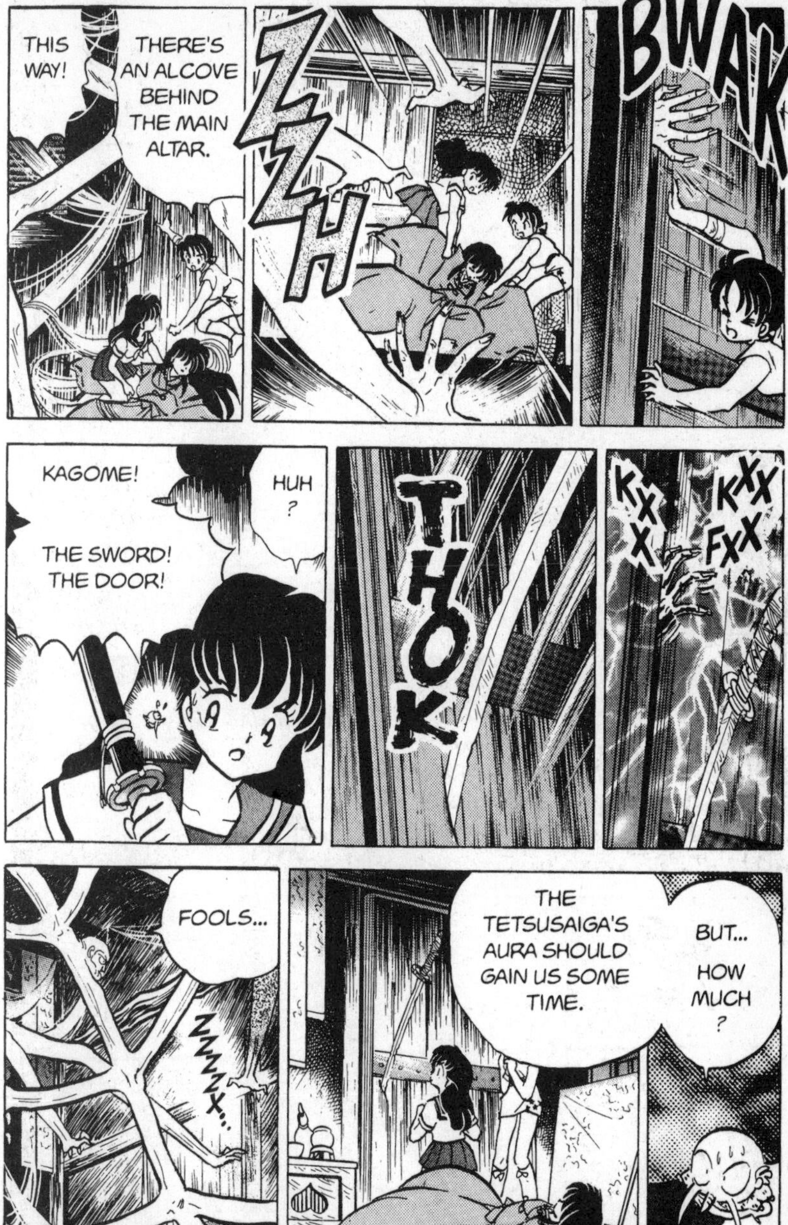
THIS WAY!
THERE'S AN ALCOVE BEHIND THE MAIN ALTAR.
ZZH
BWAK
KAGOME!
THE SWORD! THE DOOR!
HUH?
THOK
KXX
KXX FXX
FOOLS...
ZZZZX...
THE TETSUSAIGA'S AURA SHOULD GAIN US SOME TIME.
BUT... HOW MUCH?

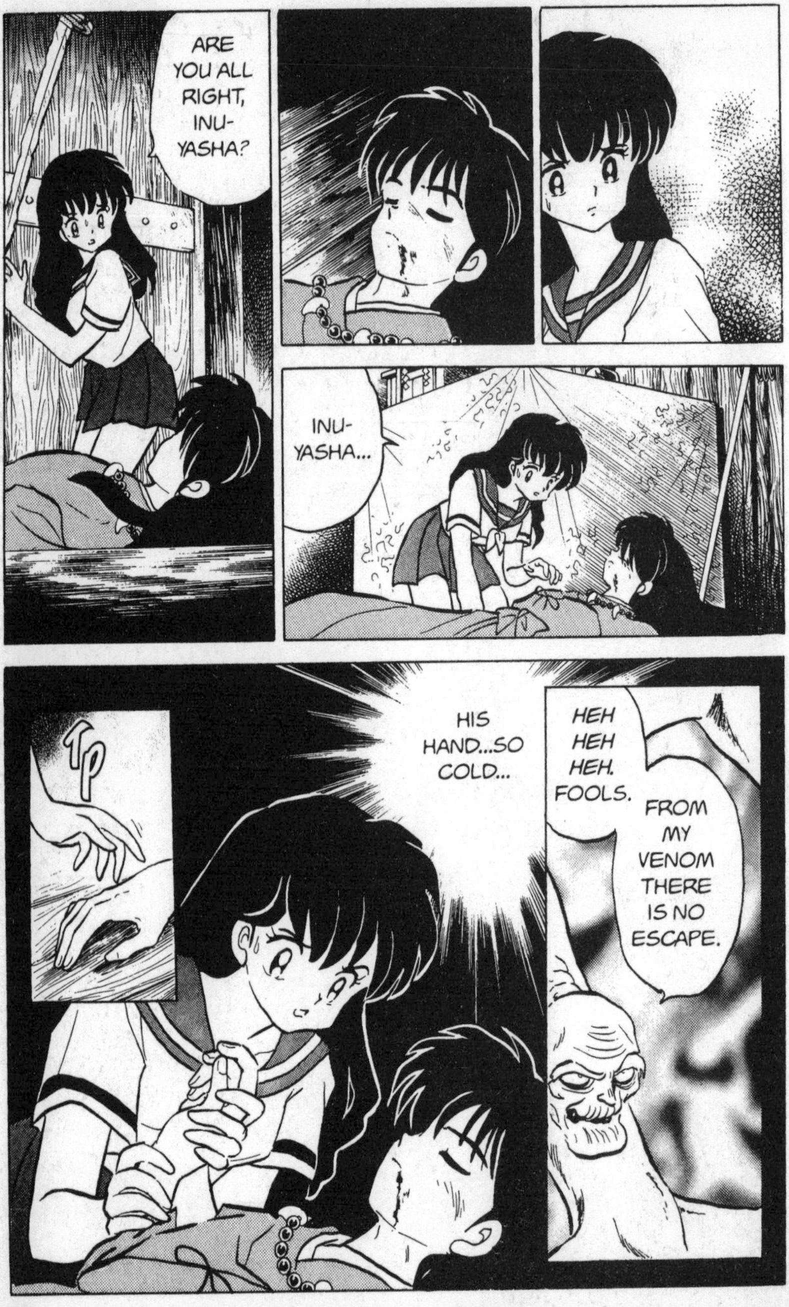
ARE YOU ALL RIGHT, INU-YASHA?
INU-YASHA...
HIS HAND...SO COLD...
HEH HEH HEH. FOOLS.
FROM MY VENOM THERE IS NO ESCAPE.

SCROLL FOUR
INSIDE THE AURA

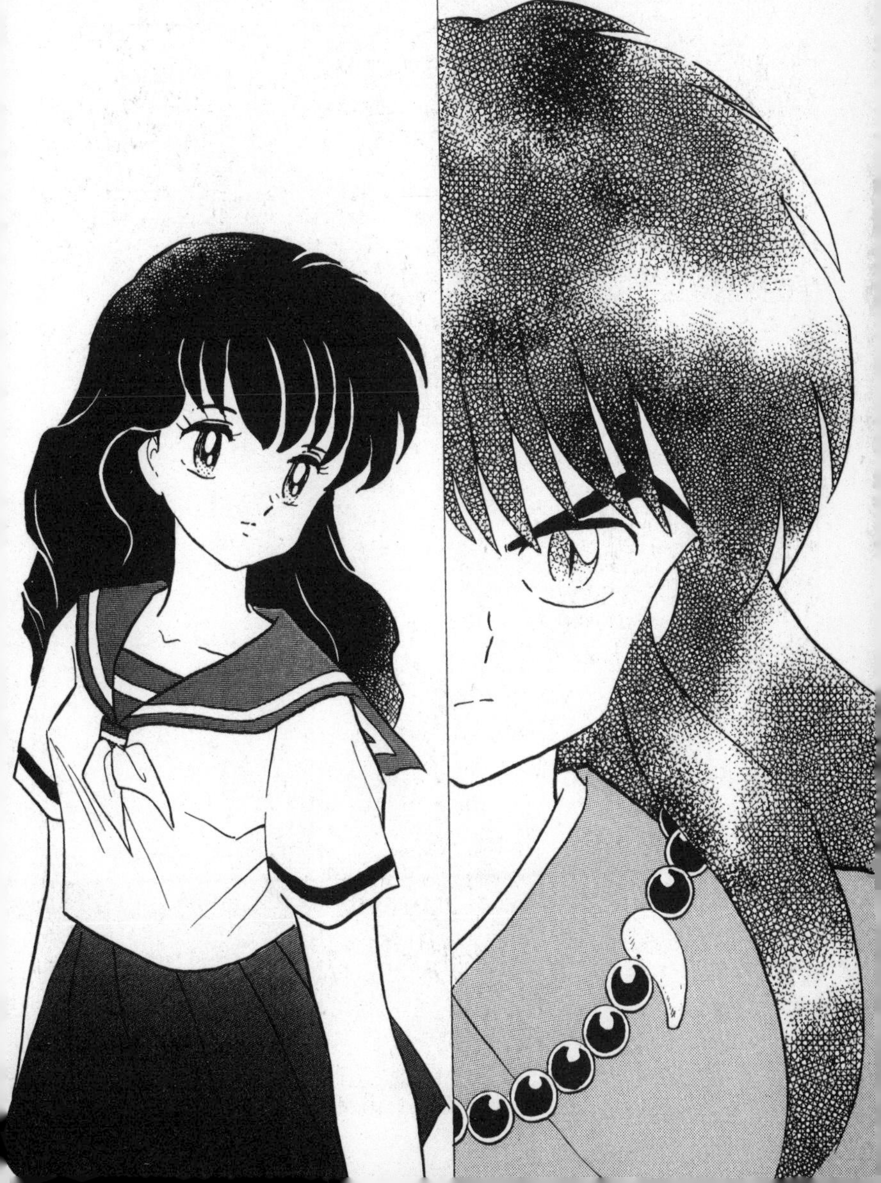

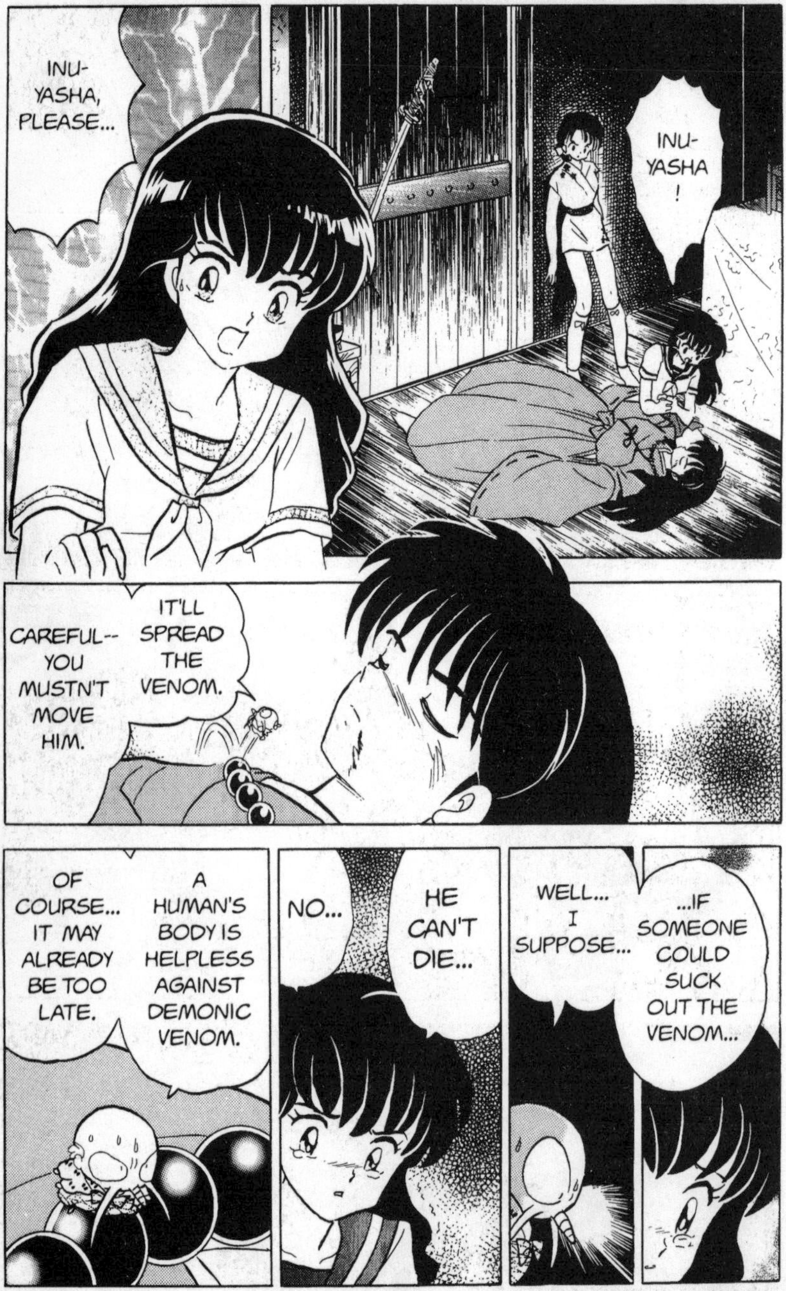
INU-YASHA, PLEASE...
INU-YASHA!
CAREFUL-- YOU MUSTN'T MOVE HIM.
IT'LL SPREAD THE VENOM.
OF COURSE... IT MAY ALREADY BE TOO LATE.
A HUMAN'S BODY IS HELPLESS AGAINST DEMONIC VENOM.
NO...
HE CAN'T DIE...
WELL... I SUPPOSE...
...IF SOMEONE COULD SUCK OUT THE VENOM...

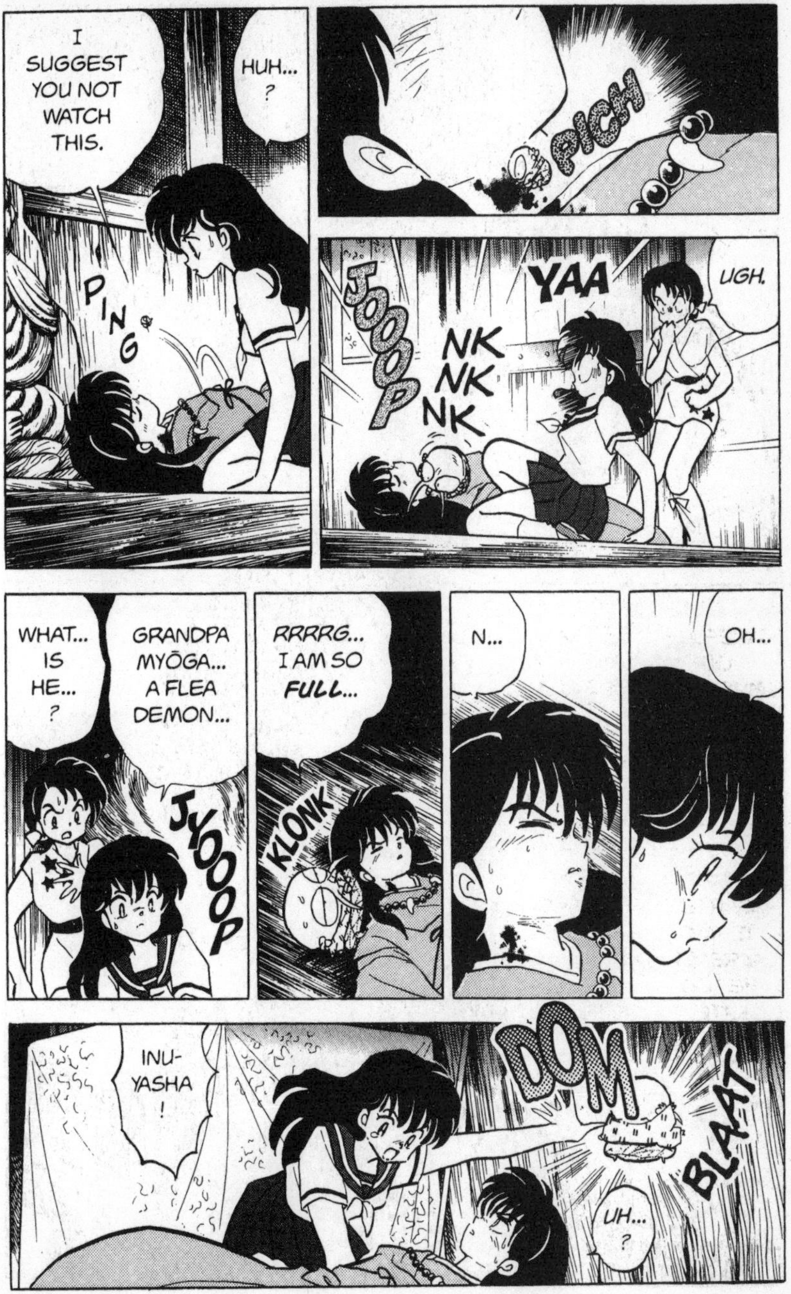
I SUGGEST YOU NOT WATCH THIS.
HUH... ?
PING
PICH
JOOOOP
NK NK NK
YAA
UGH.
WHAT... IS HE... ?
GRANDPA MYŌGA... A FLEA DEMON...
JYOOOP
RRRRG... I AM SO *FULL*...
KLONK
N...
OH...
INU-YASHA !
DOM
BLAAT
UH... ?

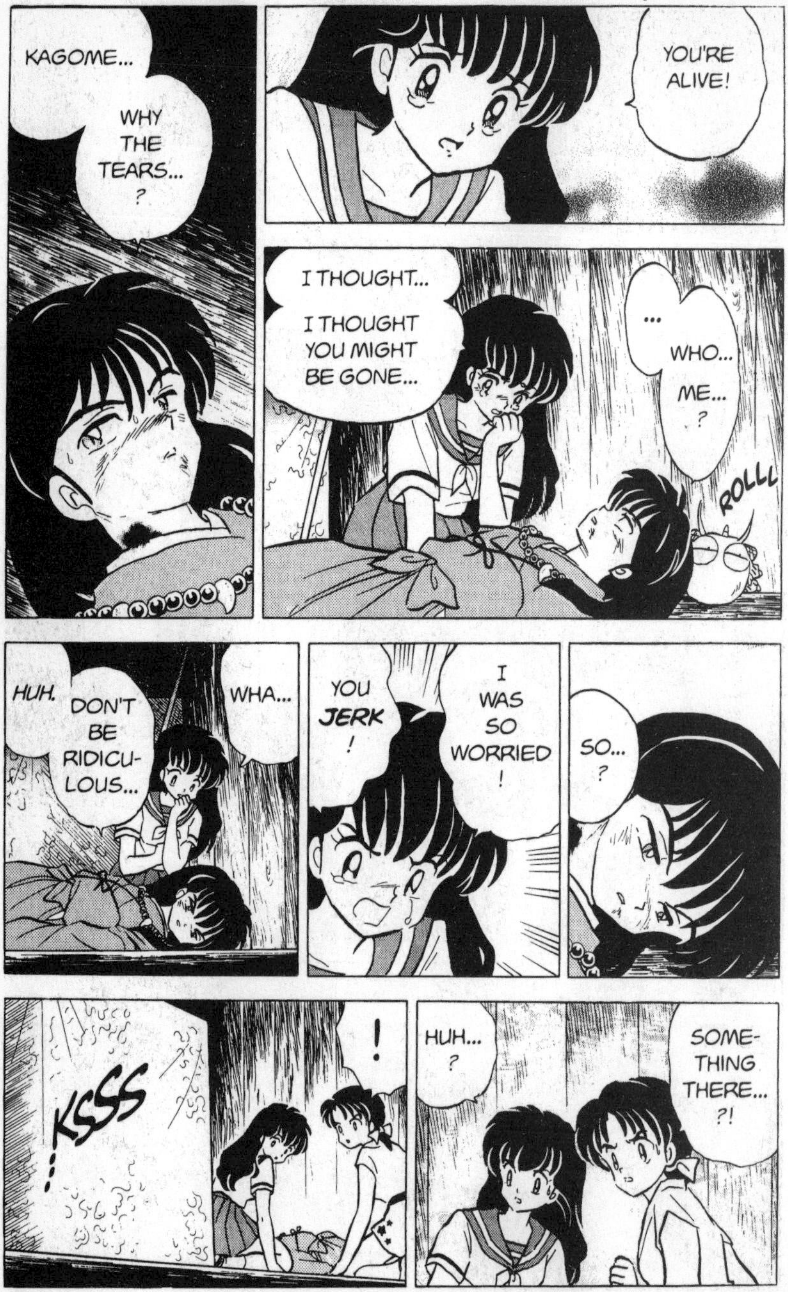
KAGOME...
WHY THE TEARS... ?
YOU'RE ALIVE!
I THOUGHT...
I THOUGHT YOU MIGHT BE GONE...
... WHO... ME... ?
ROLLL
HUH.
DON'T BE RIDICU-LOUS...
WHA...
YOU JERK!
I WAS SO WORRIED!
SO... ?
KSSS
!
HUH... ?
SOME-THING THERE... ?!

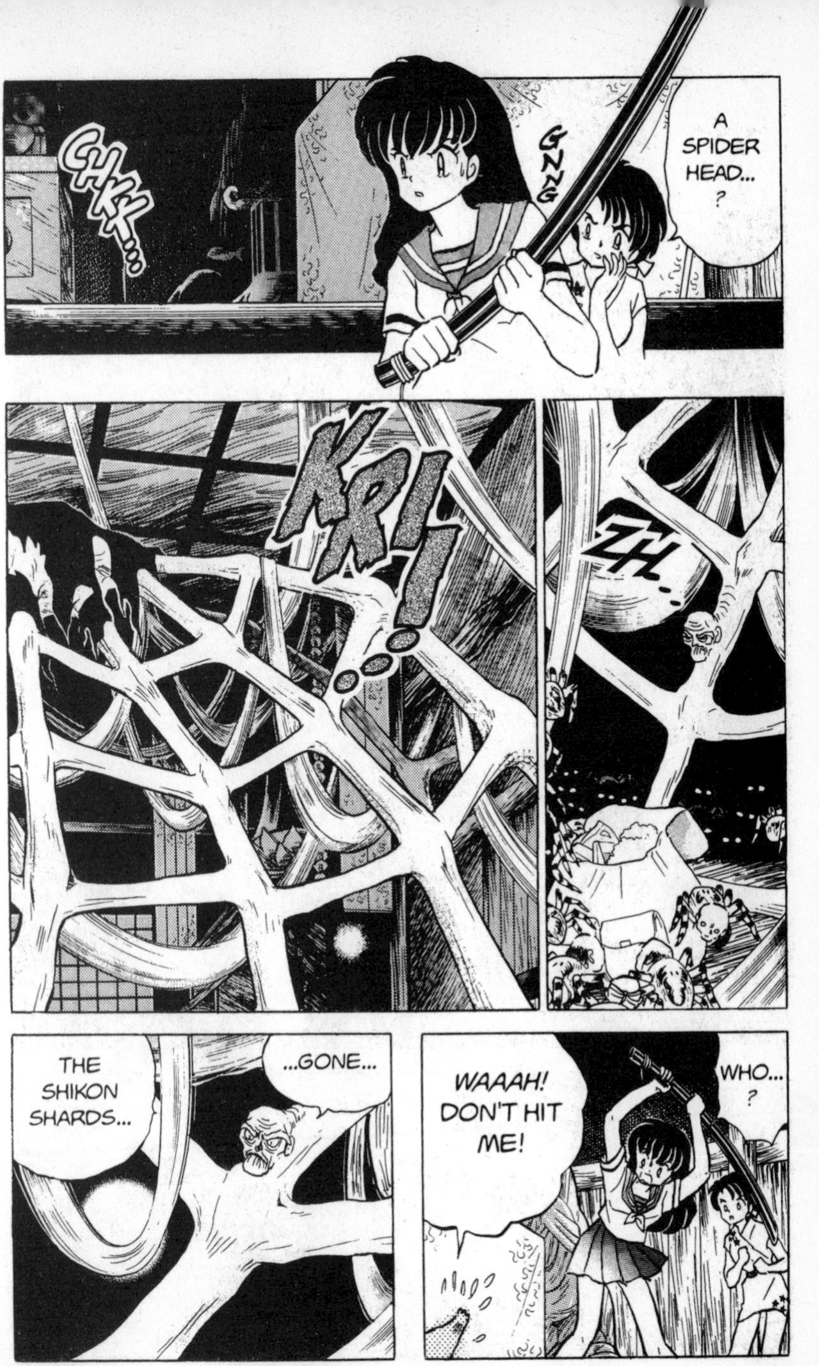
CHKK...
GNNG
A SPIDER HEAD... ?
KRI...!
ZH...
THE SHIKON SHARDS...
...GONE...
WAAAH! DON'T HIT ME!
WHO... ?

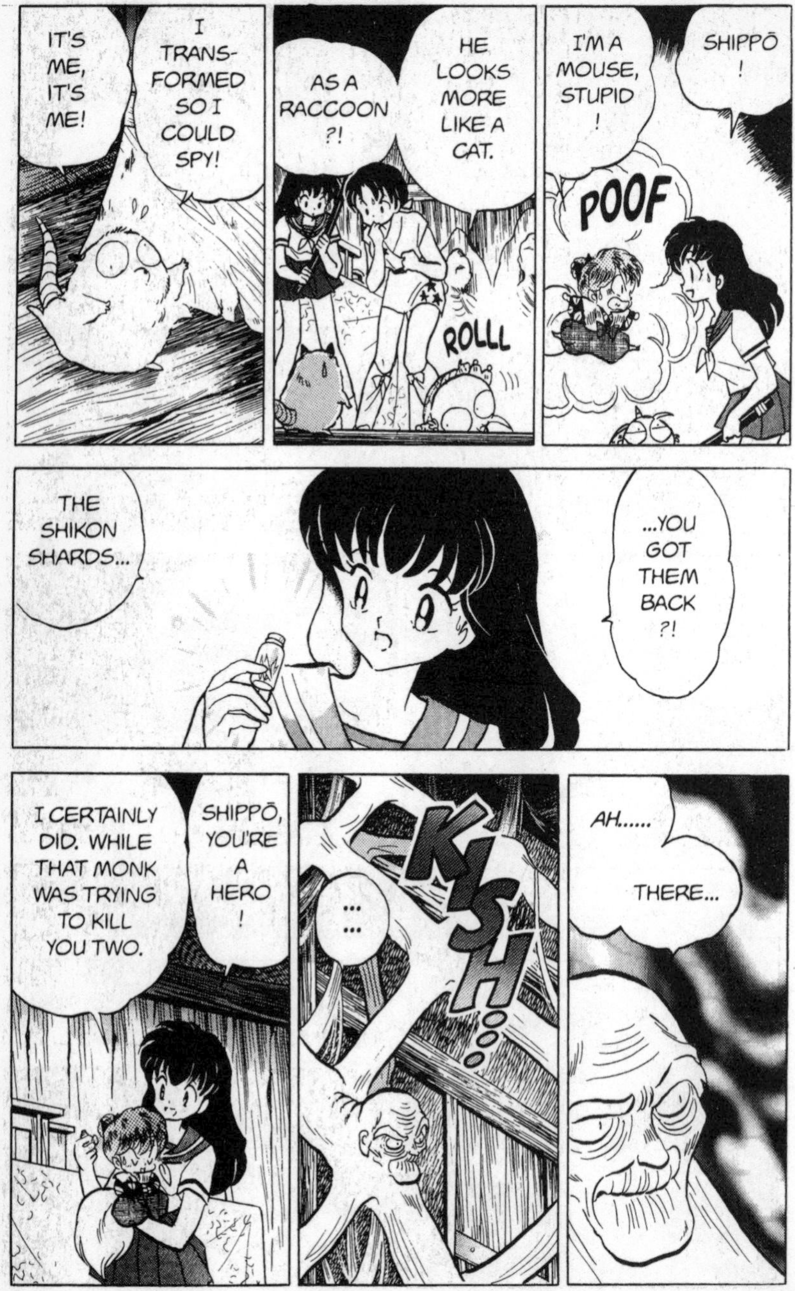
IT'S ME, IT'S ME!
I TRANSFORMED SO I COULD SPY!
AS A RACCOON ?!
HE LOOKS MORE LIKE A CAT.
ROLLL
I'M A MOUSE, STUPID !
SHIPPŌ !
POOF
THE SHIKON SHARDS...
...YOU GOT THEM BACK ?!
I CERTAINLY DID. WHILE THAT MONK WAS TRYING TO KILL YOU TWO.
SHIPPŌ, YOU'RE A HERO !
KISHOOO
......
AH......
THERE...

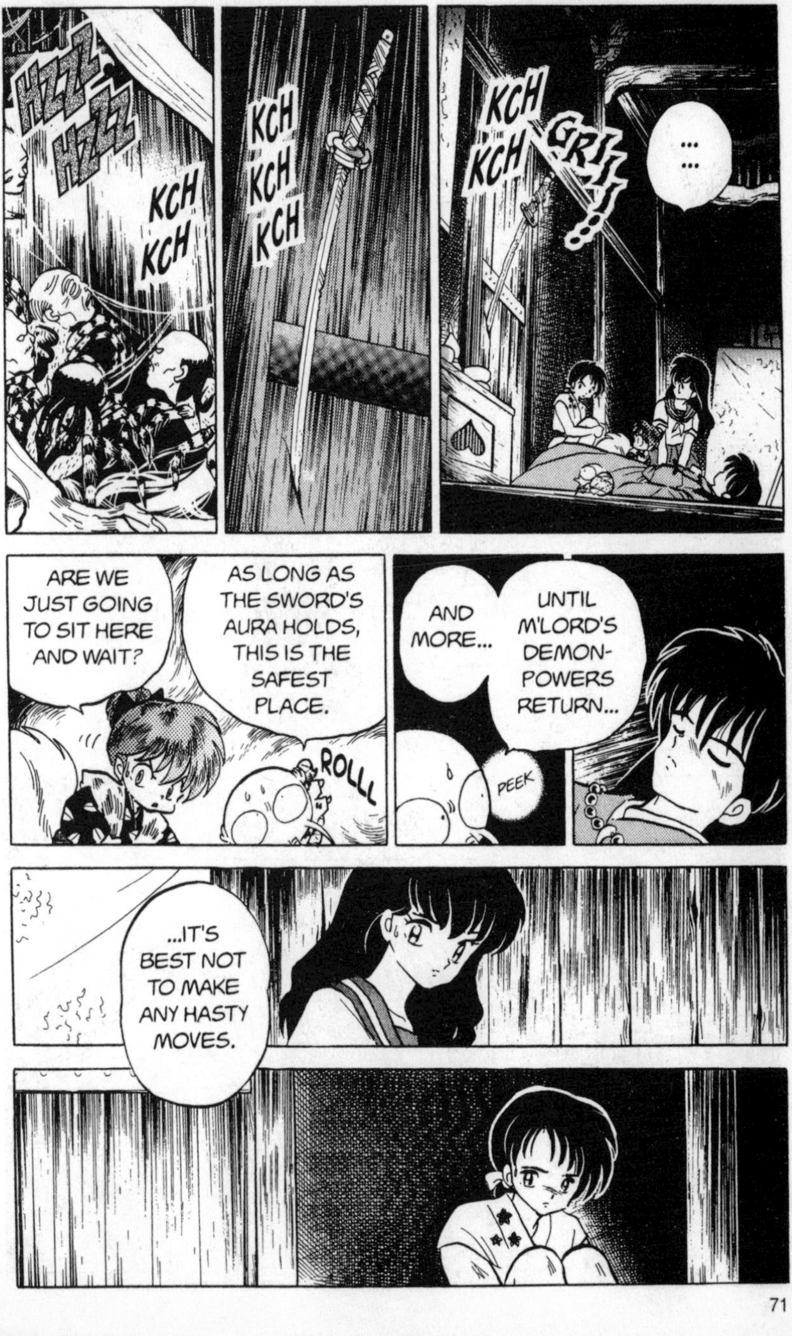
HZZZ HZZZ
KCH KCH
KCH KCH KCH
KCH KCH
GRI...!!
...
...
ARE WE JUST GOING TO SIT HERE AND WAIT?
AS LONG AS THE SWORD'S AURA HOLDS, THIS IS THE SAFEST PLACE.
ROLLL
AND MORE...
PEEK
UNTIL M'LORD'S DEMON-POWERS RETURN...
...IT'S BEST NOT TO MAKE ANY HASTY MOVES.

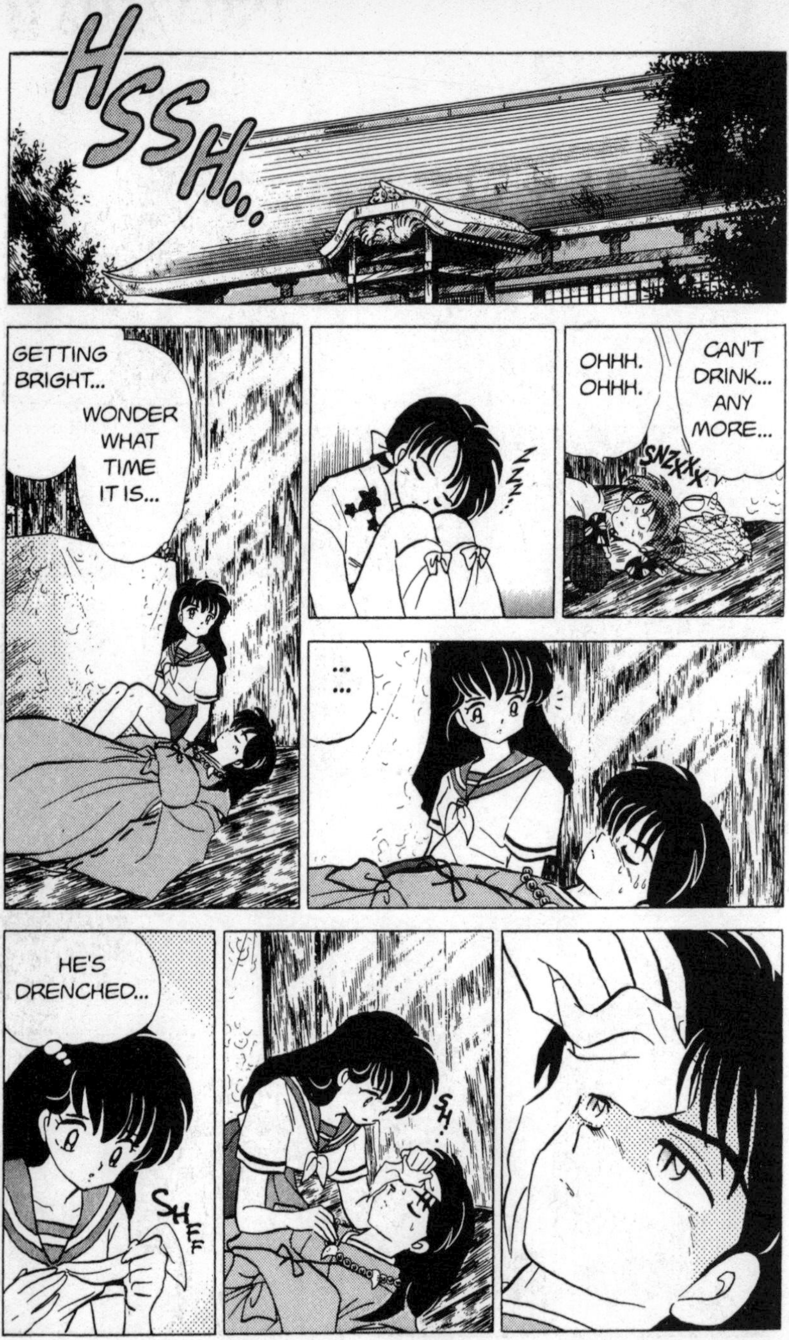
HSSH...
GETTING BRIGHT...
WONDER WHAT TIME IT IS...
OHHH. OHHH.
CAN'T DRINK... ANY MORE...
SNZXXX
...
...
HE'S DRENCHED...
SHH
SH...

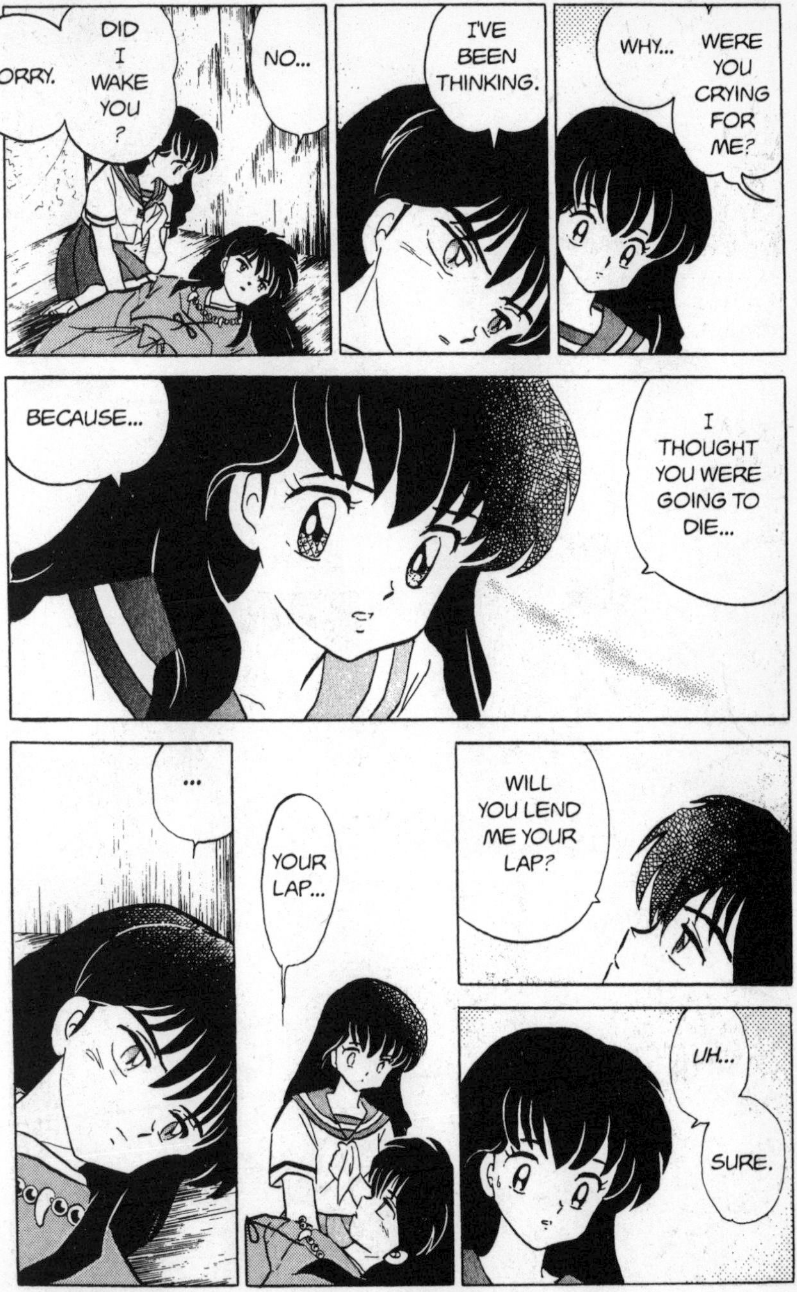
SORRY.
DID I WAKE YOU?
NO...
I'VE BEEN THINKING.
WHY...
WERE YOU CRYING FOR ME?
BECAUSE...
I THOUGHT YOU WERE GOING TO DIE...
...
YOUR LAP...
WILL YOU LEND ME YOUR LAP?
UH...
SURE.

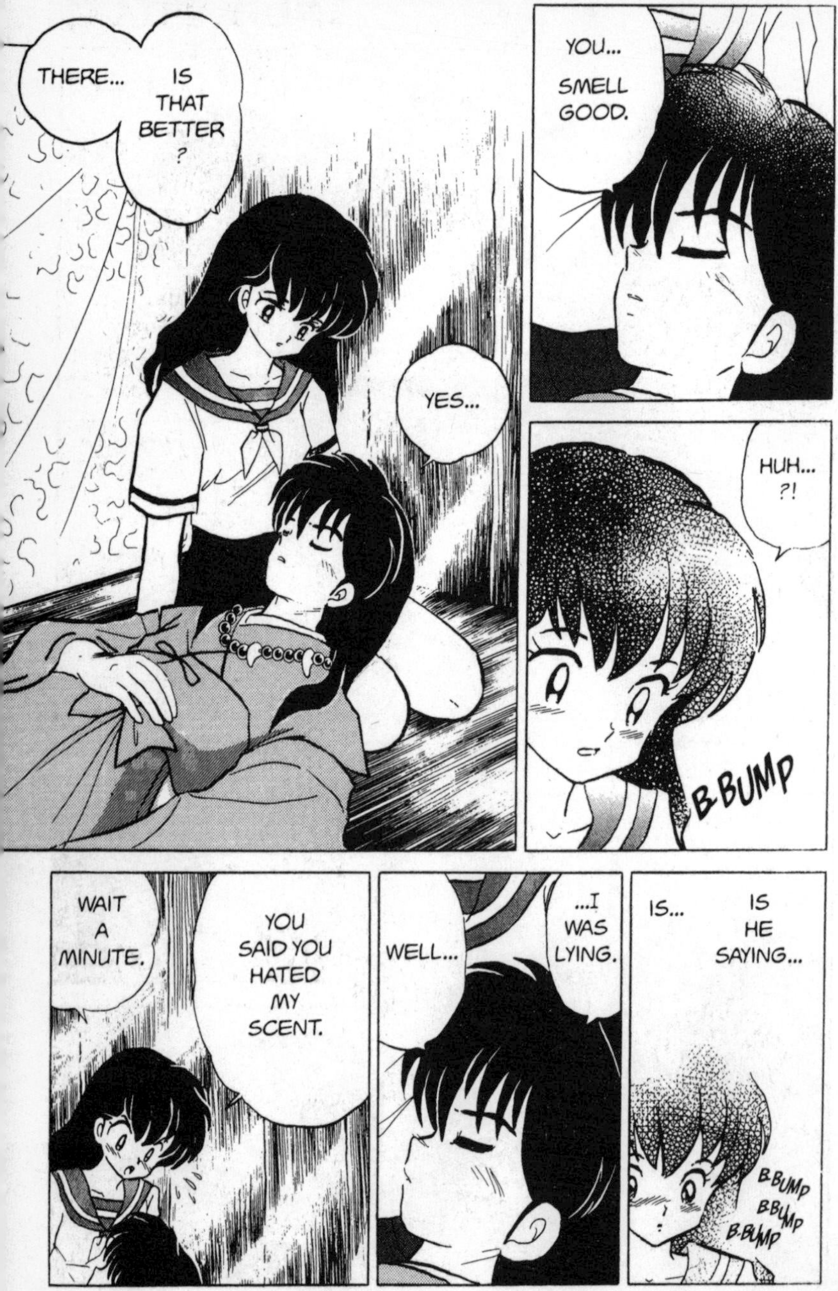
THERE... IS THAT BETTER ?
YES...
YOU... SMELL GOOD.
HUH... ?!
B-BUMP
WAIT A MINUTE.
YOU SAID YOU HATED MY SCENT.
WELL...
...I WAS LYING.
IS... IS HE SAYING...
B-BUMP
B-BUMP
B-BUMP

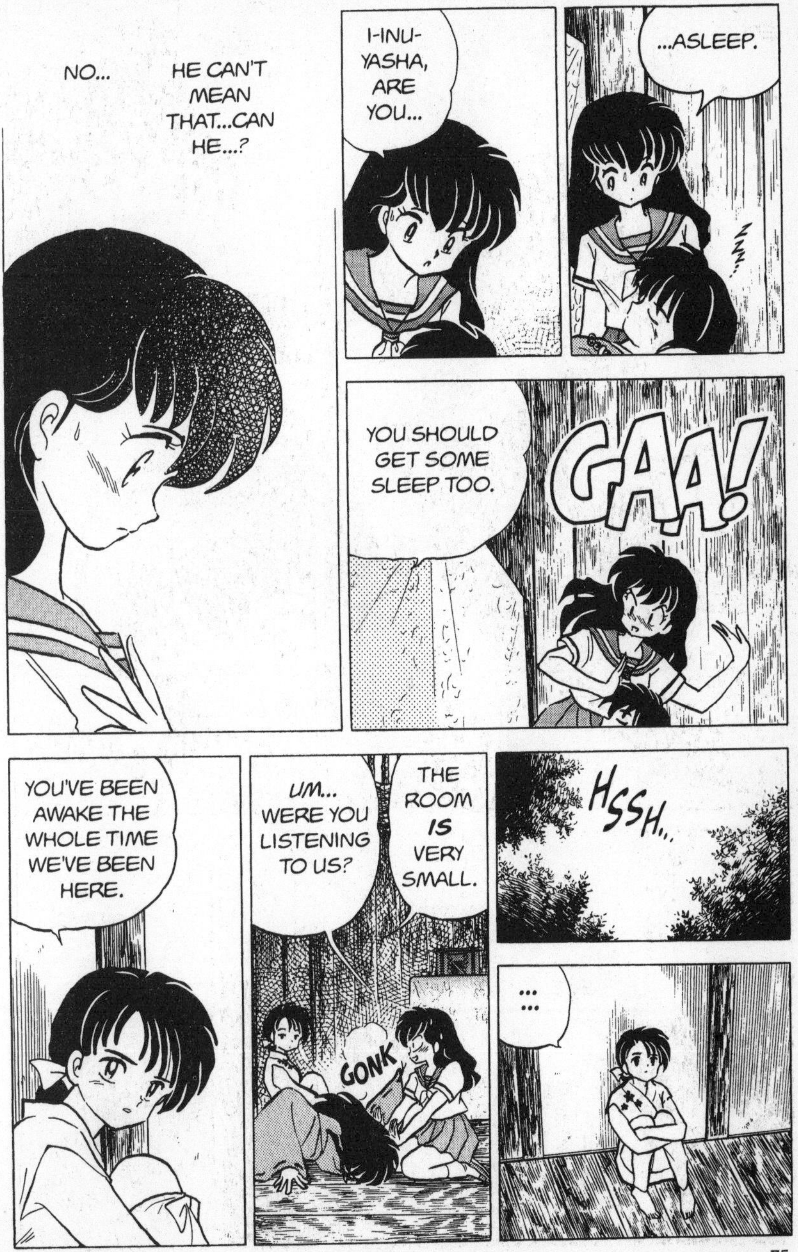
NO...
HE CAN'T MEAN THAT...CAN HE...?
I-INU-YASHA, ARE YOU...
...ASLEEP.
ZZZ
YOU SHOULD GET SOME SLEEP TOO.
GAA!
YOU'VE BEEN AWAKE THE WHOLE TIME WE'VE BEEN HERE.
UM... WERE YOU LISTENING TO US?
THE ROOM IS VERY SMALL.
GONK
HSSH...
...
...

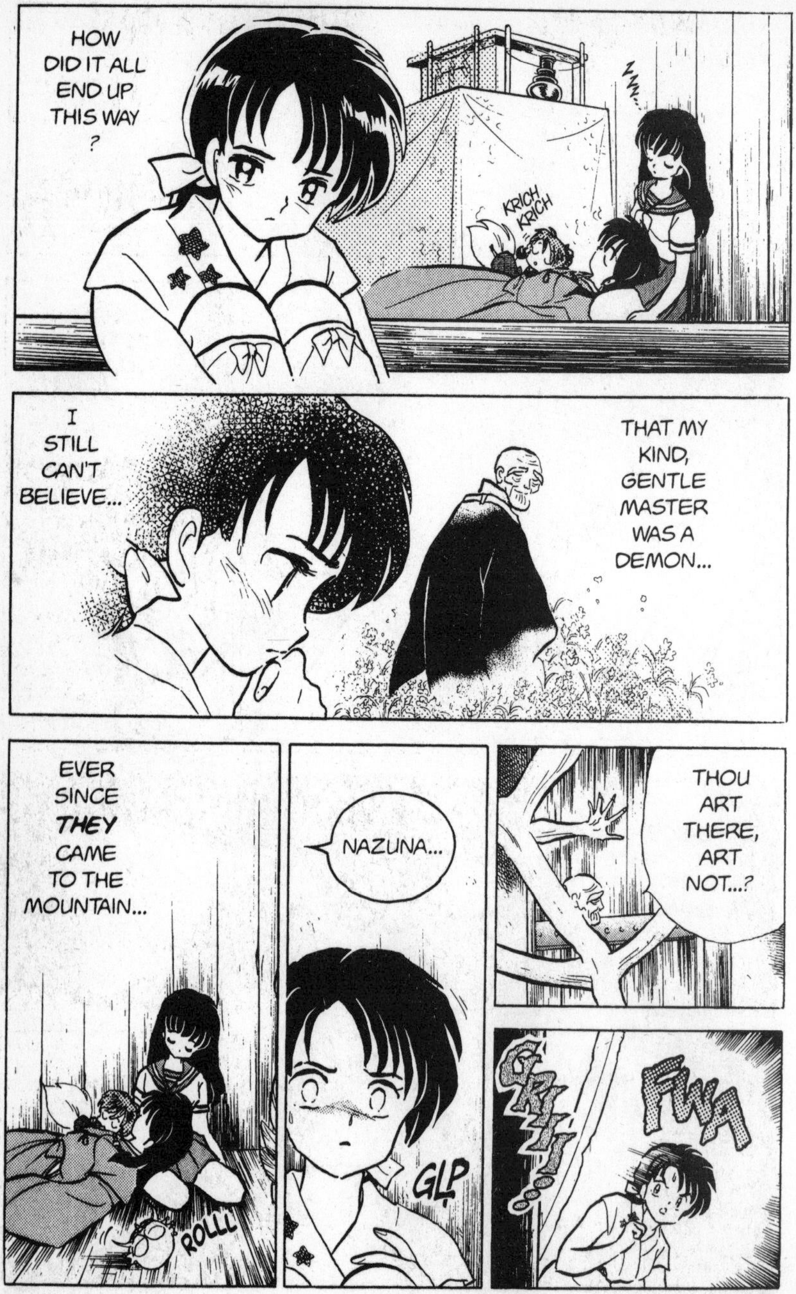
HOW DID IT ALL END UP THIS WAY ?
KRICH KRICH
I STILL CAN'T BELIEVE...
THAT MY KIND, GENTLE MASTER WAS A DEMON...
EVER SINCE ***THEY*** CAME TO THE MOUNTAIN...
ROLLL
NAZUNA...
GLP
THOU ART THERE, ART NOT...?
FWA

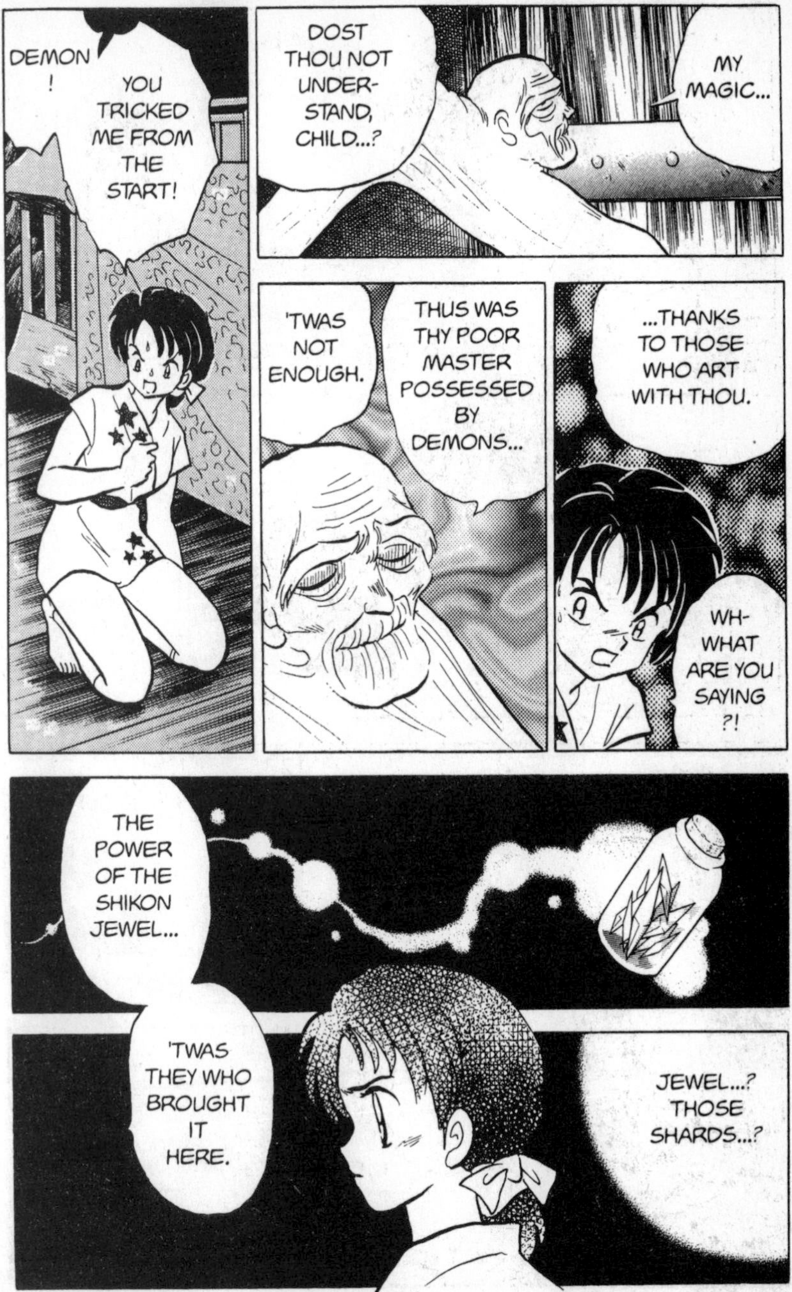
DEMON!
YOU TRICKED ME FROM THE START!
DOST THOU NOT UNDERSTAND, CHILD...?
MY MAGIC...
'TWAS NOT ENOUGH.
THUS WAS THY POOR MASTER POSSESSED BY DEMONS...
...THANKS TO THOSE WHO ART WITH THOU.
WH-WHAT ARE YOU SAYING?!
THE POWER OF THE SHIKON JEWEL...
'TWAS THEY WHO BROUGHT IT HERE.
JEWEL...? THOSE SHARDS...?

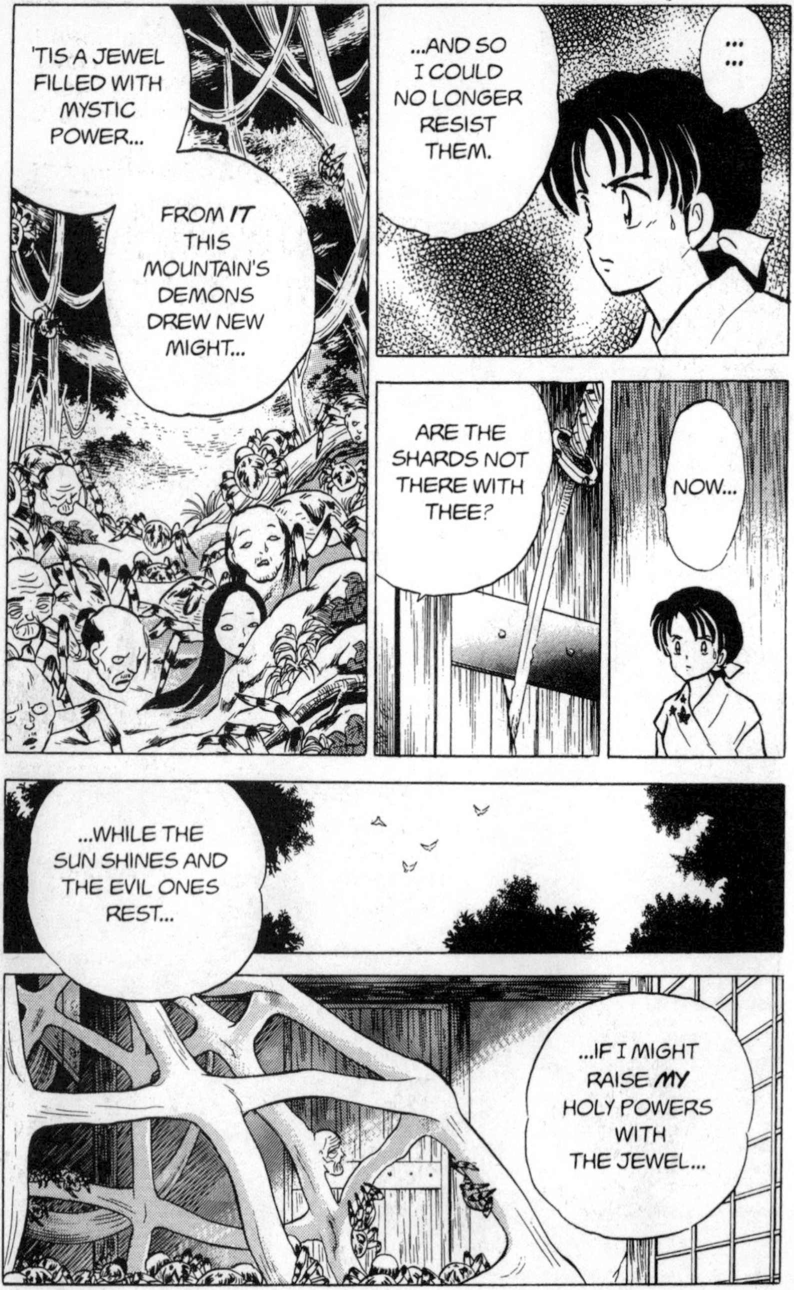
'TIS A JEWEL FILLED WITH MYSTIC POWER...
FROM *IT* THIS MOUNTAIN'S DEMONS DREW NEW MIGHT...
...AND SO I COULD NO LONGER RESIST THEM.
...
...
ARE THE SHARDS NOT THERE WITH THEE?
NOW...
...WHILE THE SUN SHINES AND THE EVIL ONES REST...
...IF I MIGHT RAISE *MY* HOLY POWERS WITH THE JEWEL...

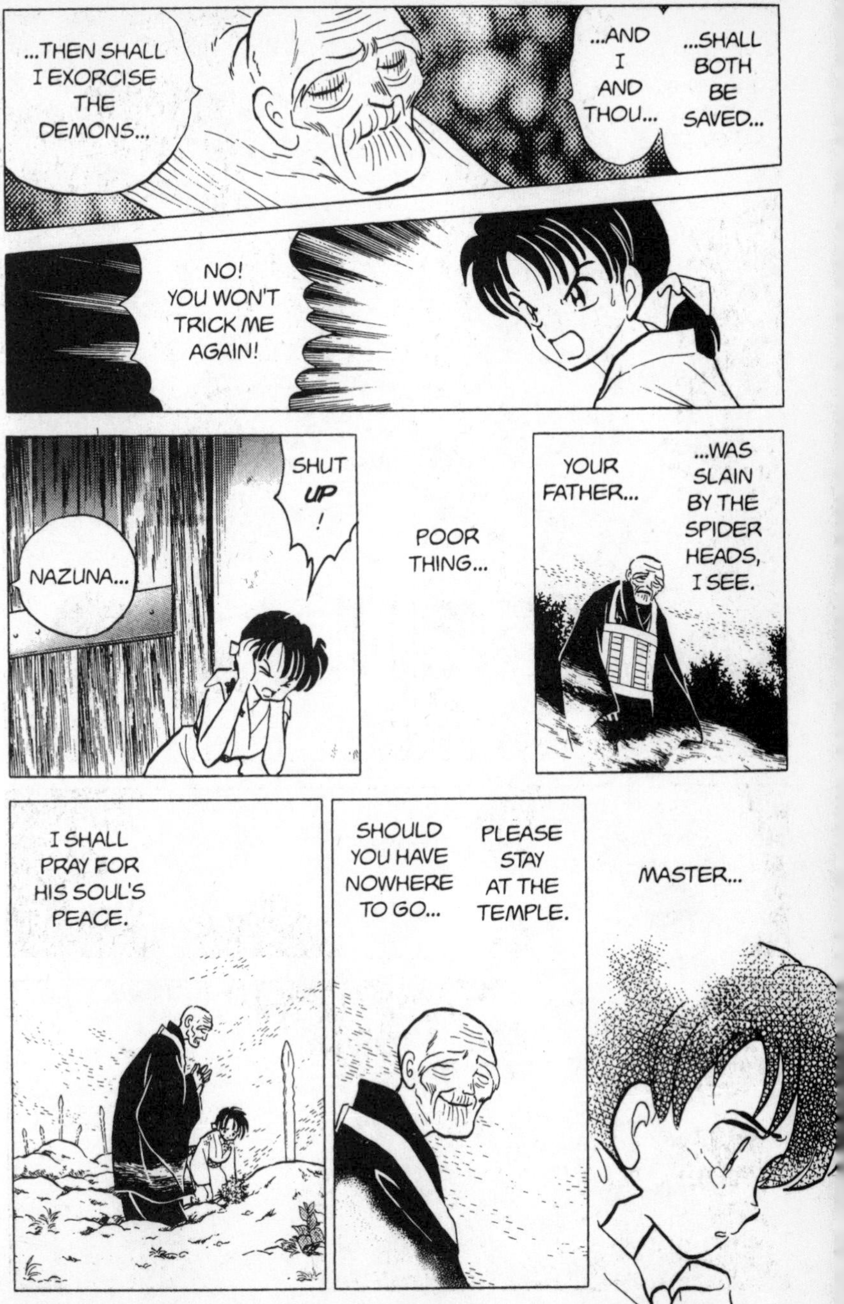
...THEN SHALL I EXORCISE THE DEMONS...
...AND I AND THOU...
...SHALL BOTH BE SAVED...
NO! YOU WON'T TRICK ME AGAIN!
NAZUNA...
SHUT UP!
POOR THING...
YOUR FATHER...
...WAS SLAIN BY THE SPIDER HEADS, I SEE.
I SHALL PRAY FOR HIS SOUL'S PEACE.
SHOULD YOU HAVE NOWHERE TO GO...
PLEASE STAY AT THE TEMPLE.
MASTER...

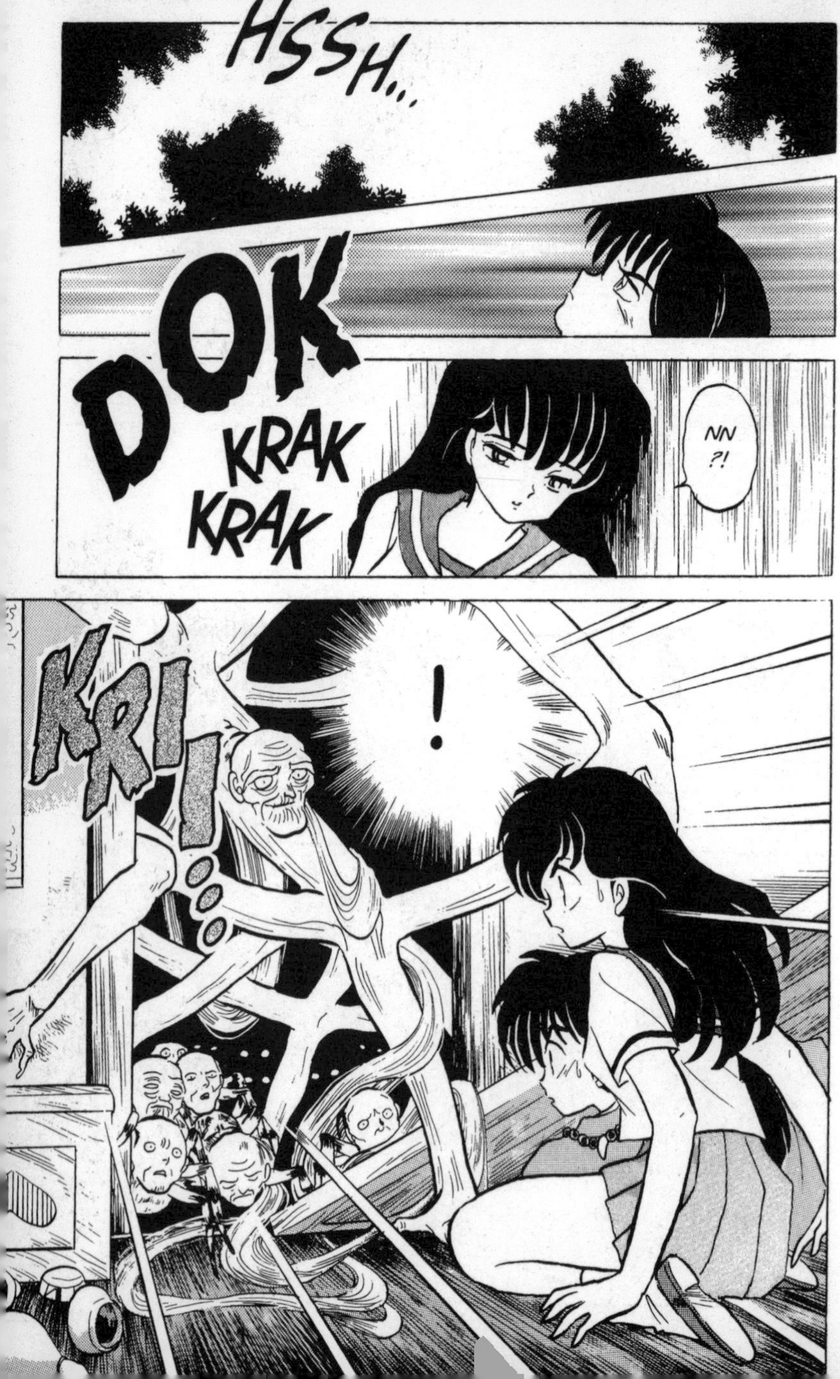
HSSH...
DOK
KRAK
KRAK
NN ?!
KRI
!

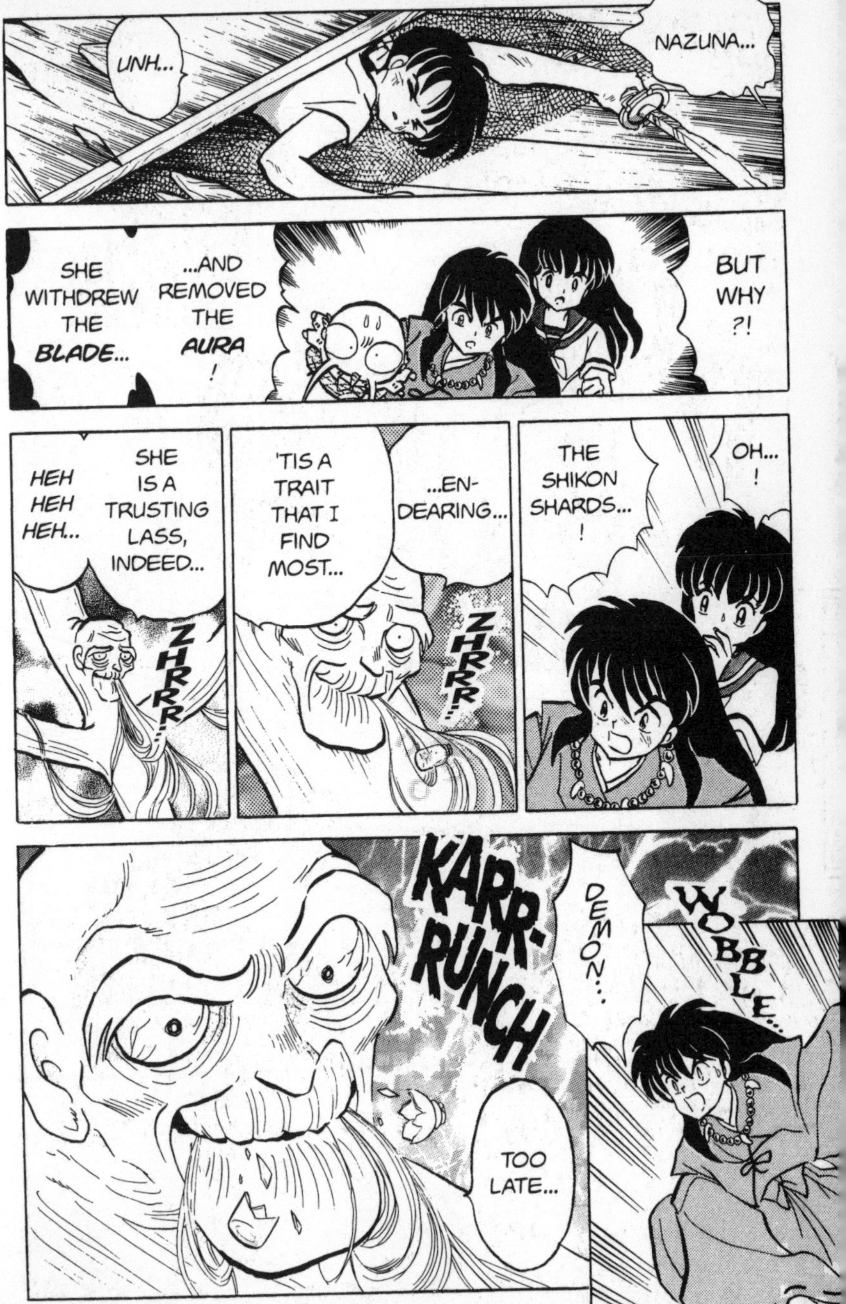

UNH...
NAZUNA...
SHE WITHDREW THE BLADE...
...AND REMOVED THE AURA!
BUT WHY?!
HEH HEH HEH...
SHE IS A TRUSTING LASS, INDEED...
ZHRRR!
'TIS A TRAIT THAT I FIND MOST...
...EN-DEARING...
ZHRRR!
THE SHIKON SHARDS...!
OH...!
KARR-RUNCH
DEMON...
TOO LATE...
WOBBLE...

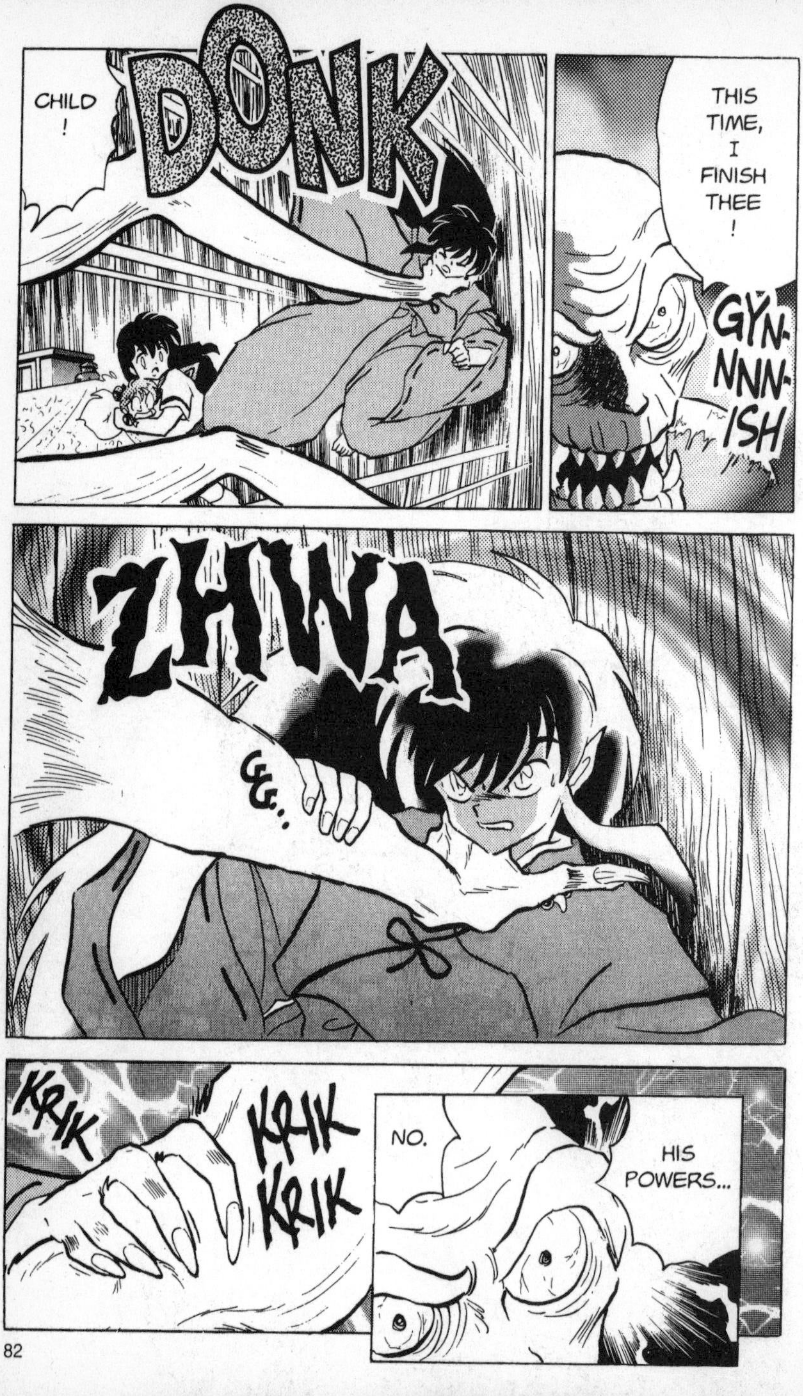
DONK
CHILD!
THIS TIME, I FINISH THEE!
GYN-NNN-ISH
ZHWA
GG...
KRIK
KRIK KRIK KRIK
NO.
HIS POWERS...

SCROLL FIVE

THE DEMON REBORN

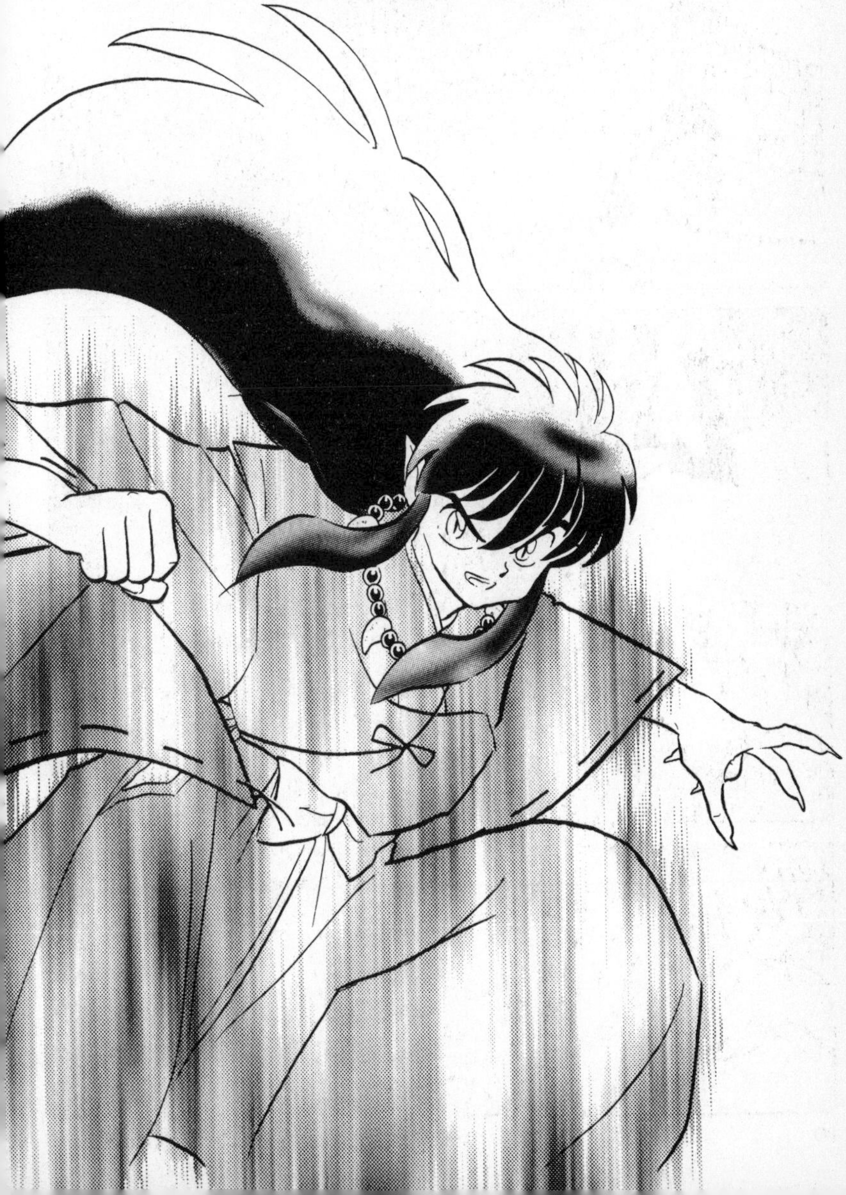

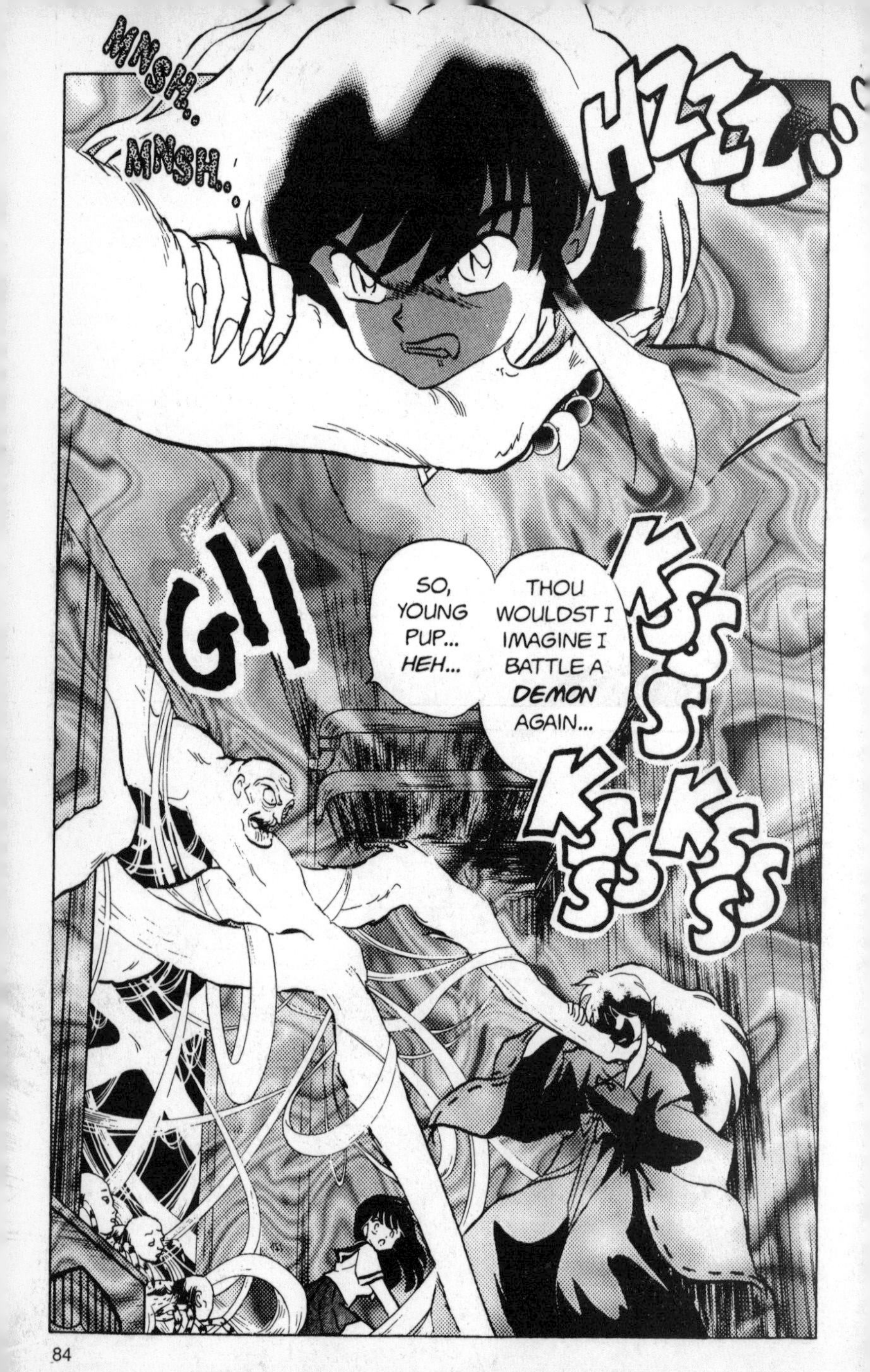
MNSH... MNSH..
HZZZZ...
GII
SO, YOUNG PUP... HEH...
THOU WOULDST I IMAGINE I BATTLE A DEMON AGAIN...
KSSS KSSS KSSS

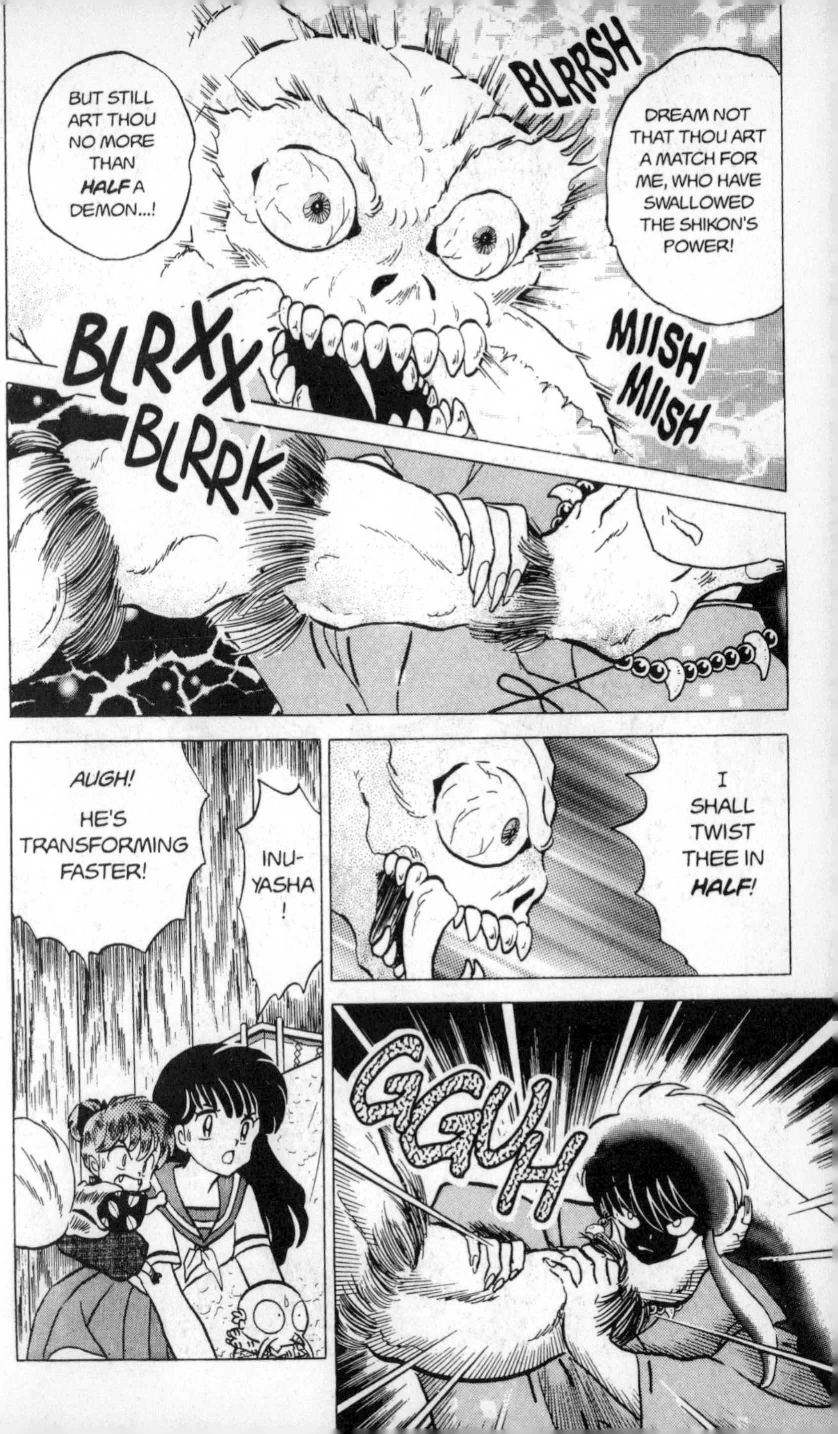
BUT STILL ART THOU NO MORE THAN HALF A DEMON...!
BLRRSH
DREAM NOT THAT THOU ART A MATCH FOR ME, WHO HAVE SWALLOWED THE SHIKON'S POWER!
BLRXX BLRRK
MIISH MIISH
AUGH!
HE'S TRANSFORMING FASTER!
INU-YASHA!
I SHALL TWIST THEE IN HALF!
GGUH

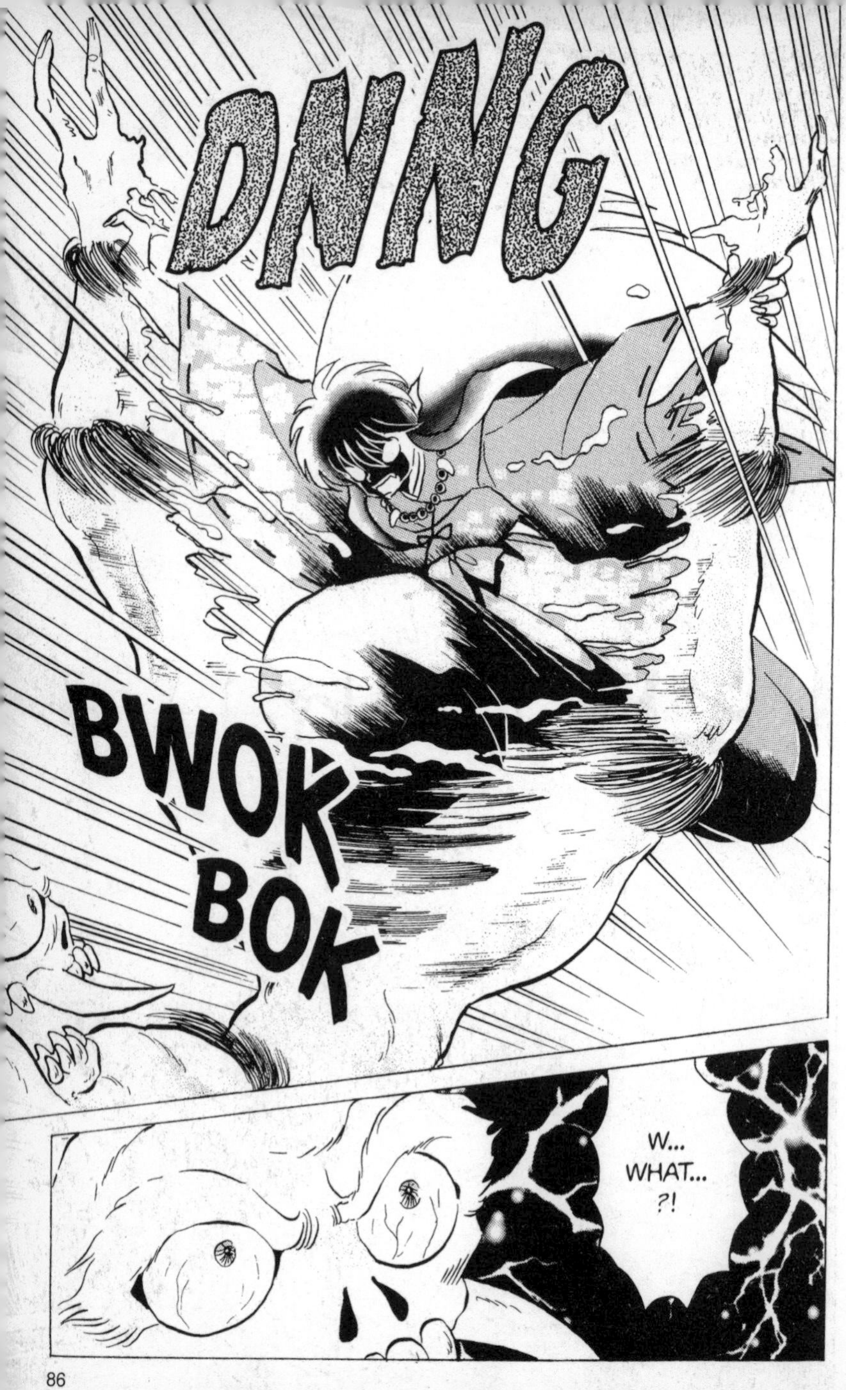
DNNG
BWOK
BOK
W... WHAT... ?!

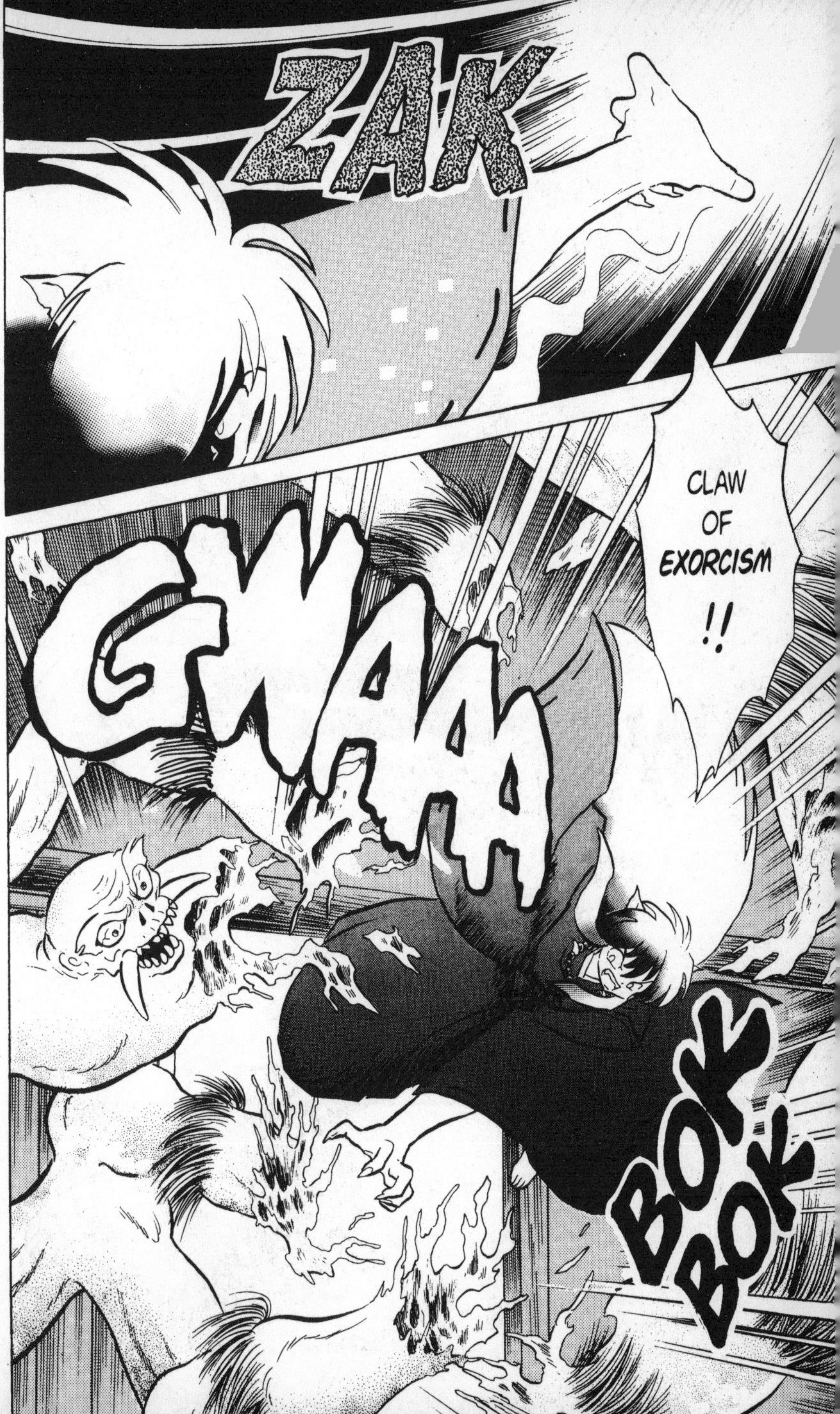
ZAK
CLAW OF EXORCISM !!
GWAA
BOK BOK

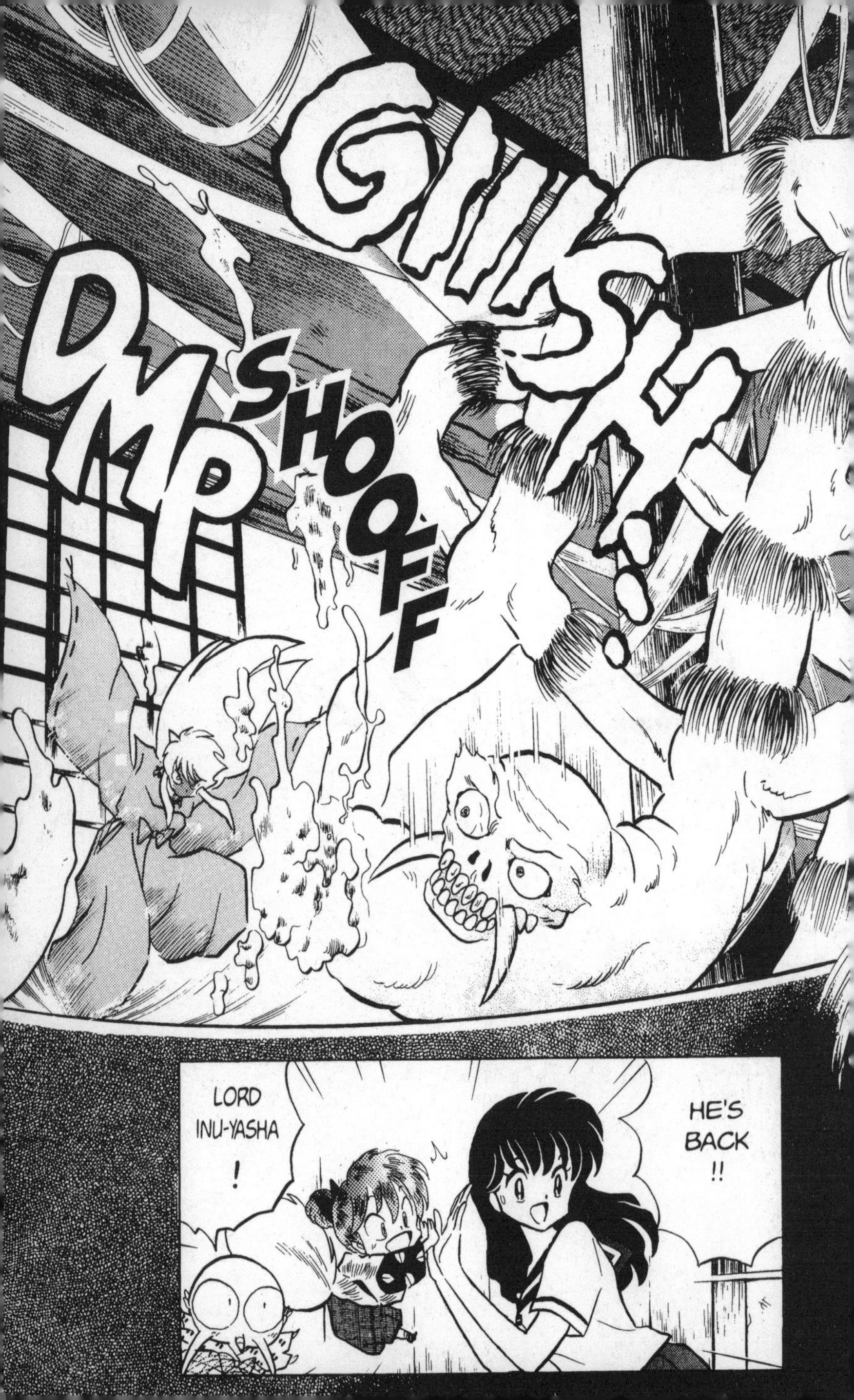
GUSH
DMP
SHOOFF
LORD INU-YASHA !
HE'S BACK !!

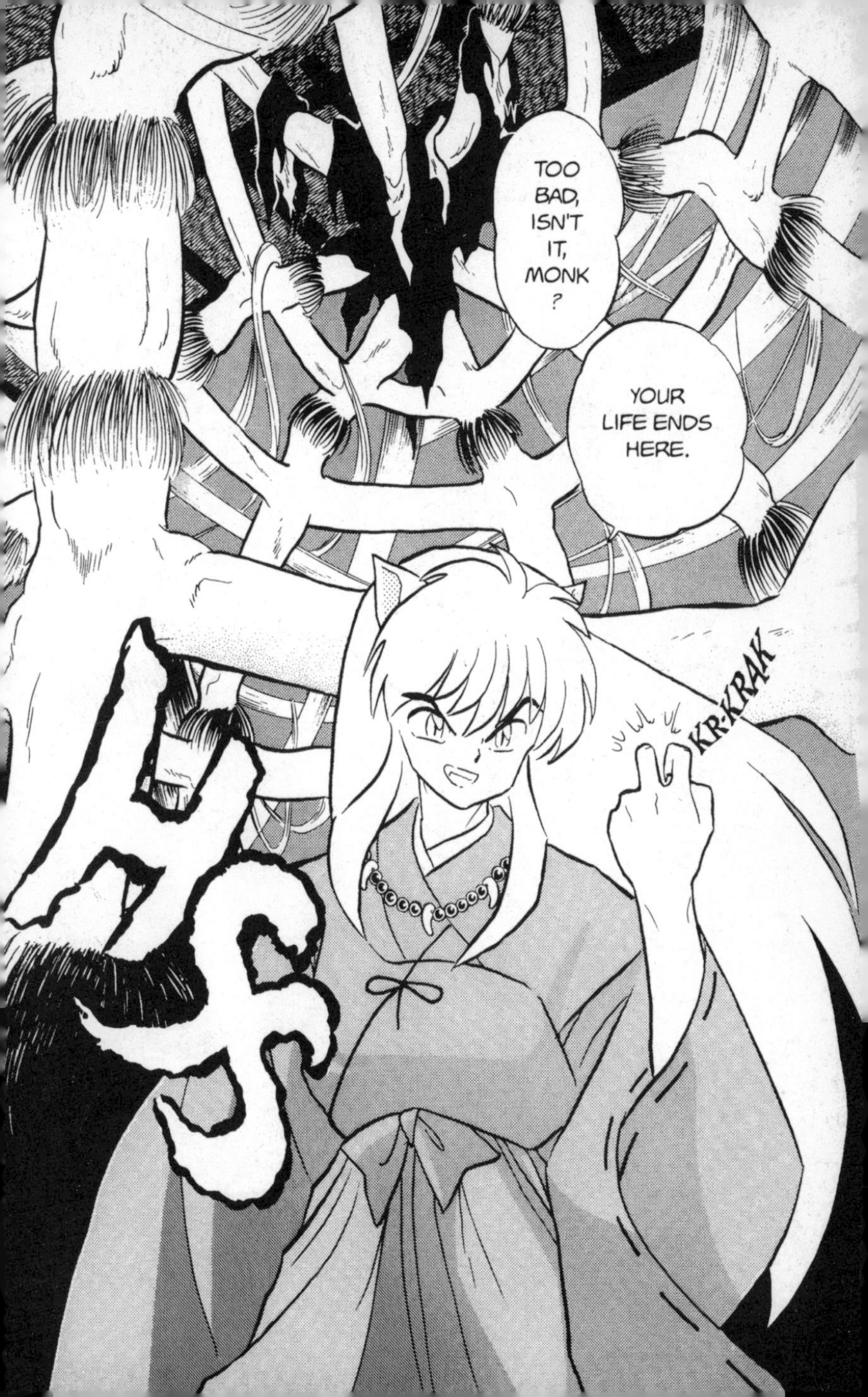
TOO BAD, ISN'T IT, MONK ?
YOUR LIFE ENDS HERE.
KR-KRAK

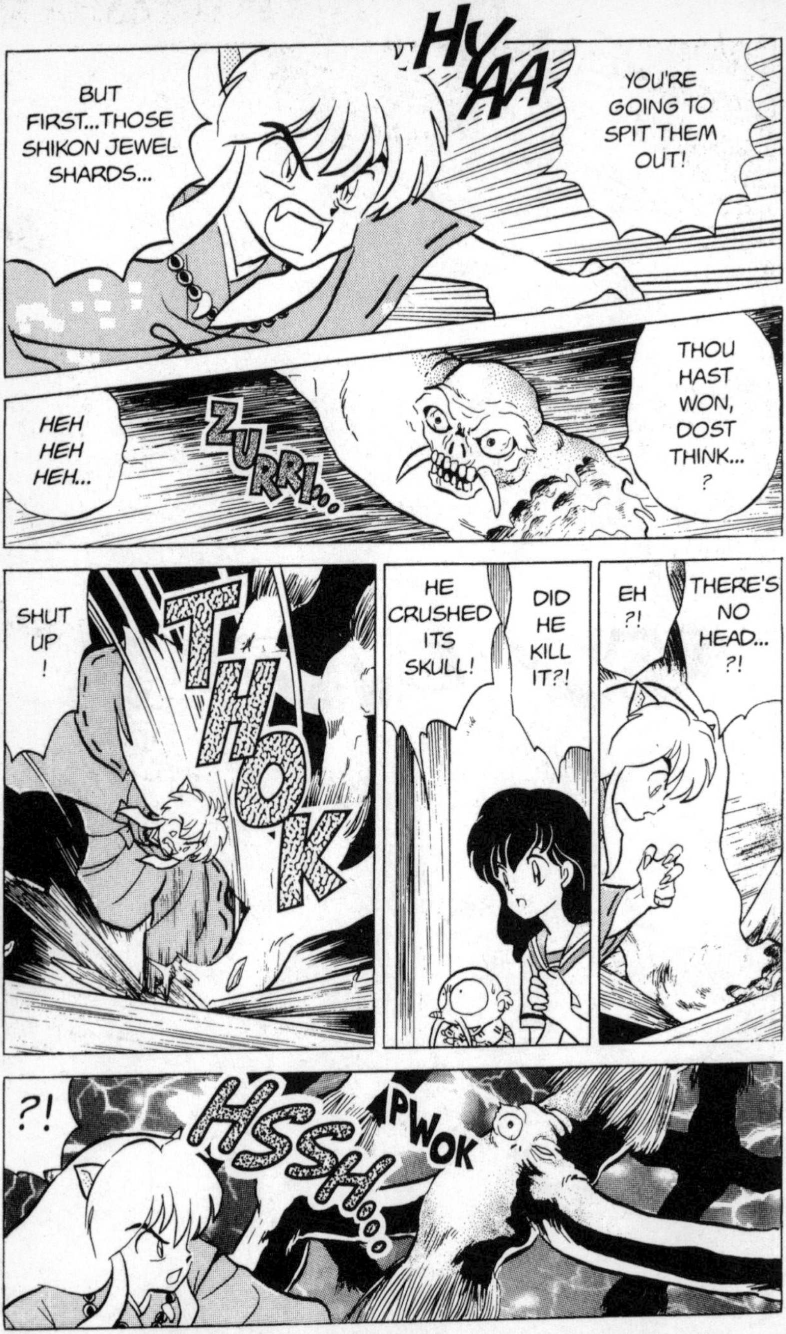
BUT FIRST...THOSE SHIKON JEWEL SHARDS...
HYAA
YOU'RE GOING TO SPIT THEM OUT!
HEH HEH HEH...
ZURRI...
THOU HAST WON, DOST THINK...?
SHUT UP!
THOK
HE CRUSHED ITS SKULL!
DID HE KILL IT?!
EH?!
THERE'S NO HEAD...?!
?!
HSSH...
PWOK

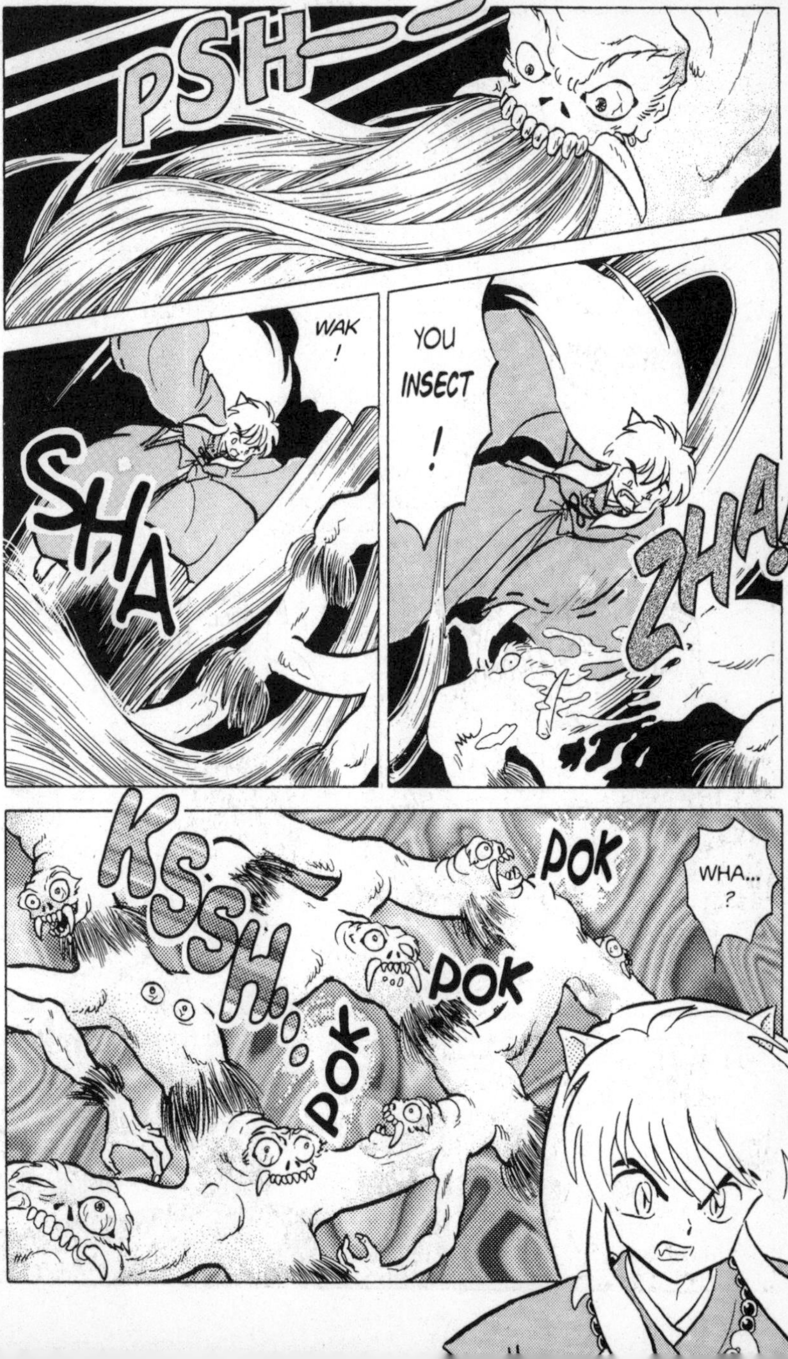
PSH——
WAK!
SHA
YOU INSECT!
ZHA!
KSSH...
POK
WHA...?
POK
POK

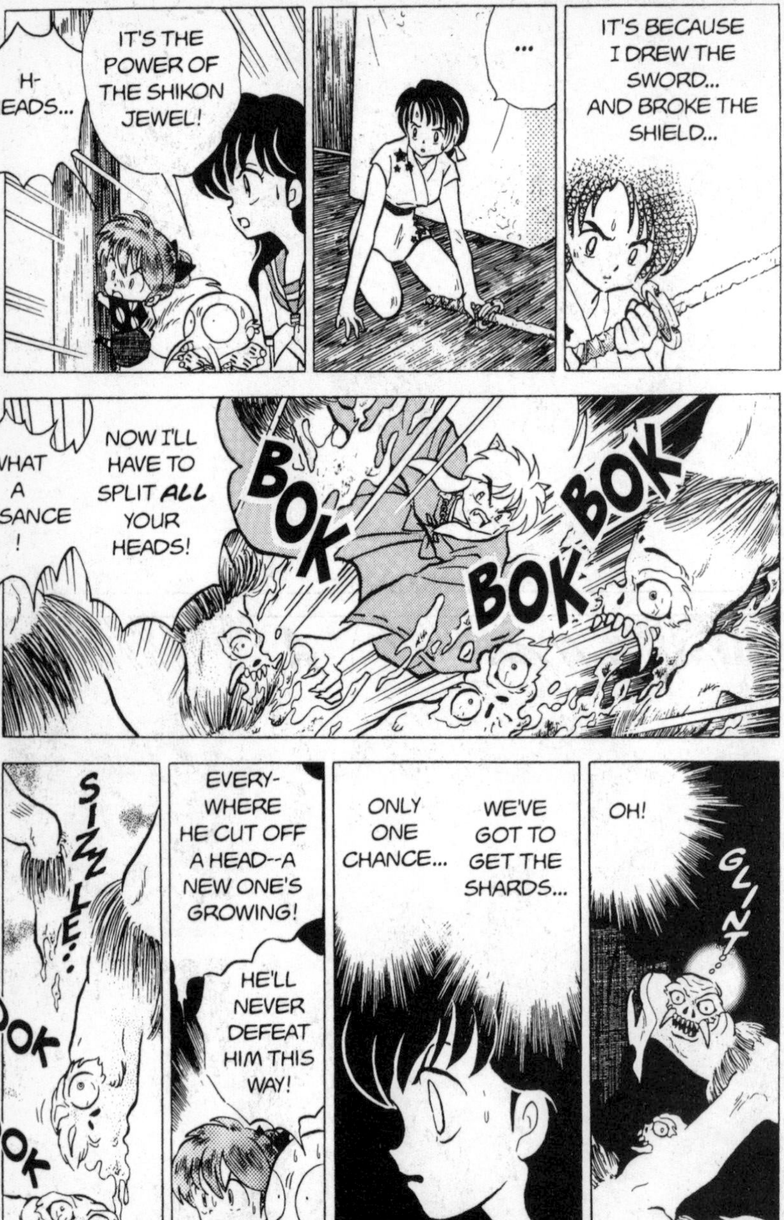
H-HEADS...
IT'S THE POWER OF THE SHIKON JEWEL!
...
IT'S BECAUSE I DREW THE SWORD... AND BROKE THE SHIELD...
WHAT A NUISANCE!
NOW I'LL HAVE TO SPLIT **ALL** YOUR HEADS!
BOK
BOK
BOK
SIZZLE...
POK
POK
EVERY-WHERE HE CUT OFF A HEAD--A NEW ONE'S GROWING!
HE'LL NEVER DEFEAT HIM THIS WAY!
ONLY ONE CHANCE...
WE'VE GOT TO GET THE SHARDS...
OH!
GLINT

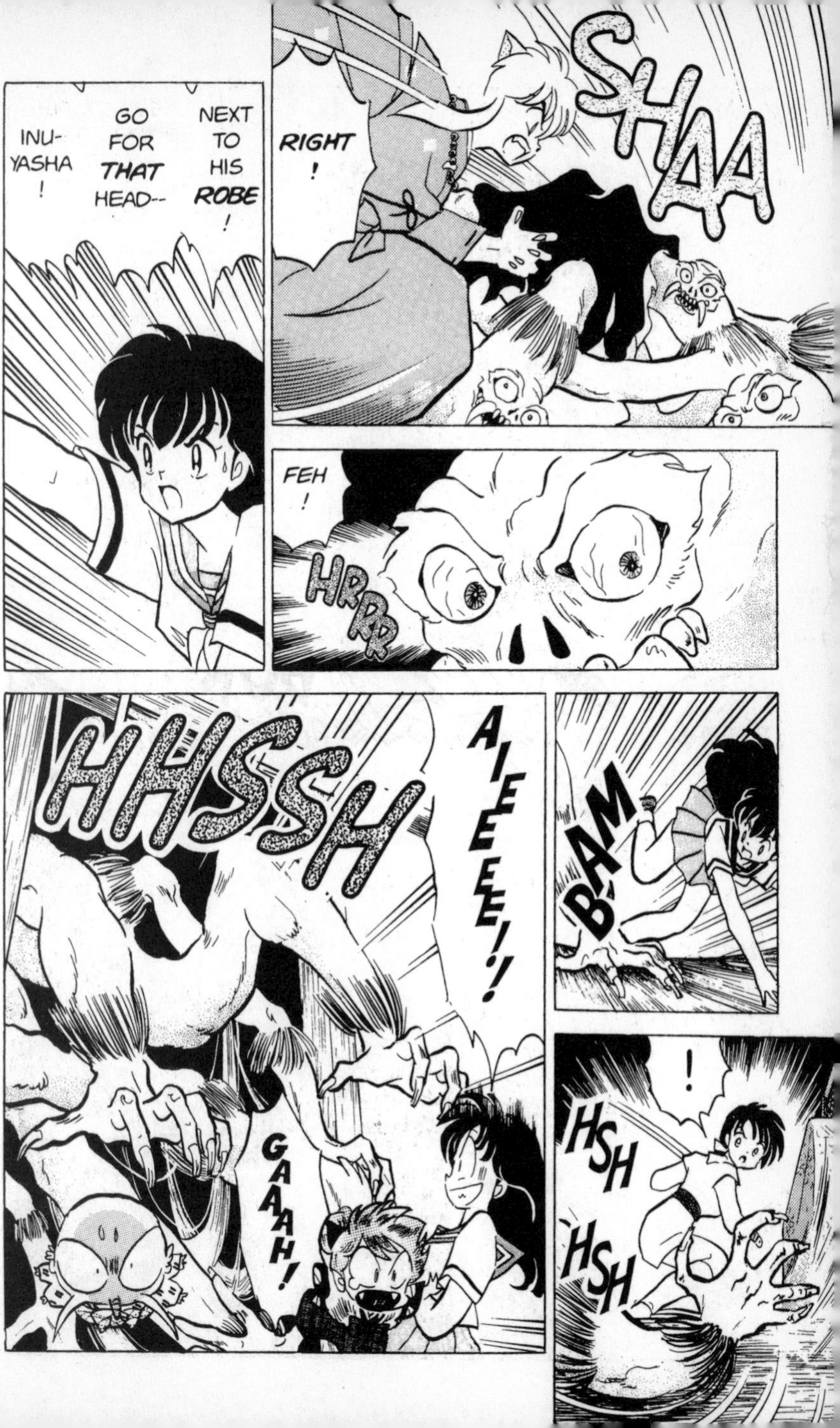

INU-YASHA!
GO FOR THAT HEAD--
NEXT TO HIS ROBE!
RIGHT!
SHAA
FEH!
HRRR
HHSSH
AIEEEE!!
GAAAH!
BAM
!
HSH
HSH

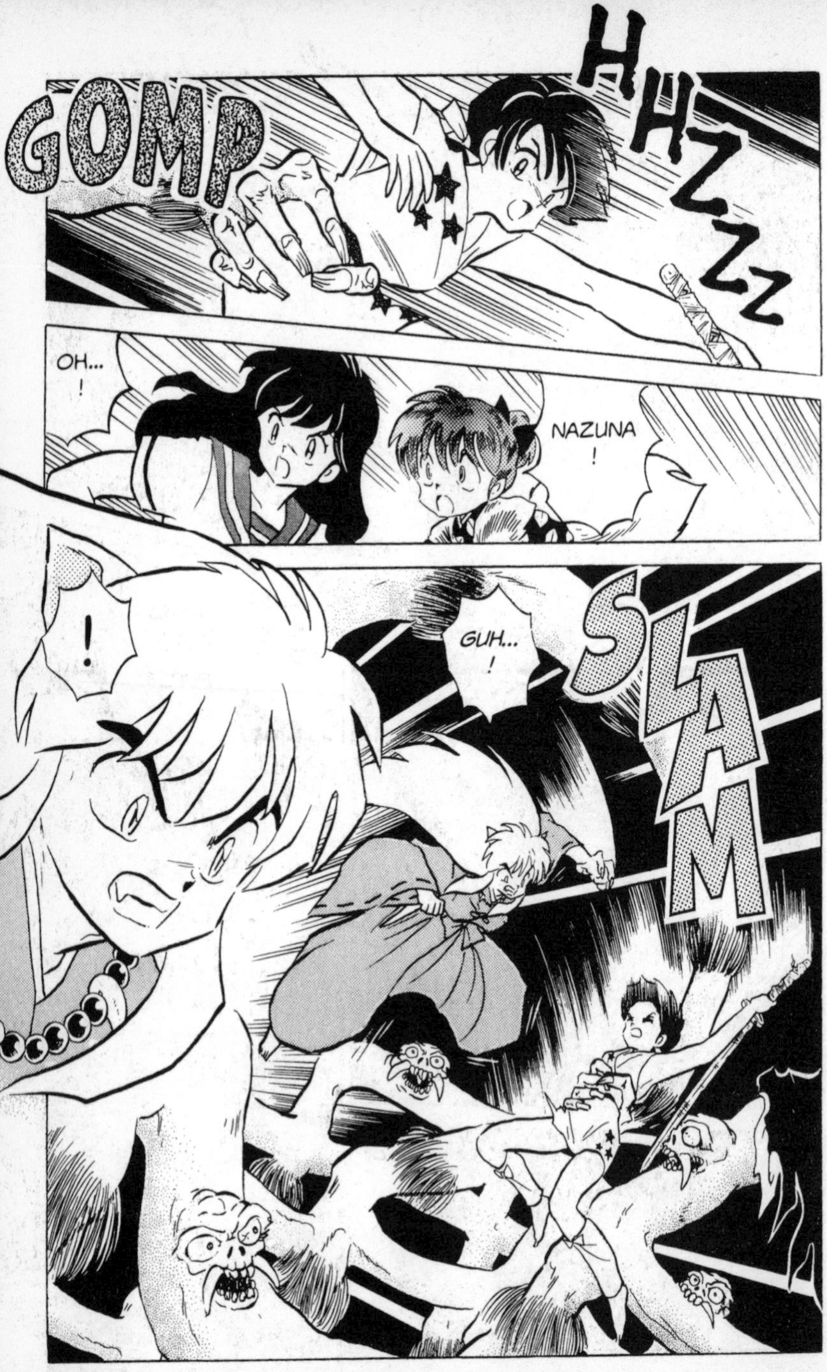
GOMP
HHZZZ
OH...!
NAZUNA!
!
GUH...!
SLAM

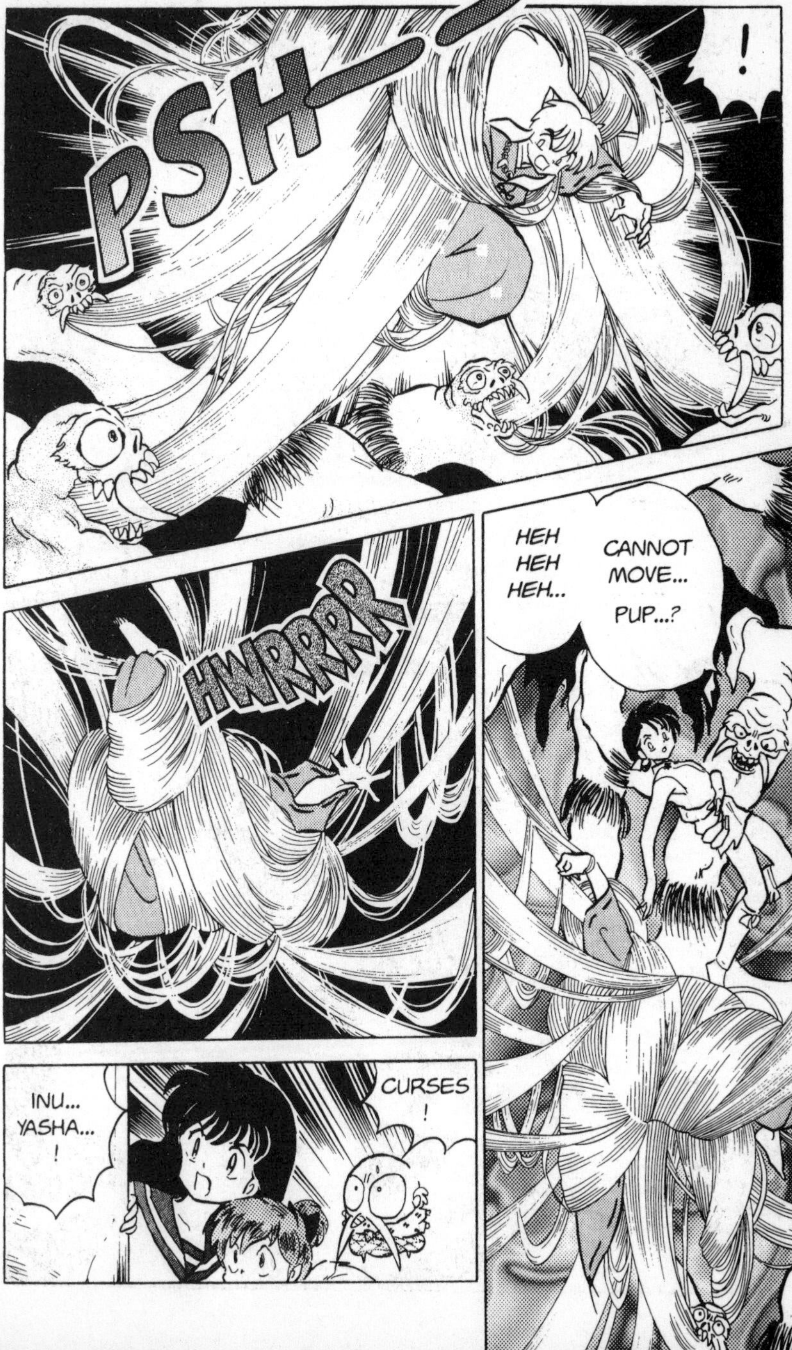
PSH—!
!
HWRRRR
INU... YASHA... !
CURSES !
HEH HEH HEH...
CANNOT MOVE... PUP...?

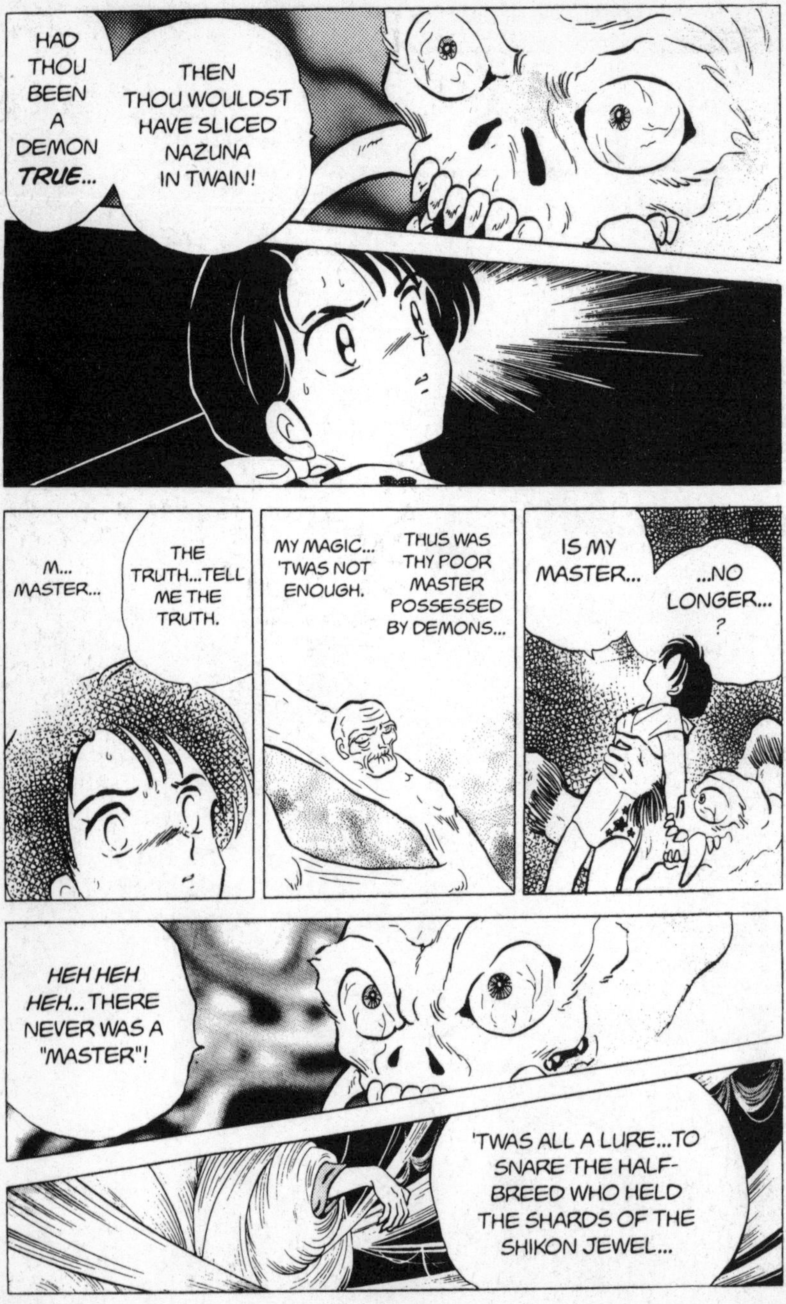
HAD THOU BEEN A DEMON *TRUE*...
THEN THOU WOULDST HAVE SLICED NAZUNA IN TWAIN!
M... MASTER...
THE TRUTH...TELL ME THE TRUTH.
MY MAGIC... 'TWAS NOT ENOUGH.
THUS WAS THY POOR MASTER POSSESSED BY DEMONS...
IS MY MASTER...
...NO LONGER...?
HEH HEH HEH... THERE NEVER WAS A "MASTER"!
'TWAS ALL A LURE...TO SNARE THE HALF-BREED WHO HELD THE SHARDS OF THE SHIKON JEWEL...

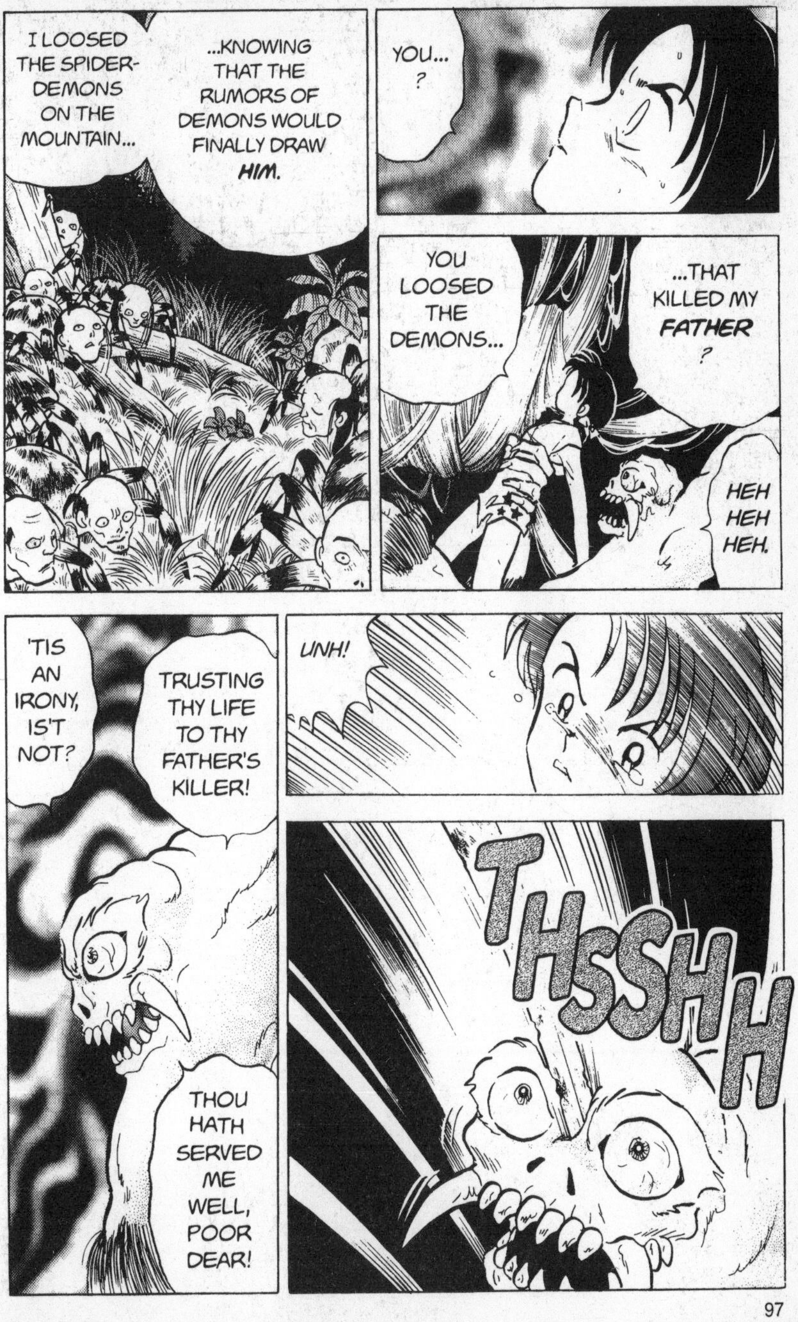
I LOOSED THE SPIDER-DEMONS ON THE MOUNTAIN...
...KNOWING THAT THE RUMORS OF DEMONS WOULD FINALLY DRAW HIM.
YOU... ?
YOU LOOSED THE DEMONS...
...THAT KILLED MY FATHER ?
HEH HEH HEH.
'TIS AN IRONY, IS'T NOT?
TRUSTING THY LIFE TO THY FATHER'S KILLER!
THOU HATH SERVED ME WELL, POOR DEAR!
UNH!
THSSHH

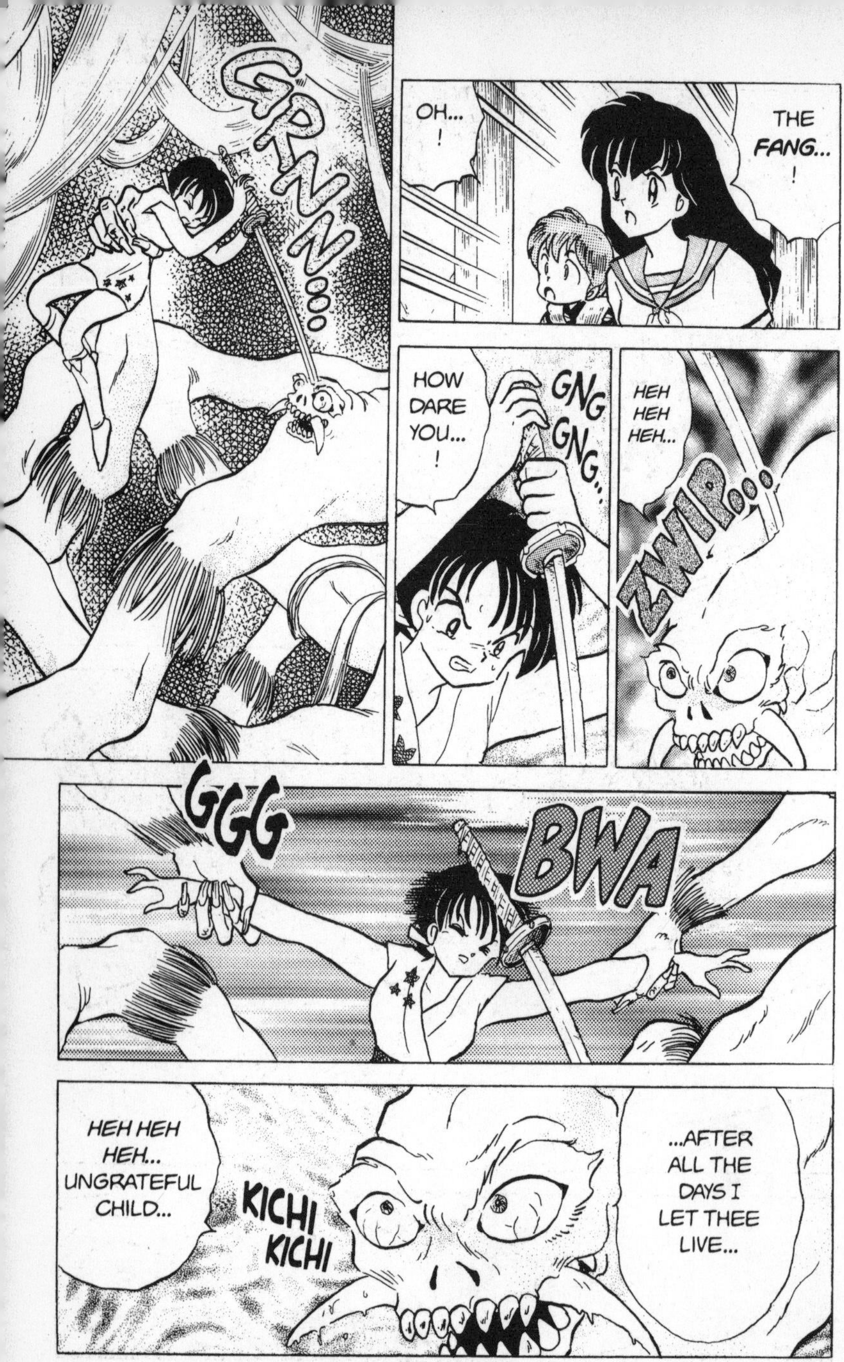
GRNN...
OH... !
THE FANG... !
HOW DARE YOU... !
GNG GNG...
HEH HEH HEH...
ZWIP...
GGG
BWA
HEH HEH HEH... UNGRATEFUL CHILD...
KICHI KICHI
...AFTER ALL THE DAYS I LET THEE LIVE...

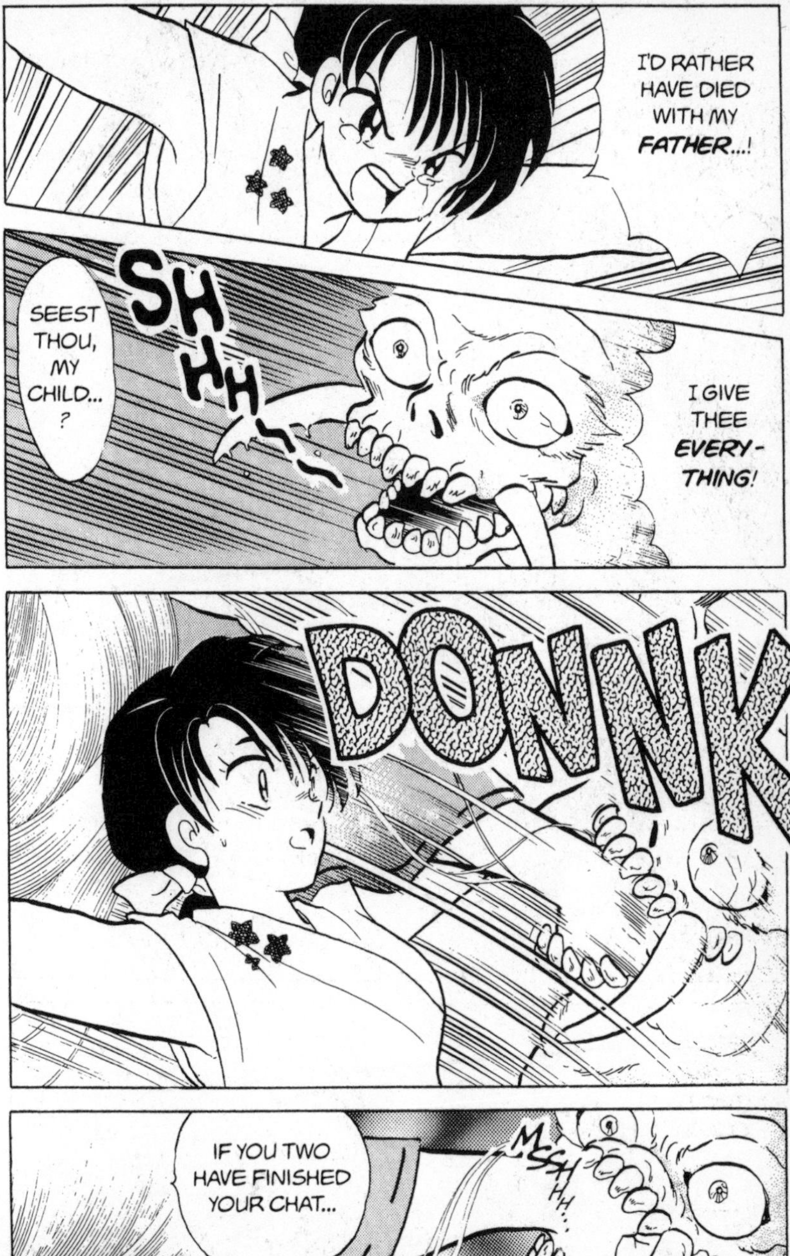
I'D RATHER HAVE DIED WITH MY FATHER...!
SEEST THOU, MY CHILD...?
SHHH
I GIVE THEE EVERYTHING!
DONNK
IF YOU TWO HAVE FINISHED YOUR CHAT...
MSSHHH...

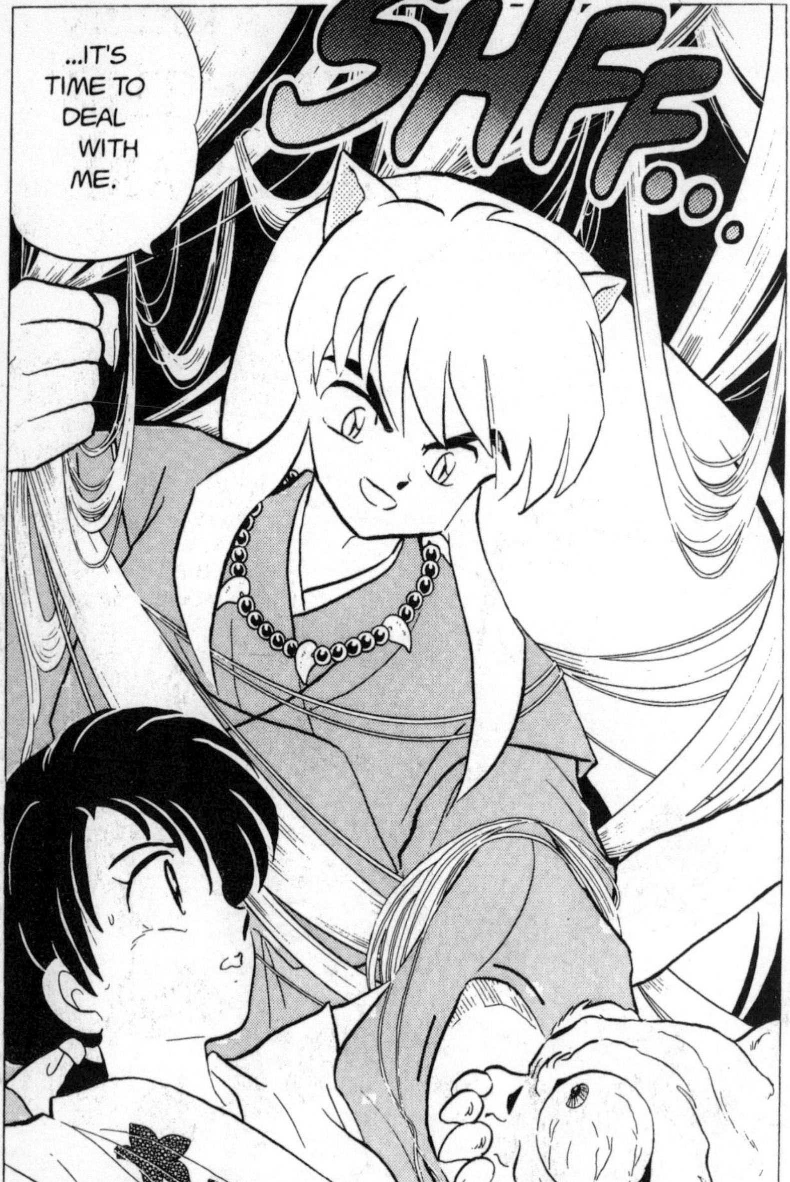
...IT'S TIME TO DEAL WITH ME.
SHFF...

SCROLL SIX

WHERE THE SHARDS ARE

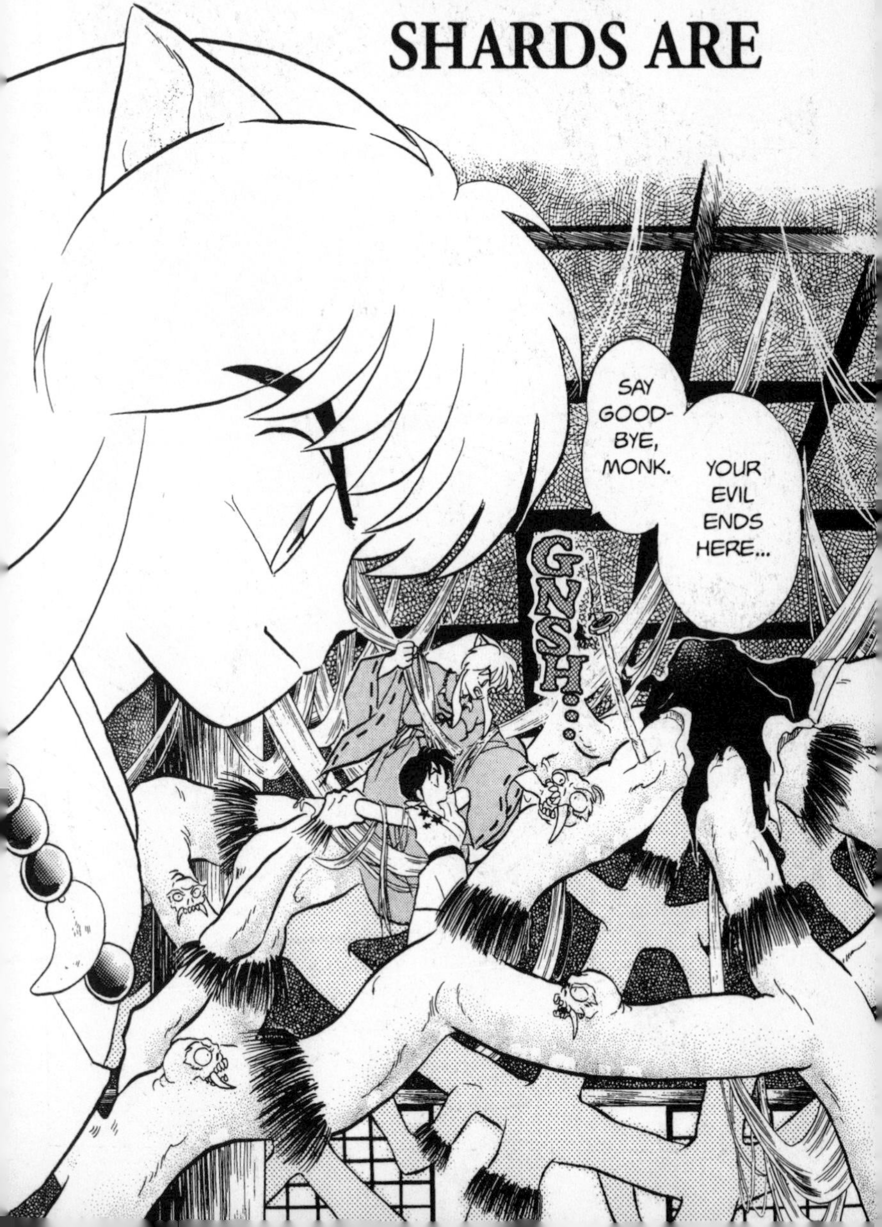

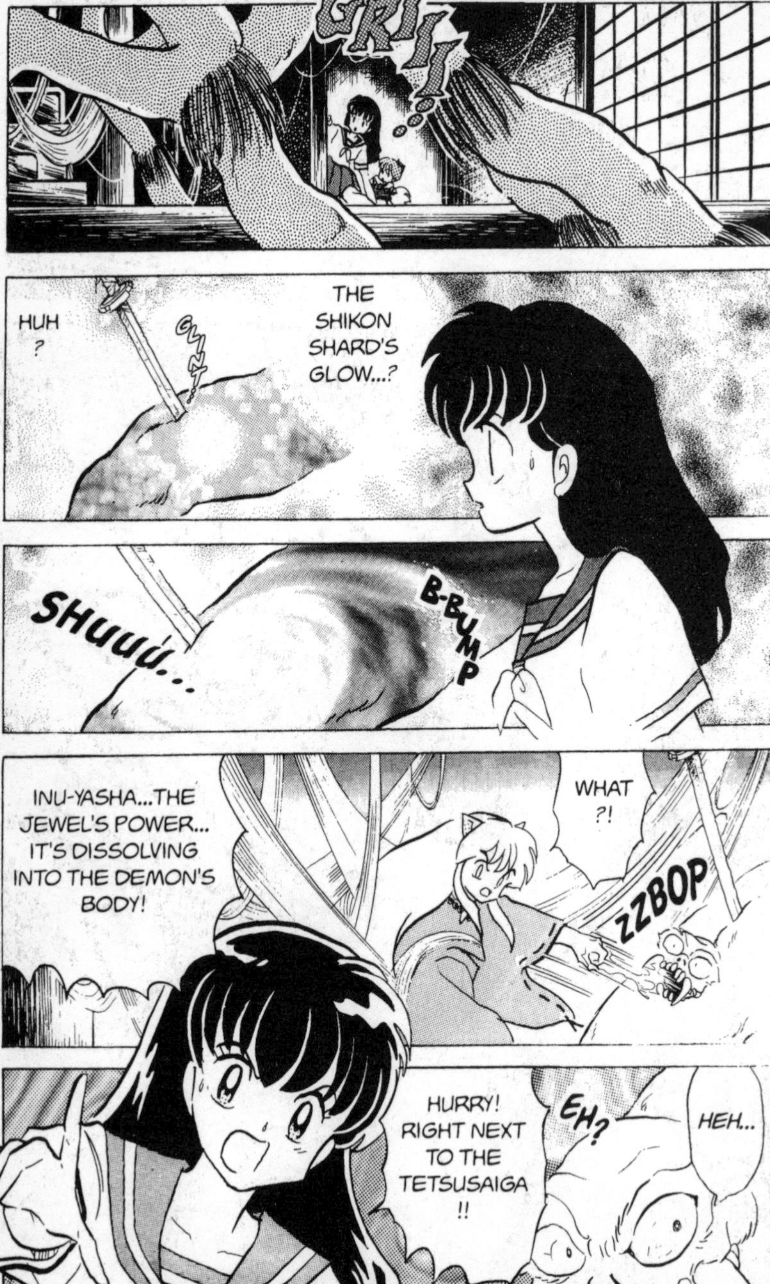
GRIII...
HUH ?
THE SHIKON SHARD'S GLOW...?
SHUUU...
B-BUMP
INU-YASHA...THE JEWEL'S POWER... IT'S DISSOLVING INTO THE DEMON'S BODY!
WHAT ?!
ZZBOP
HURRY! RIGHT NEXT TO THE TETSUSAIGA !!
EH?
HEH...

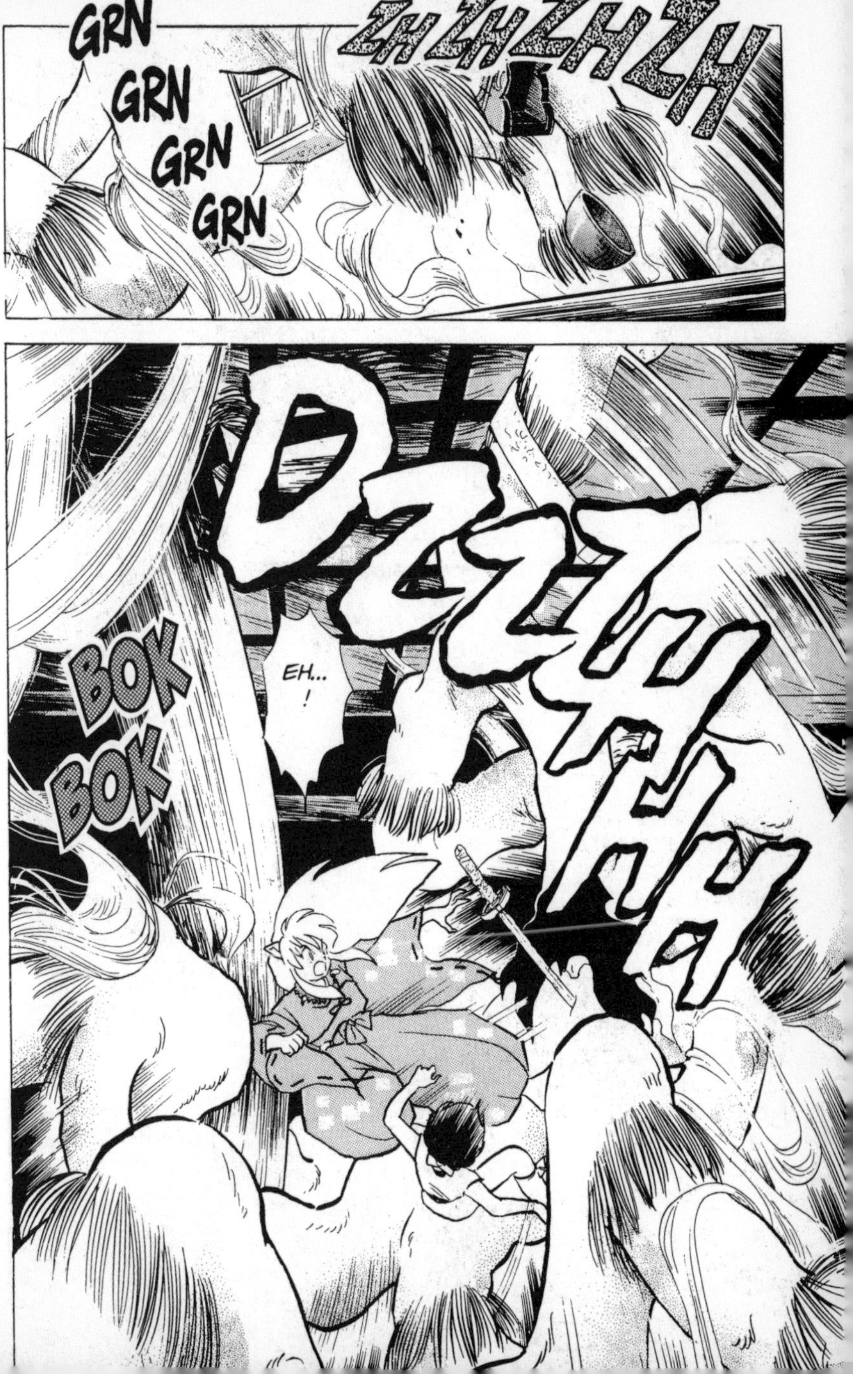
GRN
GRN
GRN
GRN
ZHZHZHZH
DZZHHH
BOK
BOK
EH...
!

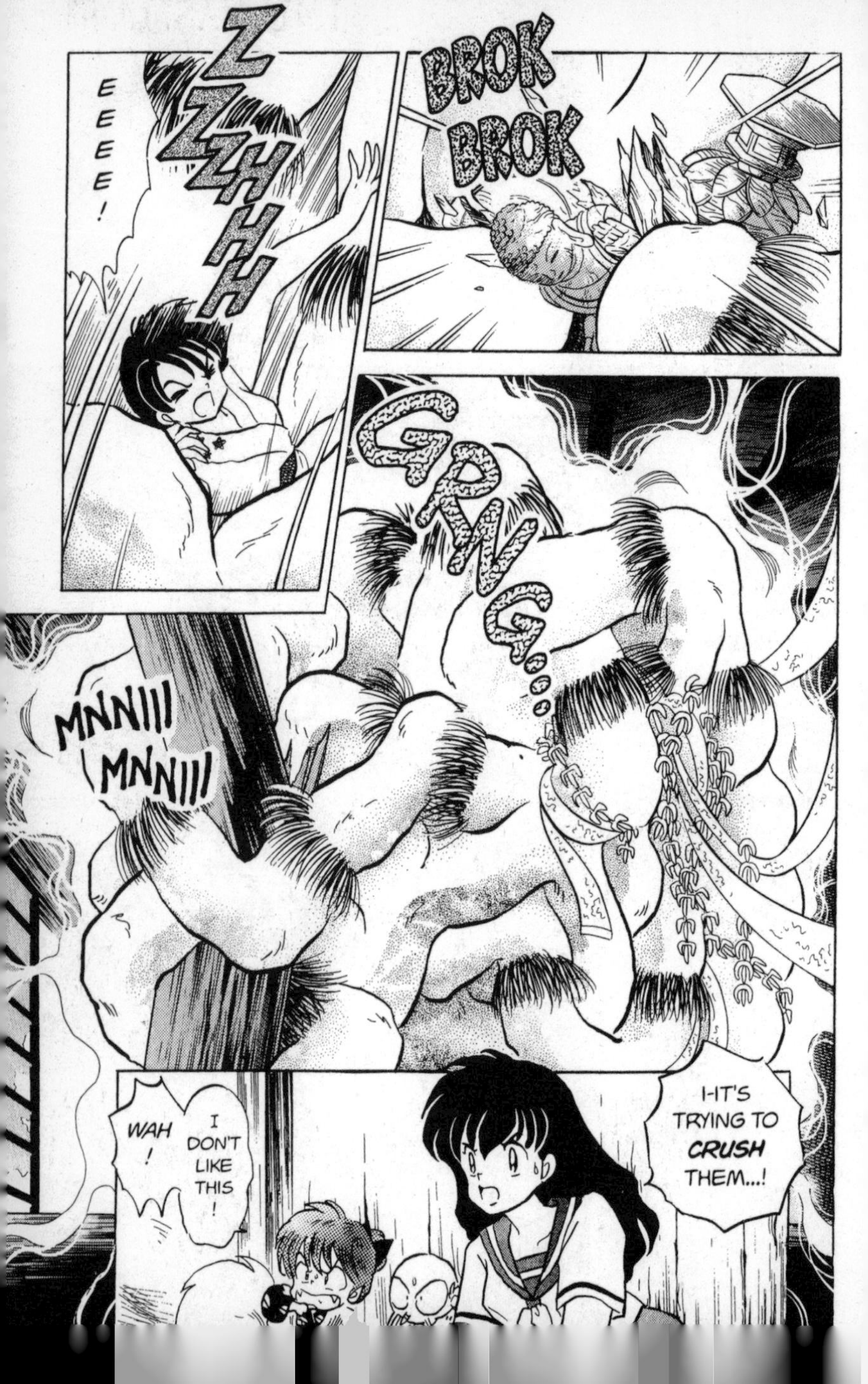
EEEEE!
ZZZHHHH
BROK BROK
GRNG...
MNIII MNIII
WAH!
I DON'T LIKE THIS!
I-IT'S TRYING TO CRUSH THEM...!

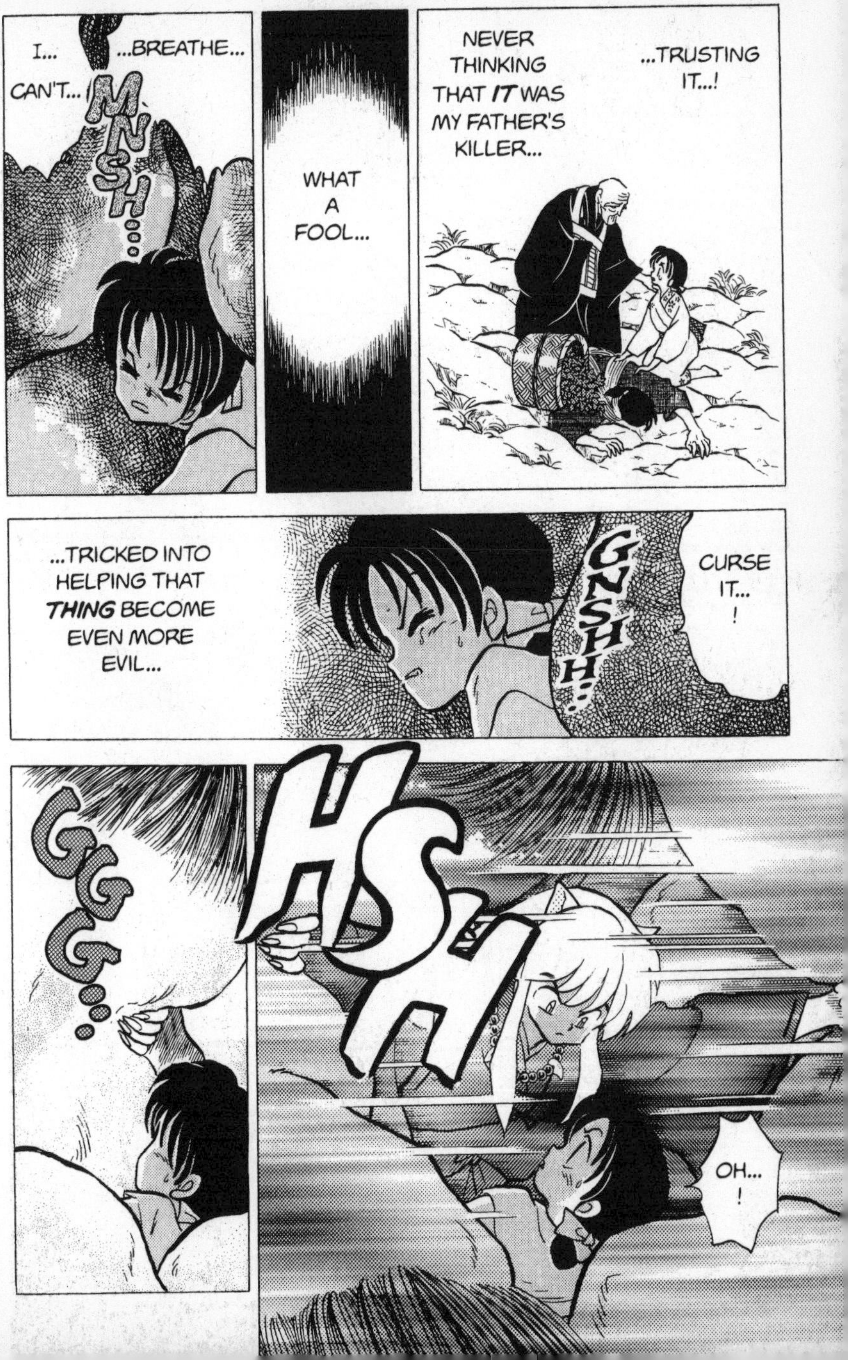
I...
CAN'T...
...BREATHE...
MNSH...
WHAT A FOOL...
NEVER THINKING THAT *IT* WAS MY FATHER'S KILLER...
...TRUSTING IT...!
...TRICKED INTO HELPING THAT **THING** BECOME EVEN MORE EVIL...
GNSHH...
CURSE IT...!
GGG...
HSH
OH...!

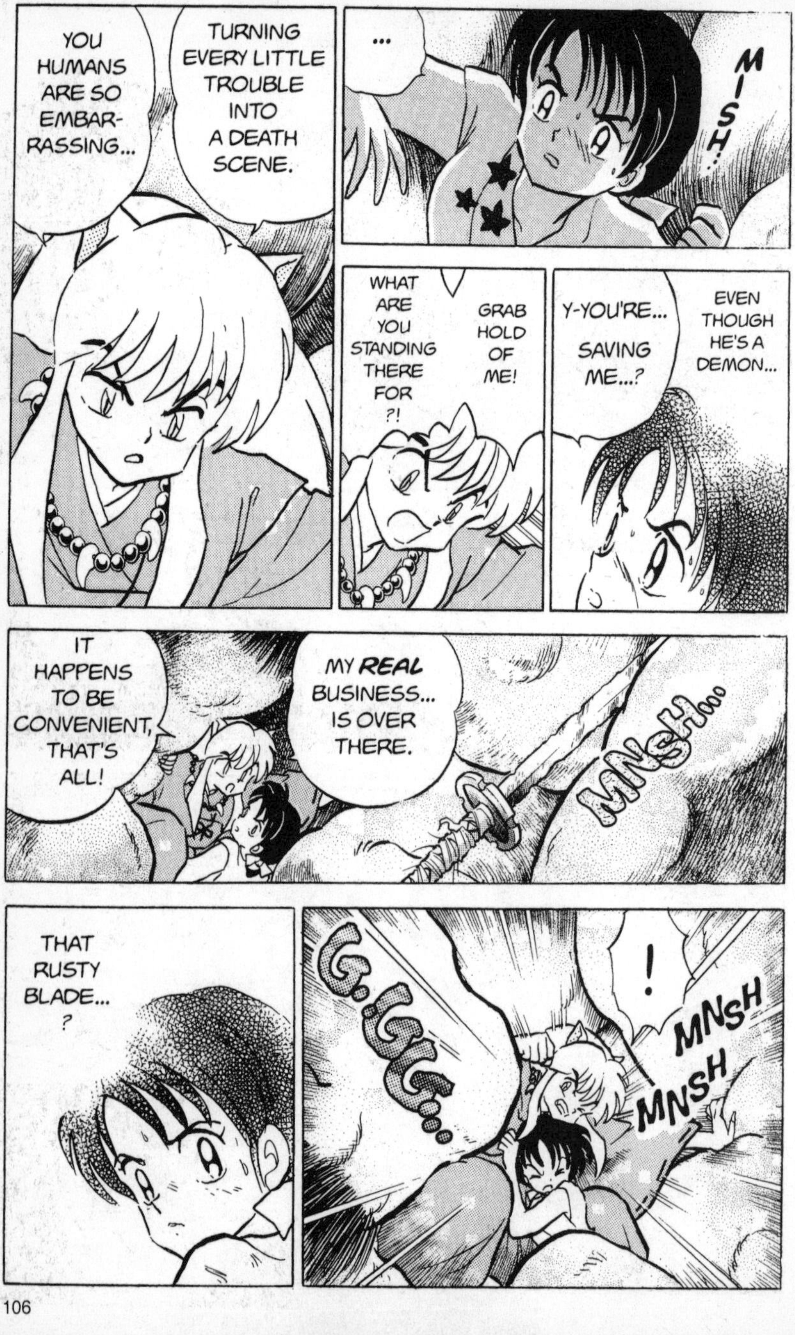

YOU HUMANS ARE SO EMBARRASSING...
TURNING EVERY LITTLE TROUBLE INTO A DEATH SCENE.
...
MISH...
WHAT ARE YOU STANDING THERE FOR ?!
GRAB HOLD OF ME!
Y-YOU'RE... SAVING ME...?
EVEN THOUGH HE'S A DEMON...
IT HAPPENS TO BE CONVENIENT, THAT'S ALL!
MY **REAL** BUSINESS... IS OVER THERE.
MNSHooo
THAT RUSTY BLADE...?
G..G..G...
!
MNSH
MNSH

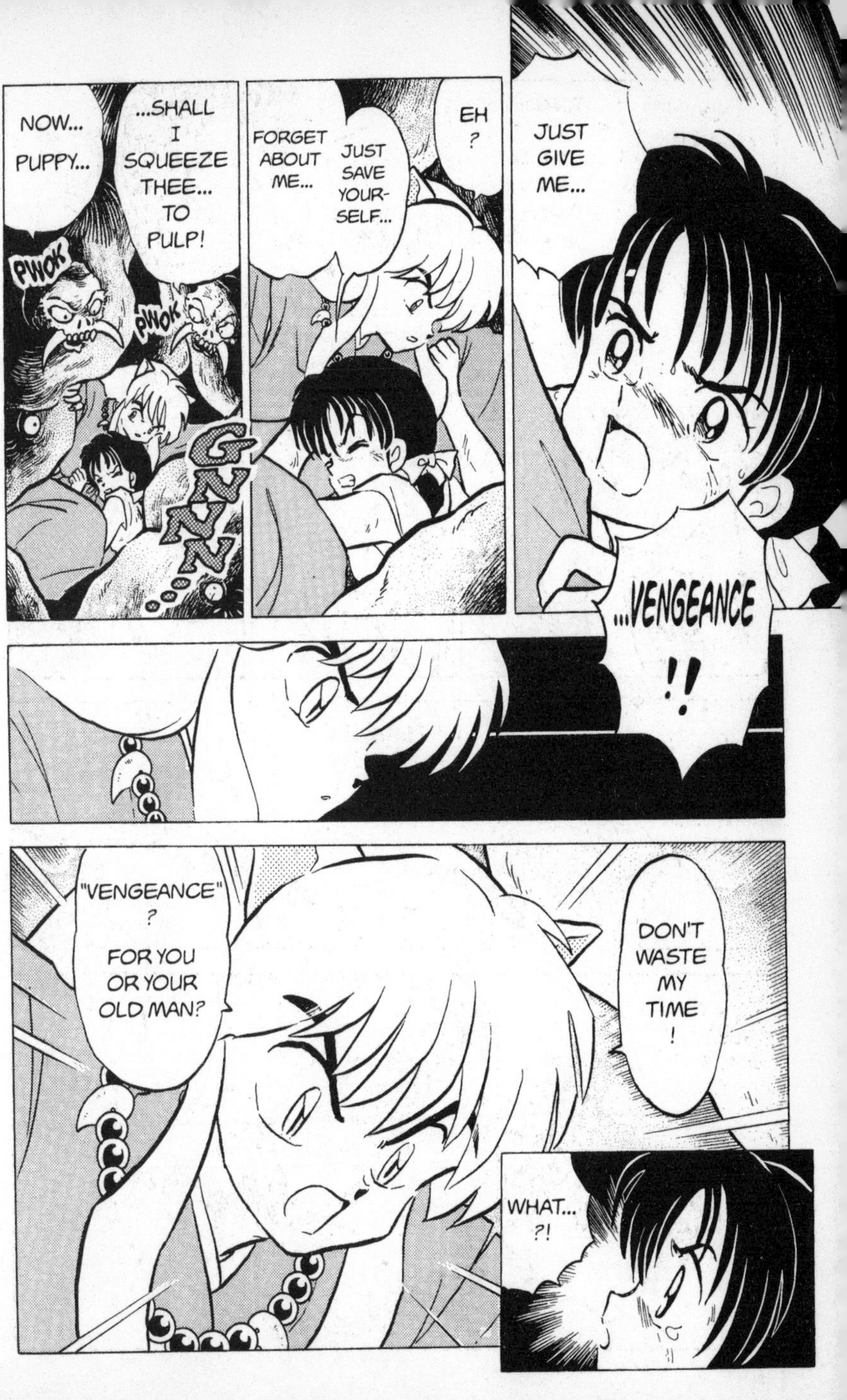
NOW... PUPPY...
...SHALL I SQUEEZE THEE... TO PULP!
PWOK
PWOK
GNNN...
FORGET ABOUT ME...
JUST SAVE YOURSELF...
EH?
JUST GIVE ME...
...VENGEANCE!!
"VENGEANCE"? FOR YOU OR YOUR OLD MAN?
DON'T WASTE MY TIME!
WHAT...?!

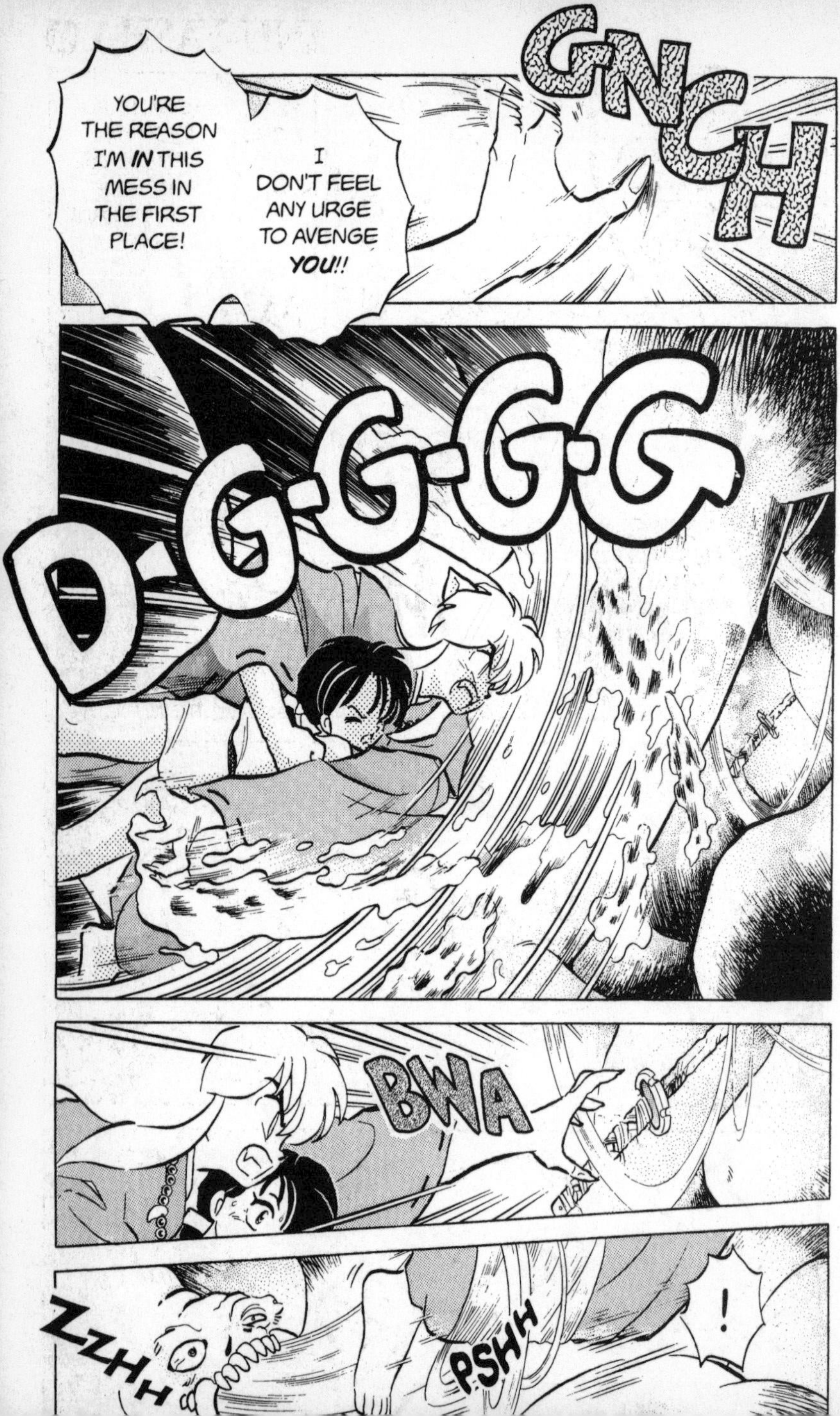

YOU'RE THE REASON I'M *IN* THIS MESS IN THE FIRST PLACE!
I DON'T FEEL ANY URGE TO AVENGE *YOU*!!
GNCH
D-G-G-G-G
BWA
ZZHHH
PSHH
!

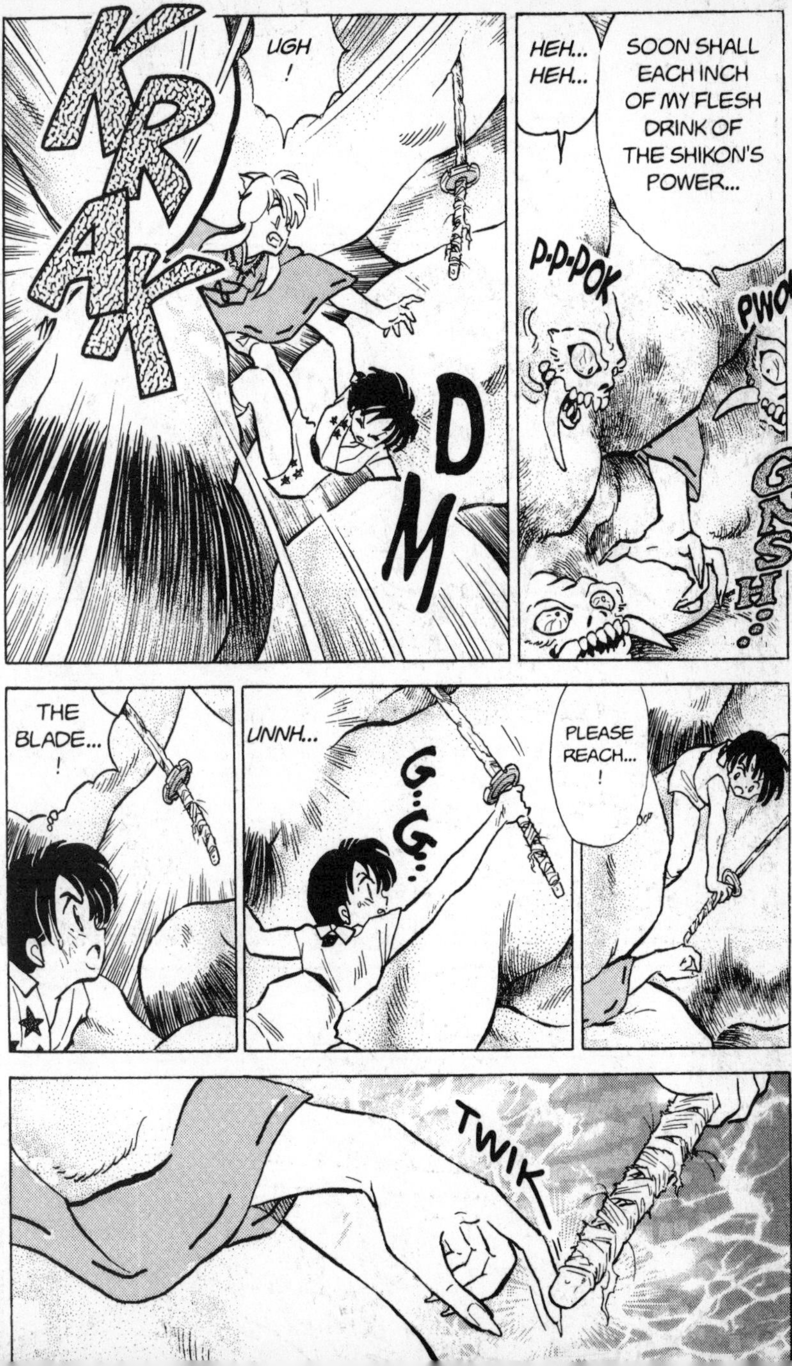
KRAK
UGH !
DM
HEH... HEH...
SOON SHALL EACH INCH OF MY FLESH DRINK OF THE SHIKON'S POWER...
P-P-POK
PWOK
GNSH
THE BLADE... !
UNNH...
G..G..
PLEASE REACH... !
TWIK

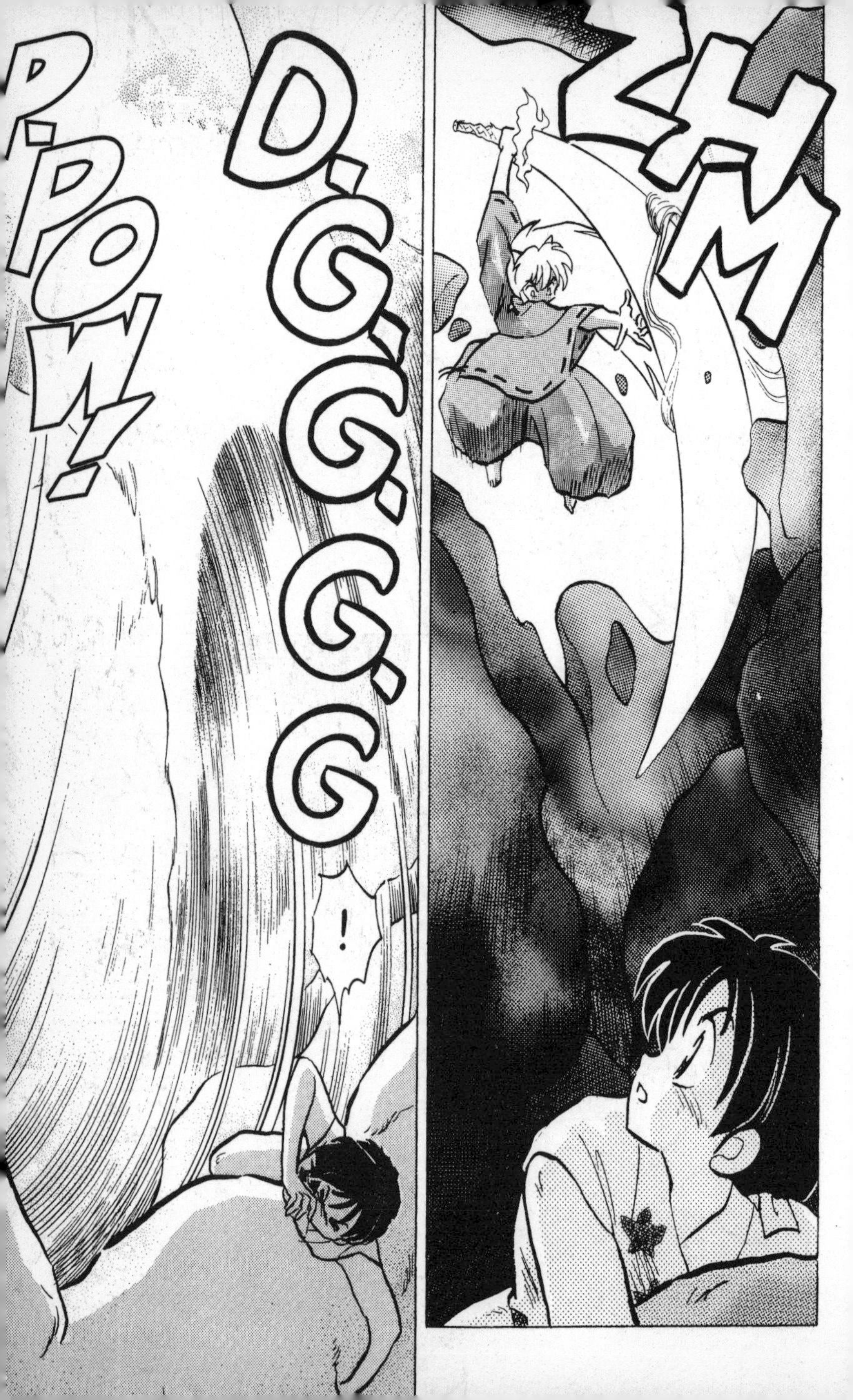
P-POW!
D-G-G-G-G
!
ZHM

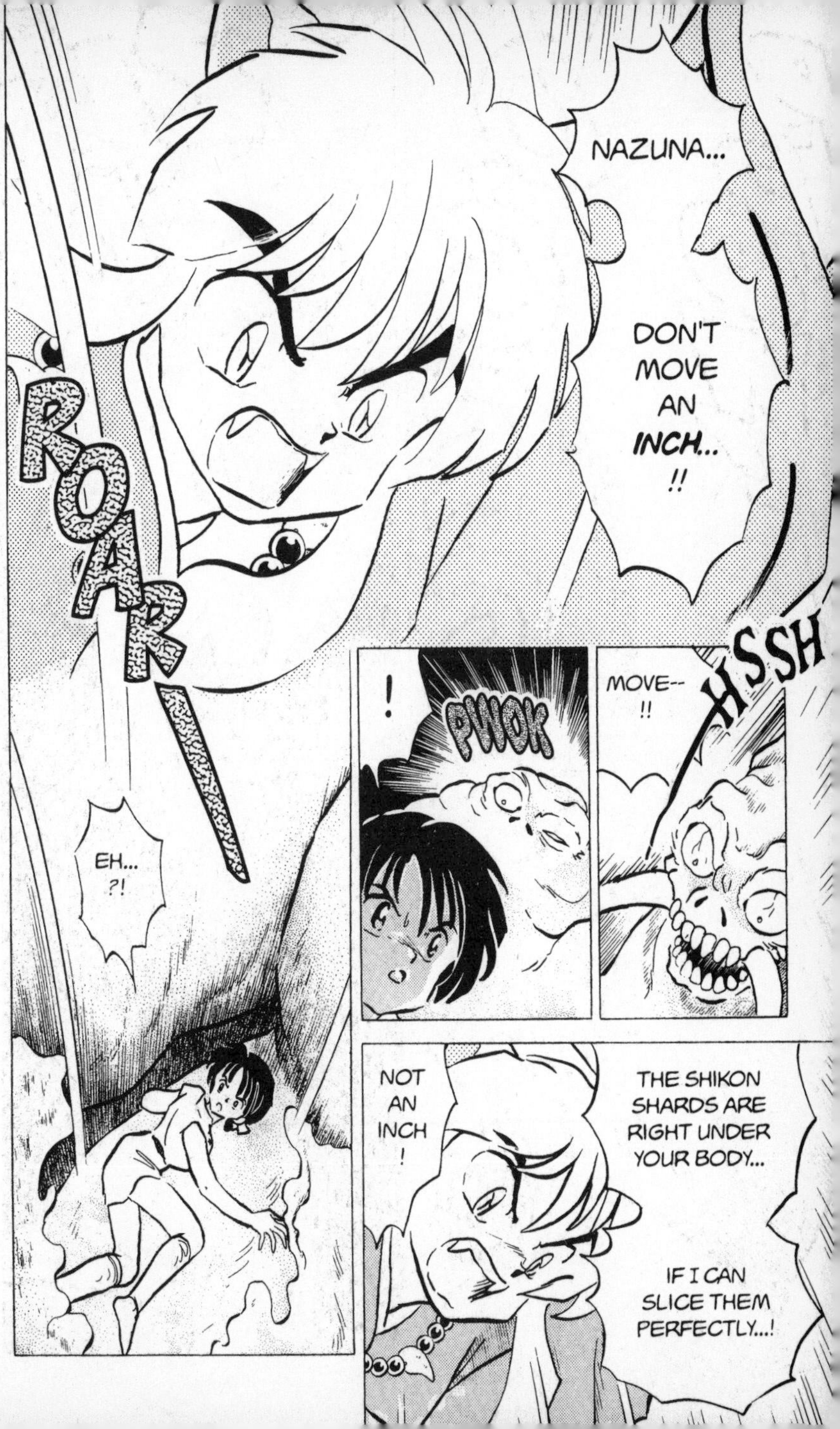
NAZUNA...
DON'T MOVE AN **INCH...** !!
ROAR!
EH... ?!
!
PWOK
MOVE-- !!
HSSH
NOT AN INCH !
THE SHIKON SHARDS ARE RIGHT UNDER YOUR BODY...
IF I CAN SLICE THEM PERFECTLY...!

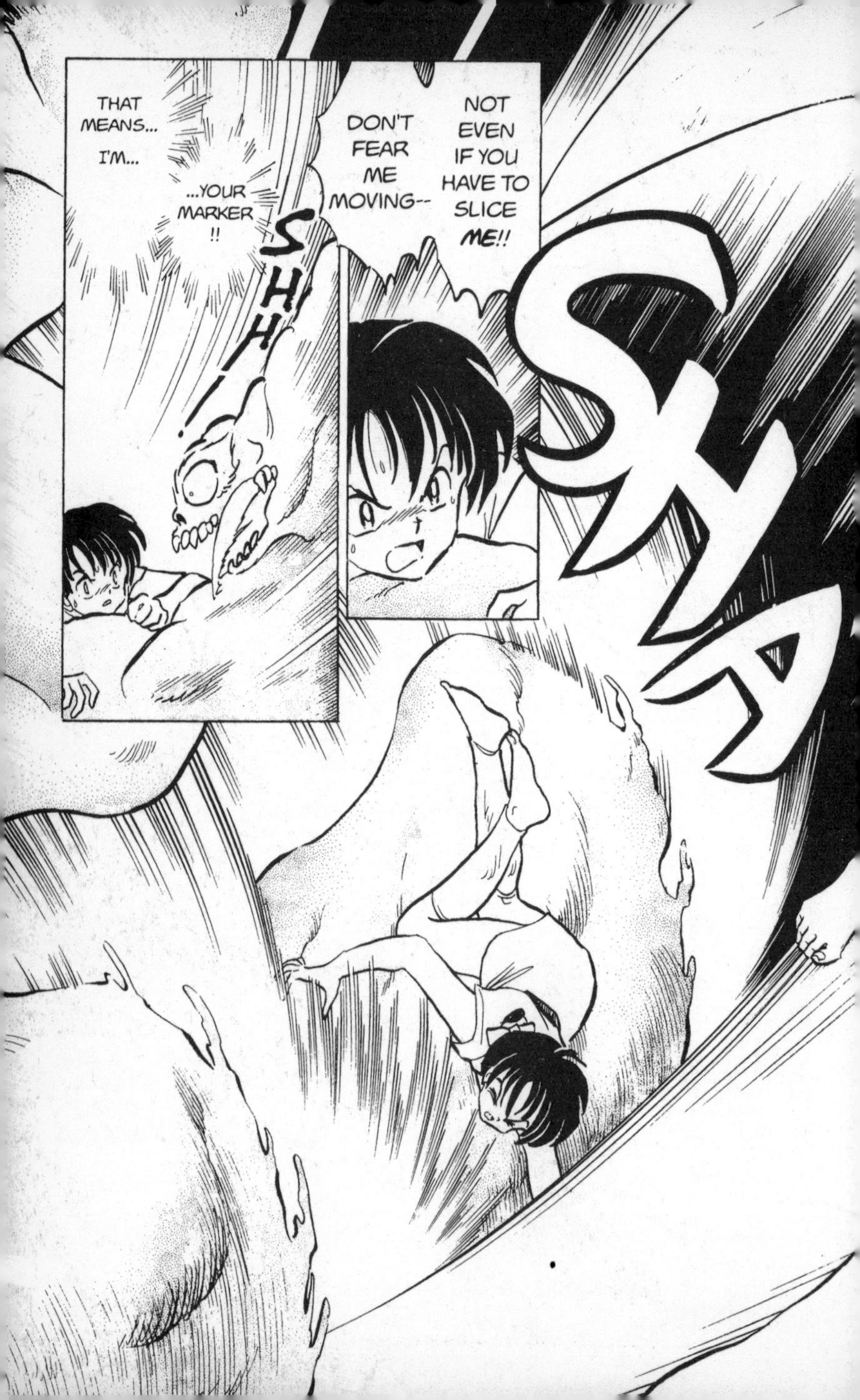
THAT MEANS...
I'M...
...YOUR MARKER !!
SHHH!!
DON'T FEAR ME MOVING--
NOT EVEN IF YOU HAVE TO SLICE ME!!
SHAA

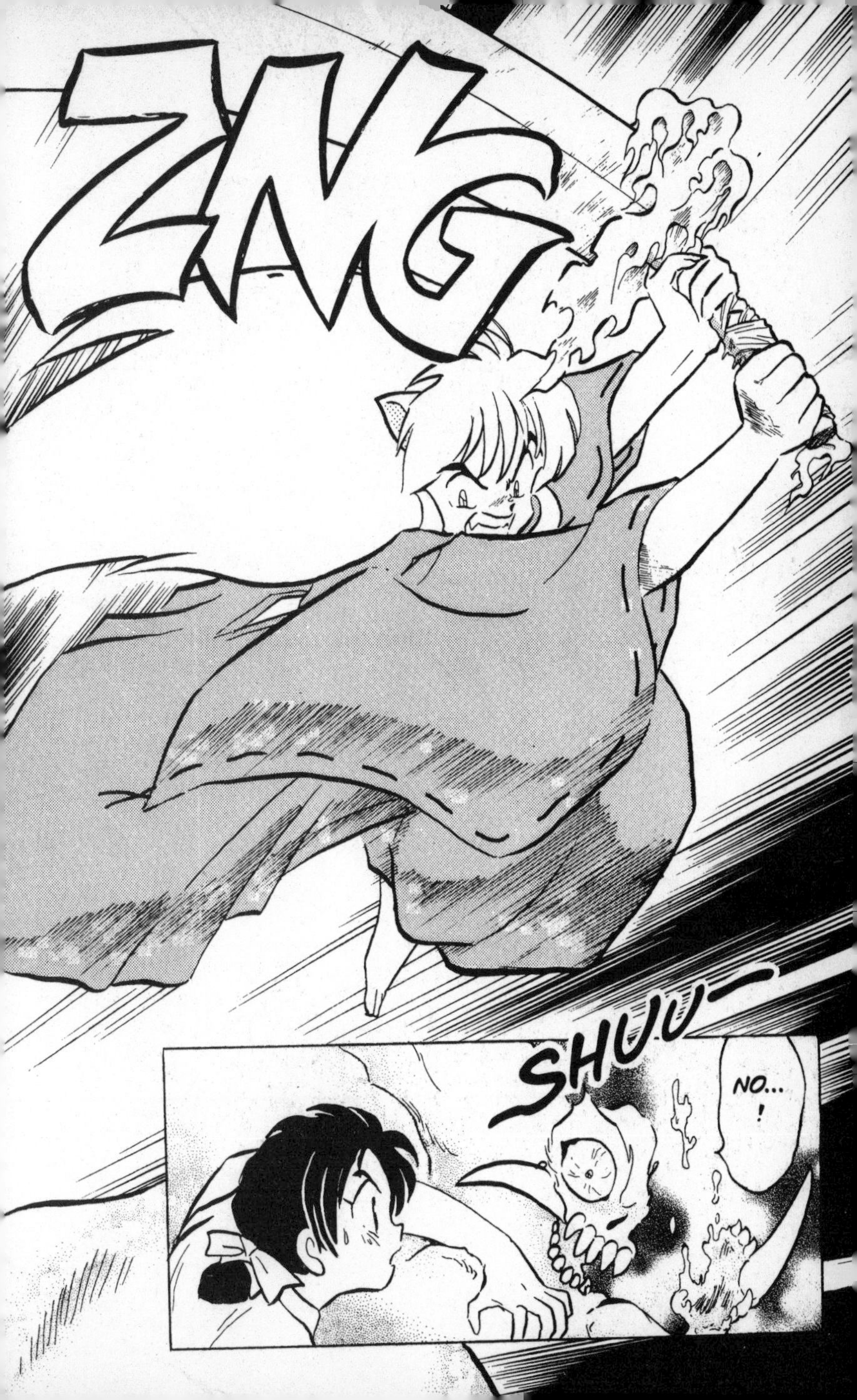
ZANG
SHUU—
NO... !

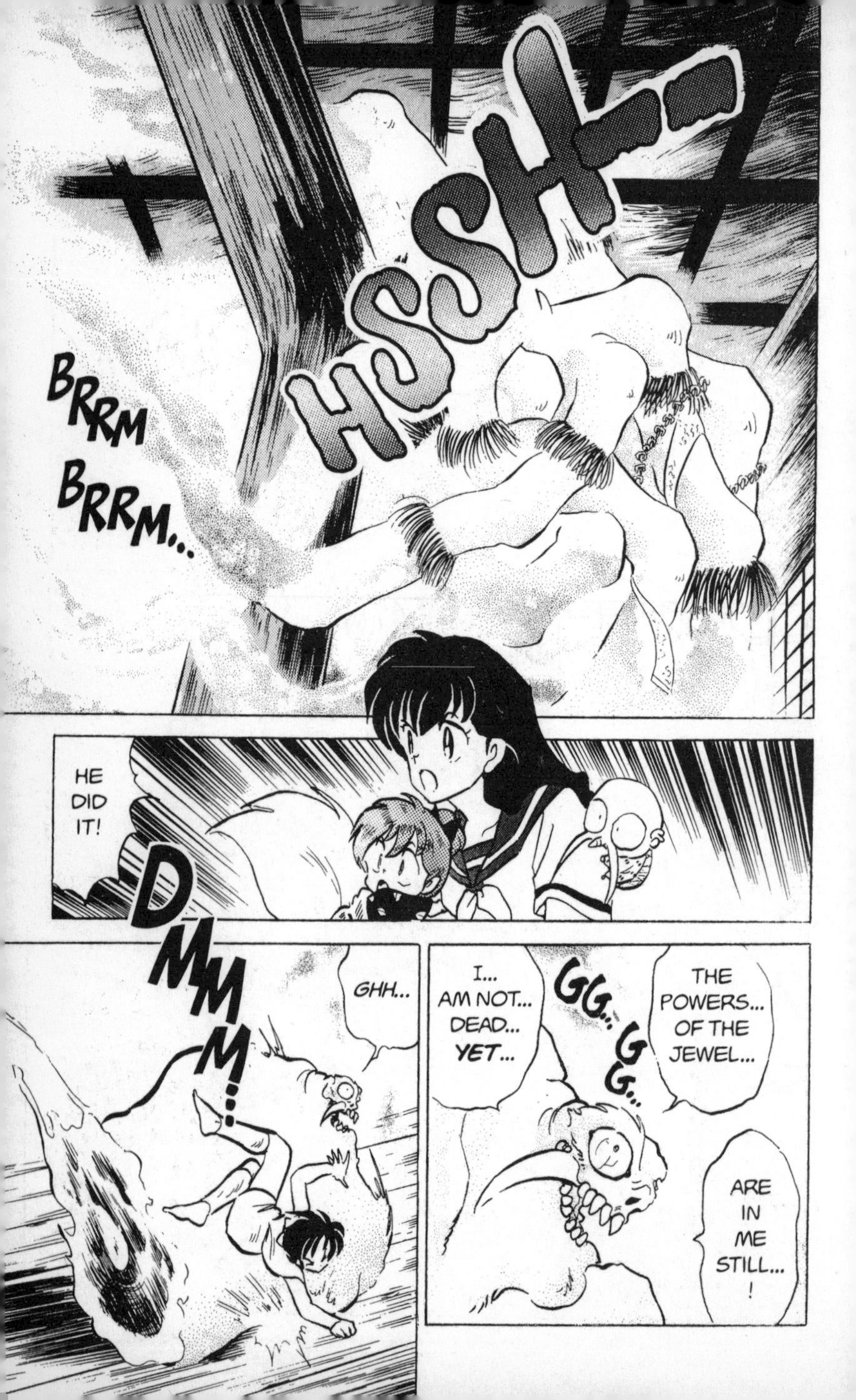
HSSH--
BRRM BRRM...
HE DID IT!
DMMM...
GHH...
I... AM NOT... DEAD... YET...
GG... G G...
THE POWERS... OF THE JEWEL...
ARE IN ME STILL...!

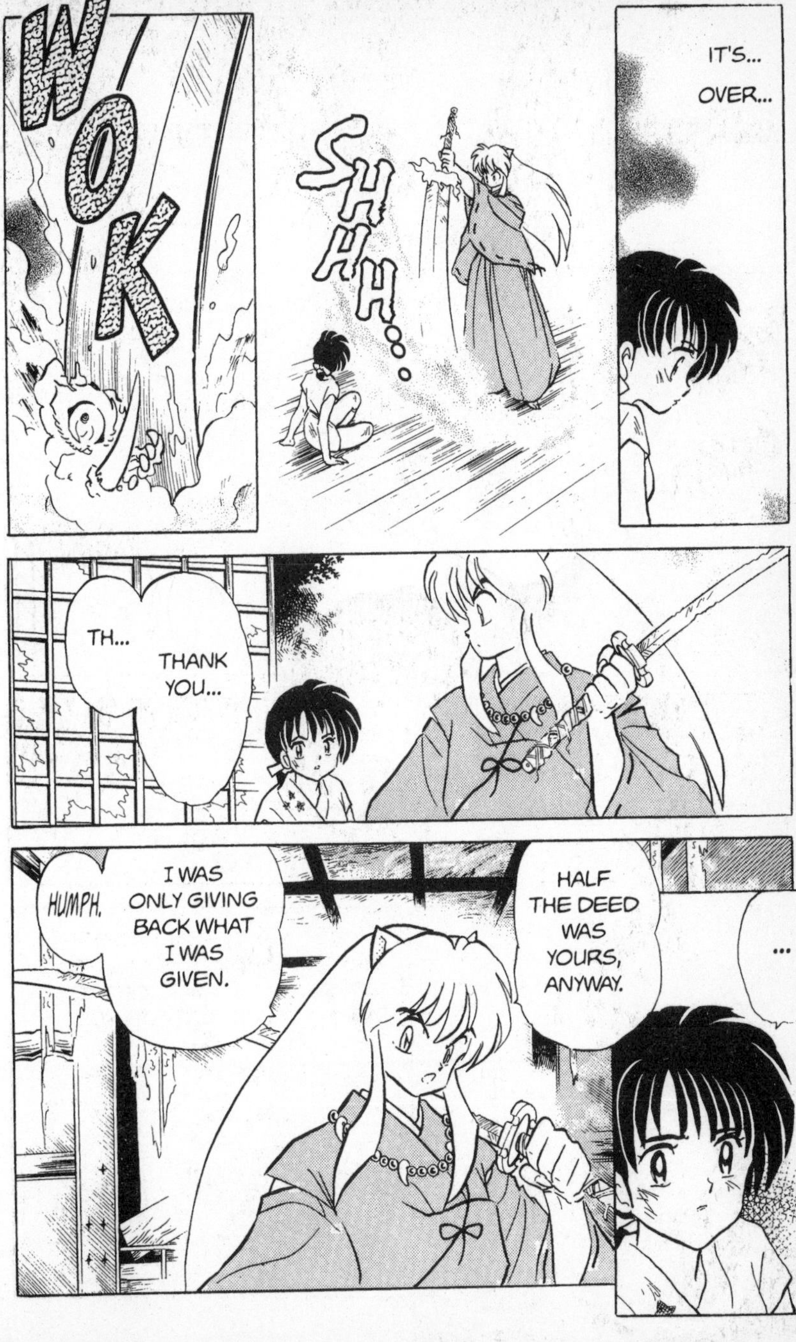
WOK
SHHHH...
IT'S... OVER...
TH...
THANK YOU...
HUMPH.
I WAS ONLY GIVING BACK WHAT I WAS GIVEN.
HALF THE DEED WAS YOURS, ANYWAY.
...

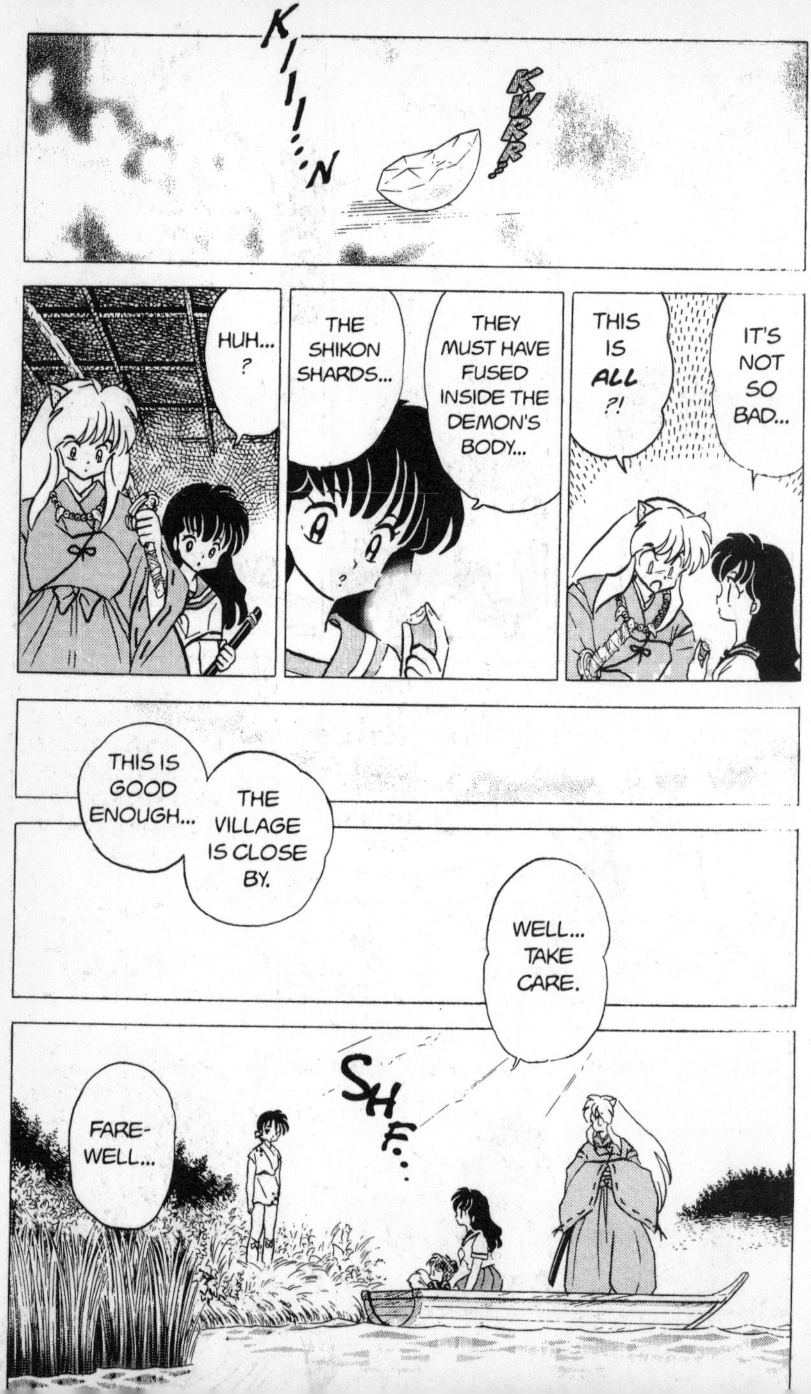
KIII...N
KWRR...
HUH...?
THE SHIKON SHARDS...
THEY MUST HAVE FUSED INSIDE THE DEMON'S BODY...
THIS IS ALL?!
IT'S NOT SO BAD...
THIS IS GOOD ENOUGH...
THE VILLAGE IS CLOSE BY.
WELL... TAKE CARE.
FARE-WELL...
SHF...

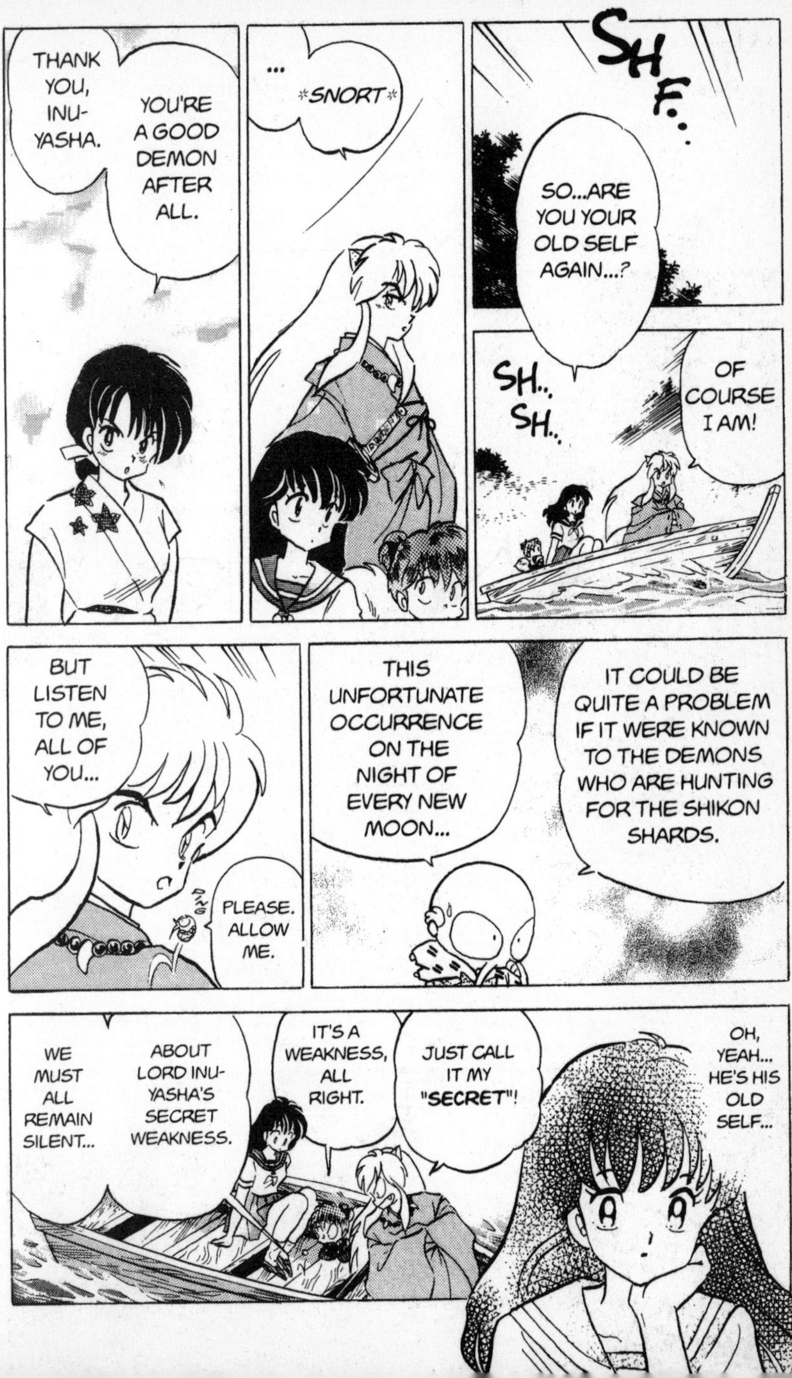
THANK YOU, INU-YASHA.
YOU'RE A GOOD DEMON AFTER ALL.
... *SNORT*
SHF...
SO...ARE YOU YOUR OLD SELF AGAIN...?
SH.. SH..
OF COURSE I AM!
BUT LISTEN TO ME, ALL OF YOU...
PLEASE. ALLOW ME.
THIS UNFORTUNATE OCCURRENCE ON THE NIGHT OF EVERY NEW MOON...
IT COULD BE QUITE A PROBLEM IF IT WERE KNOWN TO THE DEMONS WHO ARE HUNTING FOR THE SHIKON SHARDS.
WE MUST ALL REMAIN SILENT...
ABOUT LORD INU-YASHA'S SECRET WEAKNESS.
IT'S A WEAKNESS, ALL RIGHT.
JUST CALL IT MY "SECRET"!
OH, YEAH... HE'S HIS OLD SELF...

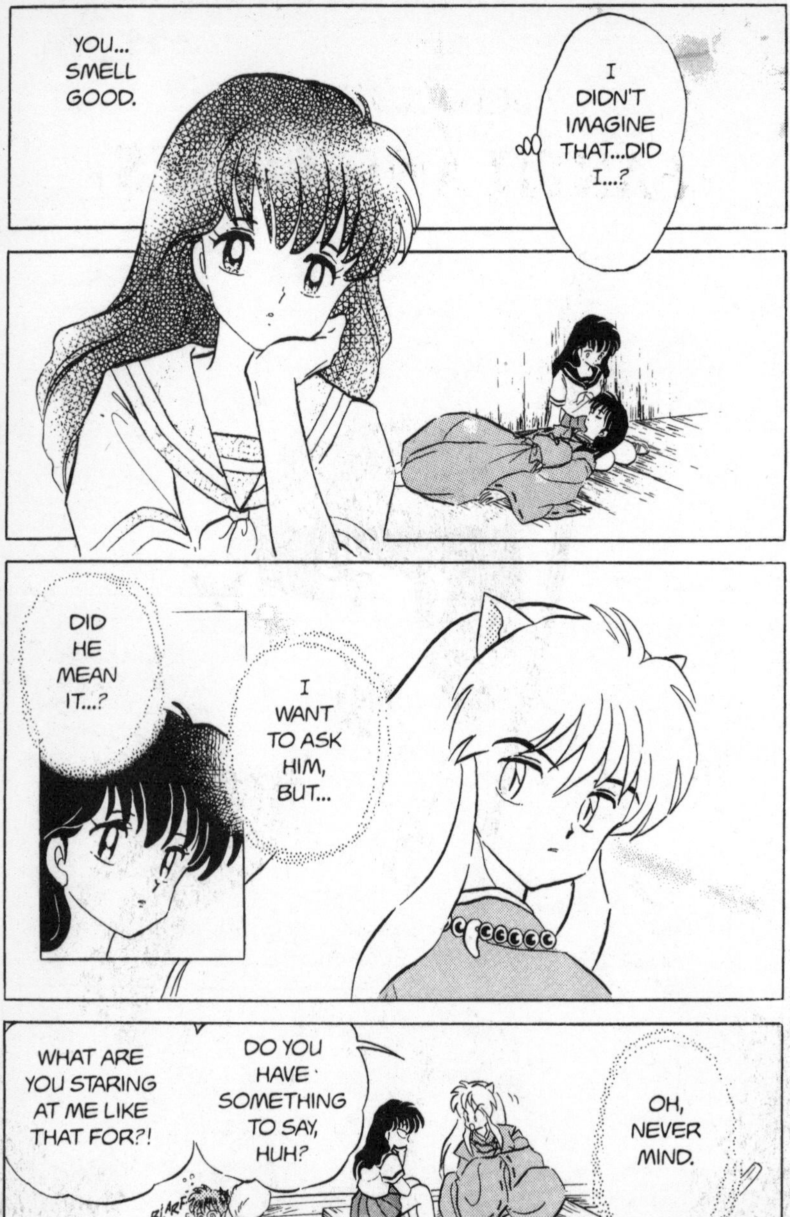
YOU... SMELL GOOD.
I DIDN'T IMAGINE THAT...DID I...?
DID HE MEAN IT...?
I WANT TO ASK HIM, BUT...
WHAT ARE YOU STARING AT ME LIKE THAT FOR?!
DO YOU HAVE SOMETHING TO SAY, HUH?
BLARF
OH, NEVER MIND.

SCROLL SEVEN

EARTH AND BONES

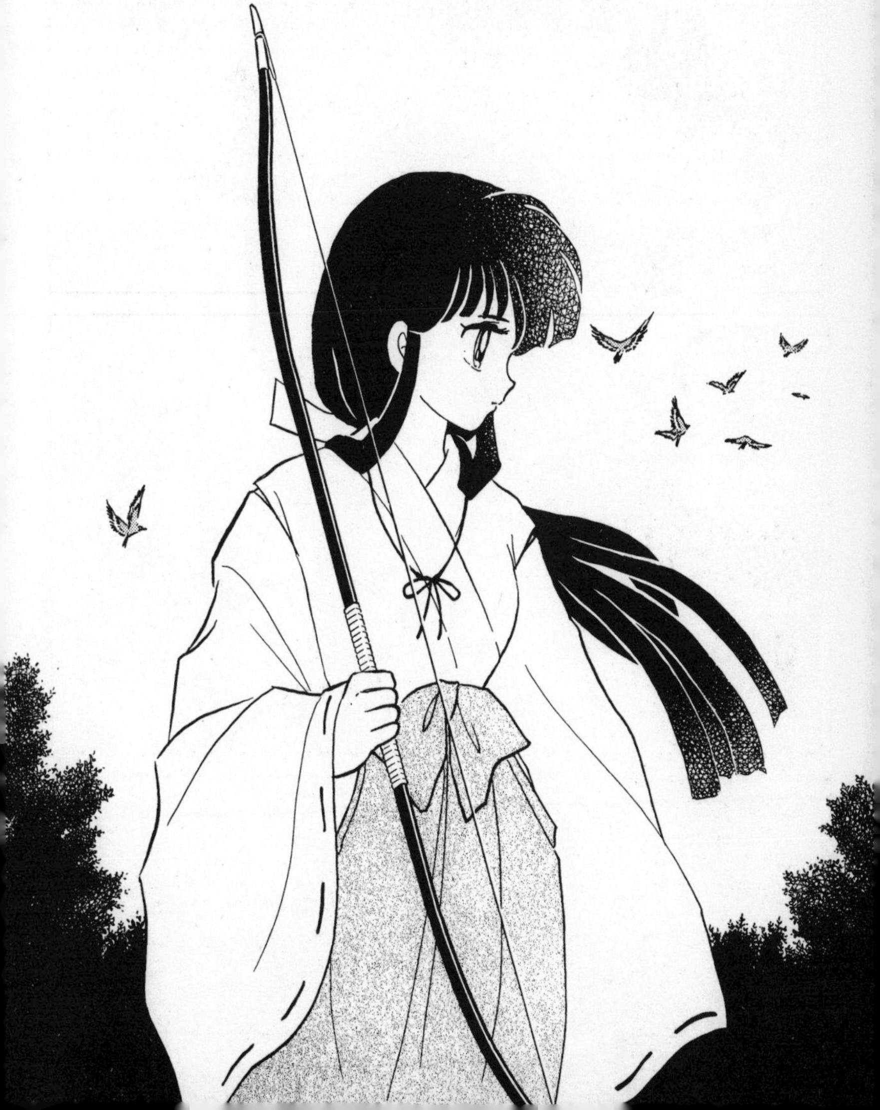

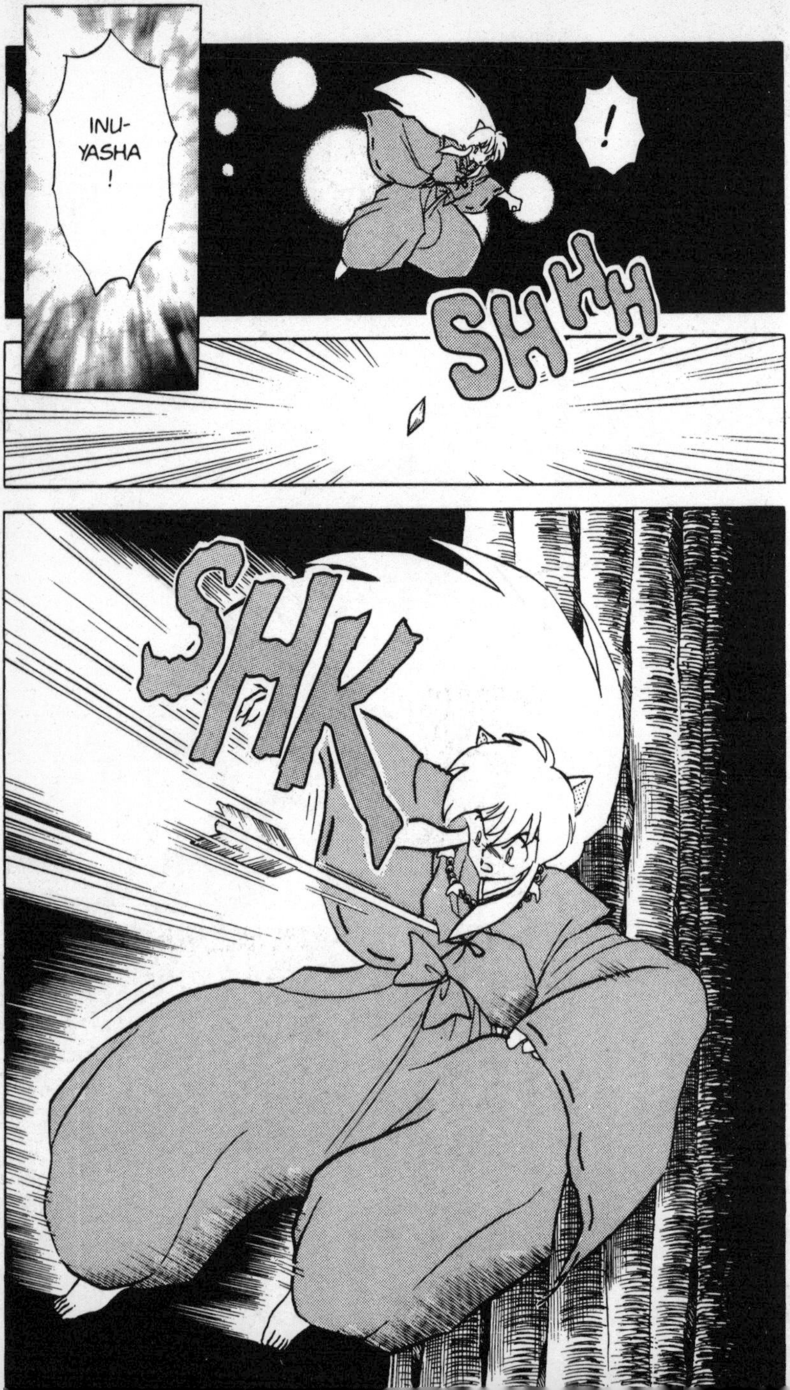
INU-YASHA
!
!
SHHH
SHK

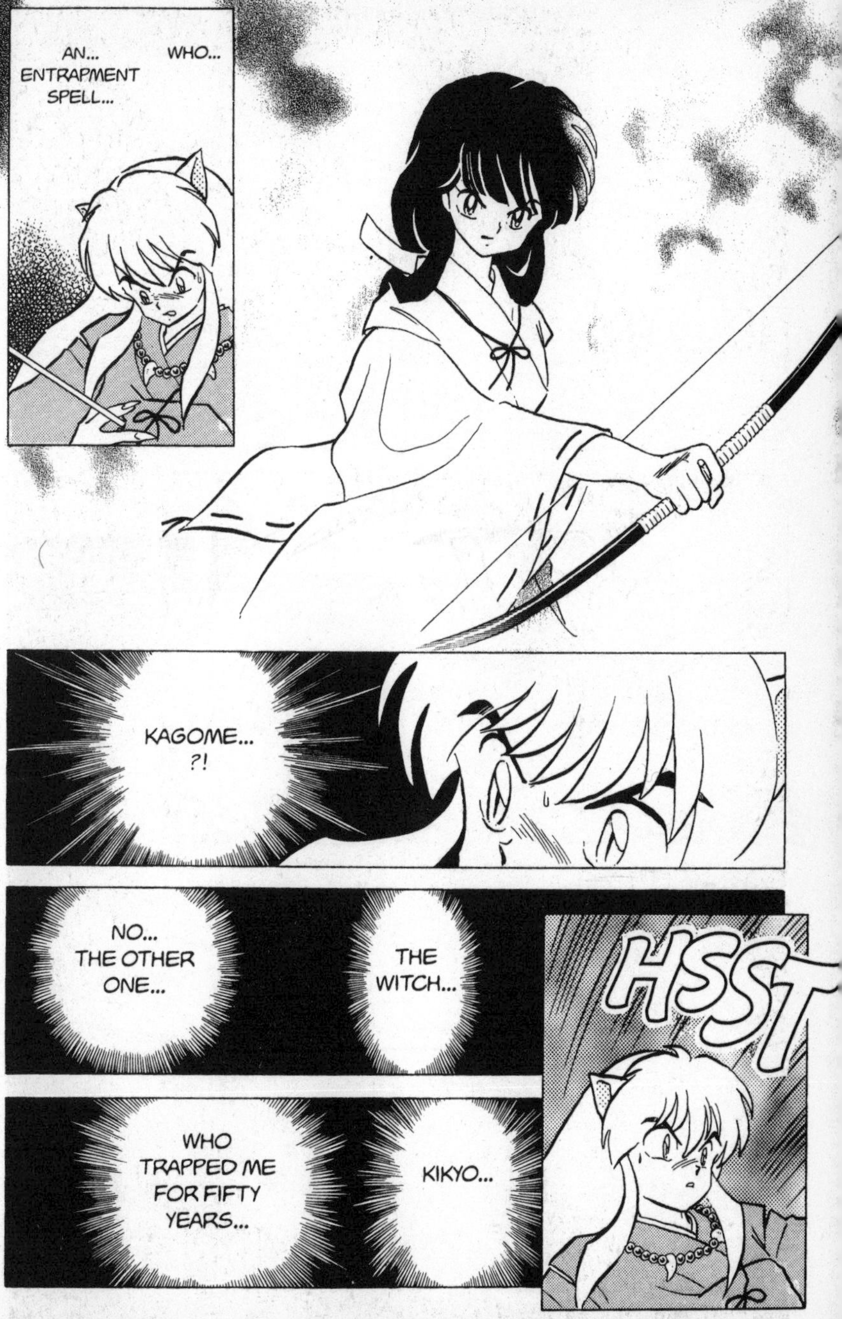

AN... ENTRAPMENT SPELL...
WHO...
KAGOME... ?!
NO... THE OTHER ONE...
THE WITCH...
HSST
WHO TRAPPED ME FOR FIFTY YEARS...
KIKYO...

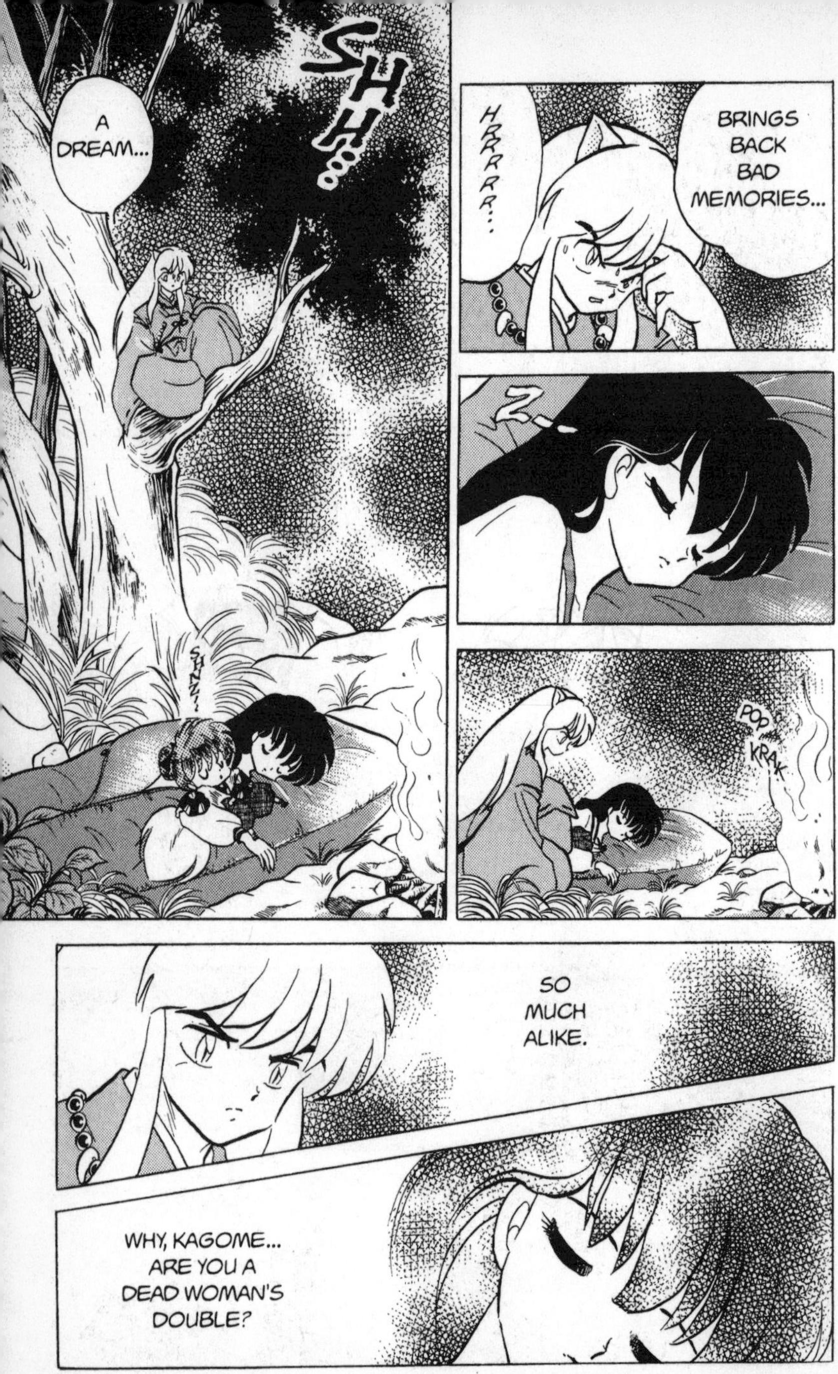
A DREAM...
SHH...
SHNZZ..
HRRRRR...
BRINGS BACK BAD MEMORIES...
Z
POP
KRAK
SO MUCH ALIKE.
WHY, KAGOME... ARE YOU A DEAD WOMAN'S DOUBLE?

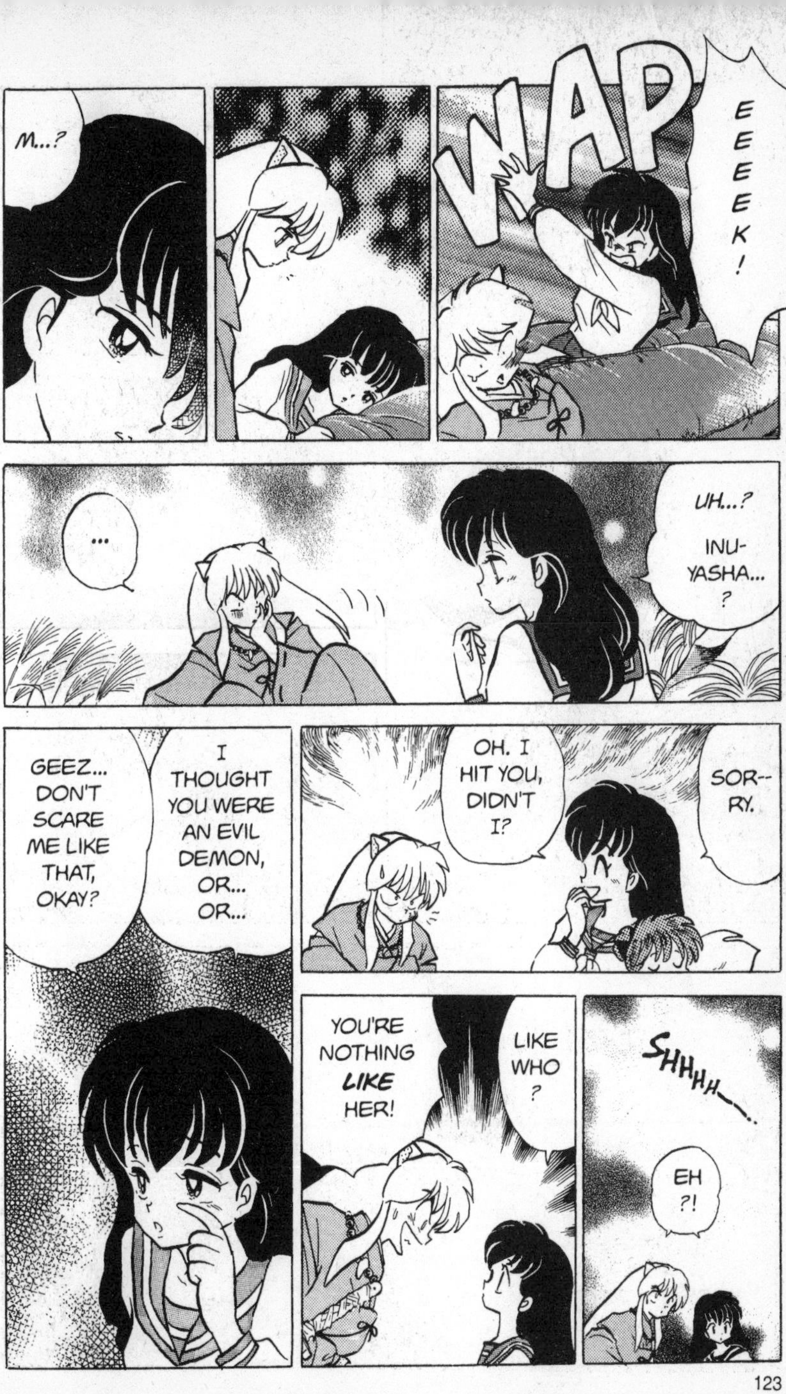
M...?
WAP
EEEEEK!
...
UH...?
INU-YASHA...?
GEEZ... DON'T SCARE ME LIKE THAT, OKAY?
I THOUGHT YOU WERE AN EVIL DEMON, OR... OR...
OH. I HIT YOU, DIDN'T I?
SOR--RY.
YOU'RE NOTHING **LIKE** HER!
LIKE WHO?
SHHHH---...
EH?!

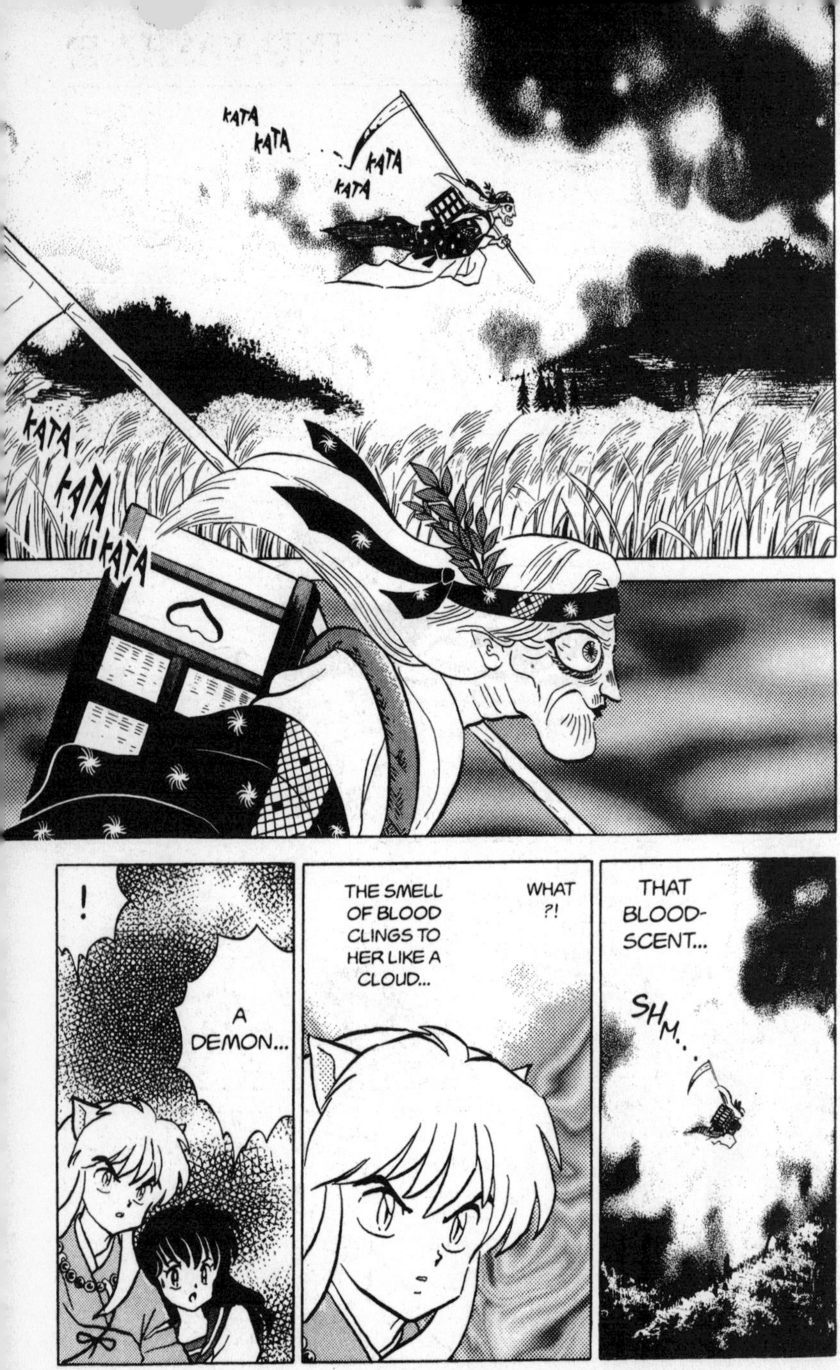
KATA
KATA
KATA
KATA
KATA
KATA
KATA
!
A DEMON...
THE SMELL OF BLOOD CLINGS TO HER LIKE A CLOUD...
WHAT ?!
THAT BLOOD-SCENT...
SHM...

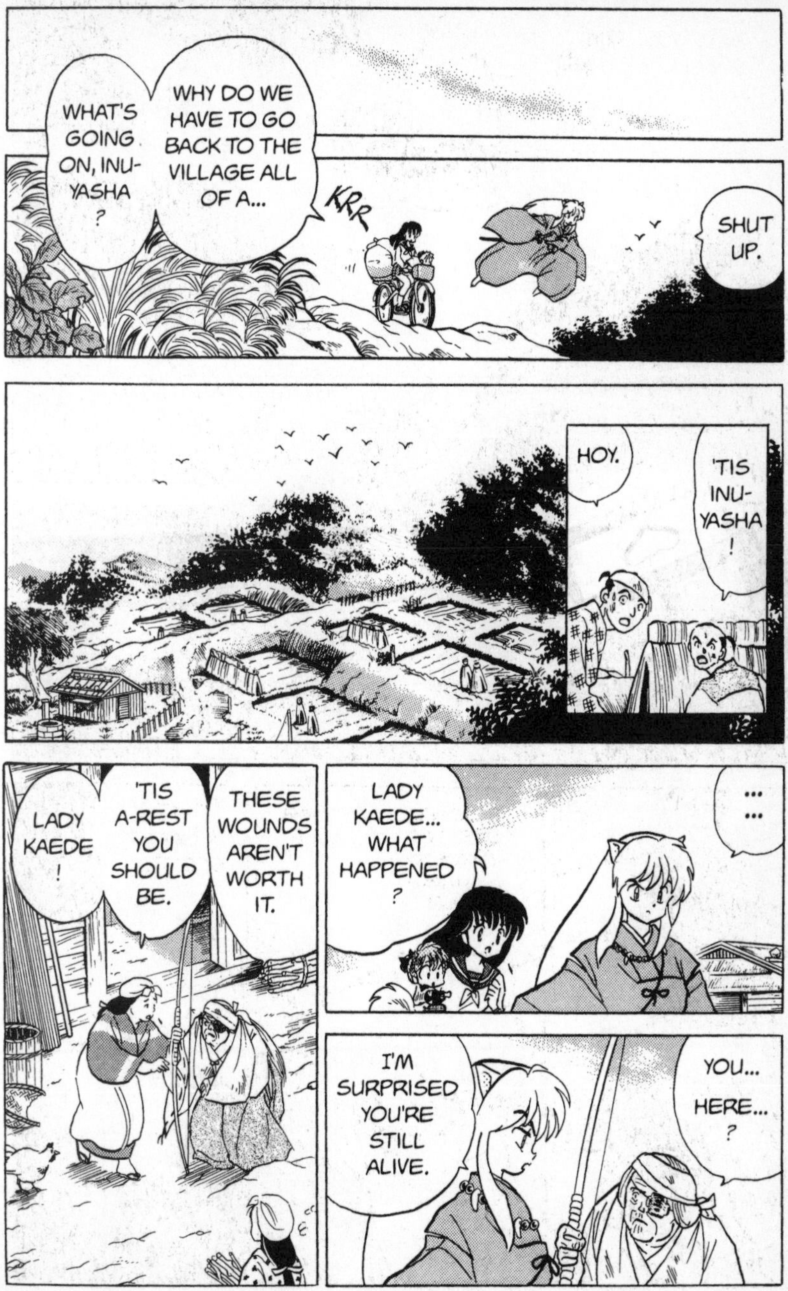
WHAT'S GOING ON, INU-YASHA?
WHY DO WE HAVE TO GO BACK TO THE VILLAGE ALL OF A...
KRR
SHUT UP.
HOY.
'TIS INU-YASHA!
LADY KAEDE!
'TIS A-REST YOU SHOULD BE.
THESE WOUNDS AREN'T WORTH IT.
LADY KAEDE... WHAT HAPPENED?
......
I'M SURPRISED YOU'RE STILL ALIVE.
YOU... HERE...?

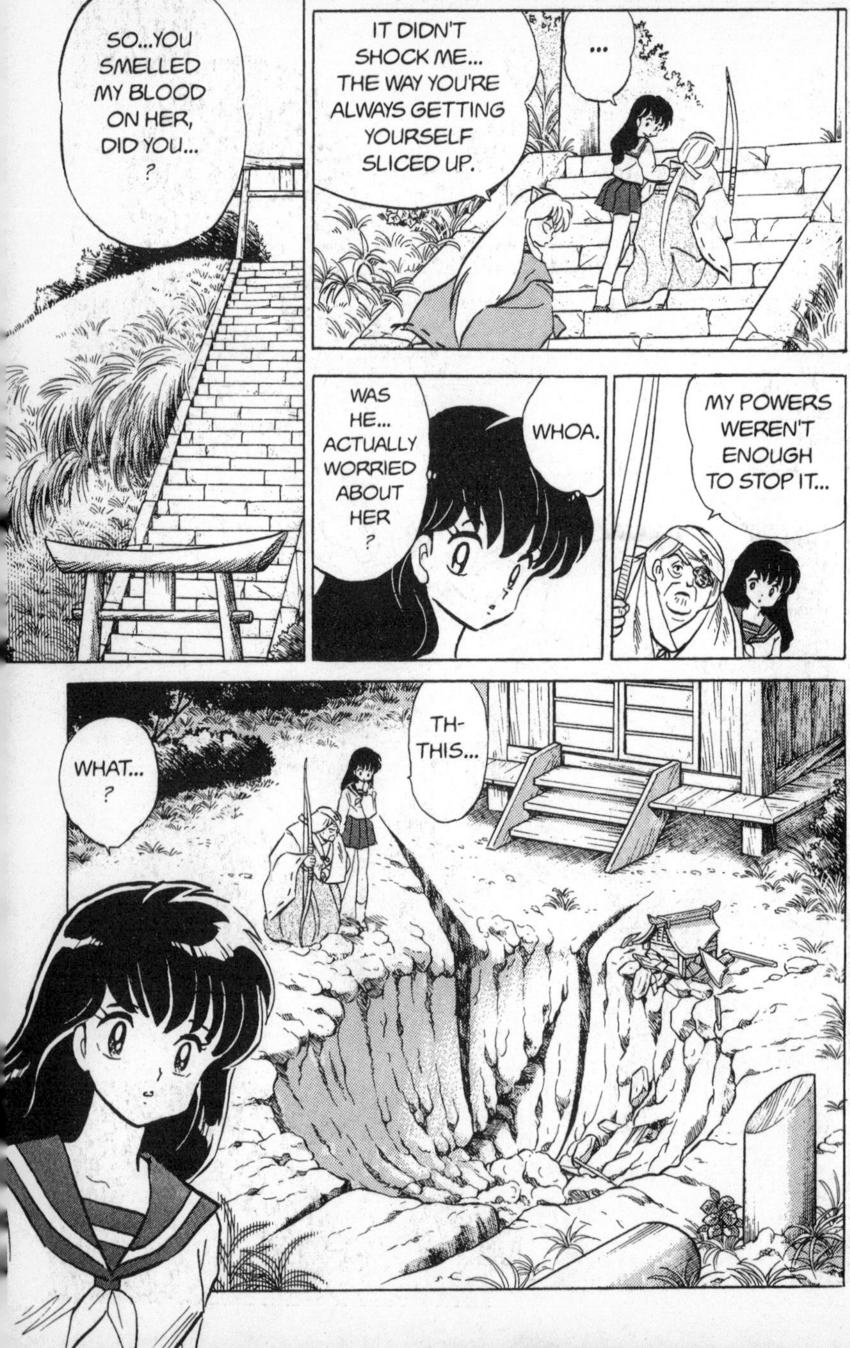
SO...YOU SMELLED MY BLOOD ON HER, DID YOU...?
IT DIDN'T SHOCK ME... THE WAY YOU'RE ALWAYS GETTING YOURSELF SLICED UP.
...
WAS HE... ACTUALLY WORRIED ABOUT HER?
WHOA.
MY POWERS WEREN'T ENOUGH TO STOP IT...
WHAT...?
TH-THIS...

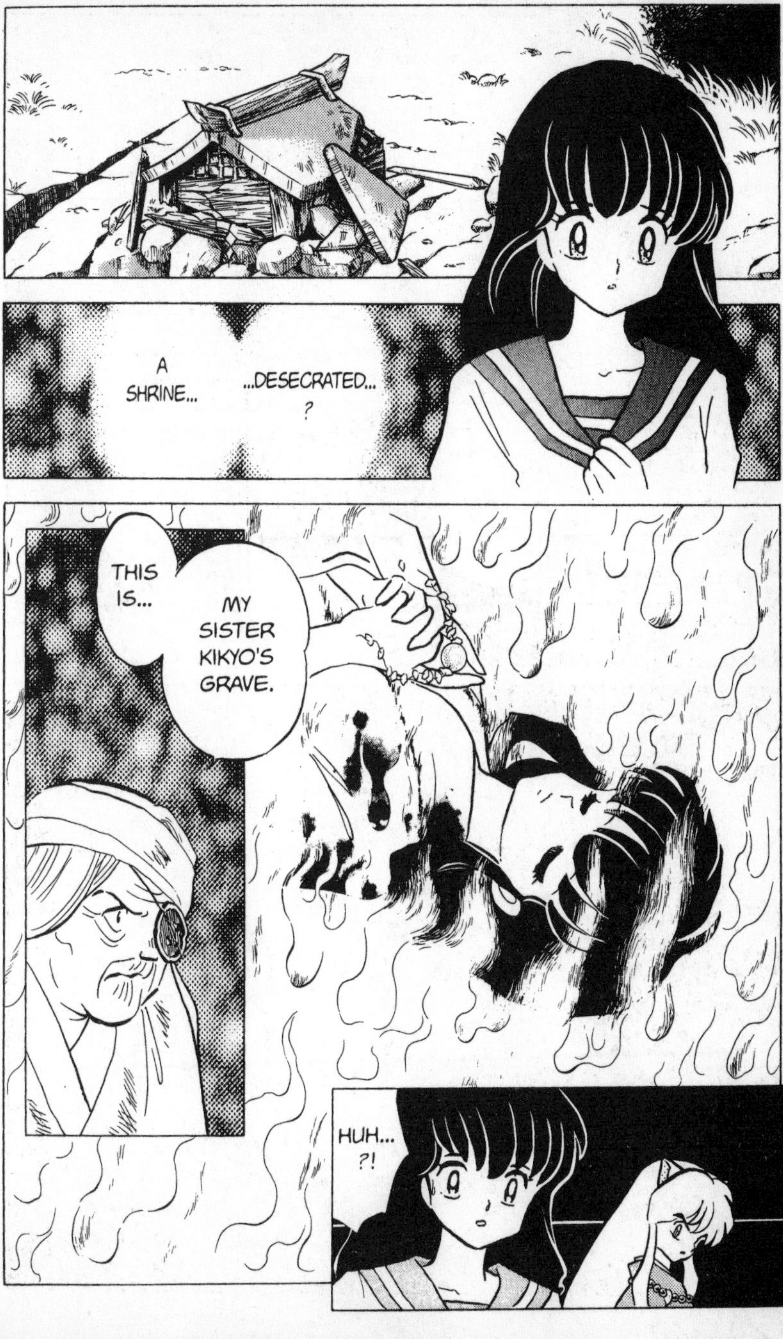
A SHRINE...
...DESECRATED...
?
THIS IS...
MY SISTER KIKYO'S GRAVE.
HUH...
?!

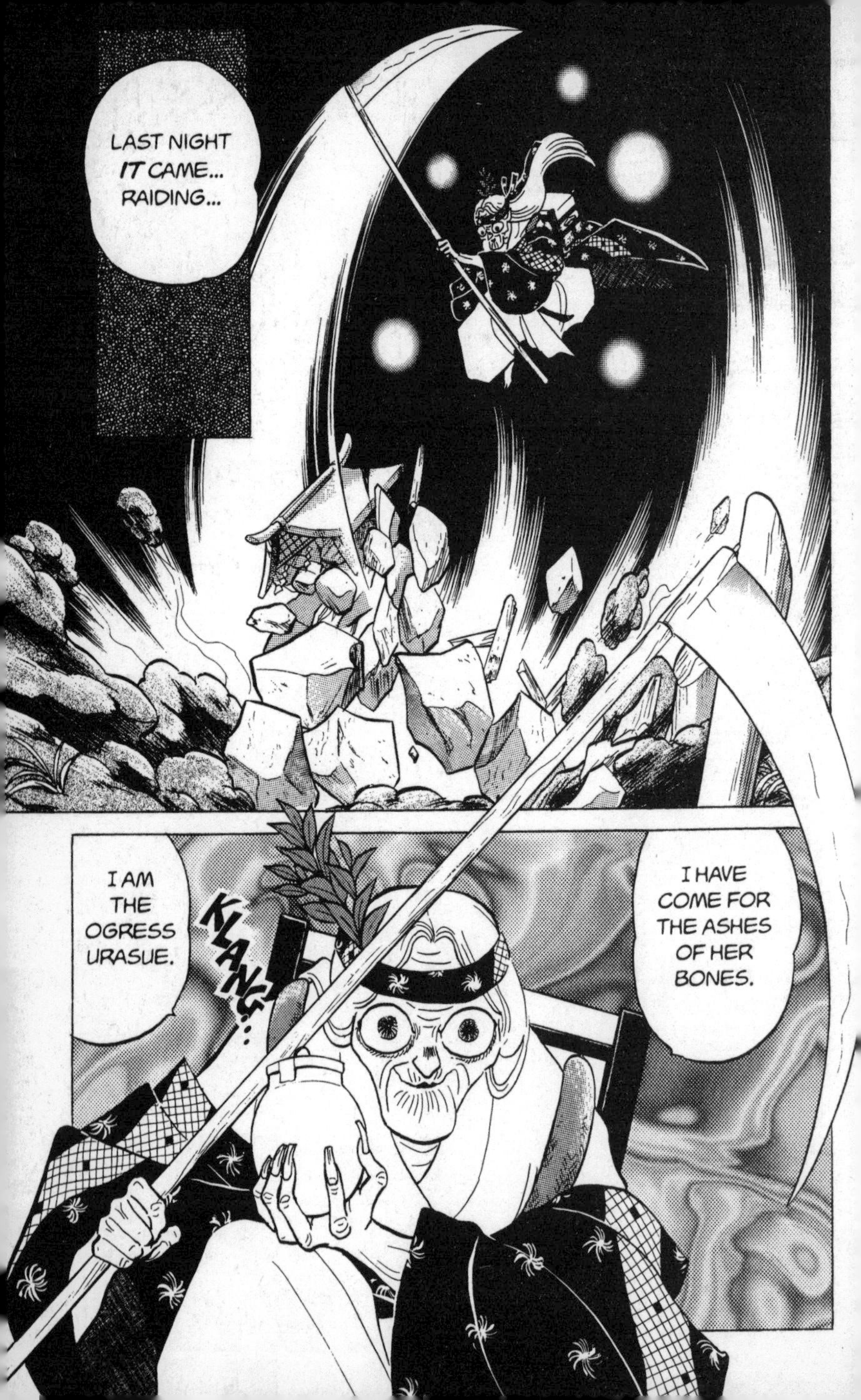
LAST NIGHT *IT* CAME... RAIDING...
I AM THE OGRESS URASUE.
KLANG...
I HAVE COME FOR THE ASHES OF HER BONES.

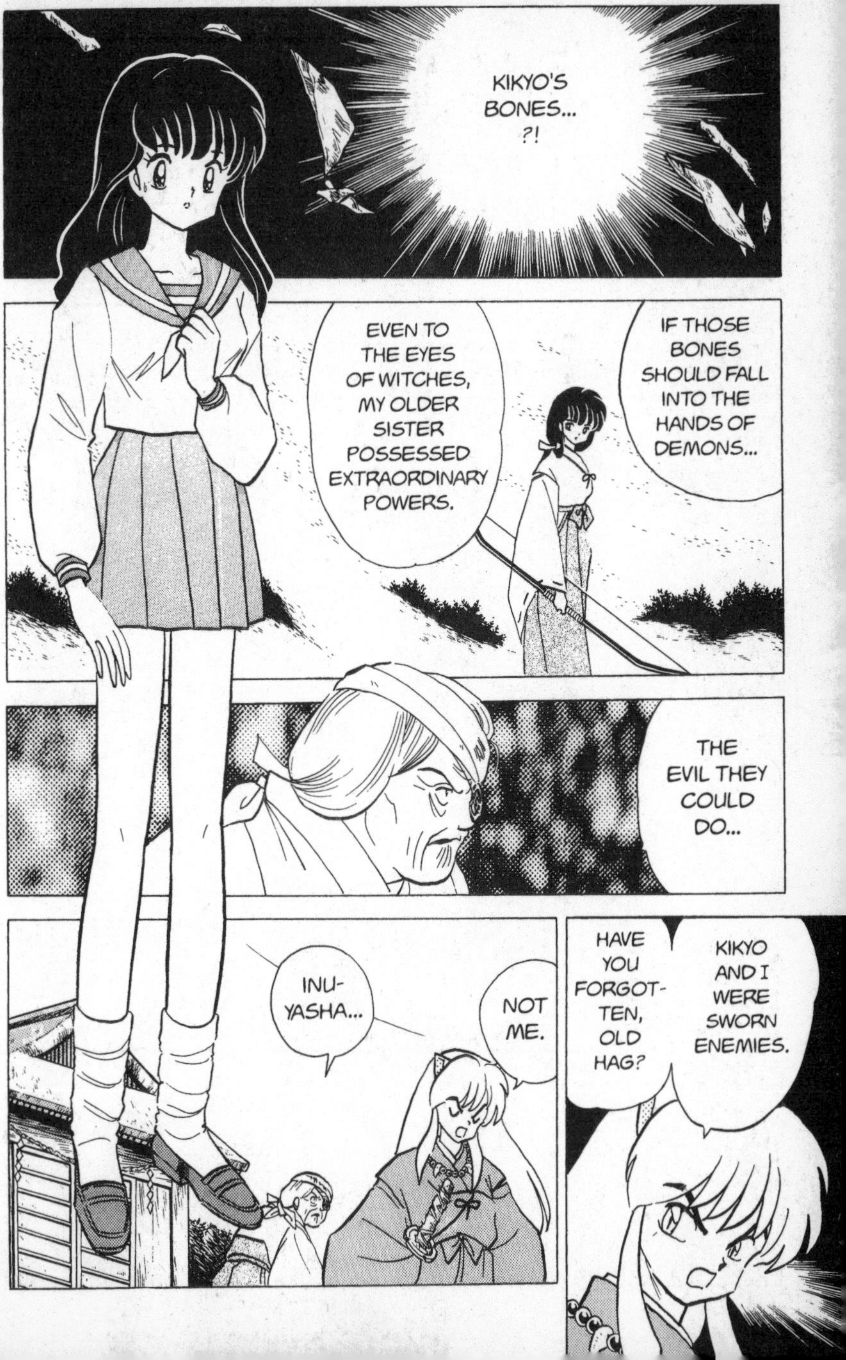
KIKYO'S BONES... ?!
EVEN TO THE EYES OF WITCHES, MY OLDER SISTER POSSESSED EXTRAORDINARY POWERS.
IF THOSE BONES SHOULD FALL INTO THE HANDS OF DEMONS...
THE EVIL THEY COULD DO...
INU-YASHA...
NOT ME.
HAVE YOU FORGOT-TEN, OLD HAG?
KIKYO AND I WERE SWORN ENEMIES.

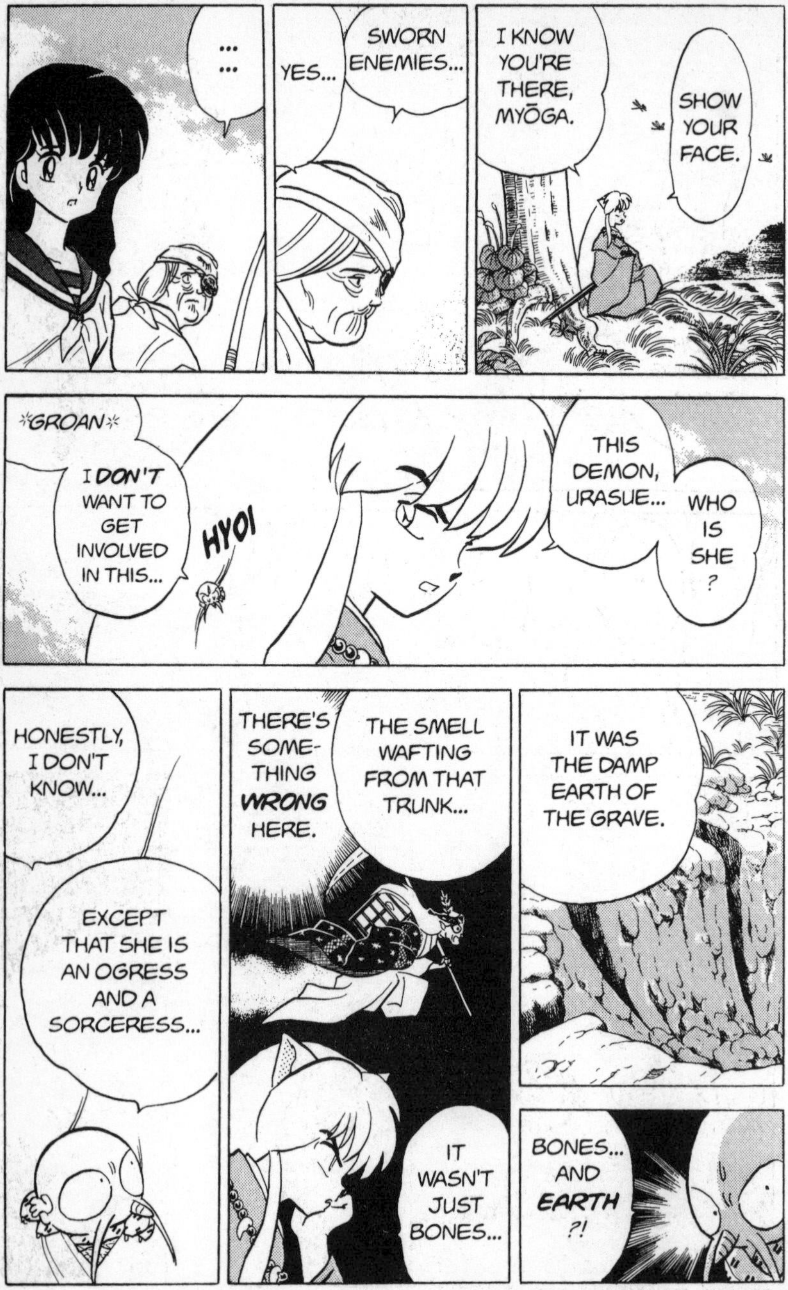
......
YES...
SWORN ENEMIES...
I KNOW YOU'RE THERE, MYŌGA.
SHOW YOUR FACE.
GROAN
I DON'T WANT TO GET INVOLVED IN THIS...
HYOI
THIS DEMON, URASUE...
WHO IS SHE?
HONESTLY, I DON'T KNOW...
EXCEPT THAT SHE IS AN OGRESS AND A SORCERESS...
THERE'S SOME-THING WRONG HERE.
THE SMELL WAFTING FROM THAT TRUNK...
IT WASN'T JUST BONES...
IT WAS THE DAMP EARTH OF THE GRAVE.
BONES... AND EARTH?!

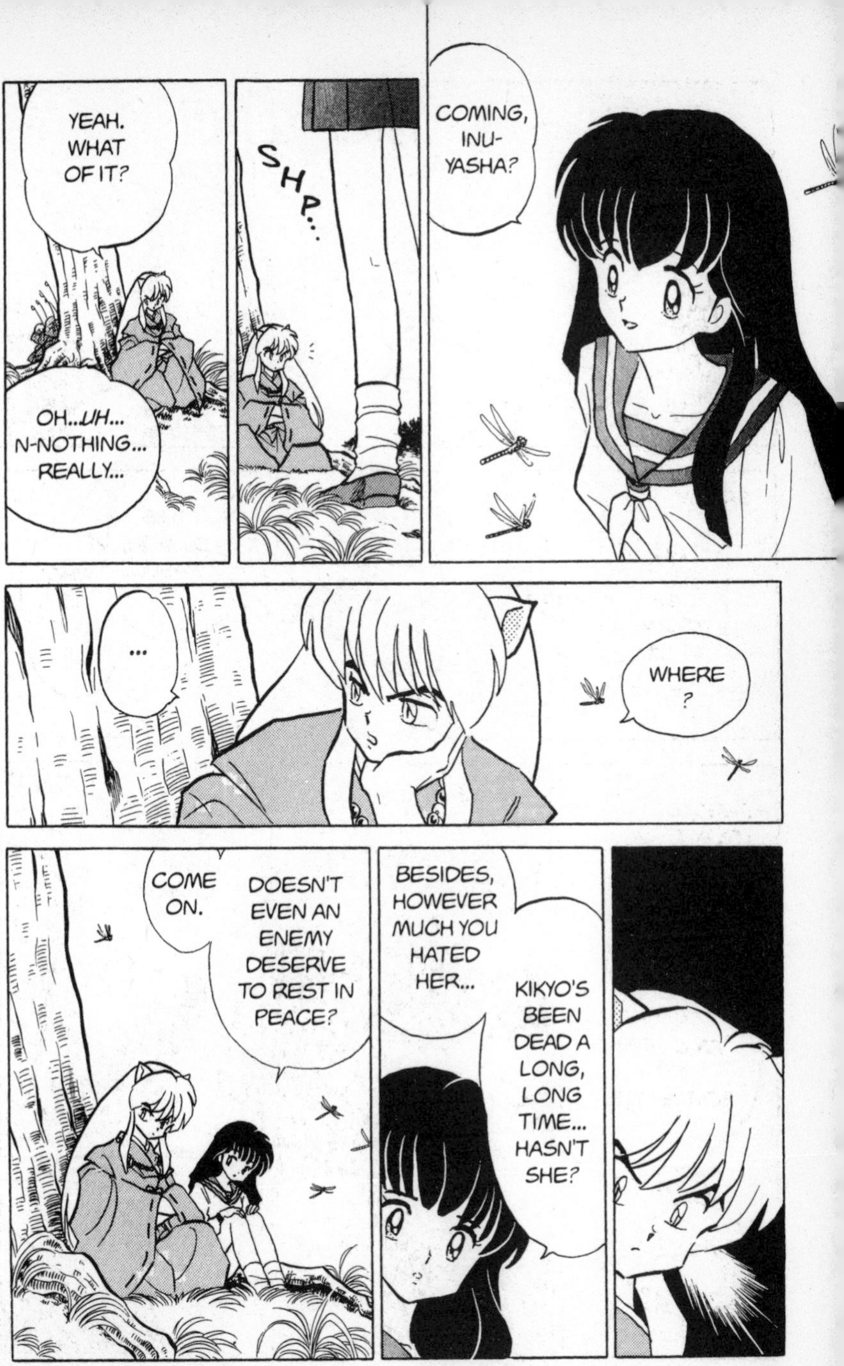
YEAH. WHAT OF IT?
OH...UH... N-NOTHING... REALLY...
SHP...
COMING, INU-YASHA?
...
WHERE?
COME ON.
DOESN'T EVEN AN ENEMY DESERVE TO REST IN PEACE?
BESIDES, HOWEVER MUCH YOU HATED HER...
KIKYO'S BEEN DEAD A LONG, LONG TIME... HASN'T SHE?

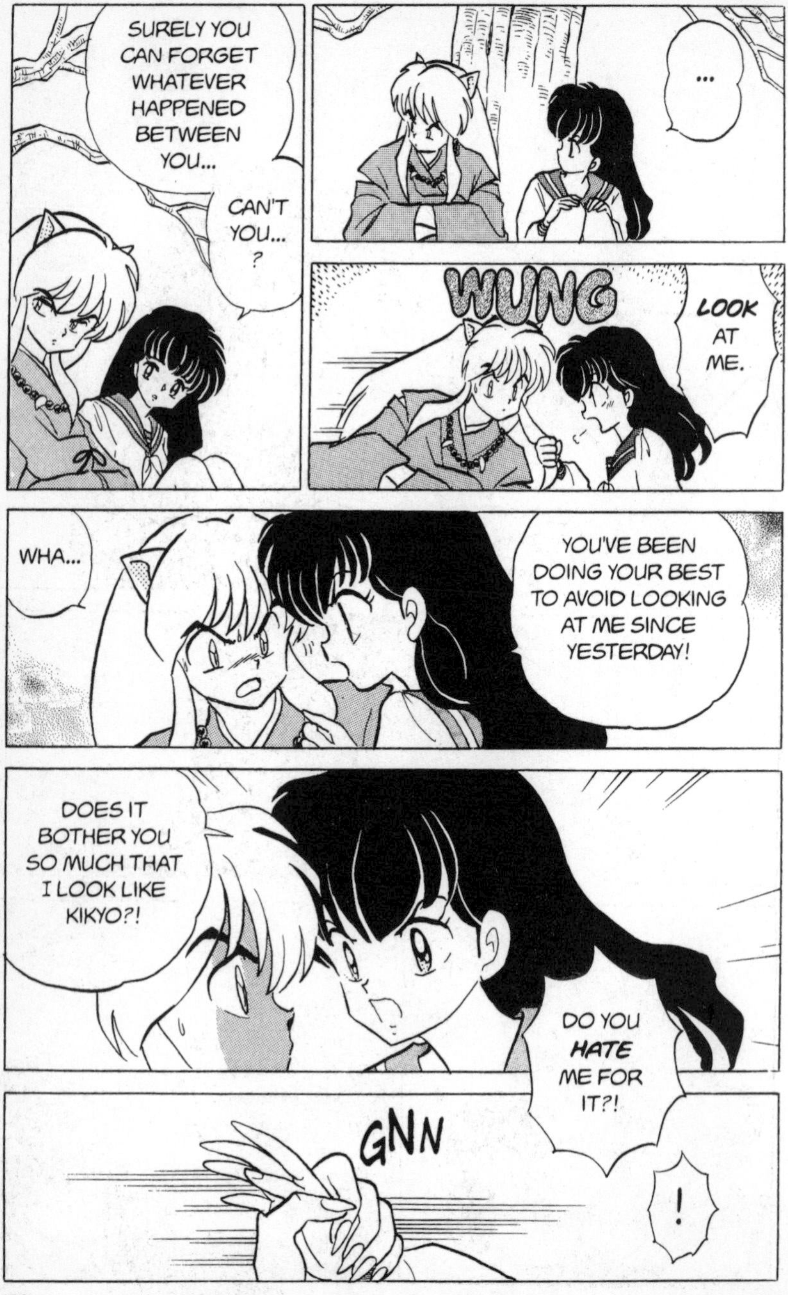
SURELY YOU CAN FORGET WHATEVER HAPPENED BETWEEN YOU...
CAN'T YOU... ?
...
WUNG
LOOK AT ME.
WHA...
YOU'VE BEEN DOING YOUR BEST TO AVOID LOOKING AT ME SINCE YESTERDAY!
DOES IT BOTHER YOU SO MUCH THAT I LOOK LIKE KIKYO?!
DO YOU HATE ME FOR IT?!
GNN
!

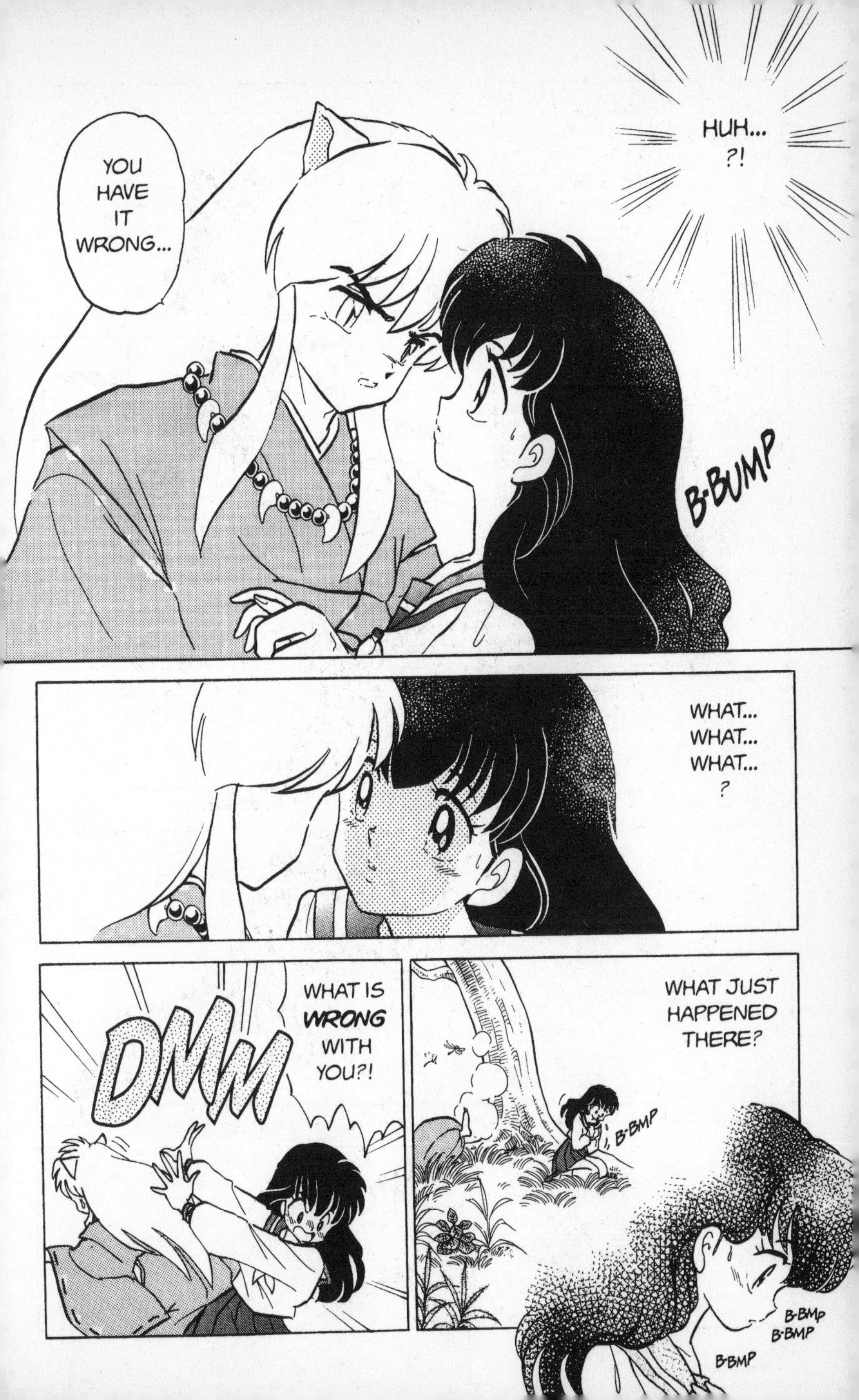
YOU HAVE IT WRONG...
HUH... ?!
B-BUMP
WHAT... WHAT... WHAT... ?
DMM
WHAT IS **WRONG** WITH YOU?!
WHAT JUST HAPPENED THERE?
B-BMP
B-BMP
B-BMP
B-BMP

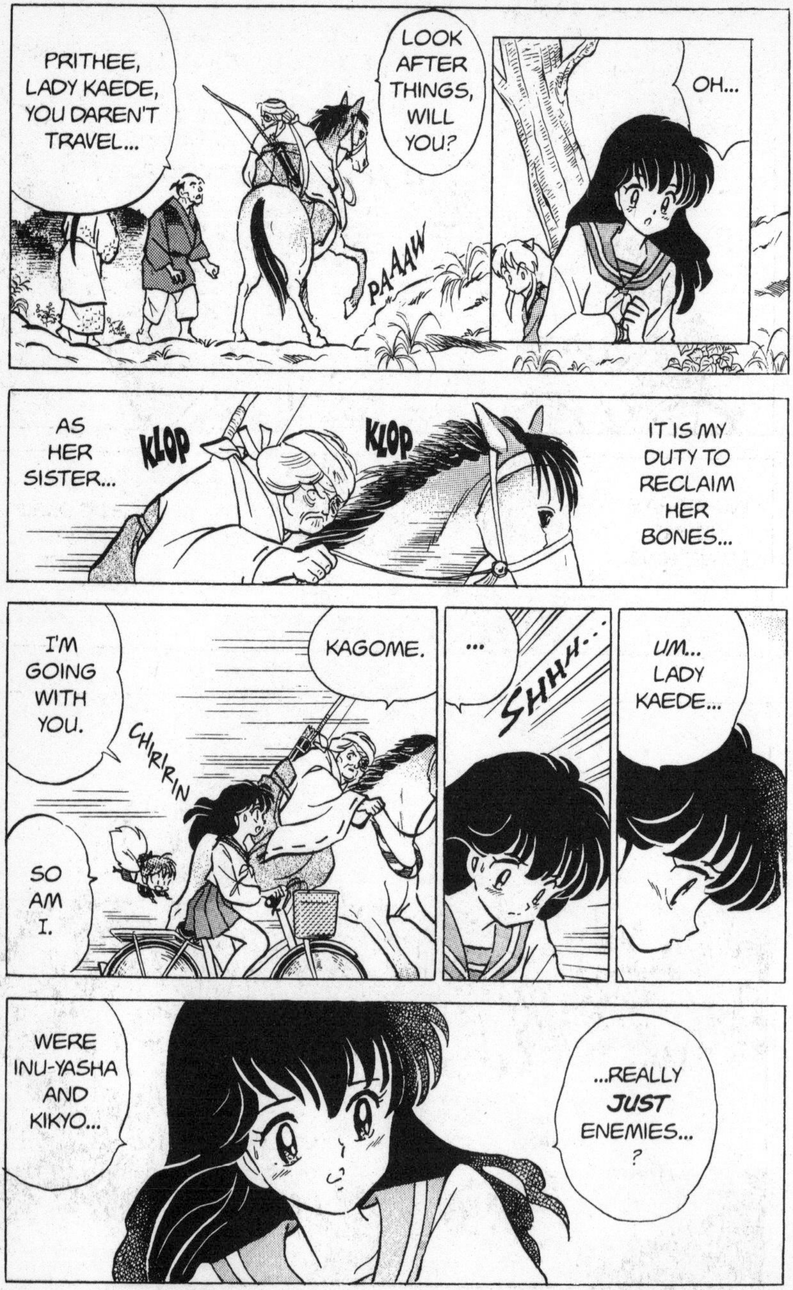
PRITHEE, LADY KAEDE, YOU DAREN'T TRAVEL...
PAAAW
LOOK AFTER THINGS, WILL YOU?
OH...
AS HER SISTER...
KLOP
KLOP
IT IS MY DUTY TO RECLAIM HER BONES...
I'M GOING WITH YOU.
CHIRIRIN
SO AM I.
KAGOME.
...
SHHH...
UM... LADY KAEDE...
WERE INU-YASHA AND KIKYO...
...REALLY **JUST** ENEMIES... ?

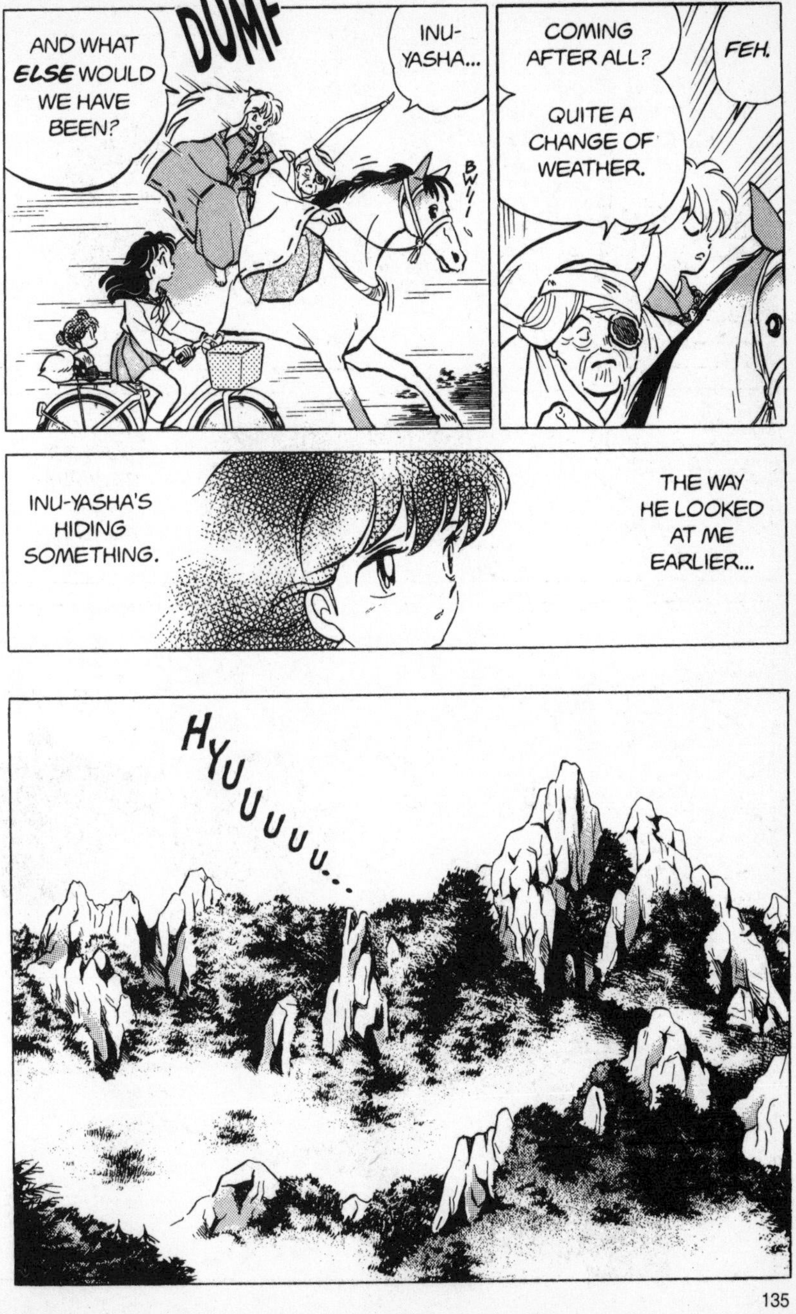
AND WHAT ELSE WOULD WE HAVE BEEN?
DUMF
INU-YASHA...
BWIII
COMING AFTER ALL?
QUITE A CHANGE OF WEATHER.
FEH.
INU-YASHA'S HIDING SOMETHING.
THE WAY HE LOOKED AT ME EARLIER...
HYUUUUUU...

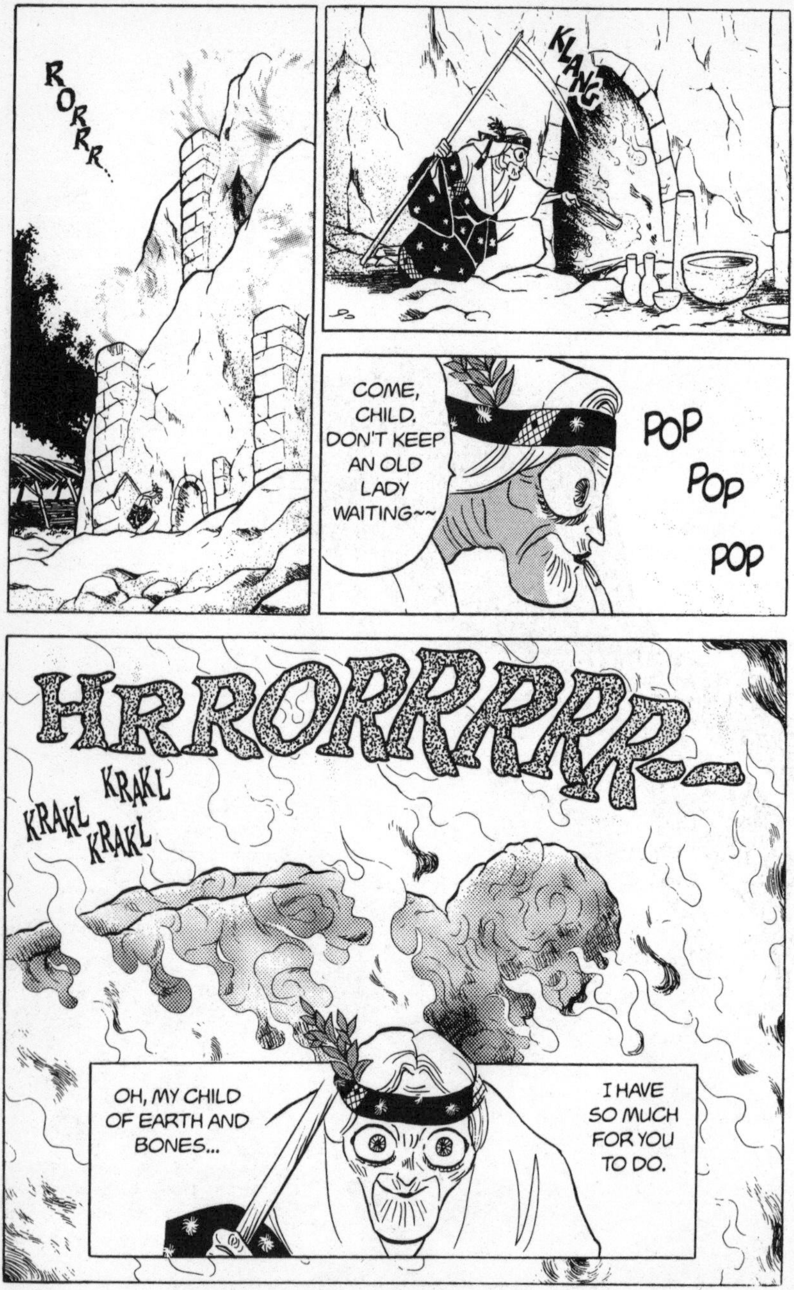
RORRR...
KLANG
COME, CHILD. DON'T KEEP AN OLD LADY WAITING~~
POP
POP
POP
HRRORRRRRR~
KRAKL
KRAKL
KRAKL
OH, MY CHILD OF EARTH AND BONES...
I HAVE SO MUCH FOR YOU TO DO.

SCROLL EIGHT
EMPTY SHELL

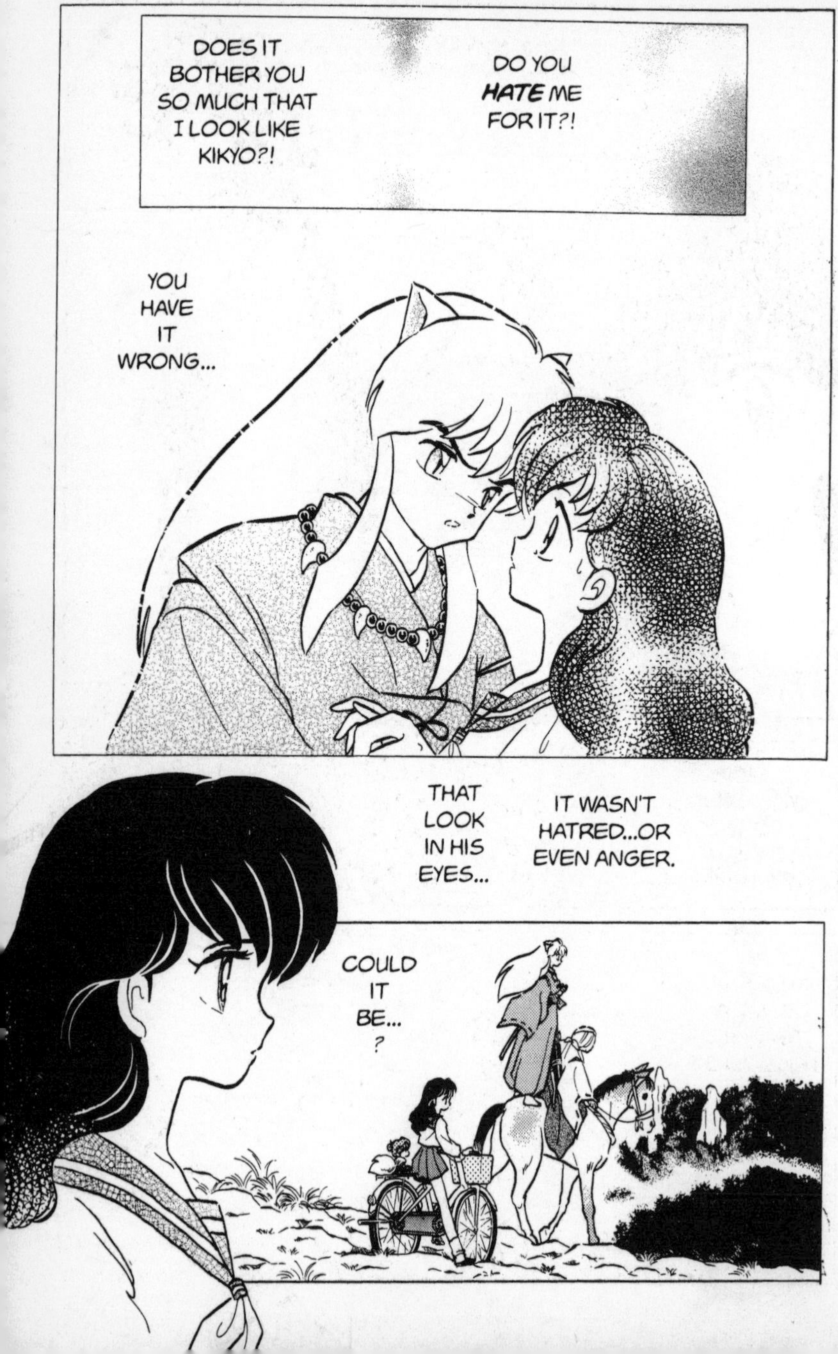
DOES IT BOTHER YOU SO MUCH THAT I LOOK LIKE KIKYO?!
DO YOU **HATE** ME FOR IT?!
YOU HAVE IT WRONG...
THAT LOOK IN HIS EYES...
IT WASN'T HATRED...OR EVEN ANGER.
COULD IT BE... ?

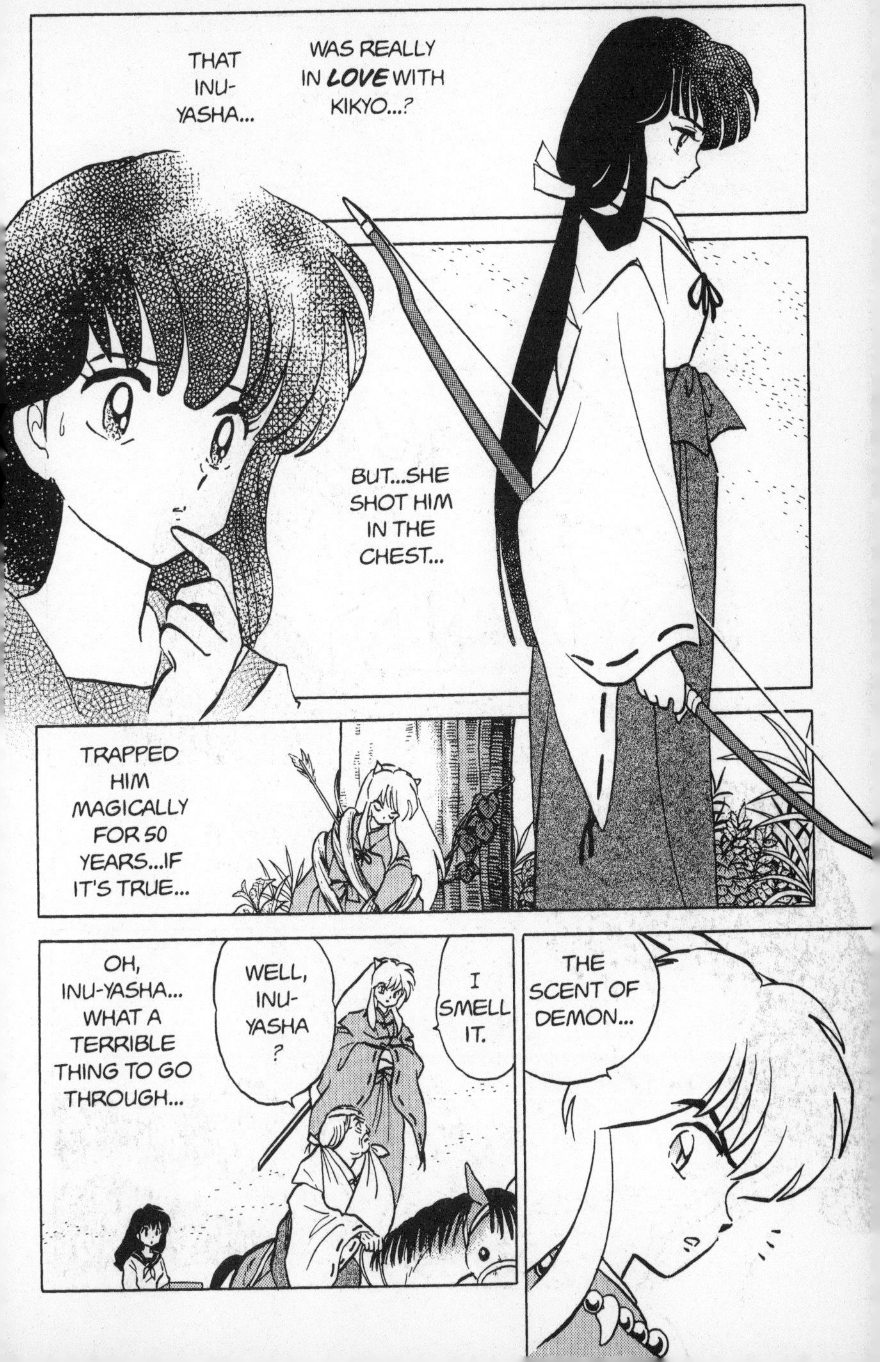
THAT INU-YASHA...
WAS REALLY IN **LOVE** WITH KIKYO...?
BUT...SHE SHOT HIM IN THE CHEST...
TRAPPED HIM MAGICALLY FOR 50 YEARS...IF IT'S TRUE...
OH, INU-YASHA... WHAT A TERRIBLE THING TO GO THROUGH...
WELL, INU-YASHA?
I SMELL IT.
THE SCENT OF DEMON...

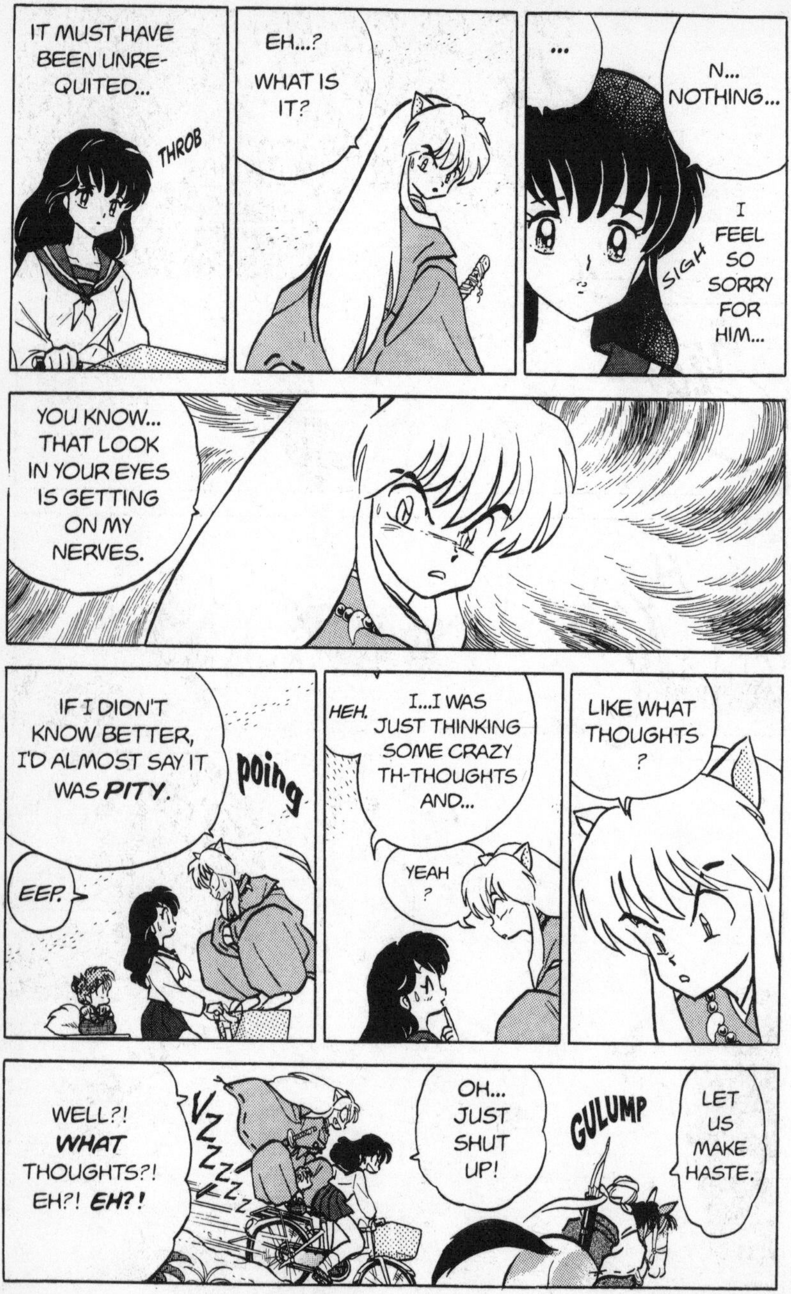
IT MUST HAVE BEEN UNRE-QUITED...
THROB
EH...?
WHAT IS IT?
...
N... NOTHING...
SIGH
I FEEL SO SORRY FOR HIM...
YOU KNOW... THAT LOOK IN YOUR EYES IS GETTING ON MY NERVES.
IF I DIDN'T KNOW BETTER, I'D ALMOST SAY IT WAS PITY.
poing
EEP.
HEH.
I...I WAS JUST THINKING SOME CRAZY TH-THOUGHTS AND...
YEAH?
LIKE WHAT THOUGHTS?
WELL?! WHAT THOUGHTS?! EH?! EH?!
VZZZZZZ
OH... JUST SHUT UP!
GULUMP
LET US MAKE HASTE.

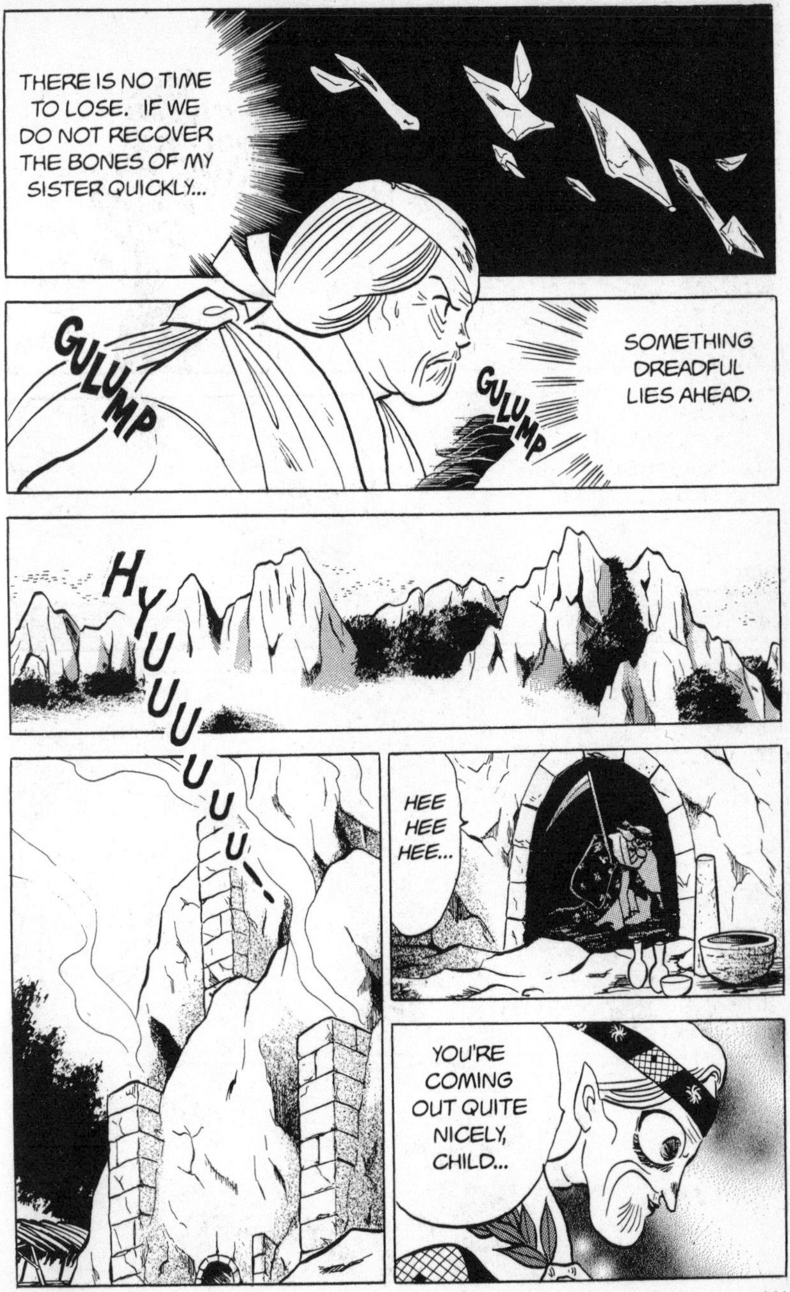
THERE IS NO TIME TO LOSE. IF WE DO NOT RECOVER THE BONES OF MY SISTER QUICKLY...
GULUMP
GULUMP
SOMETHING DREADFUL LIES AHEAD.
HYUUUUUUU...
HEE HEE HEE...
YOU'RE COMING OUT QUITE NICELY, CHILD...

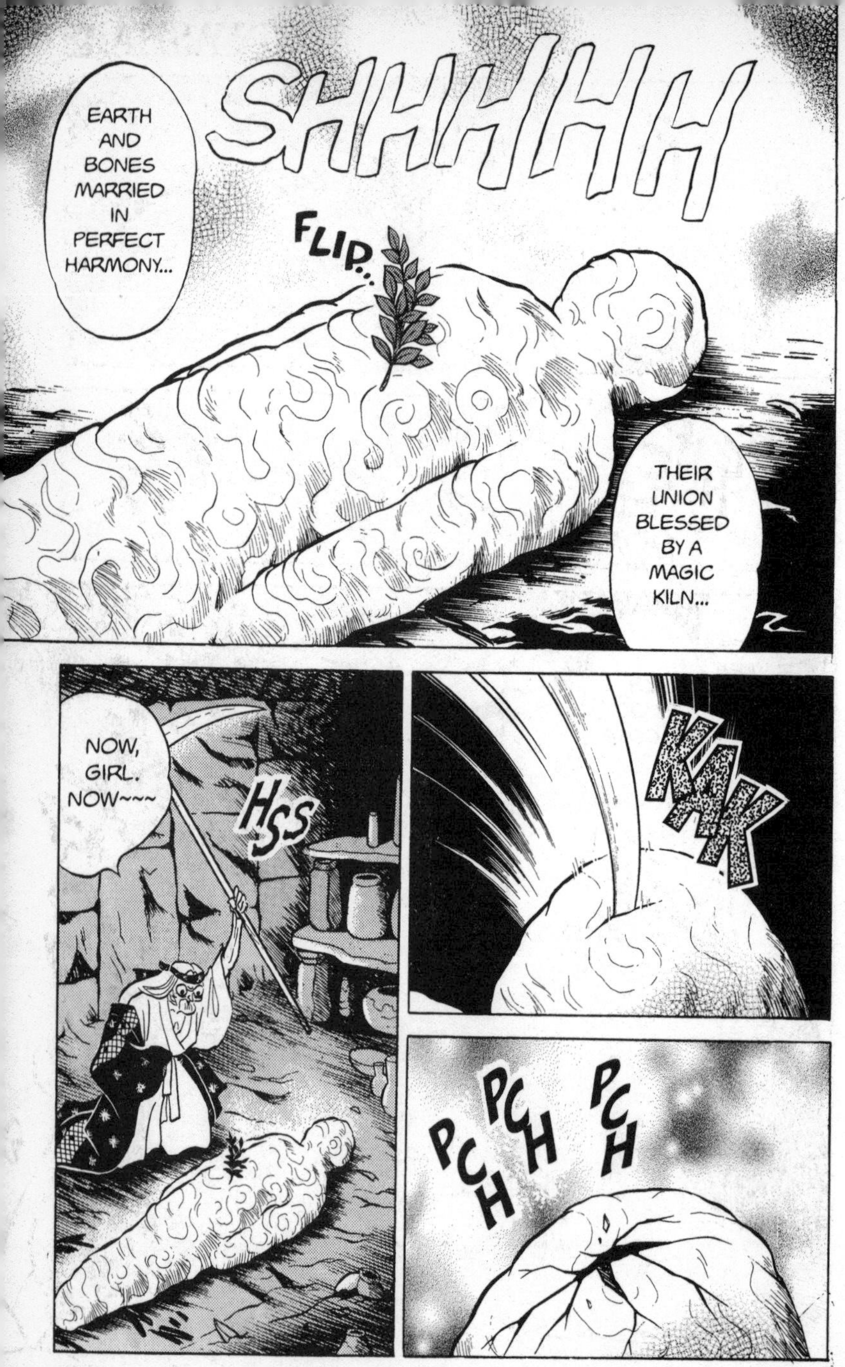

EARTH AND BONES MARRIED IN PERFECT HARMONY...
SHHHHH
FLIP...
THEIR UNION BLESSED BY A MAGIC KILN...
NOW, GIRL. NOW~~~
HSS
KAK
PCH
PCH
PCH

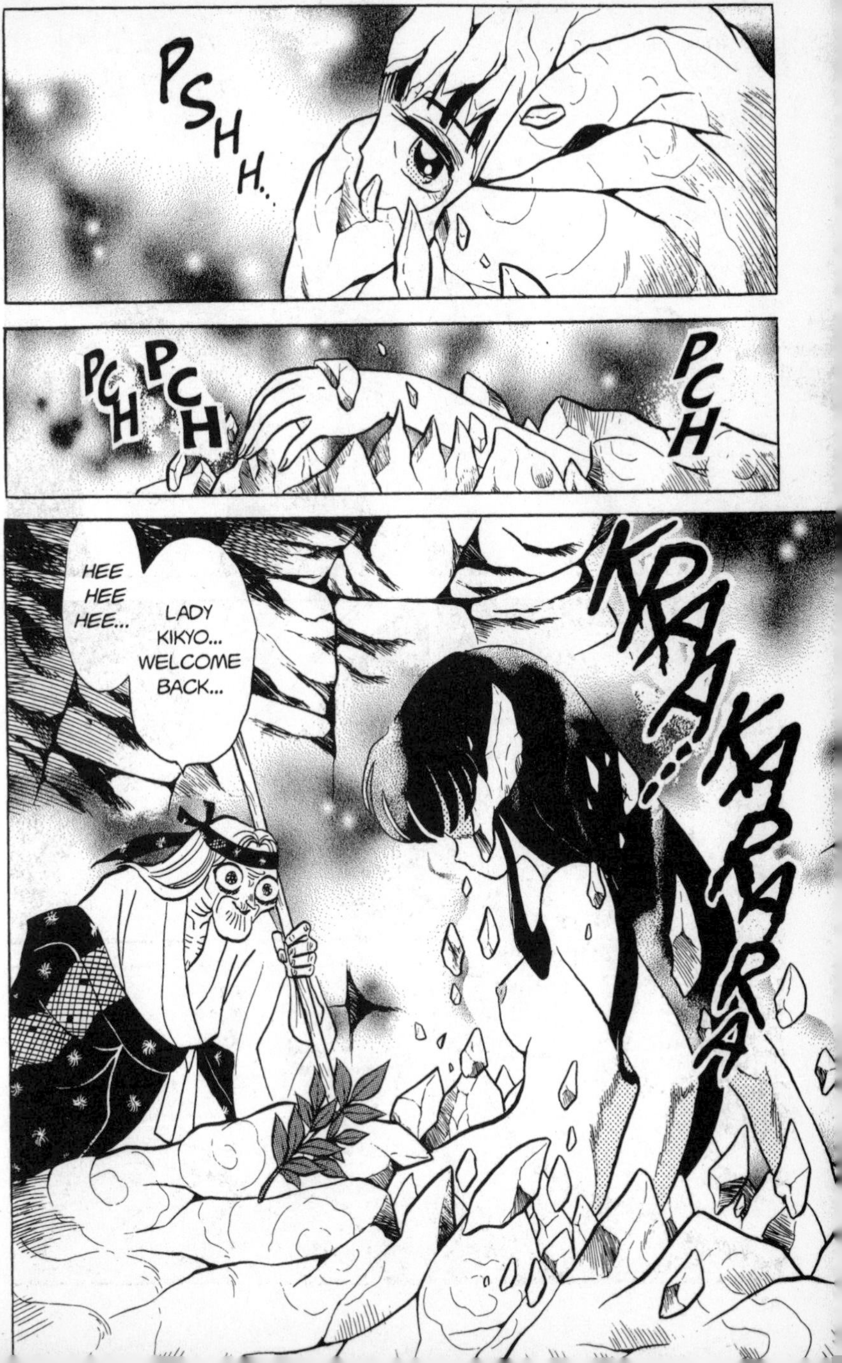
PSHH...
PCH PCH
PCH
HEE HEE HEE...
LADY KIKYO... WELCOME BACK...
KRAKAKARARA...

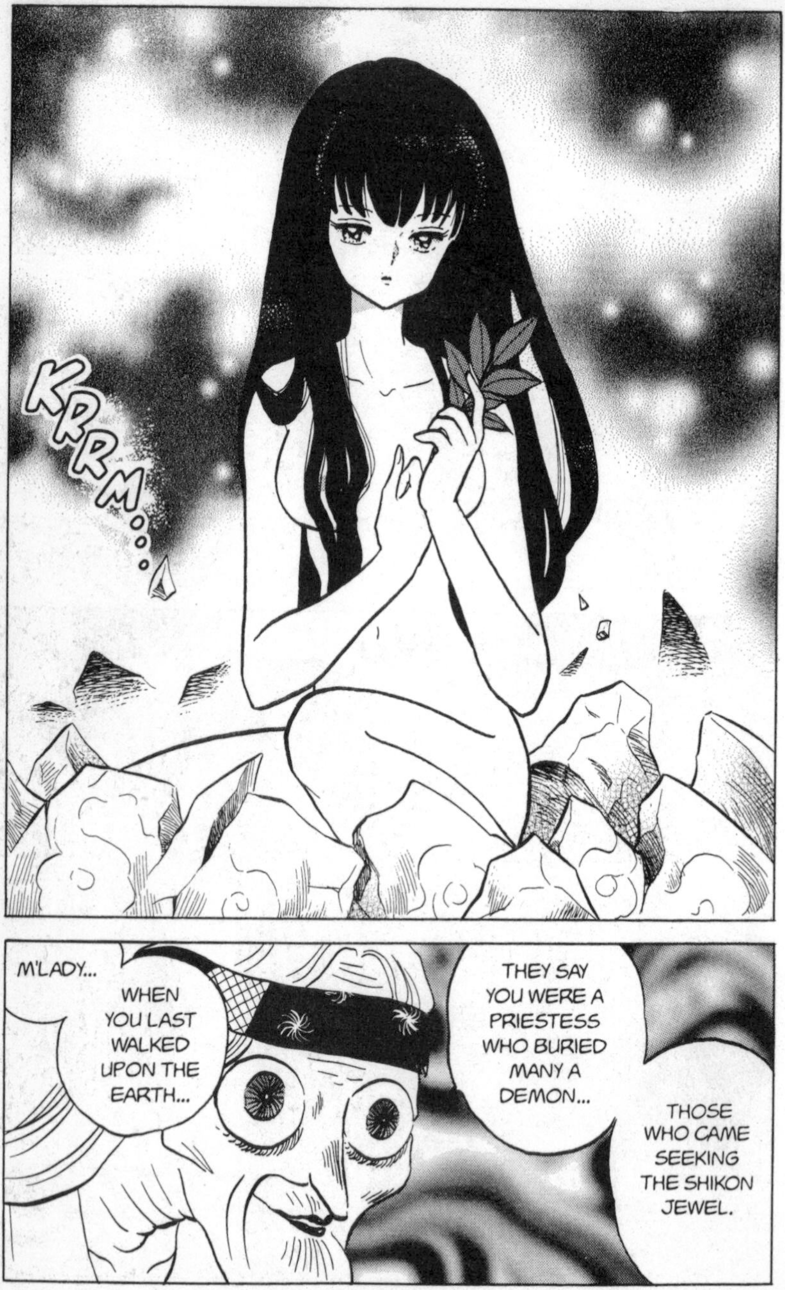
KRRM...
M'LADY...
WHEN YOU LAST WALKED UPON THE EARTH...
THEY SAY YOU WERE A PRIESTESS WHO BURIED MANY A DEMON...
THOSE WHO CAME SEEKING THE SHIKON JEWEL.

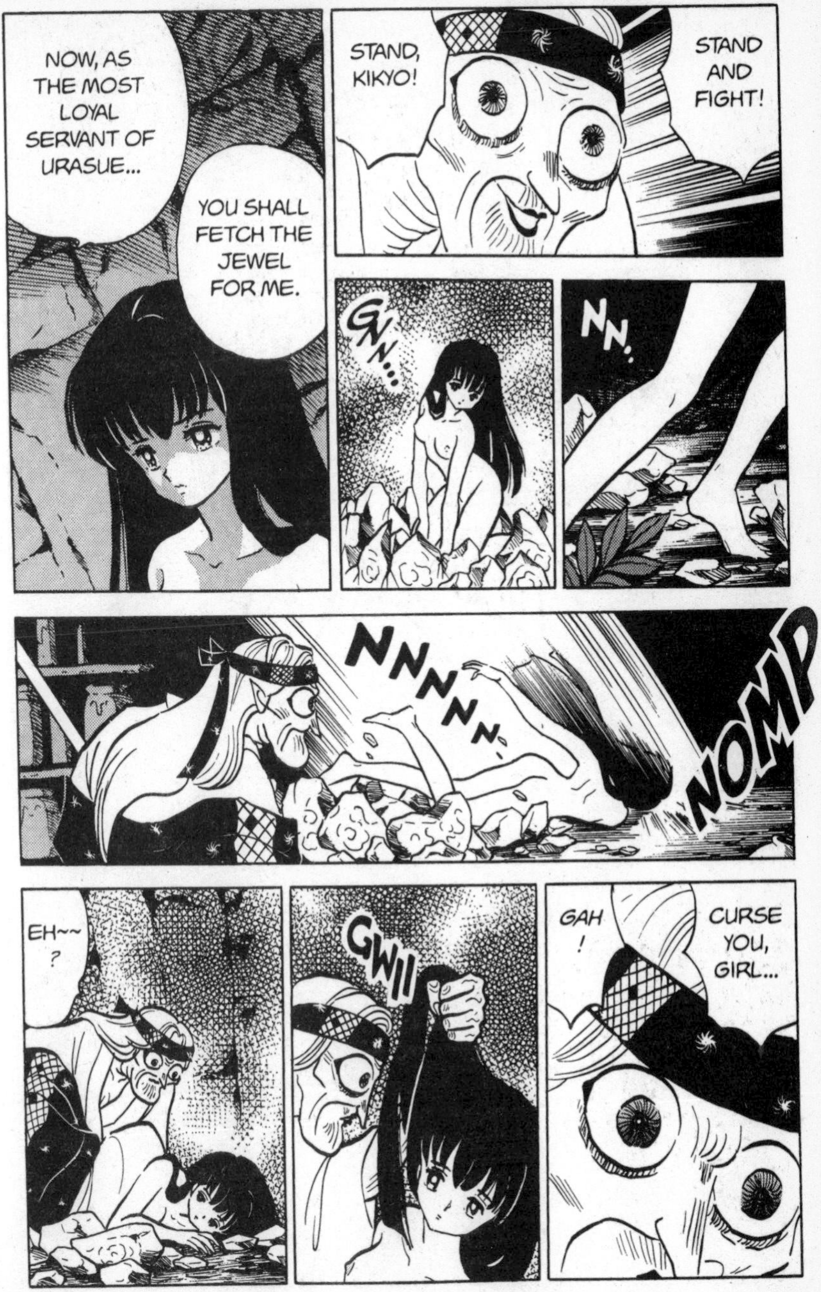
NOW, AS THE MOST LOYAL SERVANT OF URASUE...
YOU SHALL FETCH THE JEWEL FOR ME.
STAND, KIKYO!
STAND AND FIGHT!
GNN...
NN.
NNNNNN.
NOMP
EH~~?
GWII
GAH!
CURSE YOU, GIRL...

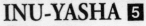

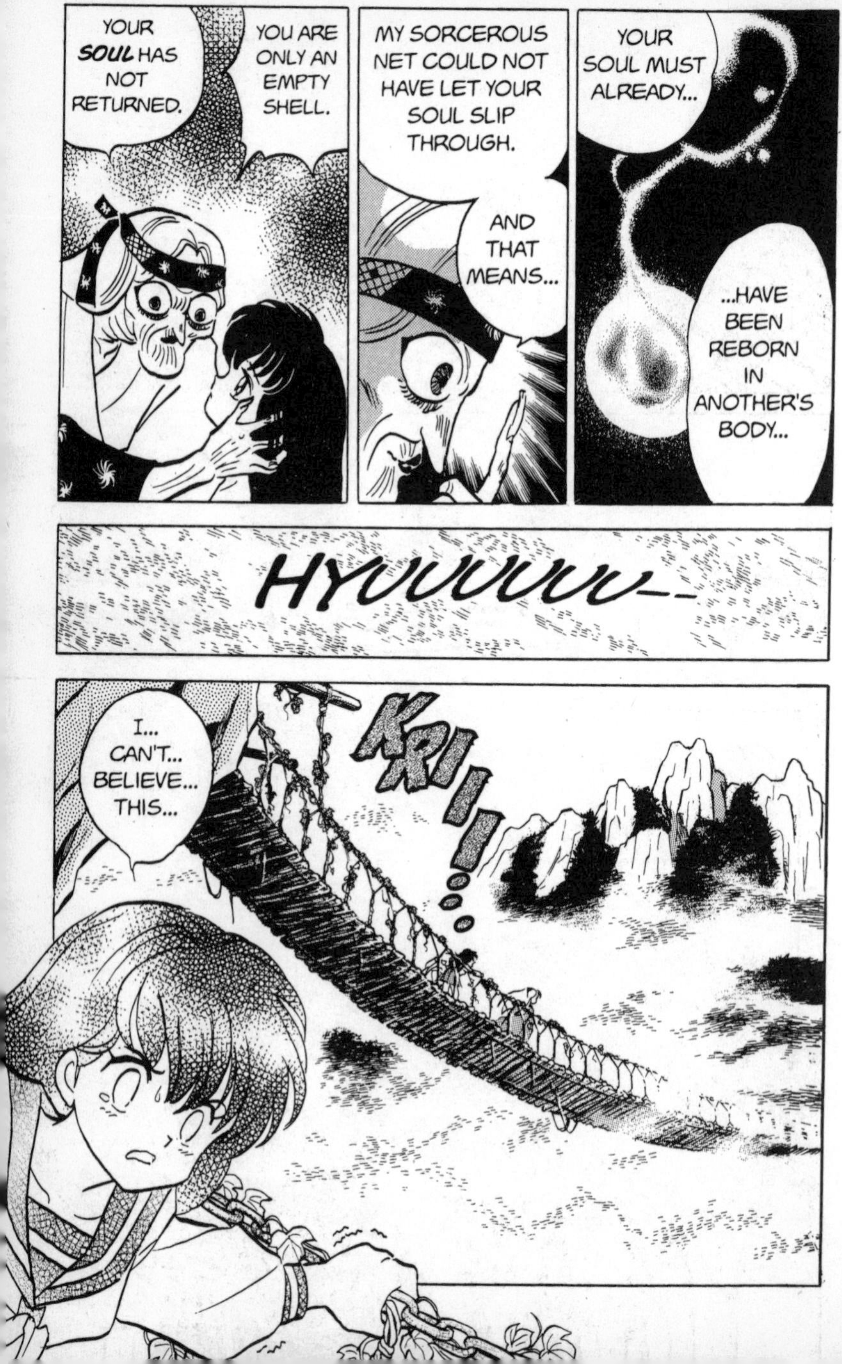
YOUR SOUL HAS NOT RETURNED.
YOU ARE ONLY AN EMPTY SHELL.
MY SORCEROUS NET COULD NOT HAVE LET YOUR SOUL SLIP THROUGH.
AND THAT MEANS...
YOUR SOUL MUST ALREADY...
...HAVE BEEN REBORN IN ANOTHER'S BODY...
HYUUUUUU--
I... CAN'T... BELIEVE... THIS...
KRIII...

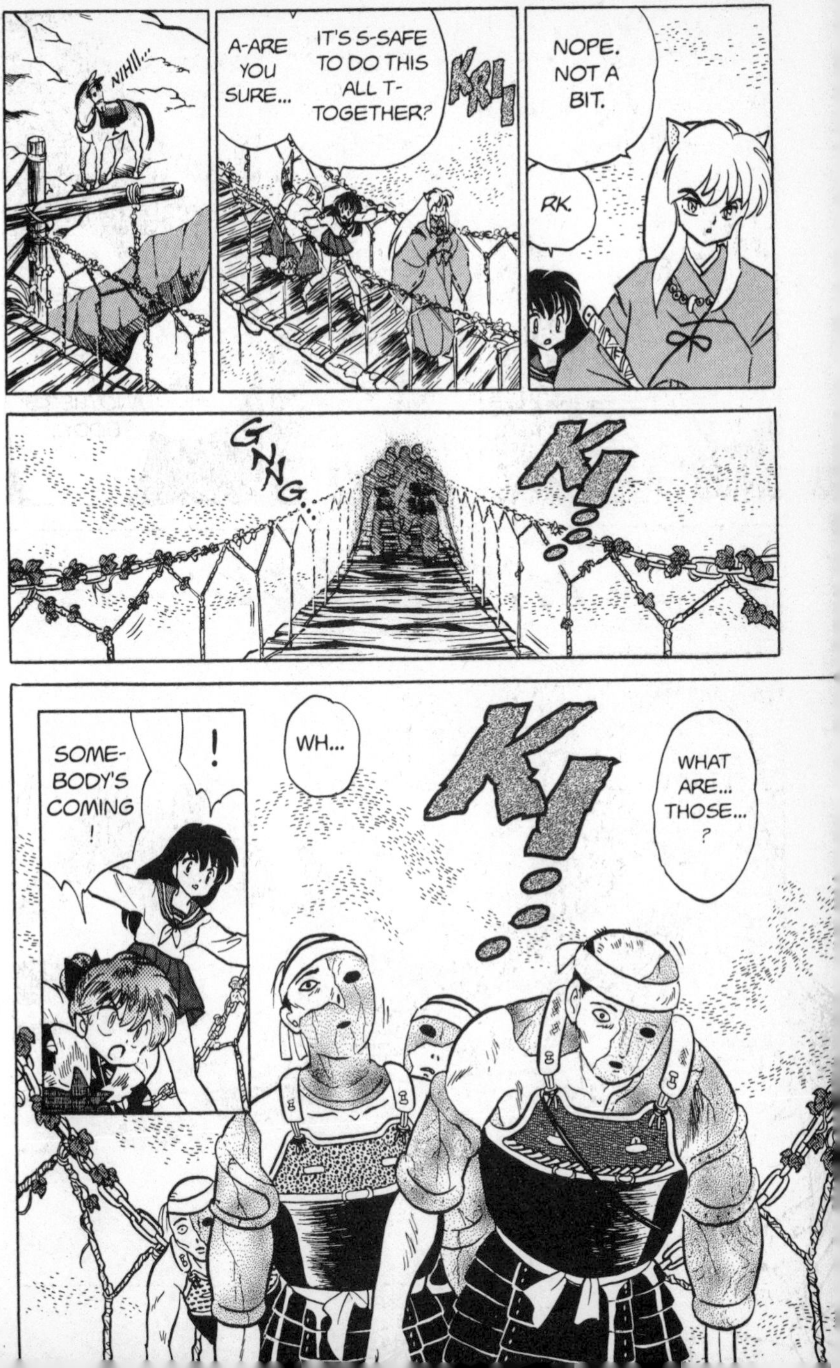
NIHI...
A-ARE YOU SURE...
IT'S S-SAFE TO DO THIS ALL T-TOGETHER?
KRI
NOPE. NOT A BIT.
RK.
GNNG...
KI...
SOME-BODY'S COMING!
!
WH...
KI...
WHAT ARE... THOSE...?

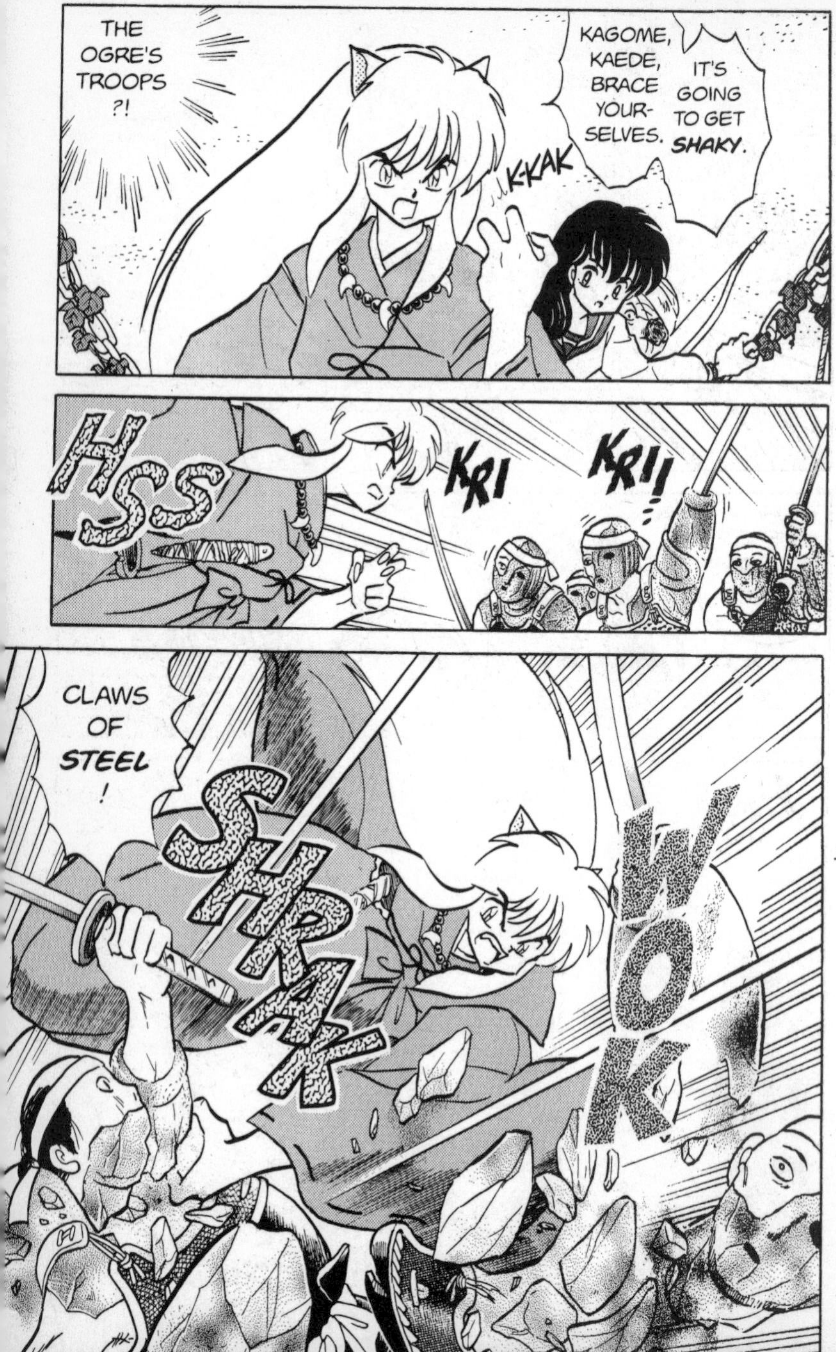
THE OGRE'S TROOPS ?!
KAGOME, KAEDE, BRACE YOUR-SELVES.
IT'S GOING TO GET SHAKY.
K-KAK
HSS
KRI
KRI!
CLAWS OF STEEL !
SHRAK
WOK

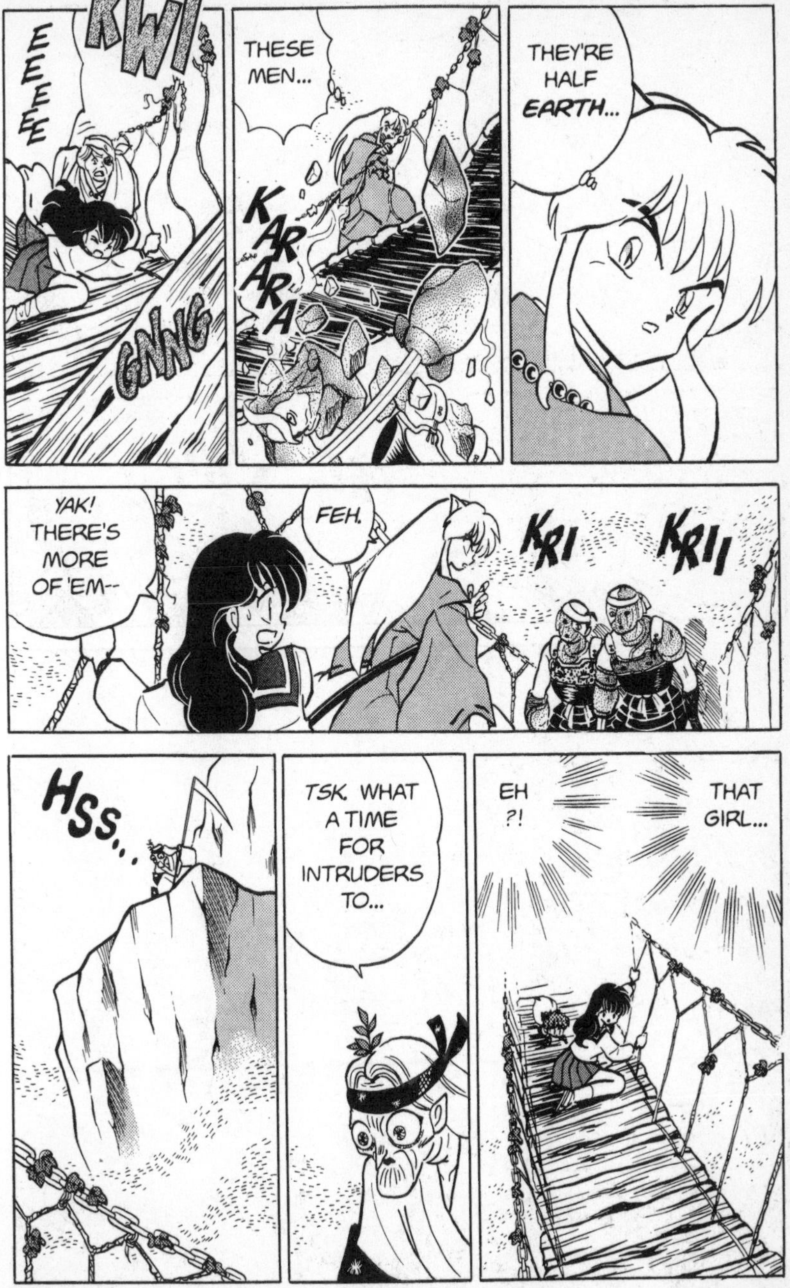
KWI
EEEEE
GNNG
THESE MEN...
KARARARA
THEY'RE HALF EARTH...
YAK! THERE'S MORE OF 'EM--
FEH.
KRI
KRII
HSS...
TSK. WHAT A TIME FOR INTRUDERS TO...
EH ?!
THAT GIRL...

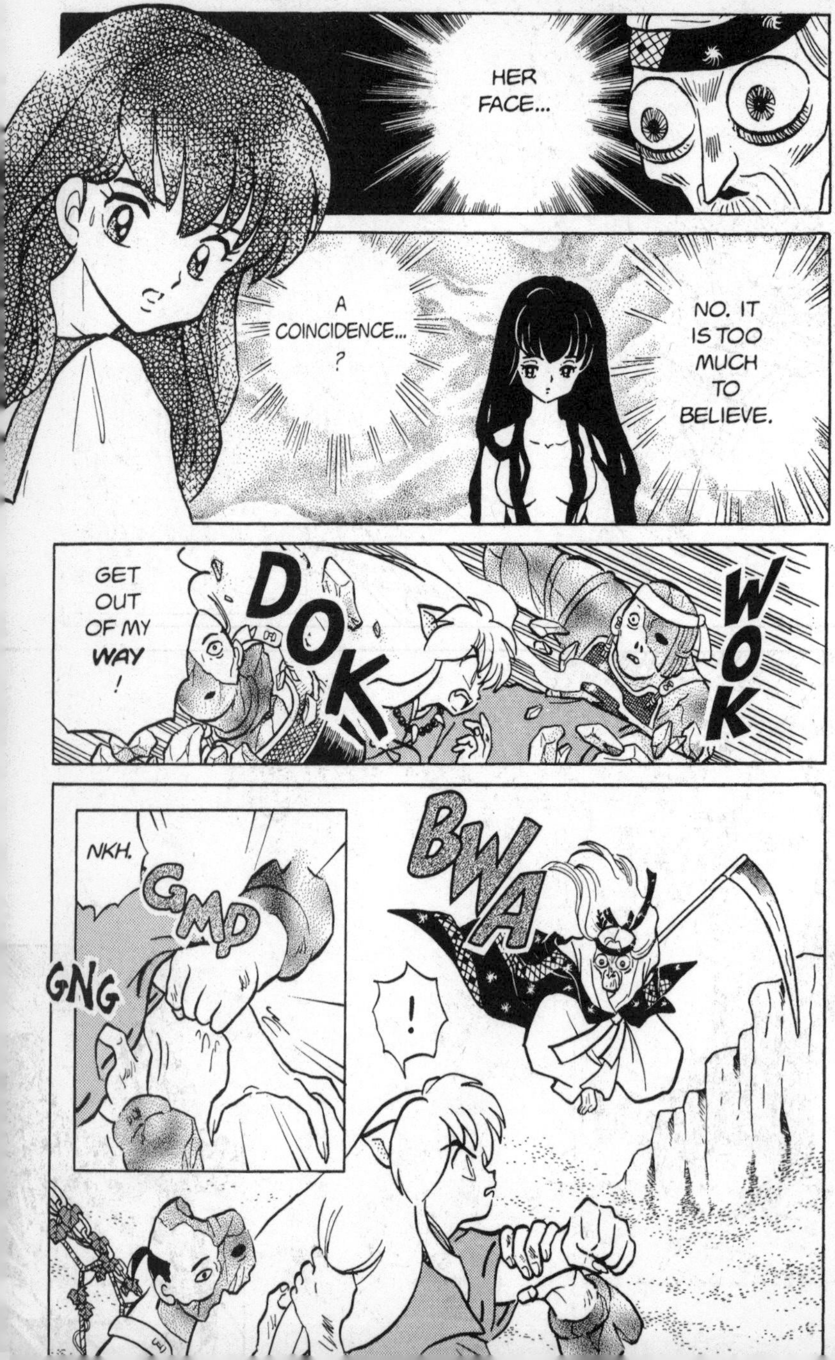
HER FACE...
A COINCIDENCE...?
NO. IT IS TOO MUCH TO BELIEVE.
GET OUT OF MY WAY!
DOK
WOK
NKH.
GMD
GNG
BWA
!

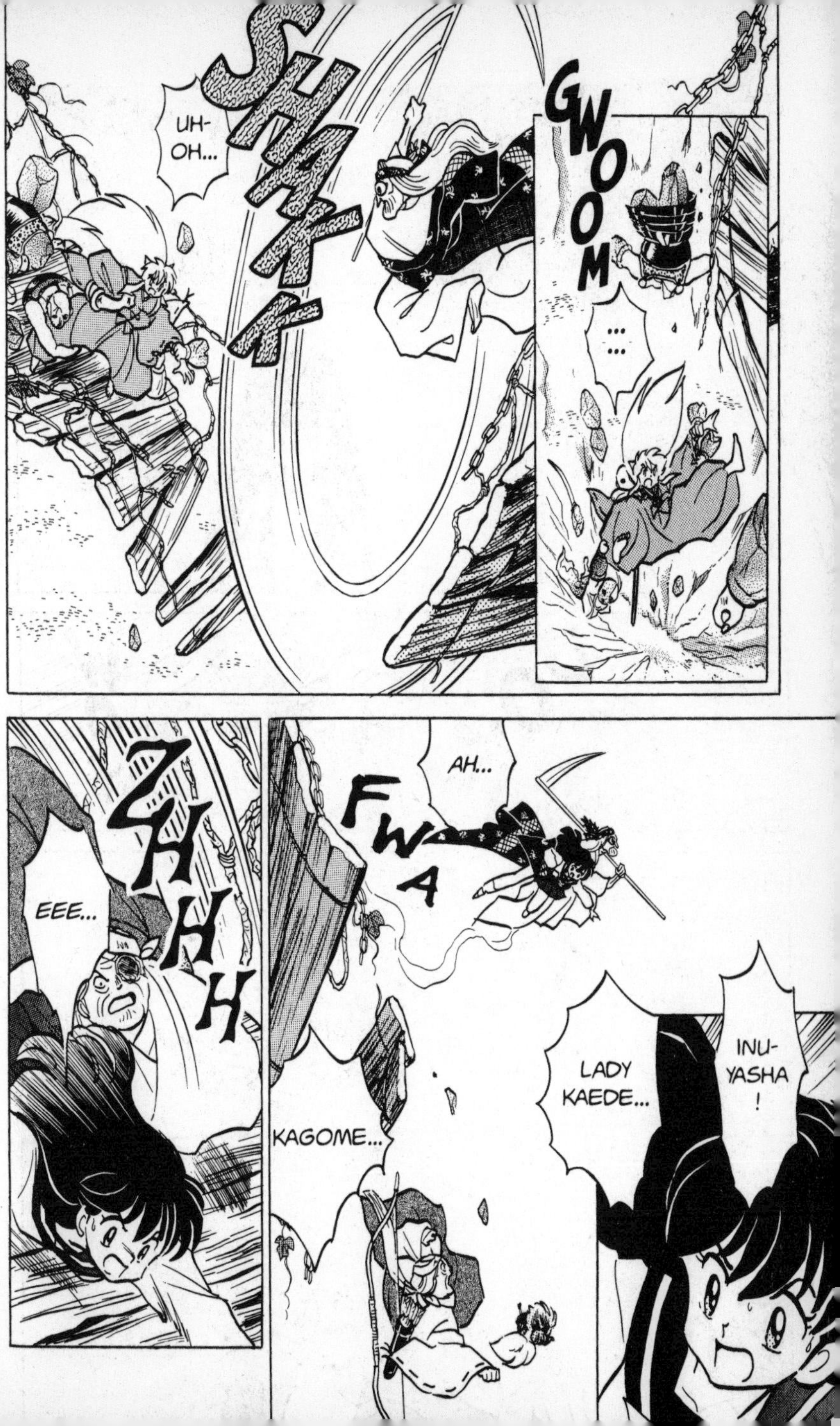
UH-OH...
SHAKKK
GWOOM
... ...
ZHHHH
EEE...
AH...
FWA
KAGOME...
LADY KAEDE...
INU-YASHA!

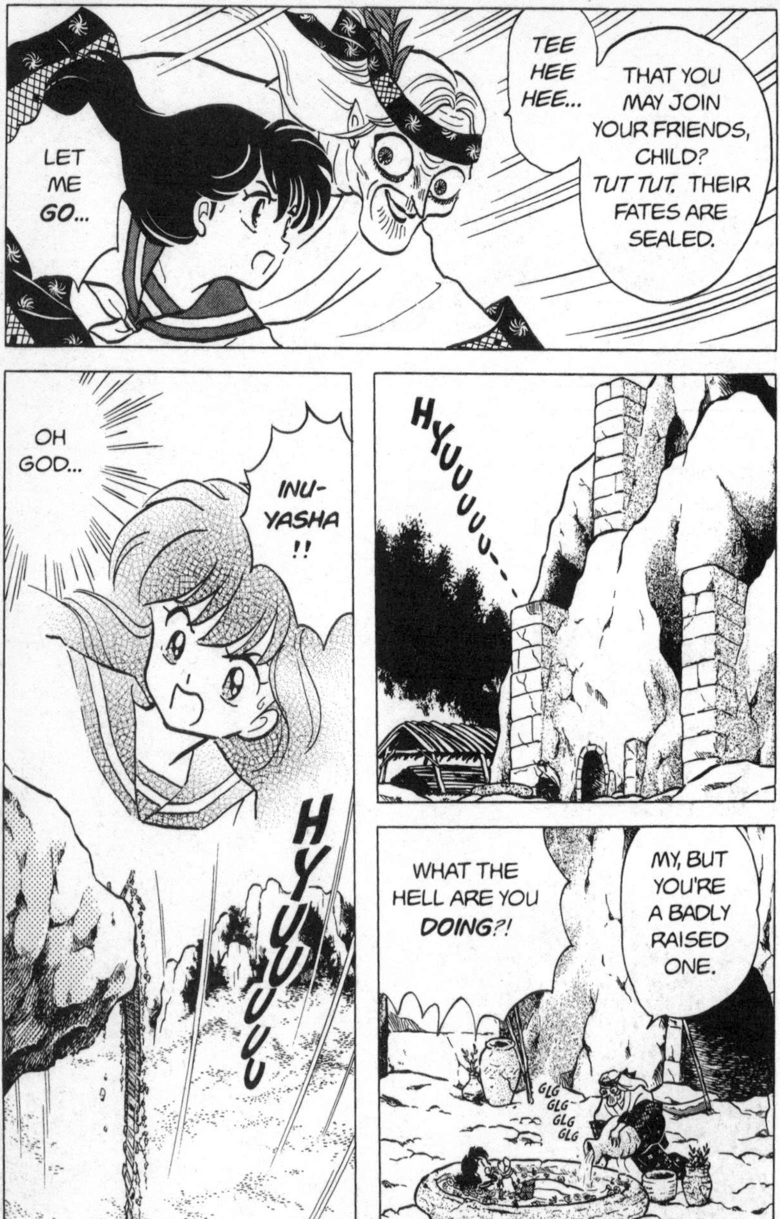
LET ME GO...
TEE HEE HEE...
THAT YOU MAY JOIN YOUR FRIENDS, CHILD? TUT TUT. THEIR FATES ARE SEALED.
OH GOD...
INU-YASHA!!
HYUUUUUUUU
HYUUUUU---
WHAT THE HELL ARE YOU DOING?!
MY, BUT YOU'RE A BADLY RAISED ONE.
GLG GLG GLG GLG

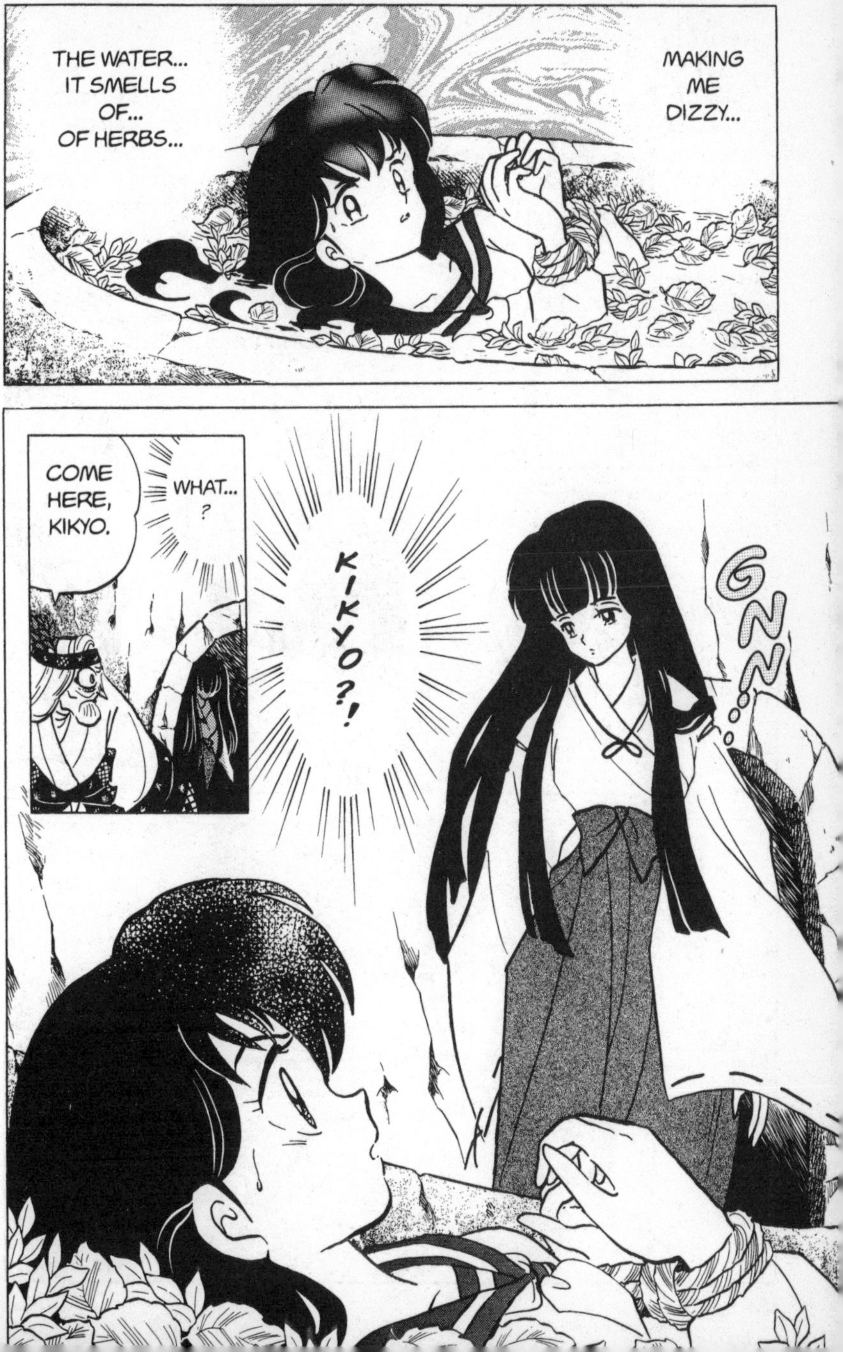
THE WATER... IT SMELLS OF... OF HERBS...
MAKING ME DIZZY...
COME HERE, KIKYO.
WHAT...?
KIKYO?!
GNN...

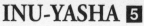

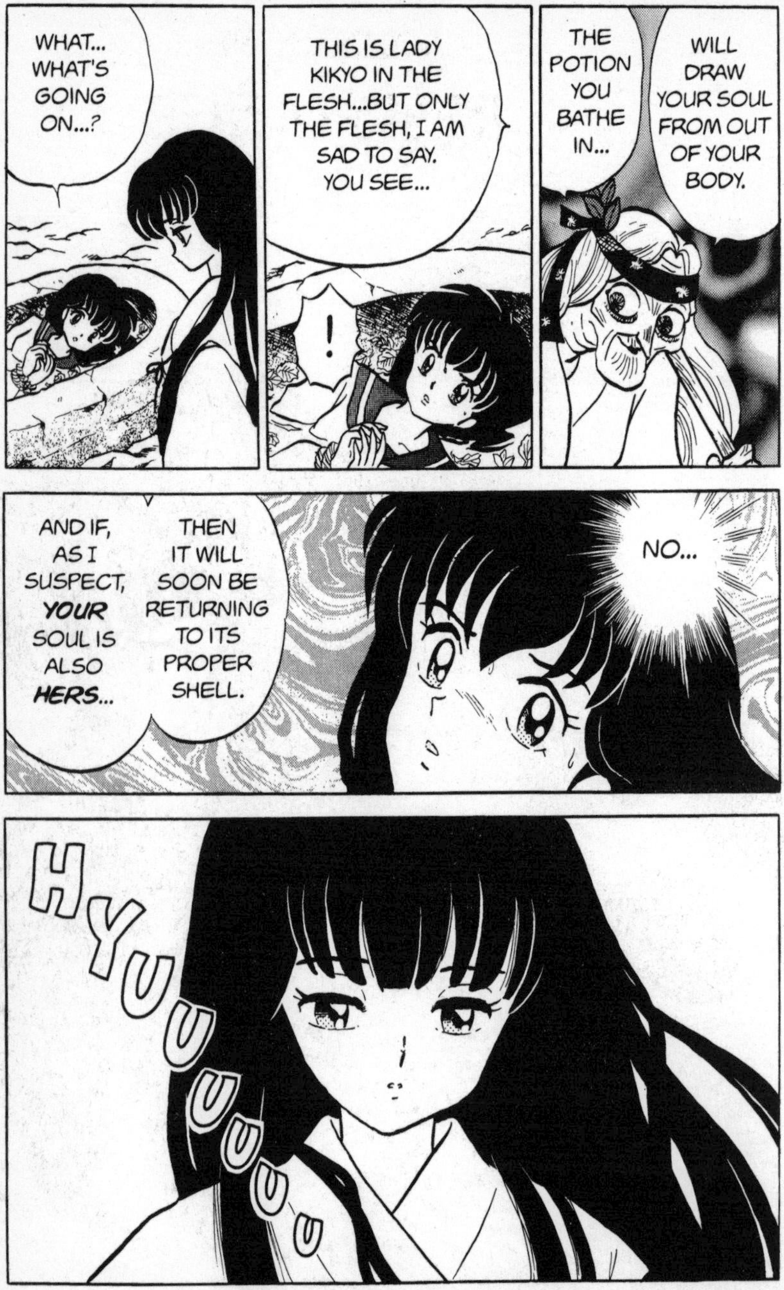
WHAT... WHAT'S GOING ON...?
THIS IS LADY KIKYO IN THE FLESH...BUT ONLY THE FLESH, I AM SAD TO SAY. YOU SEE...
!
THE POTION YOU BATHE IN...
WILL DRAW YOUR SOUL FROM OUT OF YOUR BODY.
AND IF, AS I SUSPECT, YOUR SOUL IS ALSO HERS...
THEN IT WILL SOON BE RETURNING TO ITS PROPER SHELL.
NO...
HYUUUUUUUU

SCROLL NINE
RESISTANCE

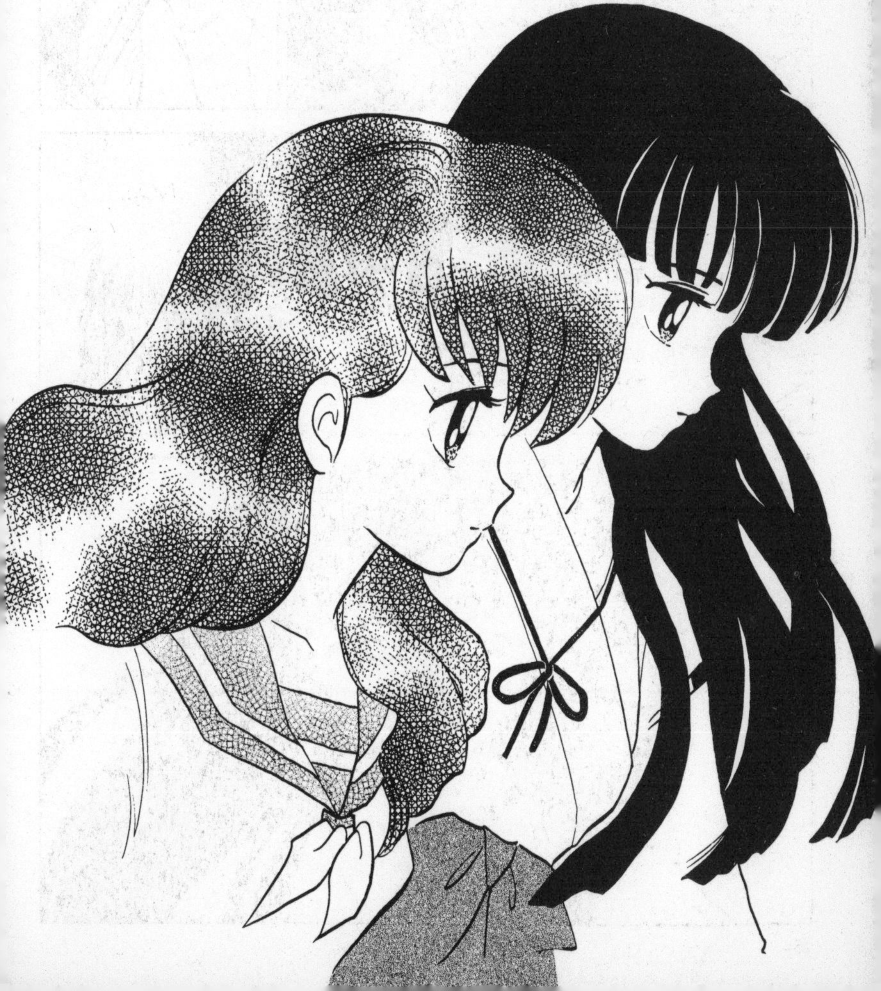

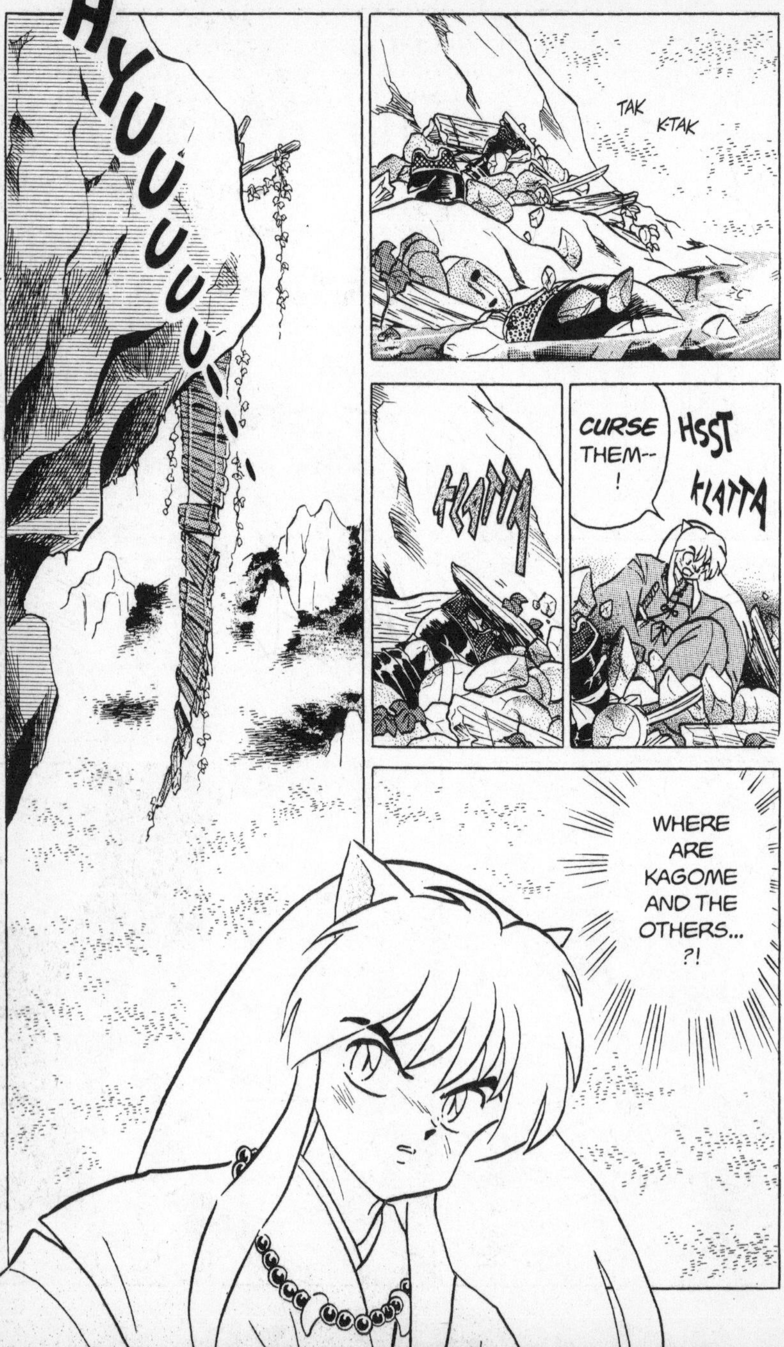
HYUUUU...
TAK
K-TAK
KLATTA
CURSE THEM--!
HSST
KLATTA
WHERE ARE KAGOME AND THE OTHERS...?!

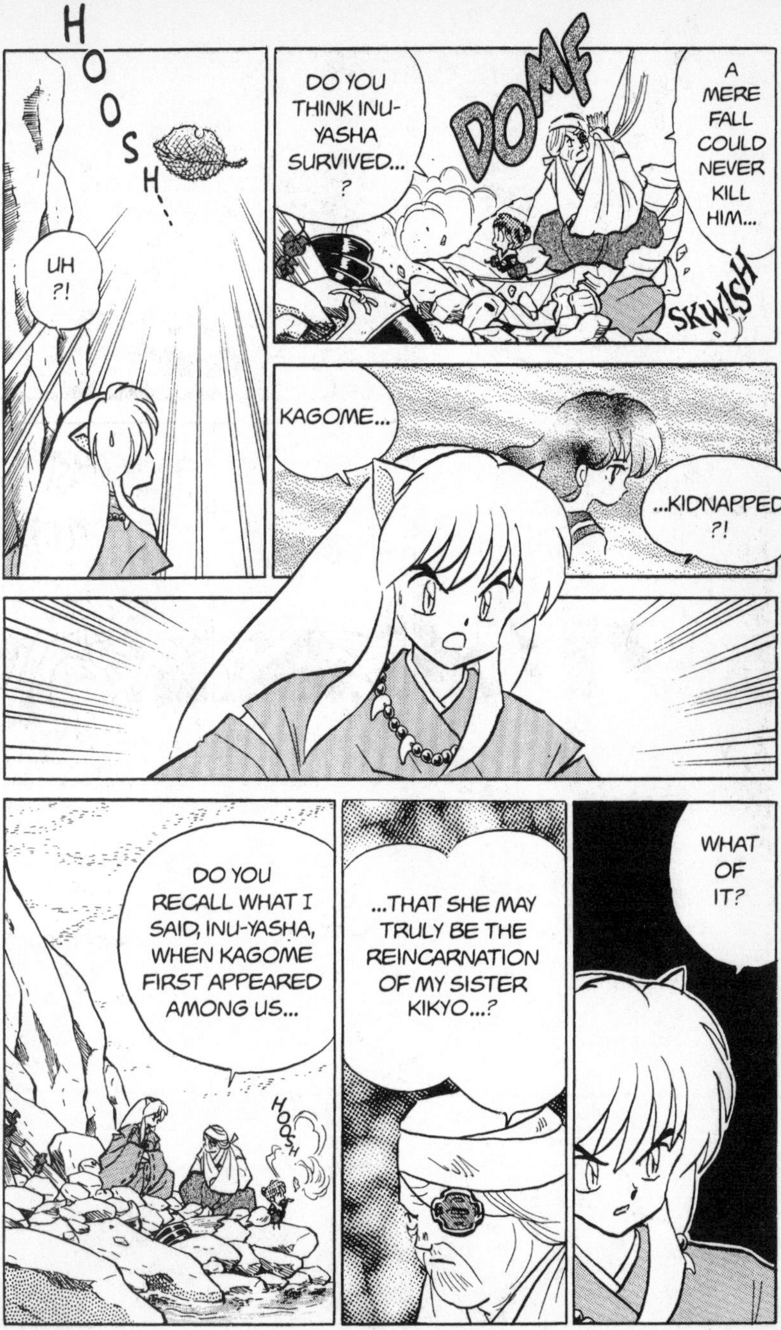
HOOSH
UH ?!
DO YOU THINK INU-YASHA SURVIVED... ?
DOMF
A MERE FALL COULD NEVER KILL HIM...
SKWISH
KAGOME...
...KIDNAPPED ?!
DO YOU RECALL WHAT I SAID, INU-YASHA, WHEN KAGOME FIRST APPEARED AMONG US...
HOOSH
...THAT SHE MAY TRULY BE THE REINCARNATION OF MY SISTER KIKYO...?
WHAT OF IT?

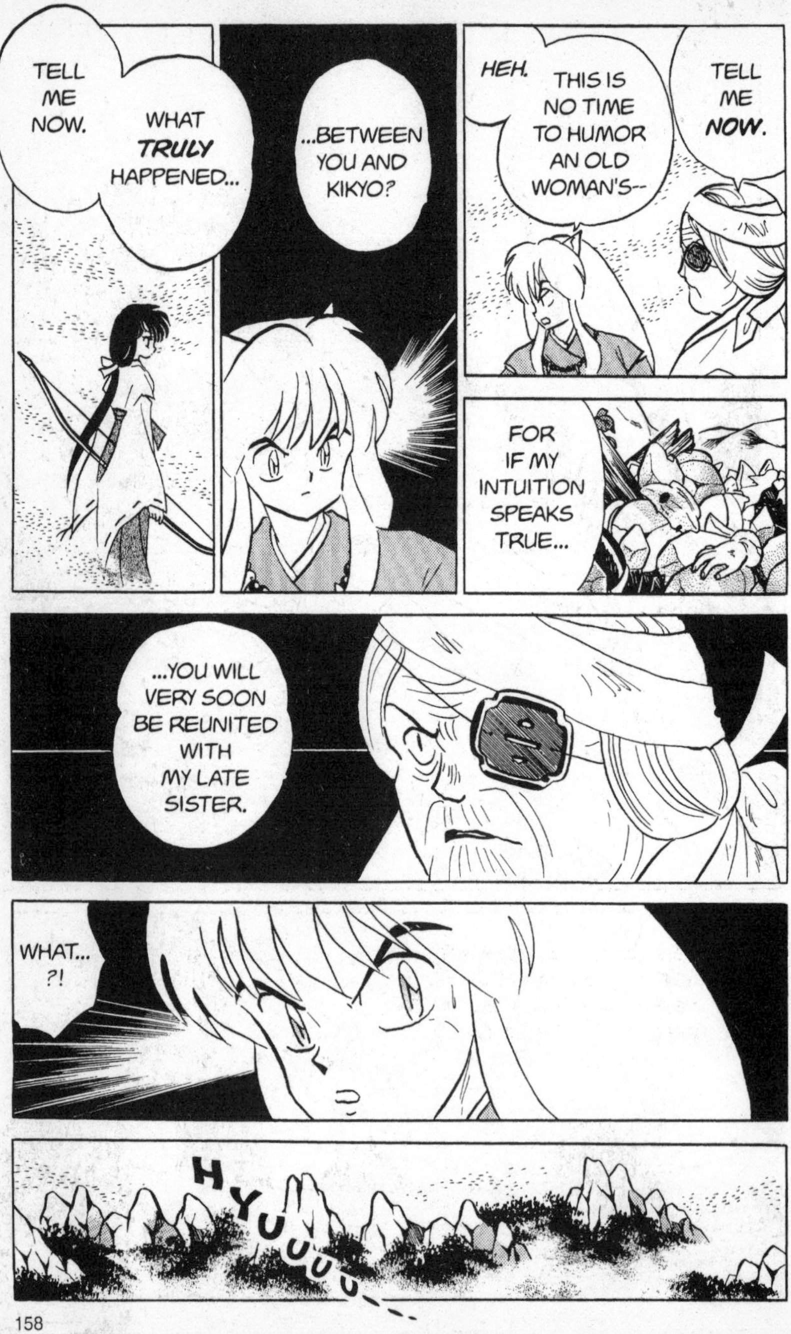
TELL ME NOW.
WHAT TRULY HAPPENED...
...BETWEEN YOU AND KIKYO?
HEH.
THIS IS NO TIME TO HUMOR AN OLD WOMAN'S--
TELL ME NOW.
FOR IF MY INTUITION SPEAKS TRUE...
...YOU WILL VERY SOON BE REUNITED WITH MY LATE SISTER.
WHAT... ?!
HYUUUUU---

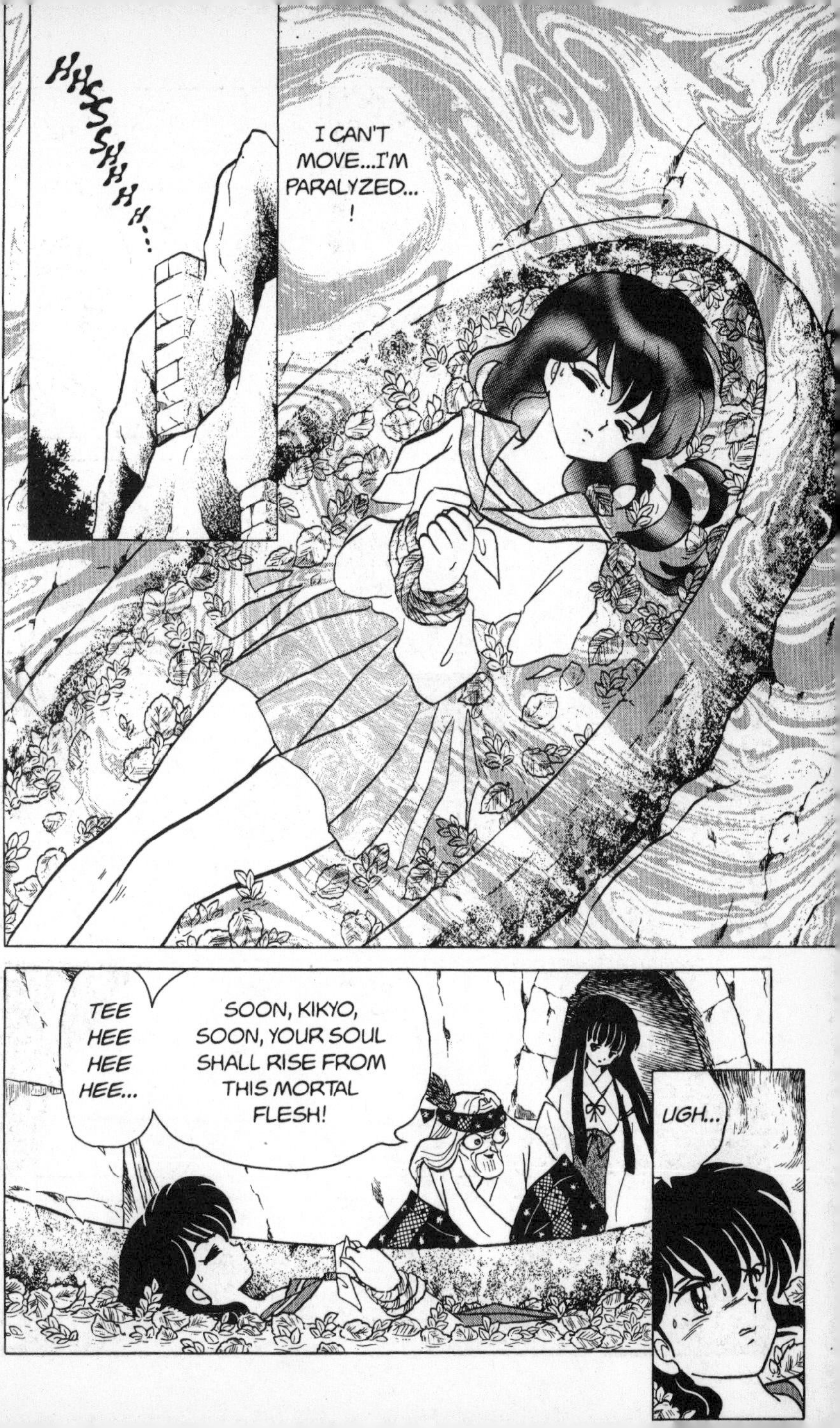
HHSSHHH...
I CAN'T MOVE...I'M PARALYZED... !
TEE HEE HEE HEE...
SOON, KIKYO, SOON, YOUR SOUL SHALL RISE FROM THIS MORTAL FLESH!
UGH...

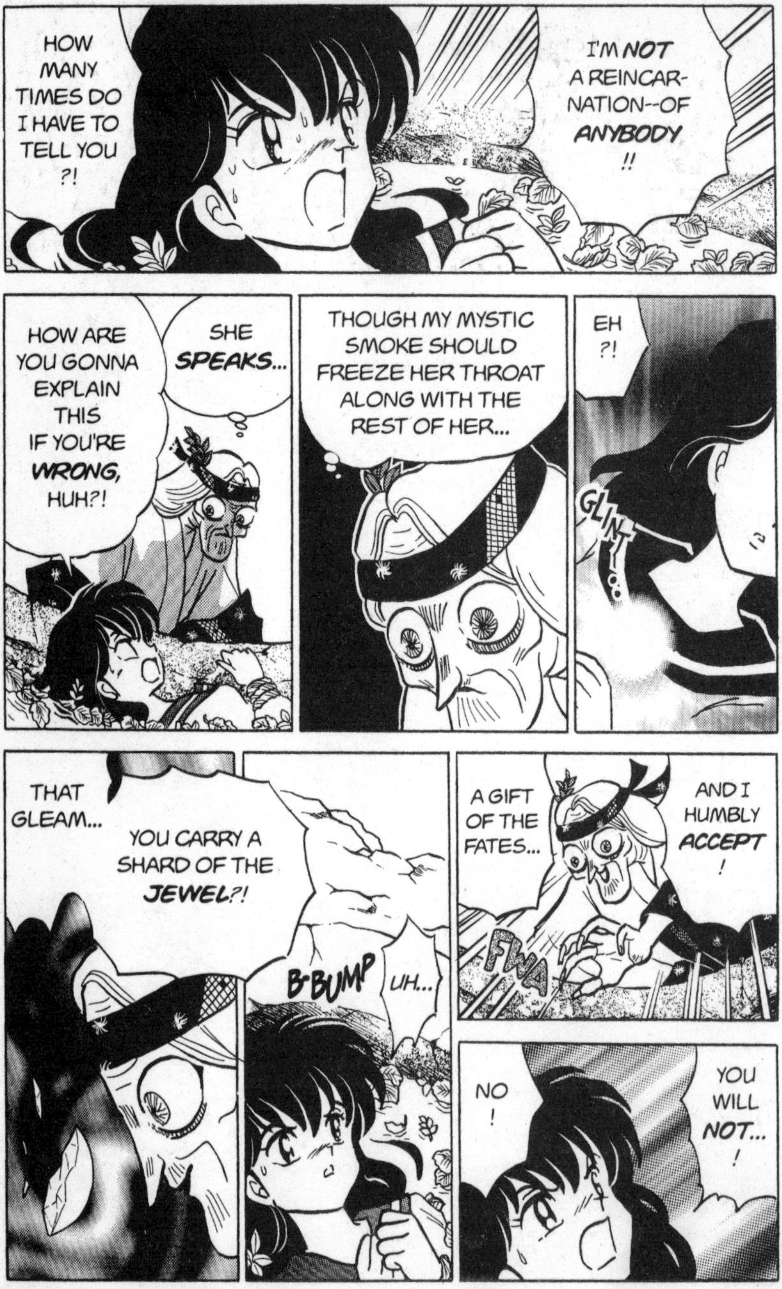
HOW MANY TIMES DO I HAVE TO TELL YOU ?!
I'M NOT A REINCAR-NATION--OF ANYBODY !!
HOW ARE YOU GONNA EXPLAIN THIS IF YOU'RE WRONG, HUH?!
SHE SPEAKS...
THOUGH MY MYSTIC SMOKE SHOULD FREEZE HER THROAT ALONG WITH THE REST OF HER...
EH ?!
GLINT
THAT GLEAM...
YOU CARRY A SHARD OF THE JEWEL?!
B-BUMP
UH...
A GIFT OF THE FATES...
AND I HUMBLY ACCEPT !
FWA
NO !
YOU WILL NOT... !

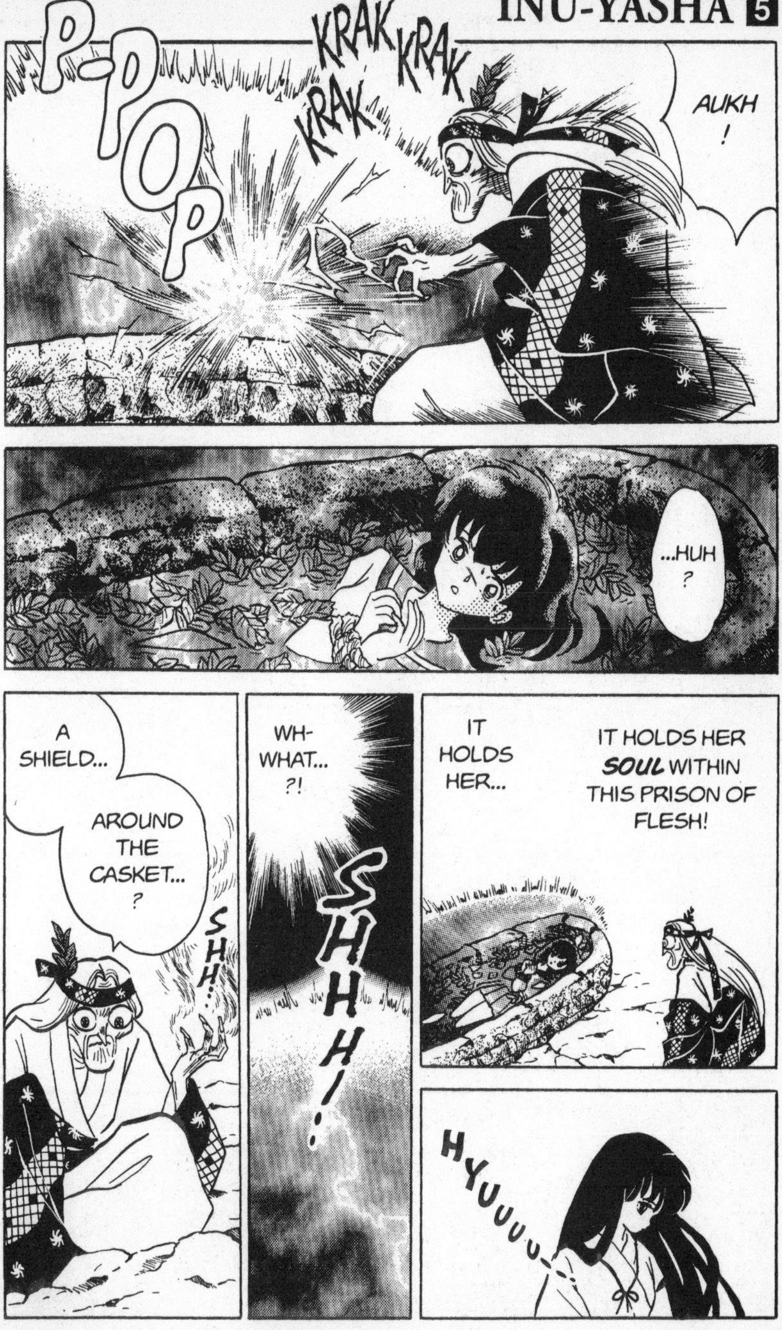
P-POP
KRAK KRAK KRAK
AUKH!
...HUH?
A SHIELD...
AROUND THE CASKET...?
SHH...
WH-WHAT...?!
SHHHH!!
IT HOLDS HER...
IT HOLDS HER **SOUL** WITHIN THIS PRISON OF FLESH!
HYUUUU...

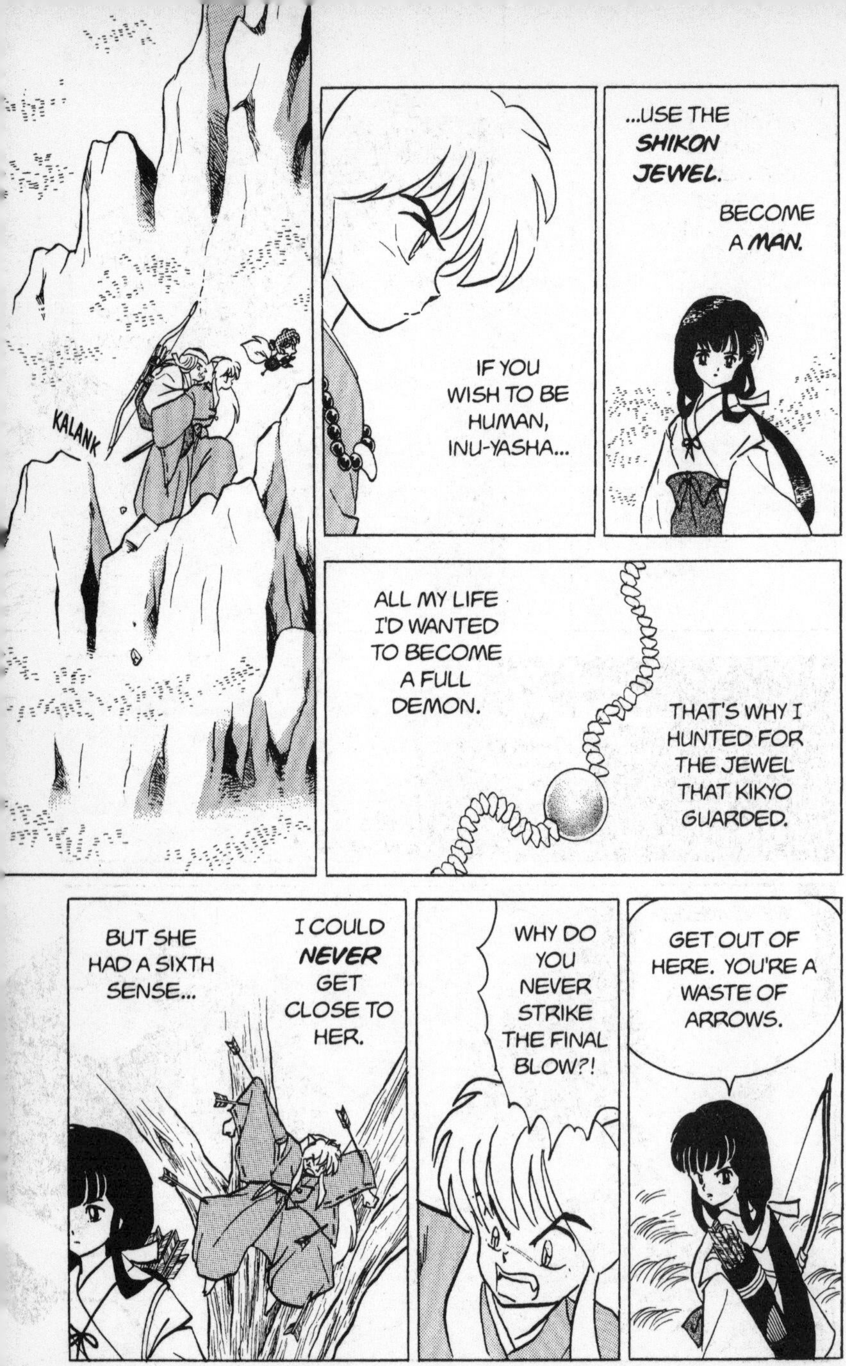
KALANK
IF YOU WISH TO BE HUMAN, INU-YASHA...
...USE THE SHIKON JEWEL.
BECOME A MAN.
ALL MY LIFE I'D WANTED TO BECOME A FULL DEMON.
THAT'S WHY I HUNTED FOR THE JEWEL THAT KIKYO GUARDED.
BUT SHE HAD A SIXTH SENSE...
I COULD NEVER GET CLOSE TO HER.
WHY DO YOU NEVER STRIKE THE FINAL BLOW?!
GET OUT OF HERE. YOU'RE A WASTE OF ARROWS.

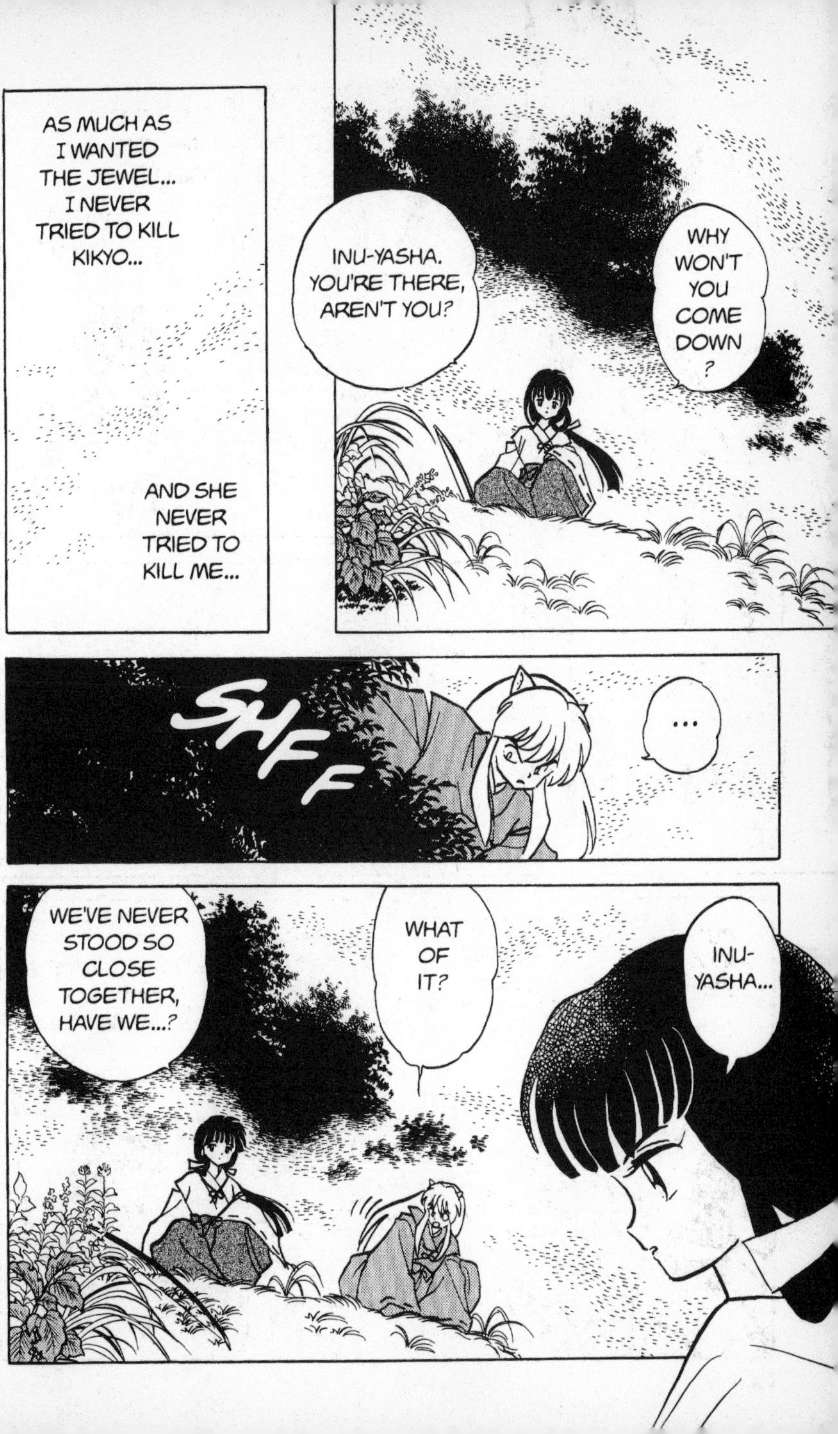
AS MUCH AS I WANTED THE JEWEL... I NEVER TRIED TO KILL KIKYO...
AND SHE NEVER TRIED TO KILL ME...
INU-YASHA. YOU'RE THERE, AREN'T YOU?
WHY WON'T YOU COME DOWN?
SHFF
...
WE'VE NEVER STOOD SO CLOSE TOGETHER, HAVE WE...?
WHAT OF IT?
INU-YASHA...

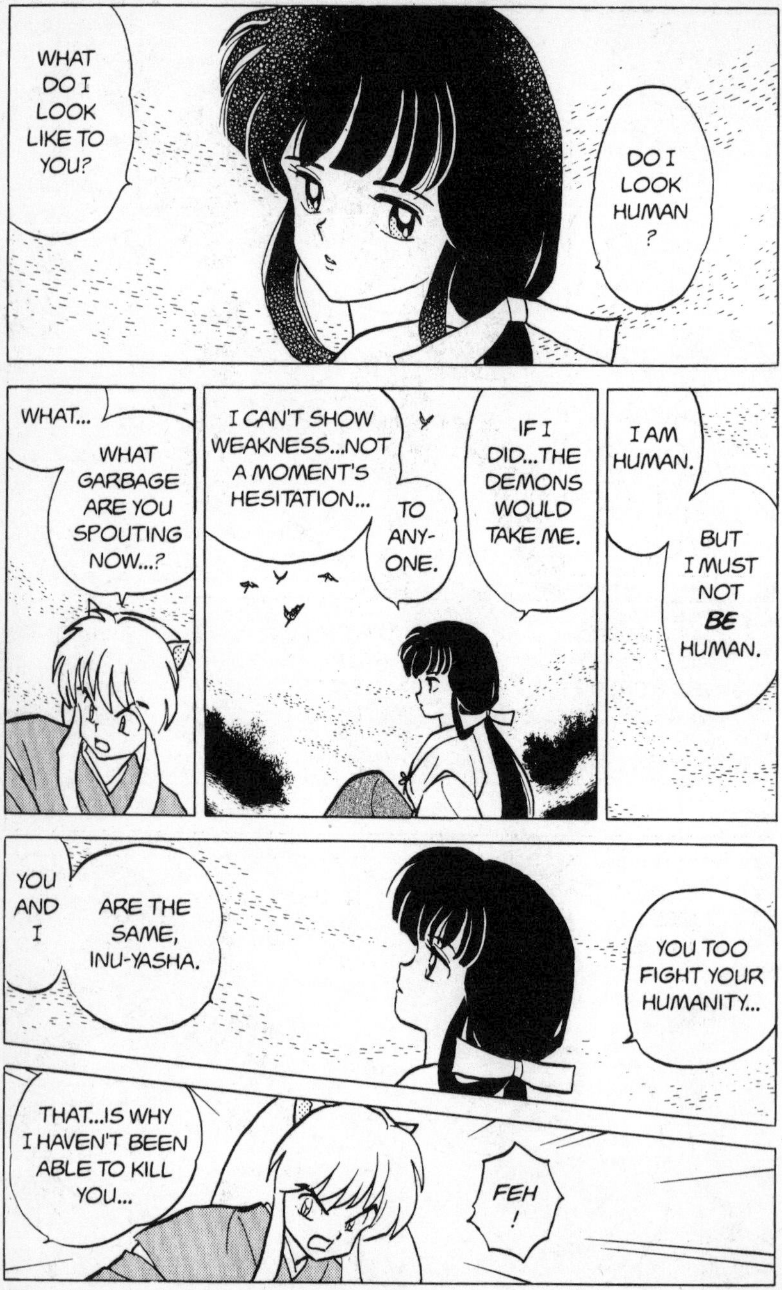
WHAT DO I LOOK LIKE TO YOU?
DO I LOOK HUMAN ?
WHAT...
WHAT GARBAGE ARE YOU SPOUTING NOW...?
I CAN'T SHOW WEAKNESS...NOT A MOMENT'S HESITATION...
TO ANY-ONE.
IF I DID...THE DEMONS WOULD TAKE ME.
I AM HUMAN.
BUT I MUST NOT *BE* HUMAN.
YOU AND I
ARE THE SAME, INU-YASHA.
YOU TOO FIGHT YOUR HUMANITY...
THAT...IS WHY I HAVEN'T BEEN ABLE TO KILL YOU...
FEH !

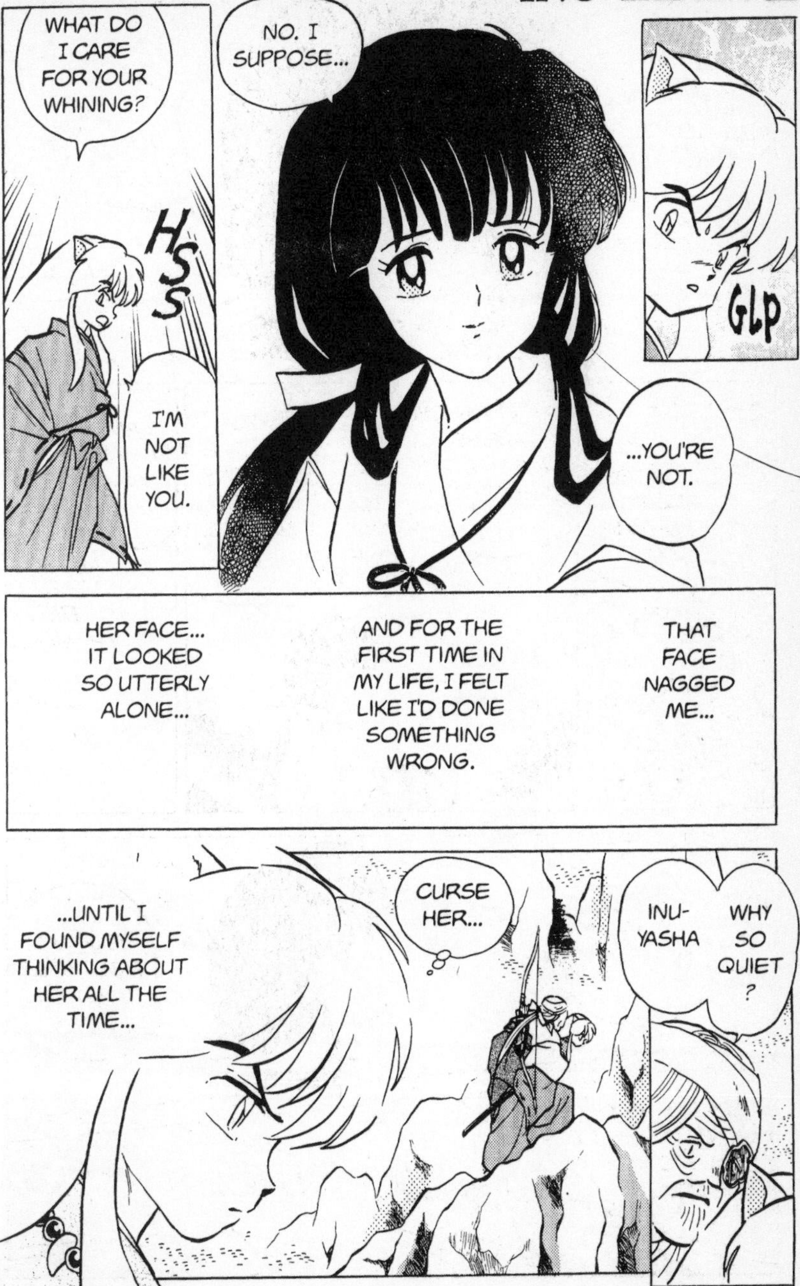
WHAT DO I CARE FOR YOUR WHINING?
HSS
I'M NOT LIKE YOU.
NO. I SUPPOSE...
...YOU'RE NOT.
GLP
HER FACE... IT LOOKED SO UTTERLY ALONE...
AND FOR THE FIRST TIME IN MY LIFE, I FELT LIKE I'D DONE SOMETHING WRONG.
THAT FACE NAGGED ME...
...UNTIL I FOUND MYSELF THINKING ABOUT HER ALL THE TIME...
CURSE HER...
INU-YASHA
WHY SO QUIET?

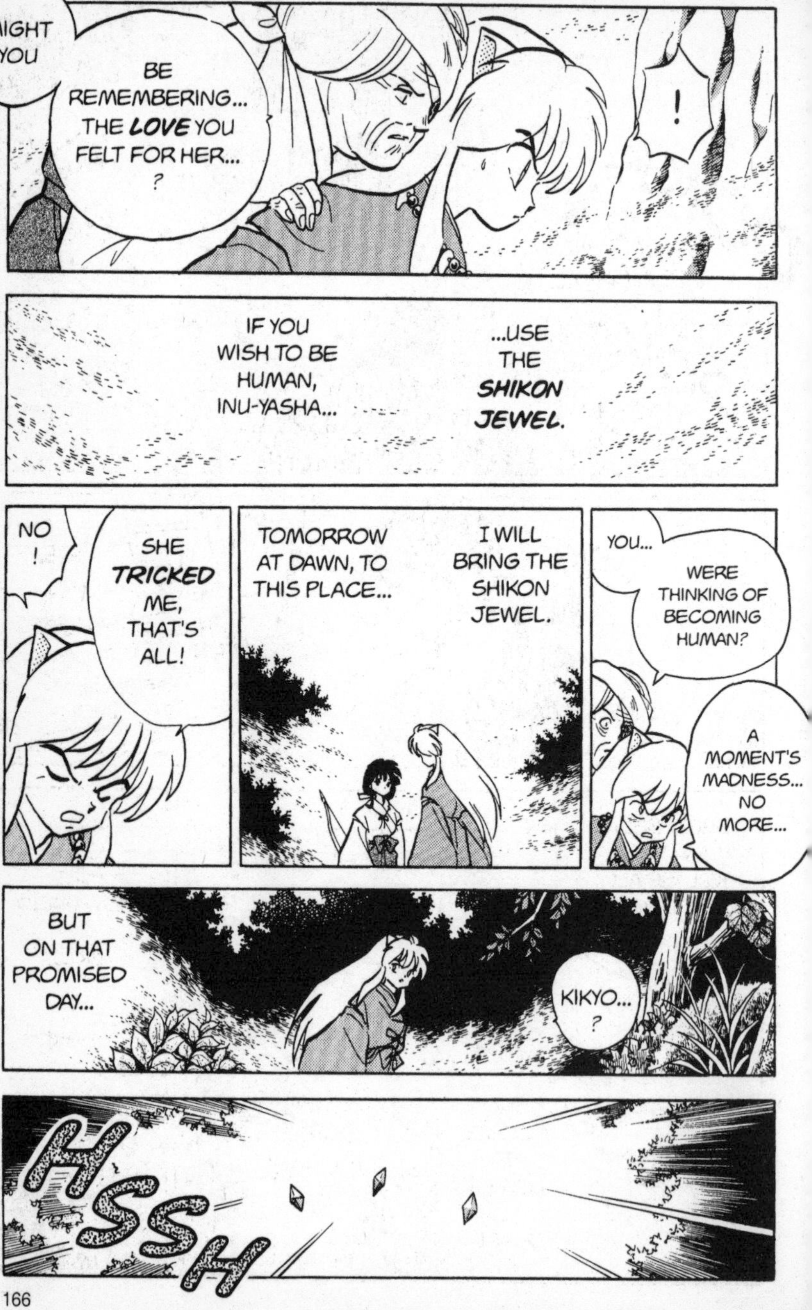
MIGHT YOU
BE REMEMBERING... THE LOVE YOU FELT FOR HER...?
!
IF YOU WISH TO BE HUMAN, INU-YASHA...
...USE THE SHIKON JEWEL.
NO!
SHE TRICKED ME, THAT'S ALL!
TOMORROW AT DAWN, TO THIS PLACE...
I WILL BRING THE SHIKON JEWEL.
YOU...
WERE THINKING OF BECOMING HUMAN?
A MOMENT'S MADNESS... NO MORE...
BUT ON THAT PROMISED DAY...
KIKYO...?
HSSH

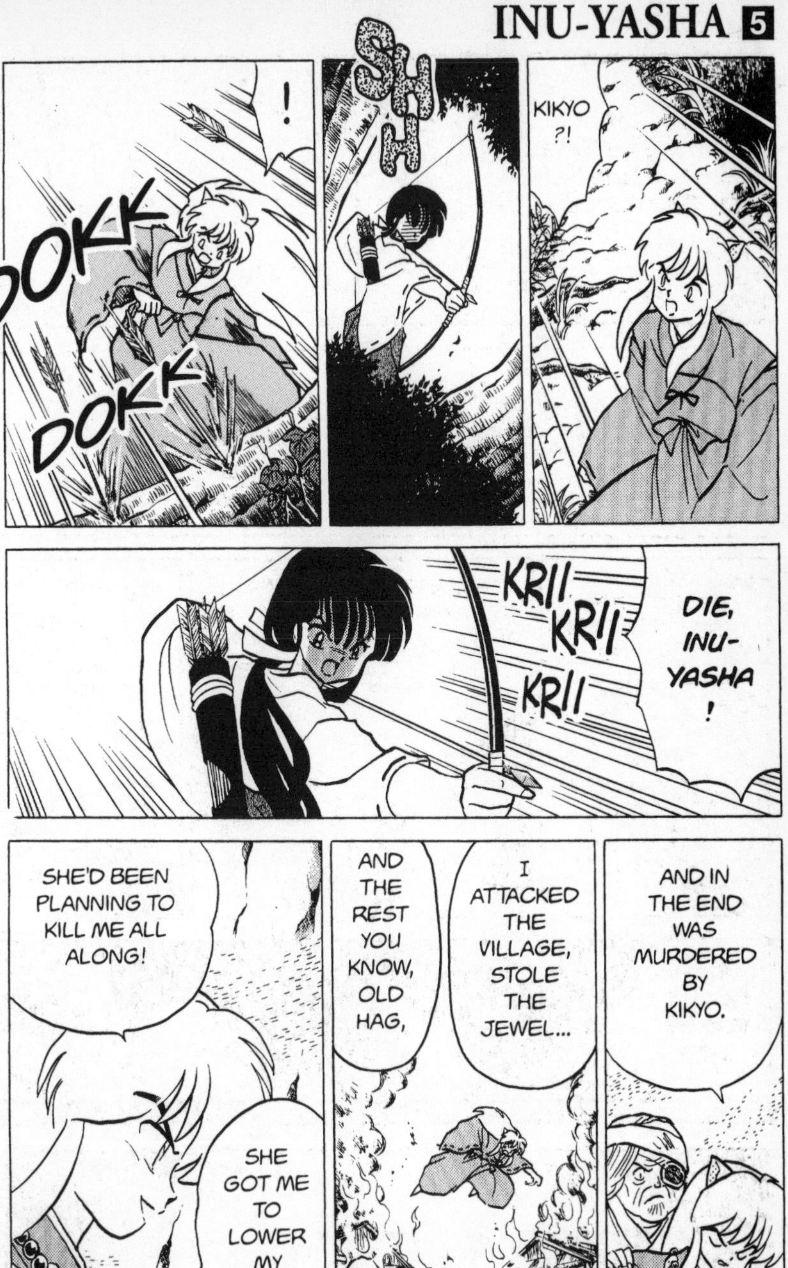
!
DOKK
DOKK
SHH
KIKYO ?!
KRII KRII KRII
DIE, INU-YASHA!
SHE'D BEEN PLANNING TO KILL ME ALL ALONG!
SHE GOT ME TO LOWER MY GUARD.
AND THE REST YOU KNOW, OLD HAG,
I ATTACKED THE VILLAGE, STOLE THE JEWEL...
AND IN THE END WAS MURDERED BY KIKYO.

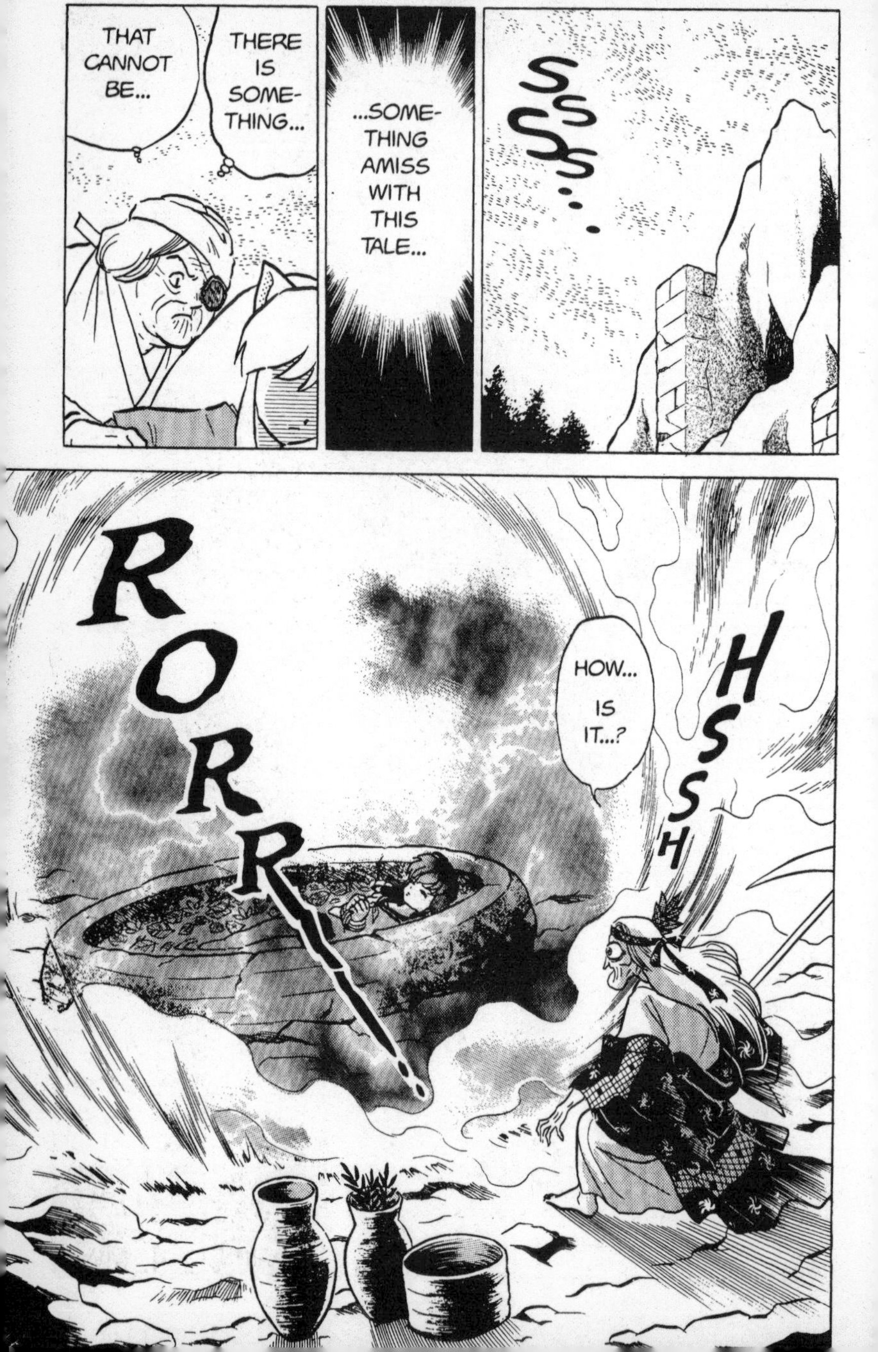
THERE IS SOMETHING...
THAT CANNOT BE...
...SOMETHING AMISS WITH THIS TALE...
SSSS...
HSSH
HOW... IS IT...?
RORRR

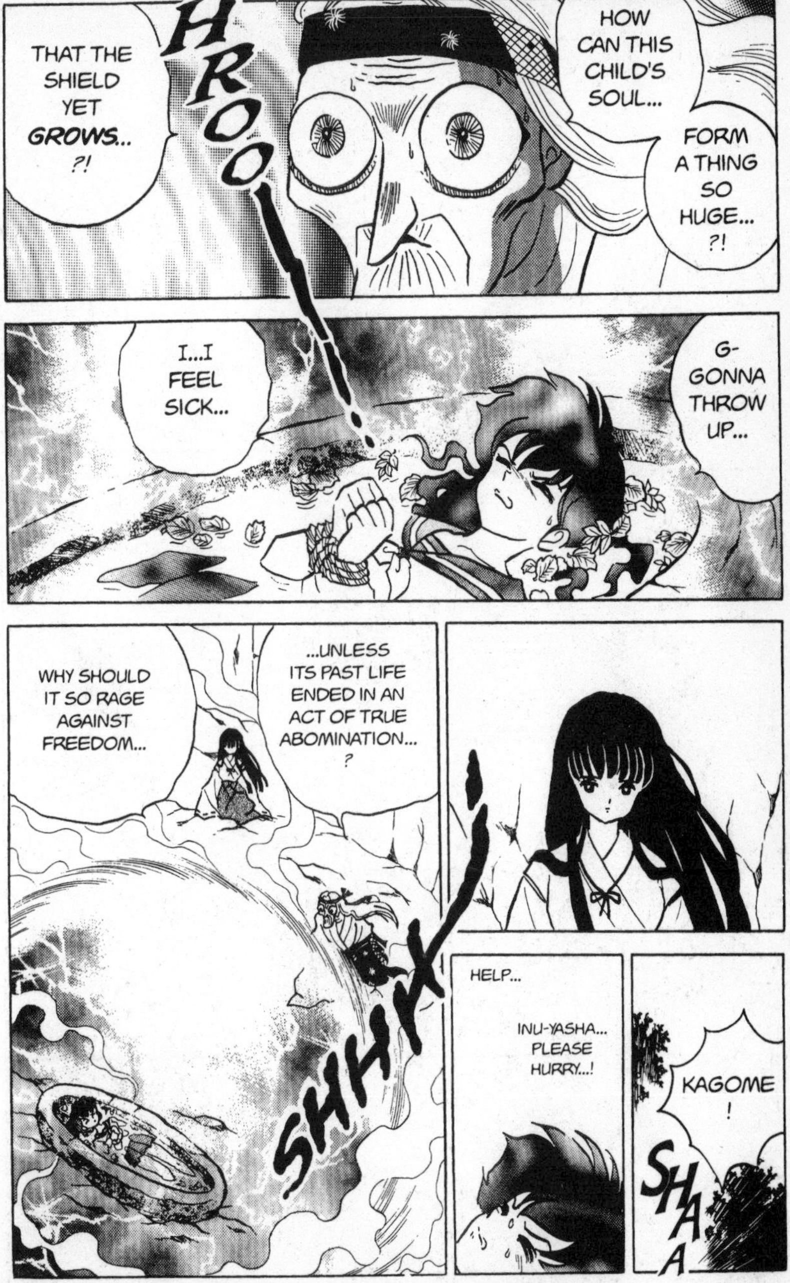
THAT THE SHIELD YET GROWS... ?!
HROO...!
HOW CAN THIS CHILD'S SOUL...
FORM A THING SO HUGE... ?!
I...I FEEL SICK...
G-GONNA THROW UP...
WHY SHOULD IT SO RAGE AGAINST FREEDOM...
...UNLESS ITS PAST LIFE ENDED IN AN ACT OF TRUE ABOMINATION... ?
SHHK!
HELP...
INU-YASHA... PLEASE HURRY...!
KAGOME!
SHAA

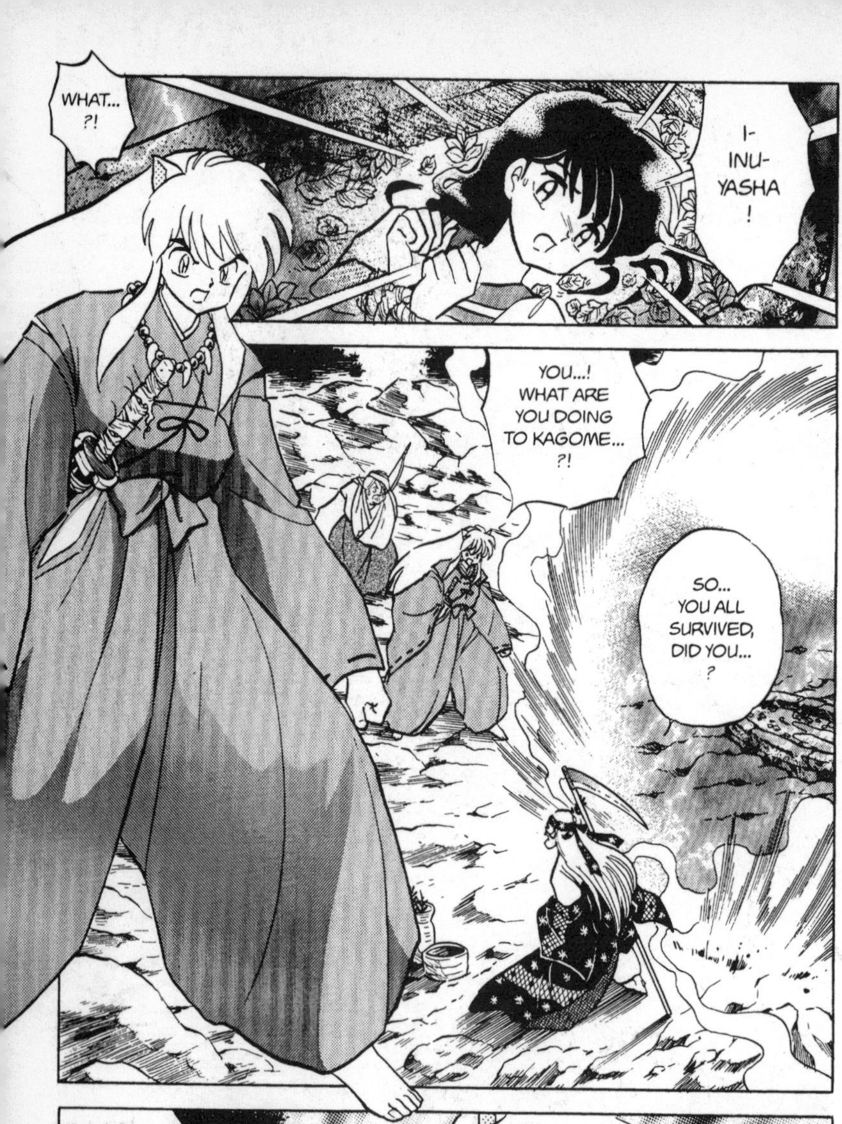

WHAT...?!
I- INU-YASHA!
YOU...! WHAT ARE YOU DOING TO KAGOME...?!
SO... YOU ALL SURVIVED, DID YOU...?
K... KIKYO...

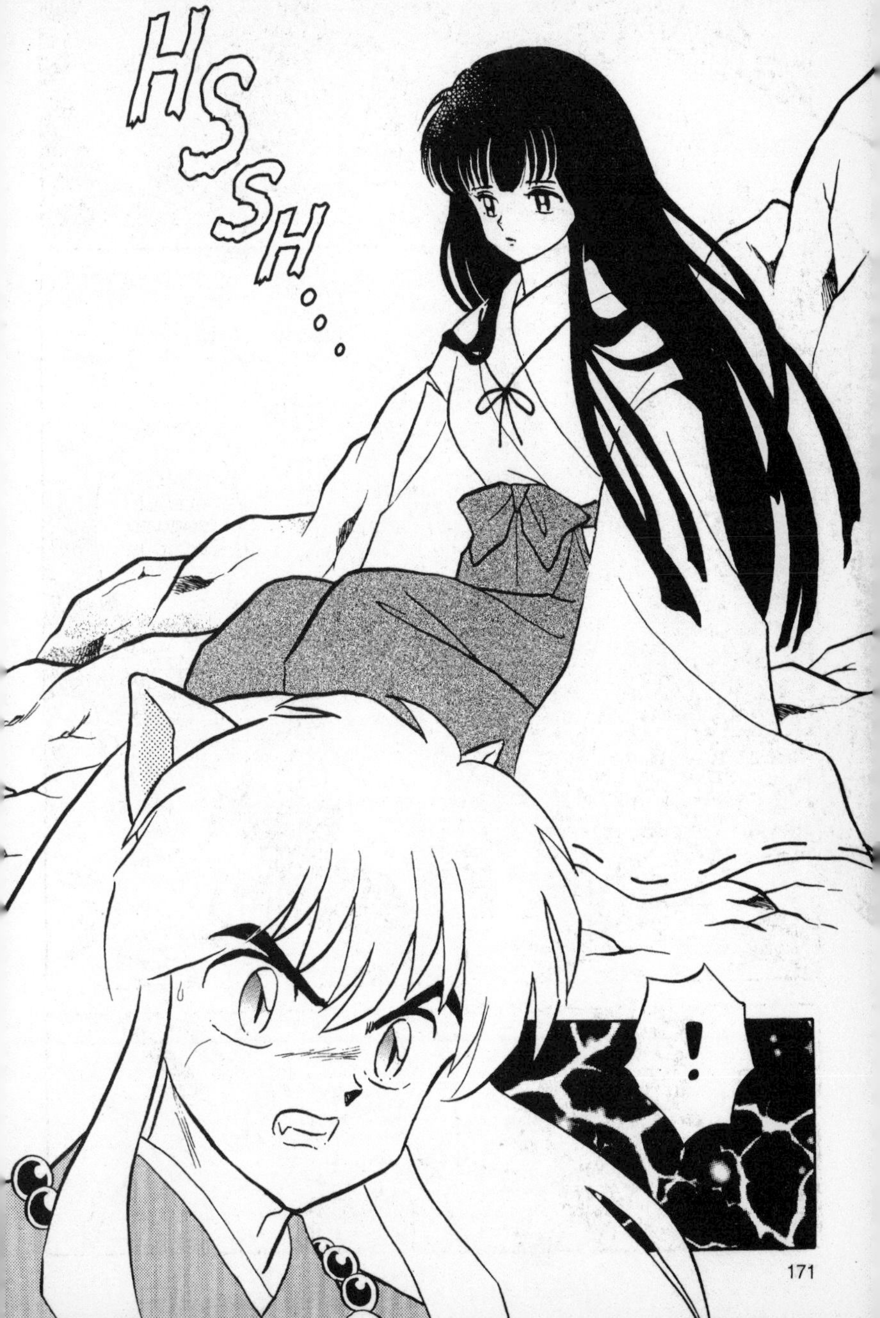
HSSH...
!

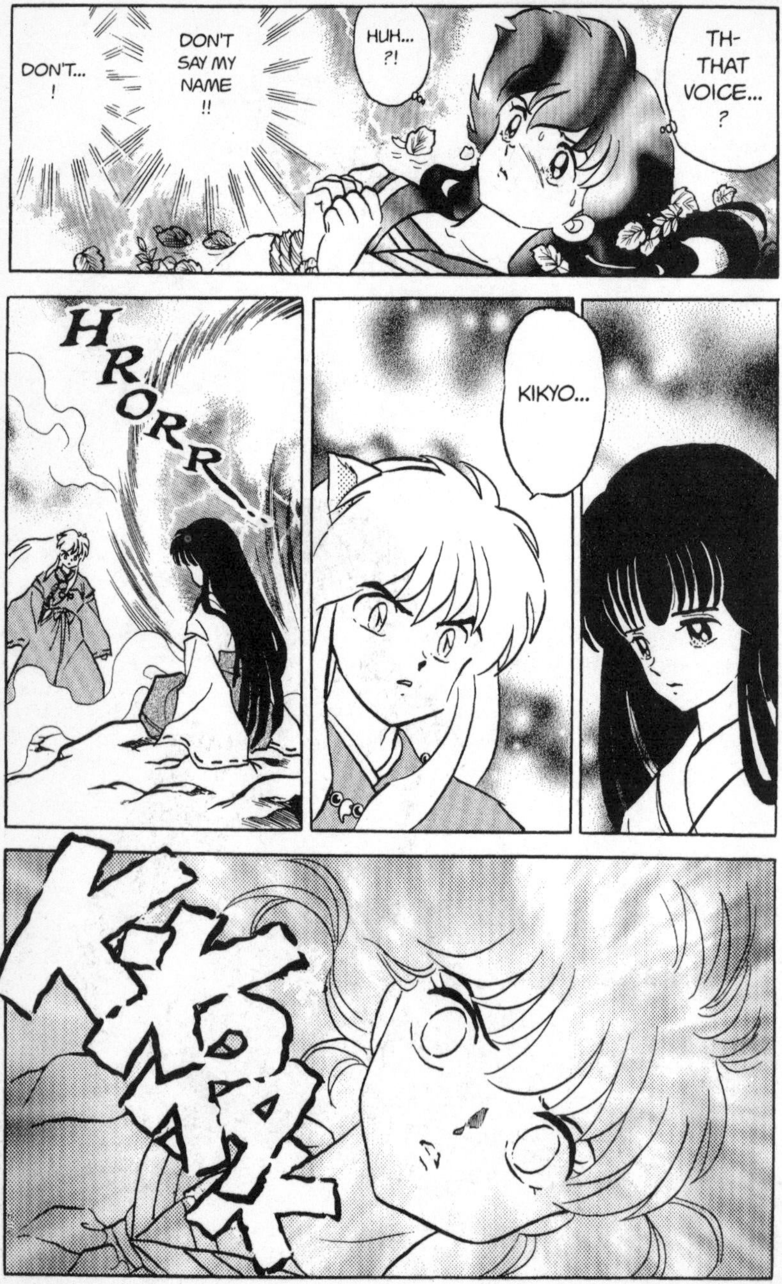
DON'T... !
DON'T SAY MY NAME !!
HUH... ?!
TH- THAT VOICE... ?
HRORR
KIKYO...

SCROLL TEN

BETRAYAL

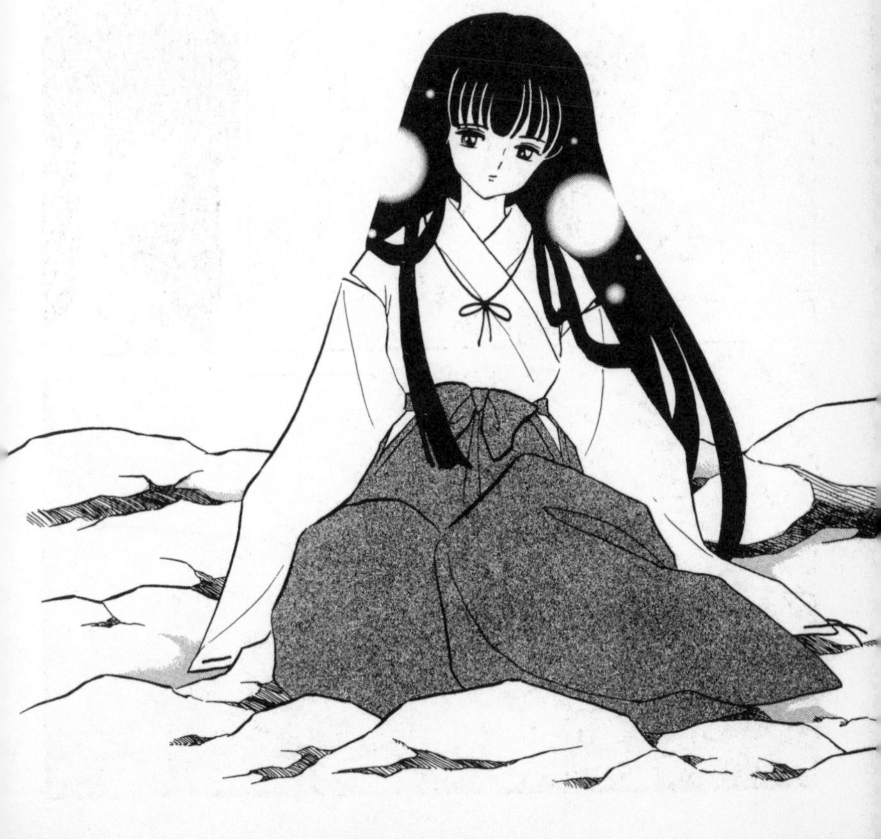

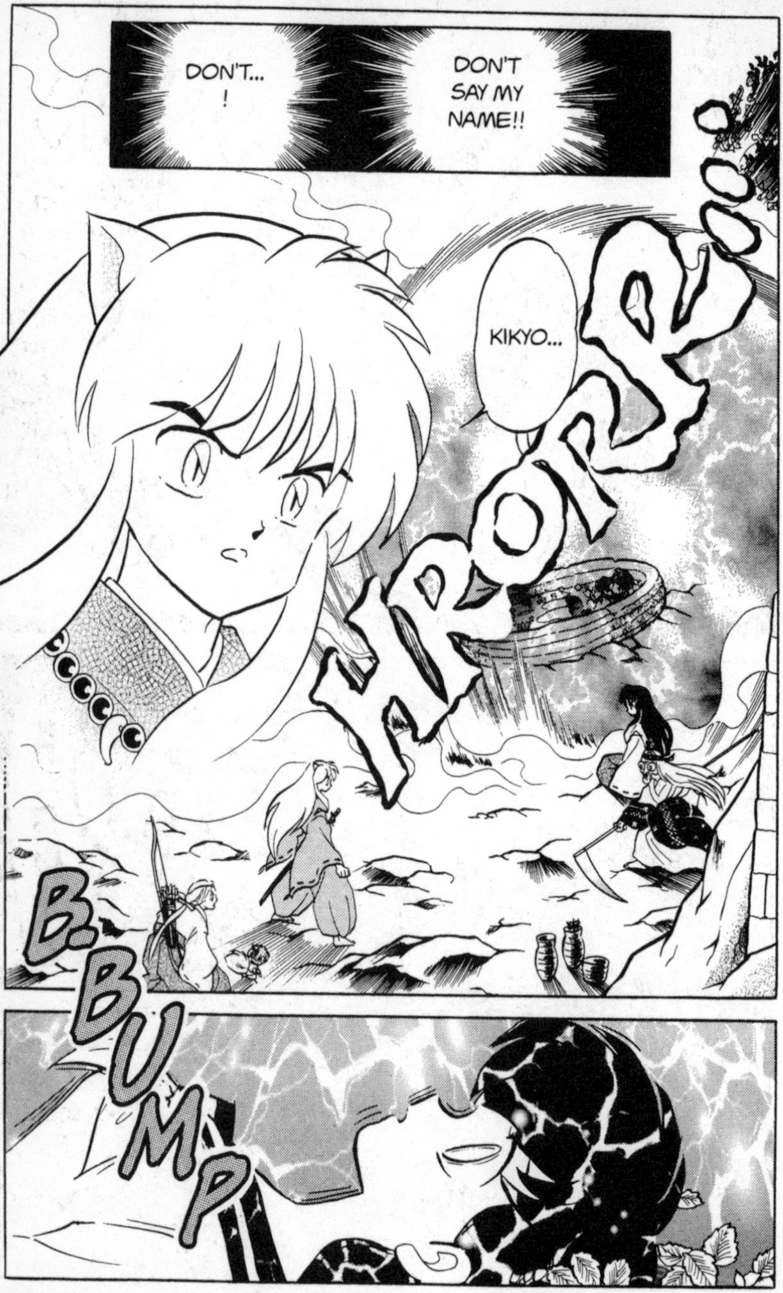
DON'T... !
DON'T SAY MY NAME!!
KIKYO...
KRORROOO
B-BUMP

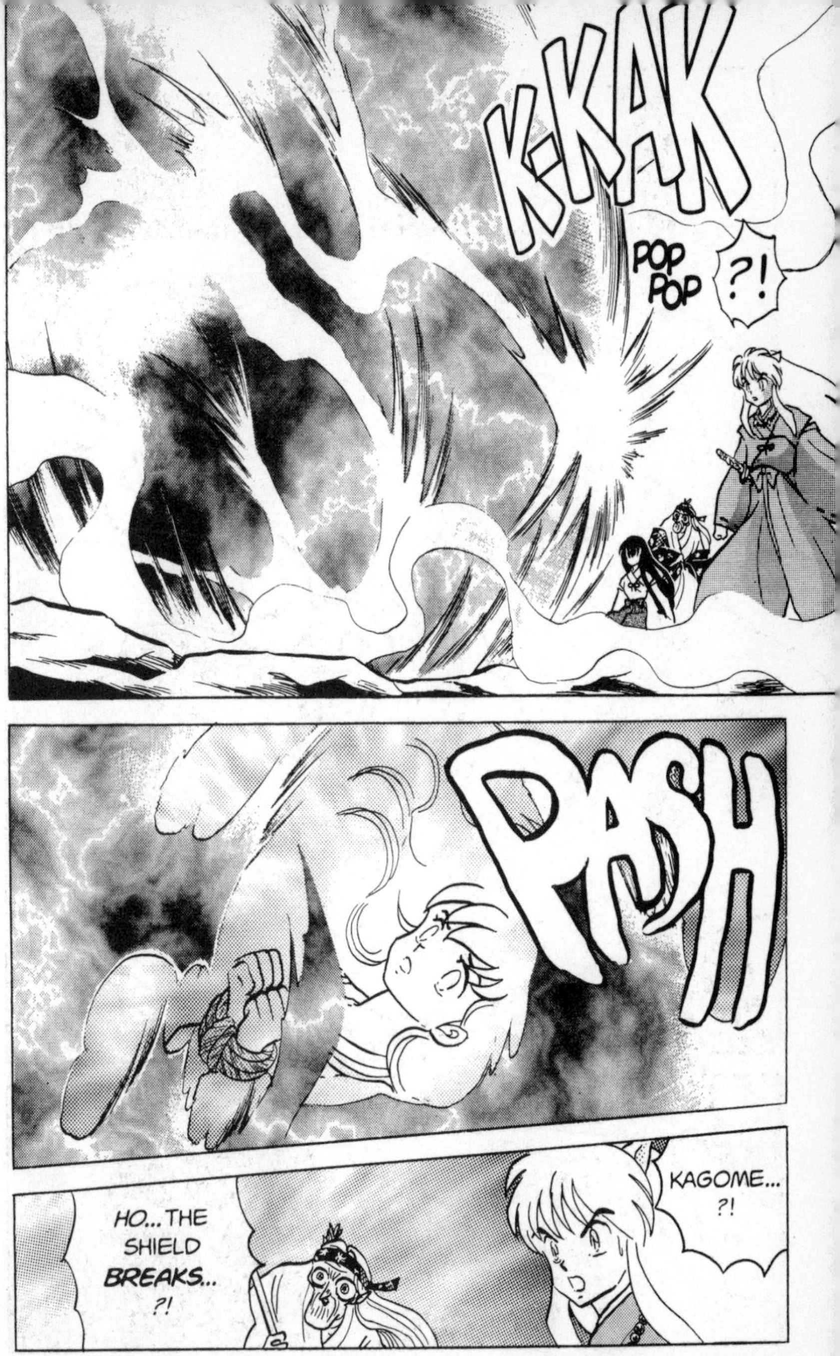

K-KAK
POP POP
?!
PASH
HO... THE SHIELD BREAKS... ?!
KAGOME... ?!

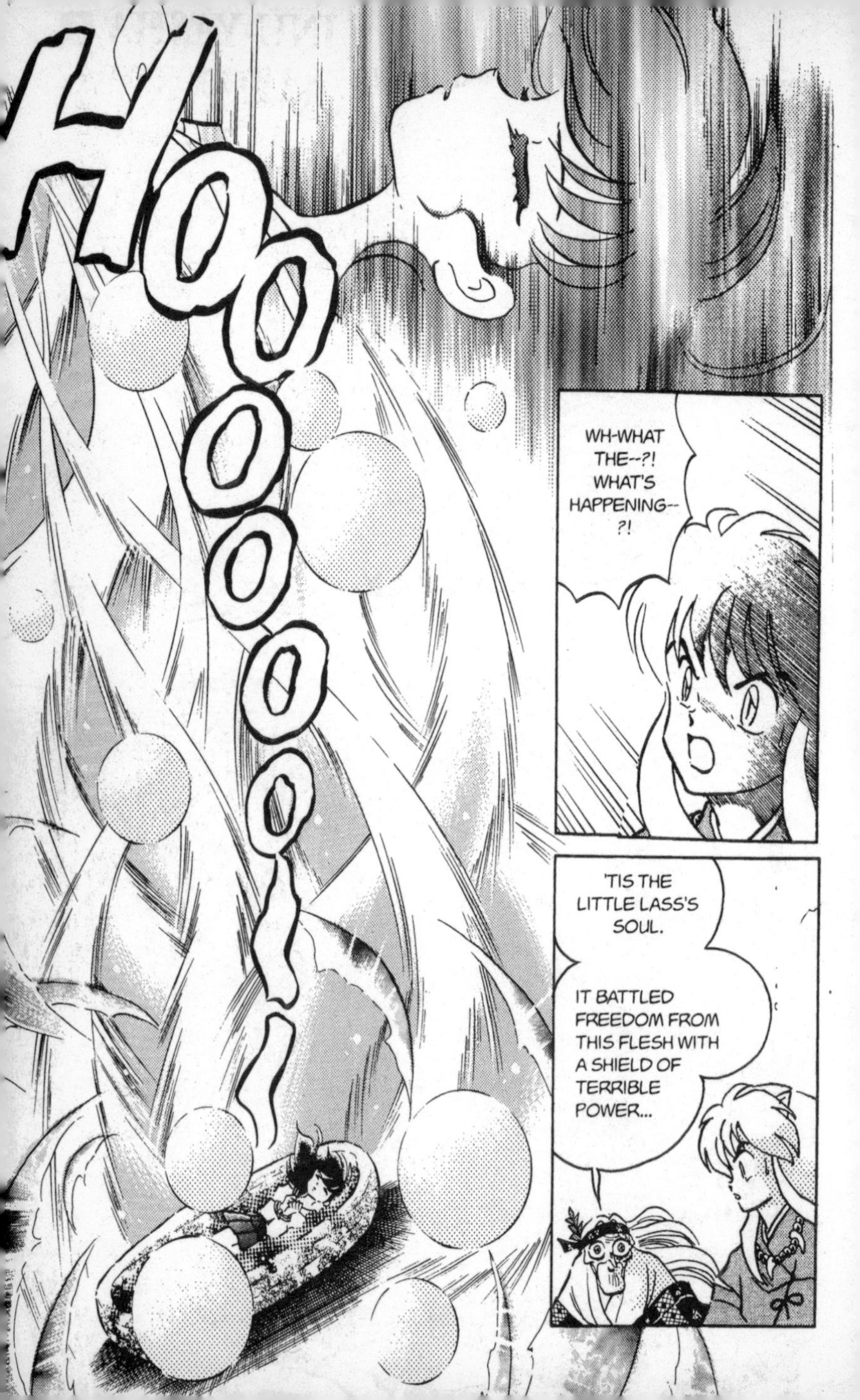
HOOOOOOO
WH-WHAT THE--?! WHAT'S HAPPENING--?!
'TIS THE LITTLE LASS'S SOUL.
IT BATTLED FREEDOM FROM THIS FLESH WITH A SHIELD OF TERRIBLE POWER...

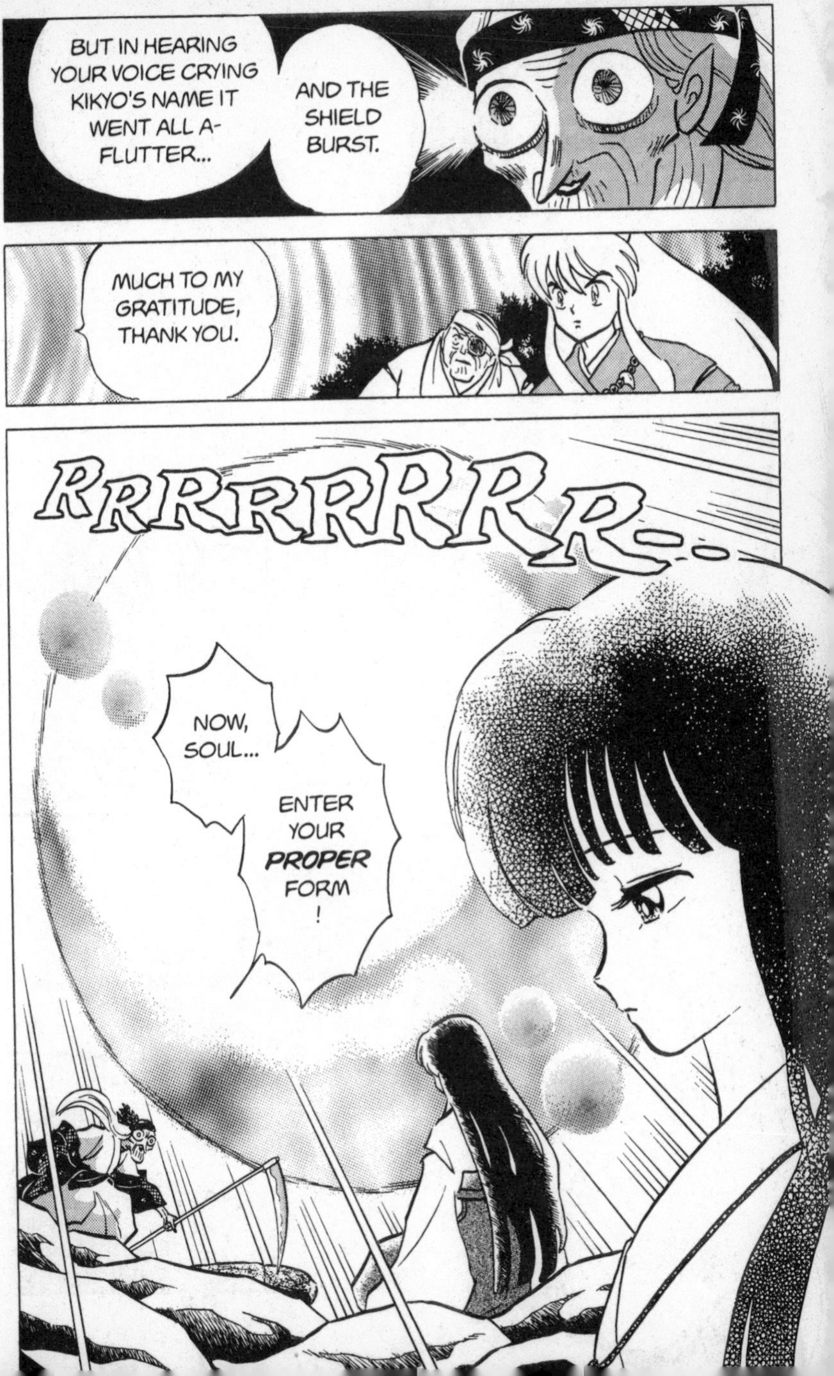
BUT IN HEARING YOUR VOICE CRYING KIKYO'S NAME IT WENT ALL A-FLUTTER...
AND THE SHIELD BURST.
MUCH TO MY GRATITUDE, THANK YOU.
RRRRRRRR...
NOW, SOUL...
ENTER YOUR **PROPER** FORM!

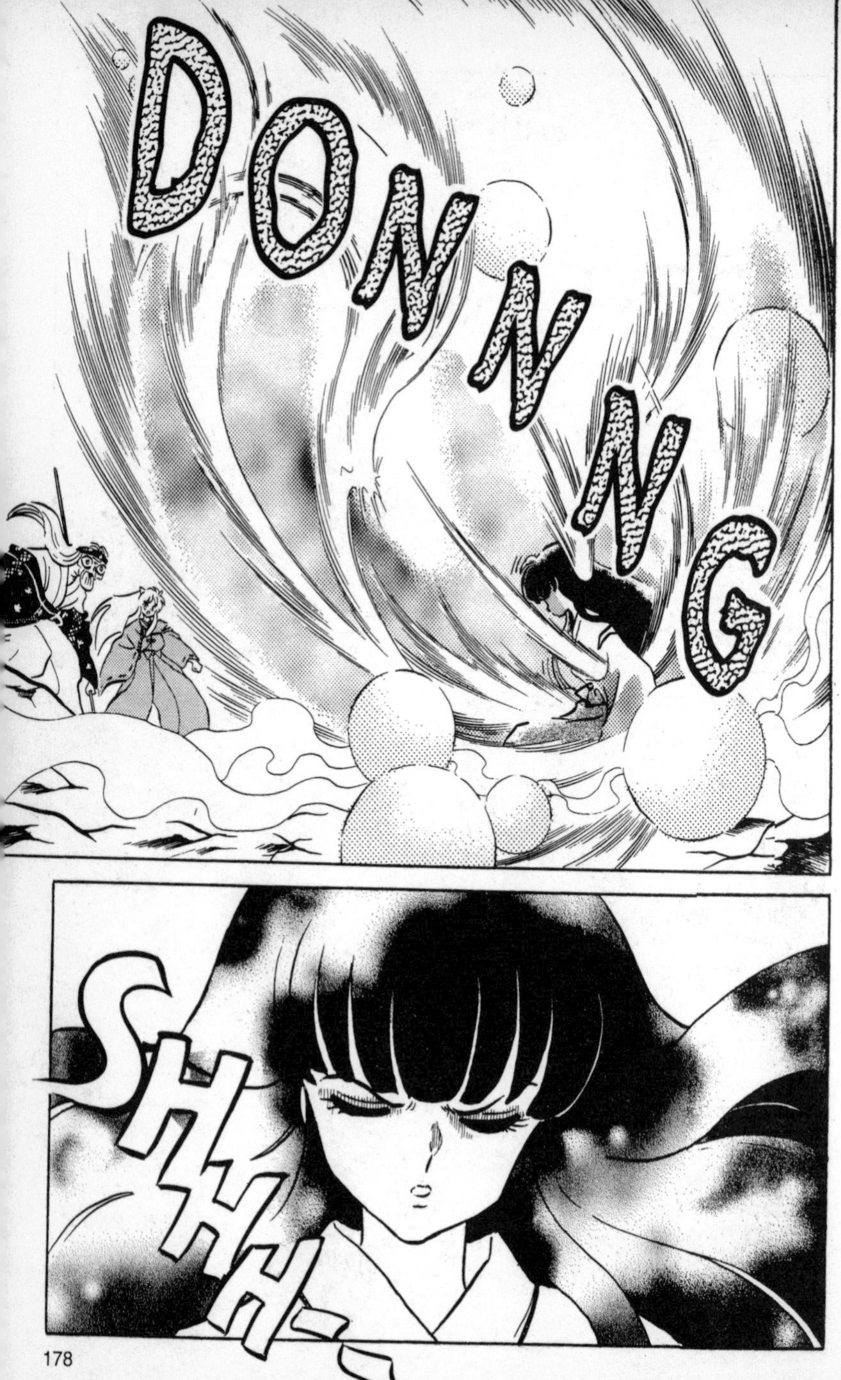
DONNNG
SHHH-

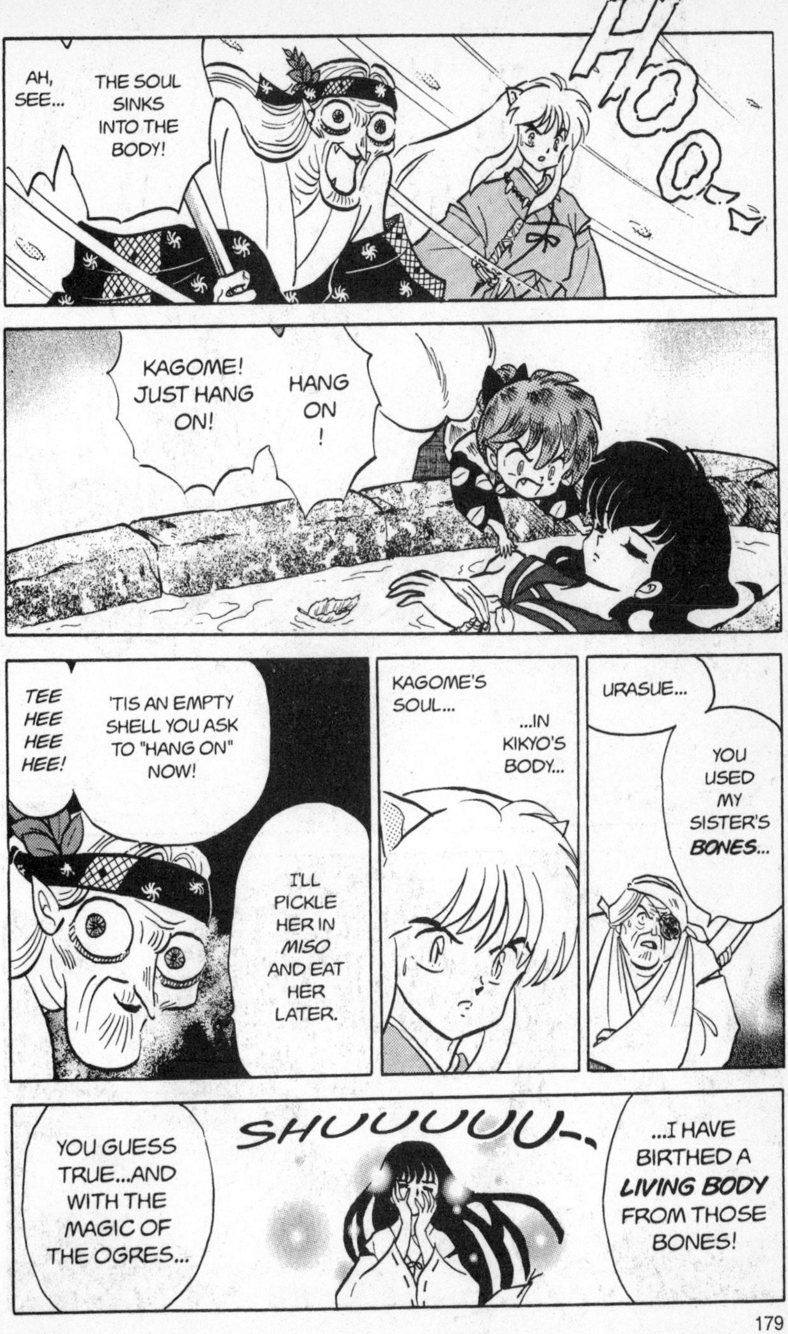

AH, SEE...
THE SOUL SINKS INTO THE BODY!
HOO...
KAGOME! JUST HANG ON!
HANG ON!
TEE HEE HEE HEE!
'TIS AN EMPTY SHELL YOU ASK TO "HANG ON" NOW!
I'LL PICKLE HER IN *MISO* AND EAT HER LATER.
KAGOME'S SOUL...
...IN KIKYO'S BODY...
URASUE...
YOU USED MY SISTER'S **BONES**...
YOU GUESS TRUE...AND WITH THE MAGIC OF THE OGRES...
SHUUUUU...
...I HAVE BIRTHED A **LIVING BODY** FROM THOSE BONES!

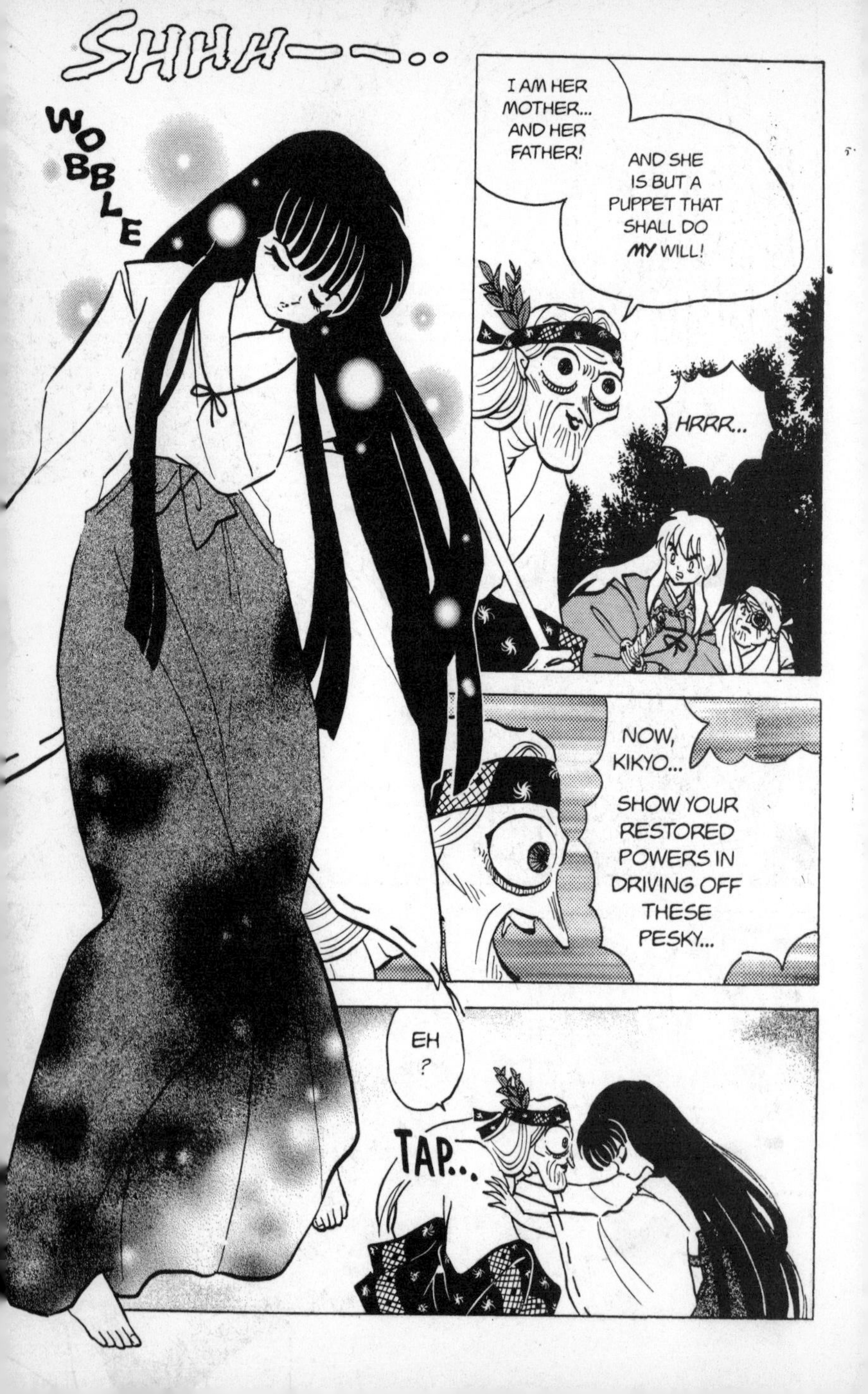
SHHH—...
WOBBLE
I AM HER MOTHER... AND HER FATHER!
AND SHE IS BUT A PUPPET THAT SHALL DO MY WILL!
HRRR...
NOW, KIKYO...
SHOW YOUR RESTORED POWERS IN DRIVING OFF THESE PESKY...
EH?
TAP...

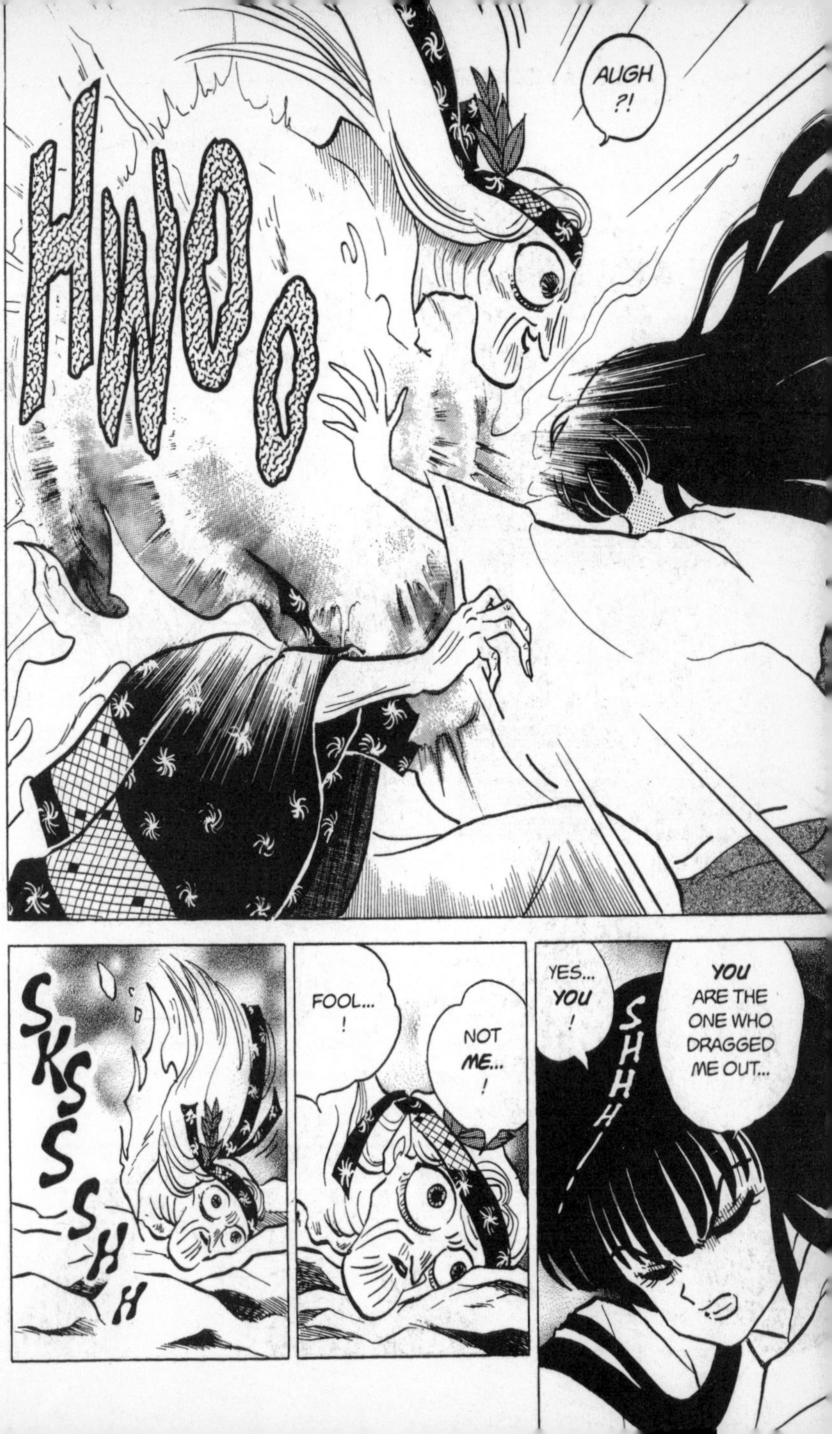
HWOO
AUGH ?!
SKSSSHH
FOOL... !
NOT ME... !
YES... YOU !
SHHHH
YOU ARE THE ONE WHO DRAGGED ME OUT...

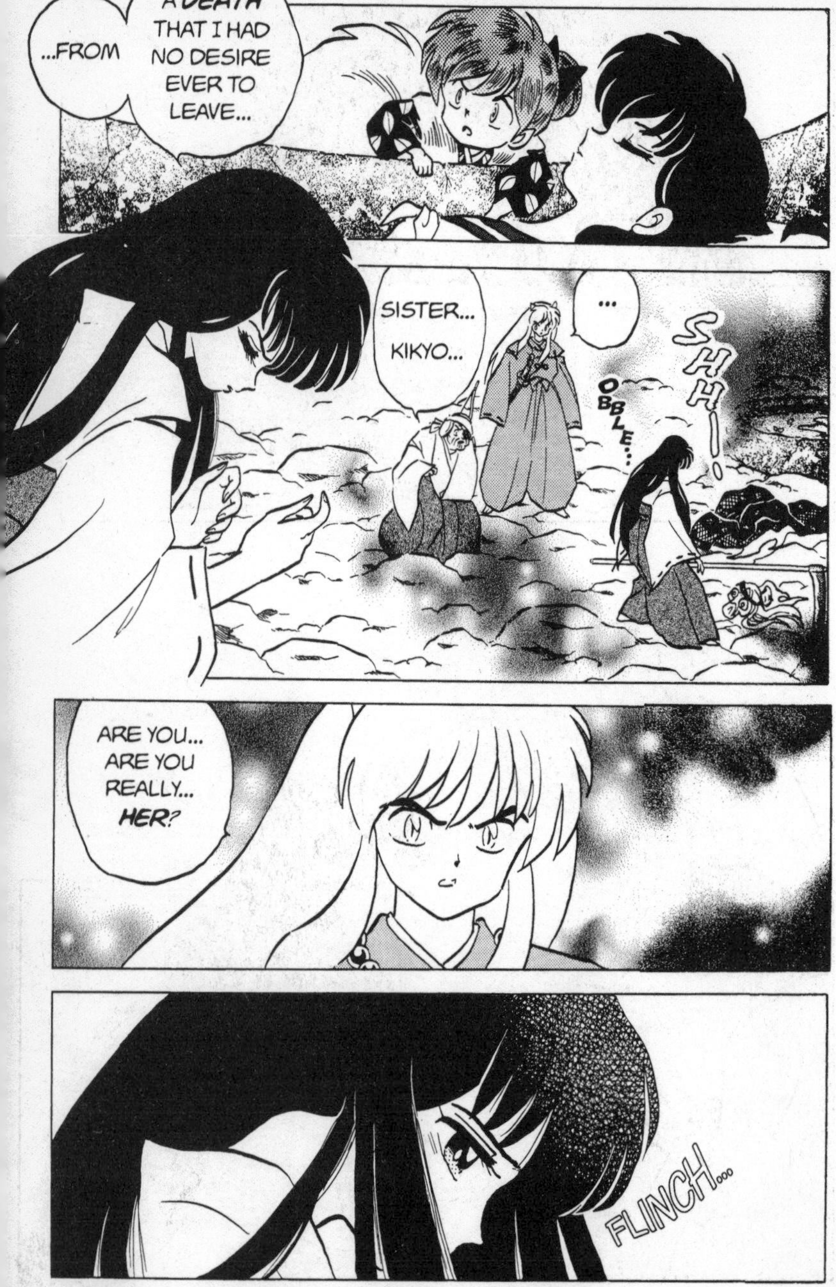

...FROM
A DEATH THAT I HAD NO DESIRE EVER TO LEAVE...
SISTER... KIKYO...
...
SHHH!!
OBBLE...
ARE YOU... ARE YOU REALLY... HER?
FLINCH...

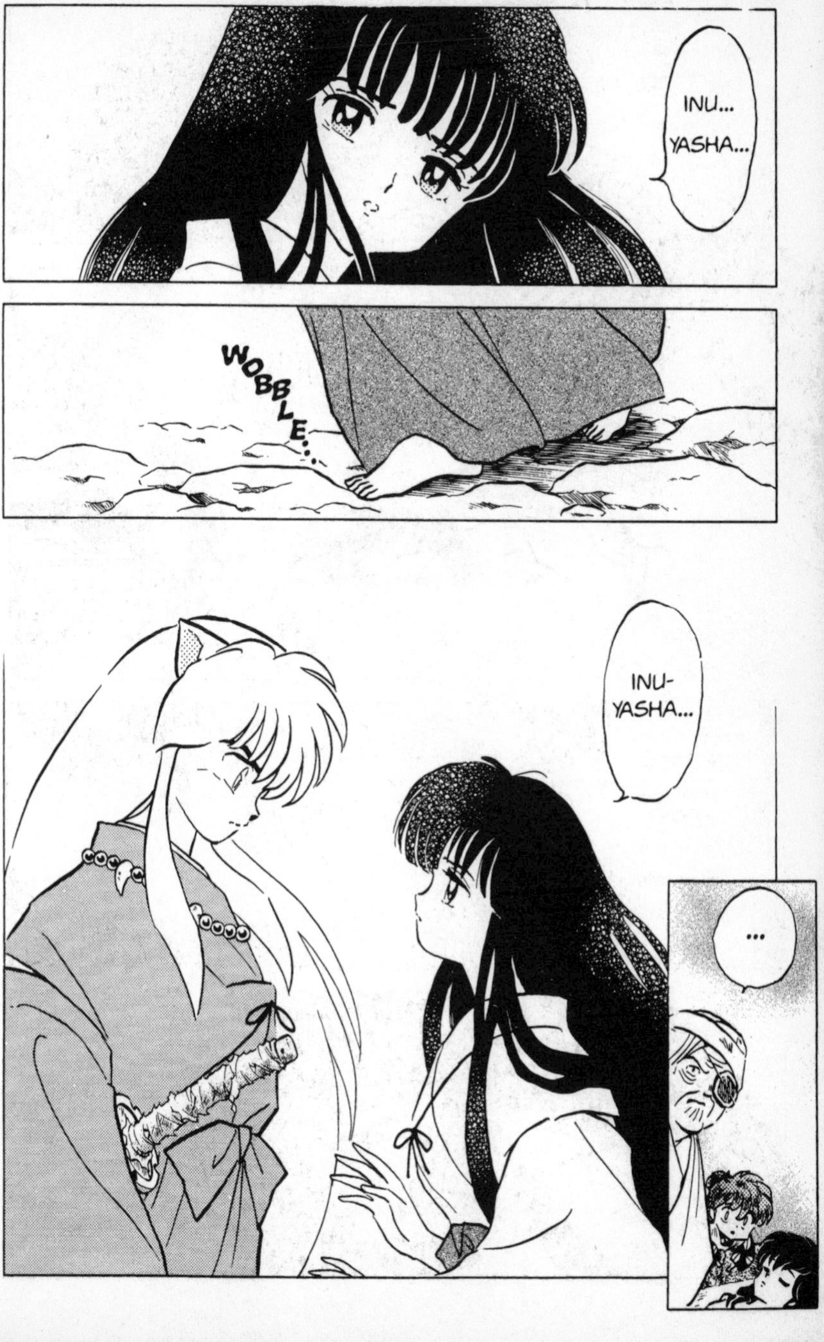
INU...
YASHA...
WOBBLE...
INU-
YASHA...
...

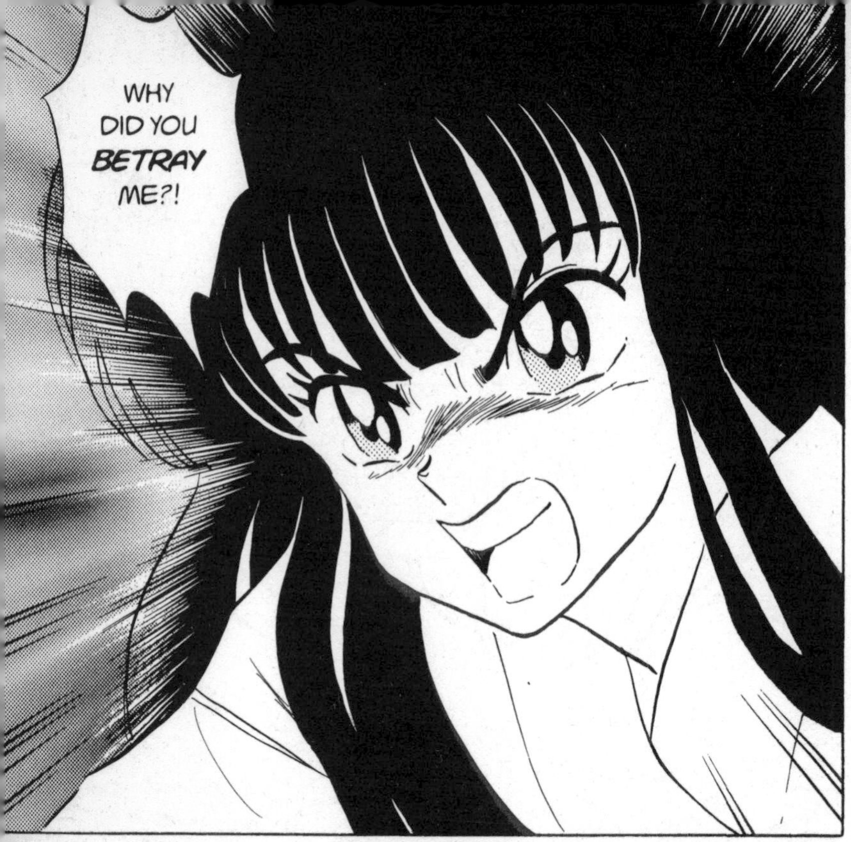
WHY DID YOU **BETRAY** ME?!

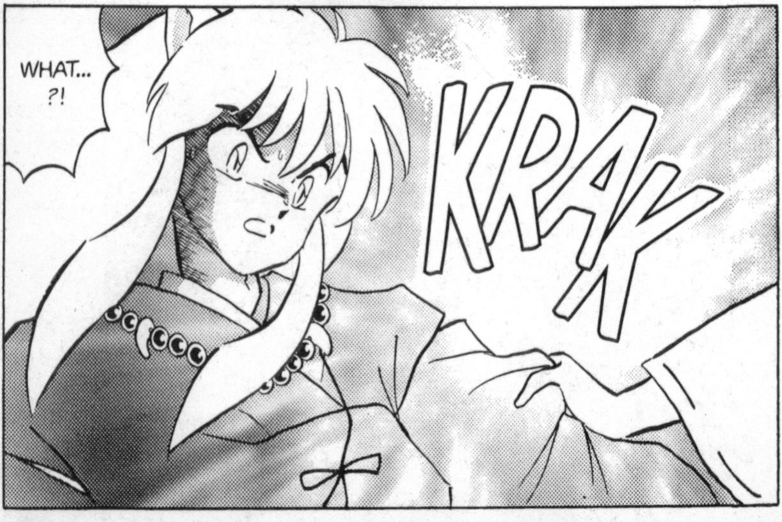
WHAT... ?!
KRAK

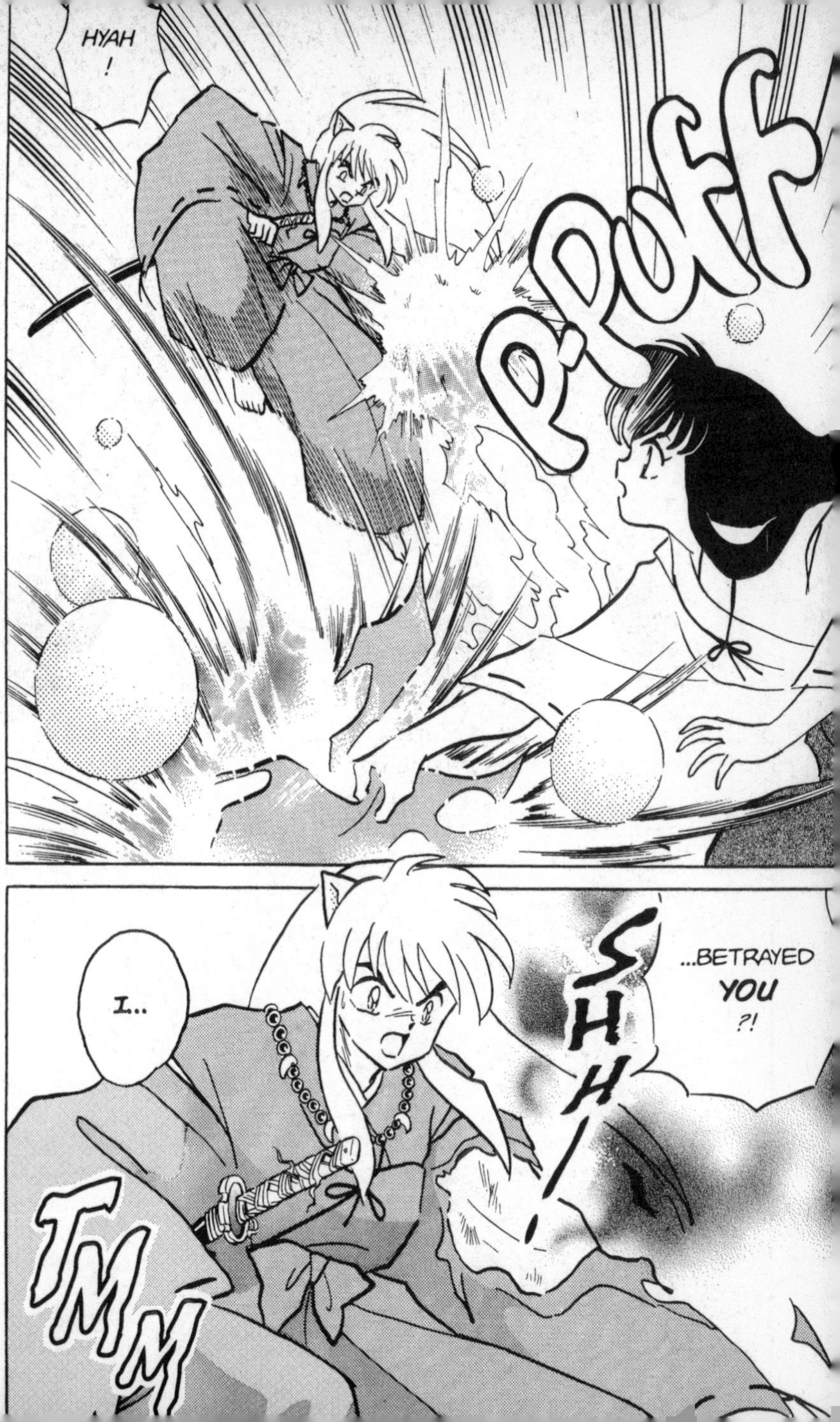
HYAH!
P-PUFF
I...
SHH!
...BETRAYED YOU?!
TMM

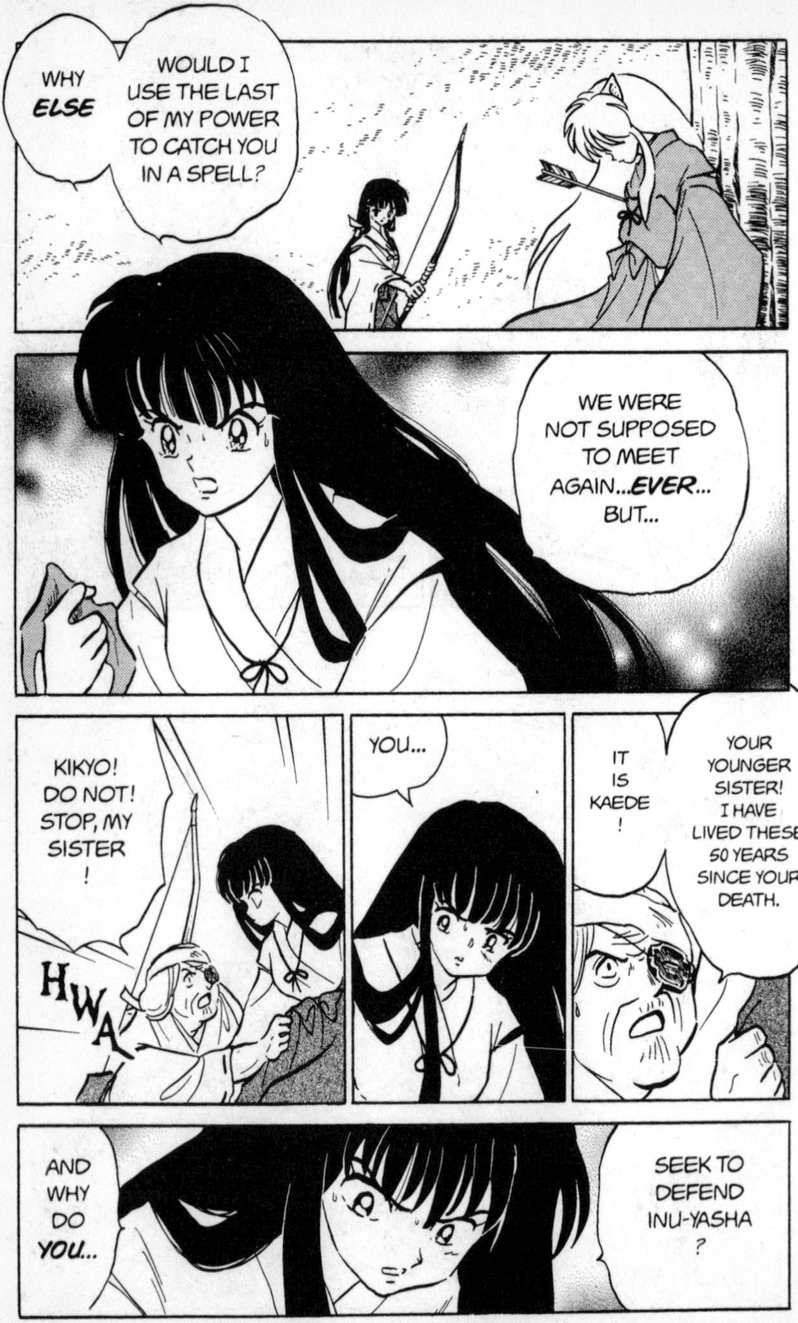
WHY ELSE
WOULD I USE THE LAST OF MY POWER TO CATCH YOU IN A SPELL?
WE WERE NOT SUPPOSED TO MEET AGAIN...EVER... BUT...
KIKYO! DO NOT! STOP, MY SISTER!
HWA
YOU...
IT IS KAEDE!
YOUR YOUNGER SISTER! I HAVE LIVED THESE 50 YEARS SINCE YOUR DEATH.
AND WHY DO YOU...
SEEK TO DEFEND INU-YASHA?

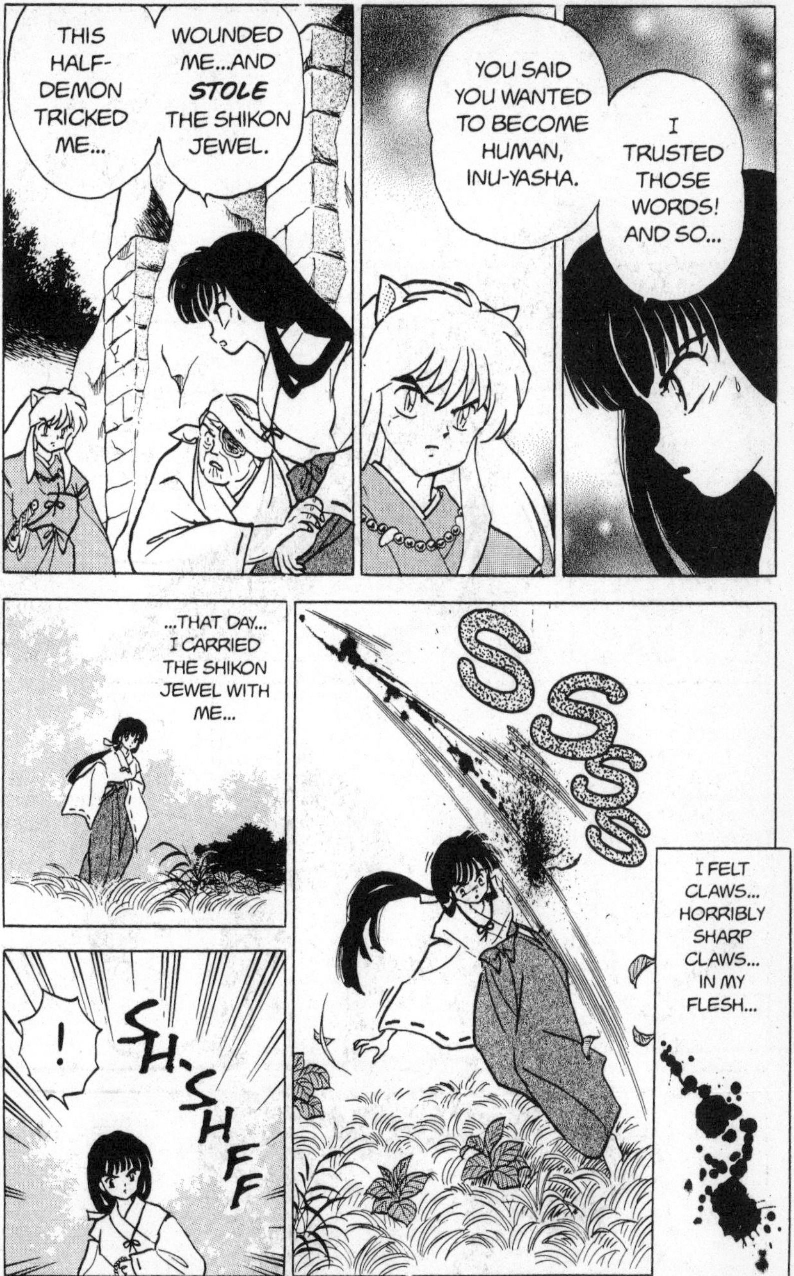
THIS HALF-DEMON TRICKED ME...
WOUNDED ME...AND STOLE THE SHIKON JEWEL.
YOU SAID YOU WANTED TO BECOME HUMAN, INU-YASHA.
I TRUSTED THOSE WORDS! AND SO...
...THAT DAY... I CARRIED THE SHIKON JEWEL WITH ME...
!
SH-SHFF
SSSSS
I FELT CLAWS... HORRIBLY SHARP CLAWS... IN MY FLESH...

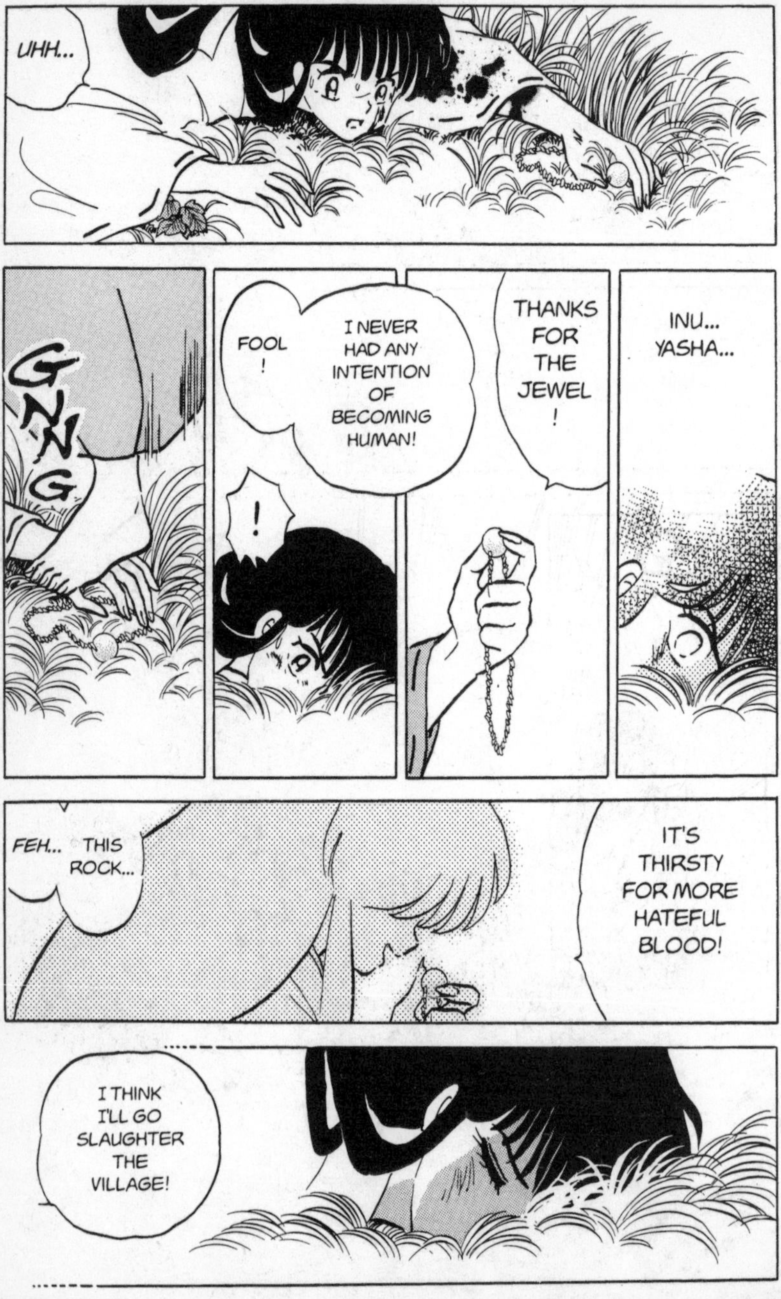
UHH...
GNNG
FOOL!
I NEVER HAD ANY INTENTION OF BECOMING HUMAN!
!
THANKS FOR THE JEWEL!
INU... YASHA...
FEH... THIS ROCK...
IT'S THIRSTY FOR MORE HATEFUL BLOOD!
I THINK I'LL GO SLAUGHTER THE VILLAGE!

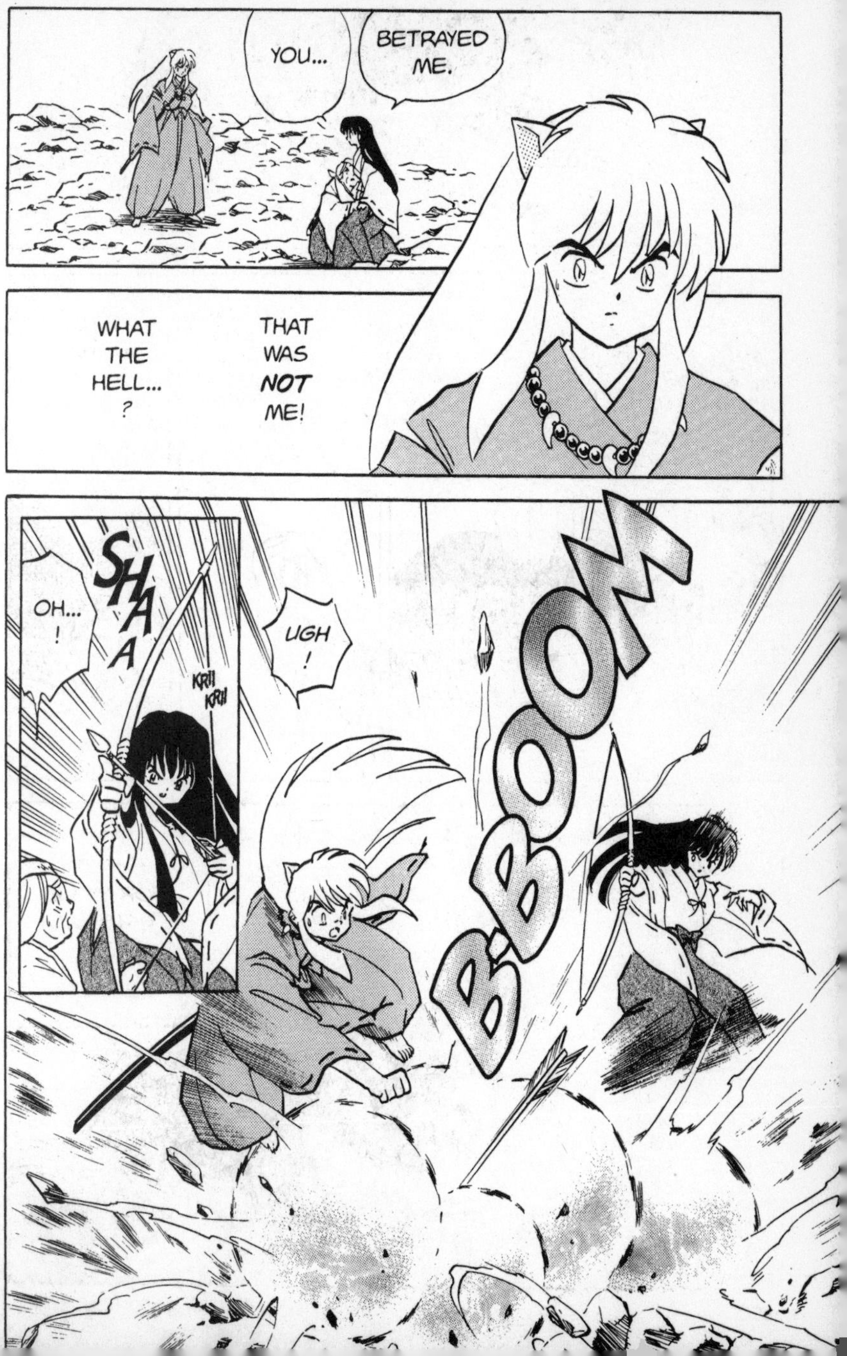
YOU...
BETRAYED ME.
WHAT THE HELL... ?
THAT WAS NOT ME!
OH... !
SHAA
KRII KRII
UGH !
B-BOOM

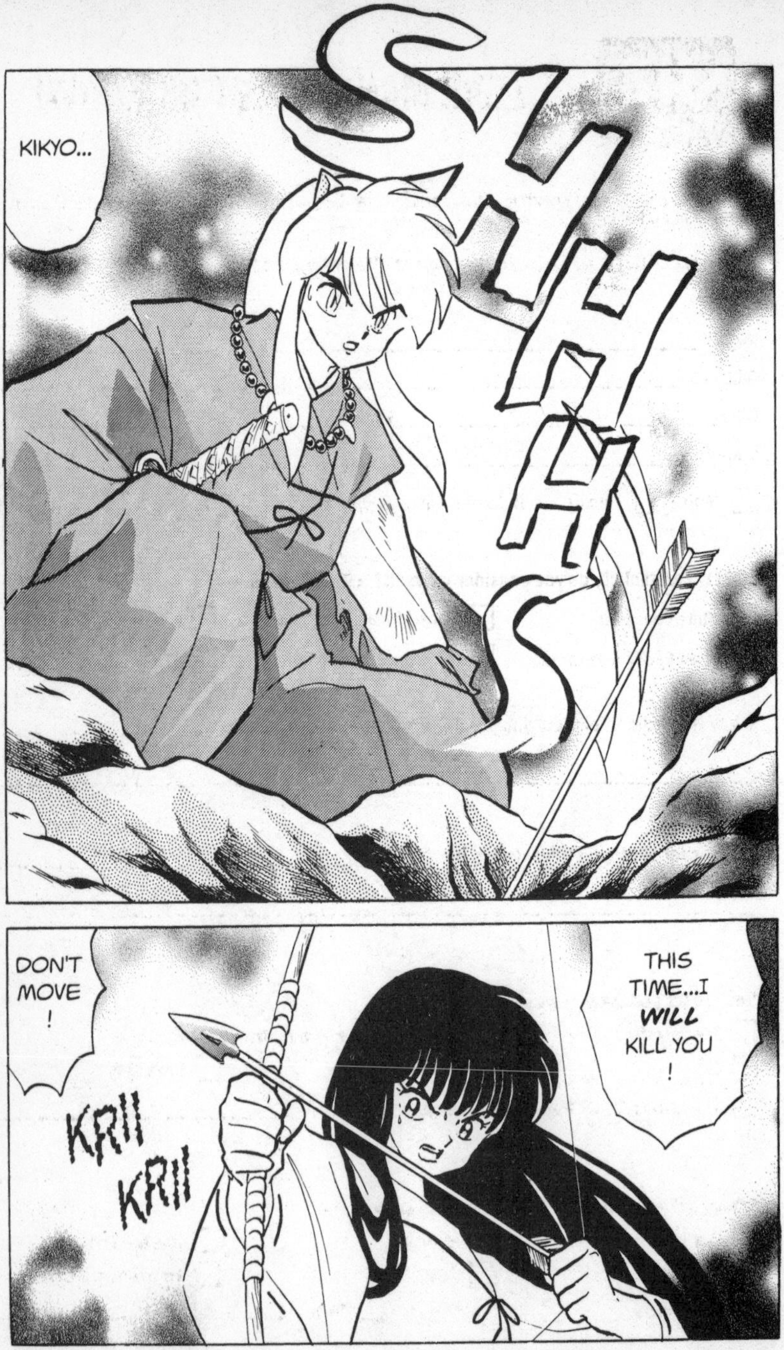
KIKYO...
SHHHS
DON'T MOVE!
KRII KRII
THIS TIME...I **WILL** KILL YOU!

TO BE CONTINUED...